T0244228

NEU KLANG

NEU KLANG

The Definitive History of Krautrock

CHRISTOPH DALLACH

translated by
Katy Derbyshire

faber

This edition first published in the UK in 2024
by Faber & Faber Limited
The Bindery, 51 Hatton Garden
London EC1N 8HN

First published in Germany in 2021
by Suhrkamp Verlag
Torstraße 44, 10119 Berlin

First published in the USA in 2024

Typeset by Ian Bahrami
Printed and bound by CPI Group (UK) Ltd, Croydon, CR0 4YY

A CIP record for this book
is available from the British Library

ISBN 978-0-571-37767-1

Printed and bound in the UK on FSC® certified paper in line with our continuing
commitment to ethical business practices, sustainability and the environment.
For further information see faber.co.uk/environmental-policy

2 4 6 8 10 9 7 5 3 1

For Maria (MoisE)

CONTENTS

INTRODUCTION

I won my first krautrock record in a competition. All I had to do was call the radio station during a narrow window of time. I got through right away.

Maybe I was lucky, or maybe I was the only caller. Whatever the case, the record arrived a week later: Holger Czukay's *Movies*, complete with a biro autograph from the artist himself.

Back then, in a dull suburb of Hamburg in 1979, the soundtrack of my youth was made up entirely of the Sex Pistols and the Stranglers. The name 'Holger Czukay' didn't exactly sound exciting and his portrait on the cover didn't improve matters. But I gave *Movies* a chance – and I was blown away. What I heard was far removed from anything I was used to, and seemed to match neither the name nor the packaging: an electrifying collage of strange sounds, the likes of which I'd only come across on John Peel's adventurous radio shows. I'd never have thought German musicians were capable of anything like it. And I was immediately so captivated that I kept playing the wondrous tracks over and over, with mounting enthusiasm. *Movies* would definitely be in my desert-island record box.

That lucky strike opened up a new world for me. I didn't know much about Czukay, but I picked up that he'd once been the bassist in a band called Can. They had to be interesting as well, then. But record shops didn't have much by Can, they didn't get airplay, and there was nothing at all to read about them. At flea markets, I tracked down albums like *Tago Mago*, *Future Days* and *Ege Bamyası*. I was happy to get hold of solo albums by Irmin Schmidt and records featuring Michael

1

Karoli or Jaki Liebezeit – and I was never disappointed. I soon started giving other German musicians a chance, people like Michael Rother, Guru Guru and La Düsseldorf. La Düsseldorf's predecessors NEU! caught my eye through their debut album's pop-art cover, which had to be worth a try. And then there was 'Hallogallo' right at the start, one of those tracks that blew my mind instantly and forever. It was all the harder for me to imagine that those ten absurd minutes could possibly come from Germany. I wouldn't have touched the krautrock section in record shops with a barge pole – that name was warning enough.

So perhaps it's no coincidence that it was a Brit, in the end, who helped me to overcome my inhibitions: Julian Cope, the singer of the Teardrop Explodes. My previous discovery of Scott Walker had been down to him, since he'd compiled a best-of from his solo records. Imagine my interest when his 1995 book with the strange title *krautrocksampler* came out, kicking up a fuss in the British music press I pored over every week. His euphoric declaration of love for German musicians like Amon Düül, NEU!, Faust, Tangerine Dream, Ash Ra Tempel, Popol Vuh, Cluster, Harmonia, Klaus Schulze, Witthüser & Westrupp and of course Can surprised me at first – how come people in the UK knew all these Germans? And where did Cope's almost insane fascination for them come from? Whatever the case, his enthusiasm encouraged me to take a deeper dive into their music. The only thing was, most records by these bands were more of a rumour than a truth, because they were impossible to get hold of anywhere. That didn't put a stop to my curiosity. If we'd once had such cool music in Germany, why was it such a secret right here?

Shortly after that I started writing about music myself, and I soon had opportunities to meet Julian Cope's legendary heroes in the flesh. I interviewed Holger Czukay, Irmin Schmidt and Jaki Liebezeit. Michael Rother often crossed my path in Hamburg anyway; I once even managed to tip a glass of red wine over his shirt when we were both watching a gig.

In 2001 came the long-overdue NEU! re-releases. I arranged to talk to Rother and his musical partner Klaus Dinger in Köln, and was surprised to find that the record company had booked them in on two different floors of the EMI office building – allegedly so they wouldn't run into each other and start fighting. As different as they were, they were both extremely interesting interview partners. What on earth had happened?

One afternoon in London not much later, I saw the American hipster-bard Beck practically buying up the whole well-stocked krautrock section at Rough Trade off Portobello Road. Chatting in foreign record shops from Tokyo to Rome, I'd often been asked about 'Kraut music' – 'What are Kraan up to these days?' 'Are Amon Düül still together?' 'Are Faust still playing gigs?' 'Who were the Kosmische Kuriere?' People were all the more disappointed when I had no answers for them.

When I involuntarily ended up at a Hamburg Red Hot Chili Peppers gig in 2008 and was about to head home, relieved, after their regular set, the Californians announced a surprise guest. As it turned out, it was their idol Michael Rother, with whom they performed a furioso version of 'Hallogallo'. What amazed me just as much were the confused faces in the audience, apparently thinking: 'Who the hell is Michael Rother?' If I hadn't realised it before, it was that evening that made me see that I absolutely had to talk to these musicians while I still could, to find out first-hand how their music came about. Once again, it all started with Can – when I revealed my plan, it was Irmin and Hildegard Schmidt who invited me to France, where they live, to tell me their story.

Thankfully, I was also able to meet Holger Czukay one more time for this book. I sat with him in his studio in Weilerswist outside Köln, over hot chocolate and melting lebkuchen on a boiling-hot day. When I told him I'd won *Movies* in a radio phone-in all those years ago, he said it was the perfect way to discover his sound world.

The best krautrock sounds came, in their time, like unheard radio waves from the future, and will go on radioing into the future. This book is about their present day and the past that came before them. And about the people who were part of it.

Christoph Dallach, Hamburg, late 2020

'KRAUT'

'You want krautrock? You'll get krautrock!'
FAUST

MICHAEL ROTHER It all starts with the fact that I don't really like the name.

ULRICH RÜTZEL 'Krautrock' sounds better than 'Deutschrock', at least.

JULIAN COPE A very brilliant term, something like punk insofar as it both takes the piss AND shows tremendous self-awareness.

JAKI LIEBEZEIT I don't mind 'Kraut'. 'Rock' is much worse! Rock doesn't stand for anything at all. You get Nazis doing rock. If [the schlager singer] Heino sings Rammstein, is that rock? Rock is a problematic term, and Can never made typical rock music. That's why we never got really famous in Germany. They wanted rock here, and rock comes from blues, but we had nothing in common with blues. I'd call Can more of a pop group than a rock band.

NIGEL HOUSE As a record dealer, I'm very grateful for the word 'krautrock', because I can put all the interesting German music from back then in one section. I know Tangerine Dream don't have much to do with Can, but from the seller's point of view, the krautrock label is useful. All that these German bands really have in common is the point in time when most of the records were made. It's the same with the so-called 'Manchester bands'. But the pigeonholes help.

SIMON DRAPER I'd even say we invented the term 'krautrock' at Virgin, though some people see that differently. When I started there in the early seventies, I was in charge of purchasing for the mail-order department. We used to get loads of letters from customers and there was huge demand for records from Germany. It was usually bands we'd never heard of. We were aware of Can, Kraftwerk and Faust, but people kept asking for things we had no idea about. One name that kept cropping up was Tangerine Dream. So I got in touch with Rolf-Ulrich Kaiser, the head of their record label Ohr. He sent us everything they'd ever released: Tangerine Dream, Popol Vuh, etc., about thirty albums. I took them home for the weekend to my flat in Ladbroke Grove, listened to them all with my younger brother and a friend, made notes and thought about how to sell them. What genre should I put them in, for our newspaper ads? If I'd just listed them alphabetically, no one would have noticed most of them. So we thought up this new name: 'krautrock'. Maybe someone else had the same idea at the same time, but we did too! And it worked: all thirty krautrock records sold like hot cakes.

GERHARD AUGUSTIN John Peel established the name 'krautrock' for this strange music. But it's completely wrong for bands like Can or Kraftwerk.

WINFRID TRENKLER The term came from one of those arrogant British music journos; there were plenty of them around in those days.

BRIAN ENO I never liked the word because for me it has associations with the war: British soldiers called their German counterparts 'Krauts', and it sounds quite offensive to me. I had been aware of German avant-garde music from the late sixties, although my preference was for the stuff that was coming out of America – the minimalists. But I knew there was a unique music scene and sensibility in Germany and I was paying attention to it.

HARALD GROSSKOPF 'Krautrock' is a wonderful name. Sure, it threw a lot of things together that don't go together: from random German bands that were just copying British and American acts to the craziest electronic musicians. The only thing that really ties them all together is the fact that they all deny having anything to do with krautrock. And it was definitely a term of abuse, originally. I remember an article in the British press when Kraftwerk were first getting successful. They'd printed above it in runic letters: 'MUZAK FROM GERMANY', with the Brandenburg Gate and flaming SA torches, really pretty bad. And the Brits didn't even know that sauerkraut is really healthy food. Whenever I heard the word 'Kraut' in England, I'd think: you come over to Germany, I'll treat you to a bratwurst and sauerkraut. And that's only fair when you've been subjected to an English breakfast.

HELLMUT HATTLER I grew up in Ulm. There were lots of US Army barracks there, and whenever you passed one of them, you'd hear the word 'Kraut'. We were still the enemy.

MANI NEUMEIER I quite like the name actually. It doesn't come from sauerkraut, the food; it's from the word *Kraut* – weed, for smoking.

DANIEL MILLER I didn't like the name at the time. The whole idea of lumping all these completely different musicians into one genre made no sense to me. I can hardly imagine two bands more different than NEU! and Amon Düül. And neither of them had anything in common with Kraftwerk. The name 'krautrock' didn't even sound like music to me, more like geography and politics. It was typical quick-fire British nonsense. These days it's an established term, of course, but I still don't feel comfortable saying it.

THOMAS KESSLER If I'd known back then that I'd fall under the term later, I'd have been very surprised.

IGGY POP It's a loathsome, stupid term but like my own first name it has eventually become a kind of affectionate positive, because the music is so good.

JÜRGEN DOLLASE Krautrock was never a particular style, the field was far too broad for that. There was exciting new music coming out almost every week at the end of the sixties. No one knew where the journey was heading.

SIGGI LOCH Everything that came out of Germany was labelled 'Kraut'. For the Brits, we've been the Krauts for more than two generations, and it's not a term of endearment.

STEVEN WILSON For me, krautrock was always a particular serious artform, with a precise ideology and philosophy, not something staged by the media. I presume none of the bands themselves see themselves as krautrock. The fact that the Faust track is called that is pure irony.

JEAN-HERVÉ PERON Our 'Krautrock' song came about by coincidence. We thought: 'You want krautrock? You'll get krautrock!' These days, the press and young audiences think the name is cool. And we even got to play in a museum. But still, it's annoying that everything that's somehow German and hip got filed under 'krautrock'. The word's history is about as complicated as our band's. At the time, we called what we were doing 'multimedia music' or 'progressive music'. But the Brits are known for their sense of humour, sometimes brilliant and sometimes rock-bottom, just like the word 'krautrock': a little bit Nazi, a little bit icky.

HOLGER CZUKAY The name is nonsense. But I never thought it referred to me anyway. Presumably like everyone they've ever lumped together under it. Whenever we went to the UK with Can, I always felt like we were respected as one of their bands.

IRMIN SCHMIDT It's not a term of abuse, for me. We were just the Krauts, for the Brits. You can't take it as an insult. The French have two names for the Germans: *Les Boches*, that's from the war and it's not that nice, and *Les Chleus*, which is much nicer. 'Chleurock' would be a great name.

STEPHEN MORRIS An ugly name that probably came about something like: 'From Germany? Just put that it's bloody krautrock, innit?' These days they'd have a whole marketing concept for it.

KLAUS SCHULZE I thought 'krautrock' was a horrible name, but it didn't matter in the end. We made electronic music – neither kraut nor rock.

PAUL WELLER I feel the term 'krautrock' doesn't do the music justice. A lot of it isn't 'rock' for a start and certainly not rock 'n' roll. It has a different groove of its own and no swing as such. It is absolutely Northern European and couldn't have come from anywhere else. There's a detachment and feeling of isolation to the music. The feeling of a new generation working outside of what was expected and finding their own path. As someone who was brought up on soul, pop and rock 'n' roll, the German music from this time has a very different form of expression and body to it, to my ears.

CHRISTIAN BURCHARD The *Sun* once wrote about Embryo: 'Some low-flying Messerschmidts.' Maybe it was meant to be funny, but it was also a bit mean. We played with Ginger Baker's Air Force in the Grugahalle in Essen, once. He wouldn't even look at us backstage, just threw his drumsticks at us, really disdainful, and said to his bandmates: 'I've had enough of these damn Bluts.' He called his German audience 'fucking Bluts'.

CHRIS KARRER We don't call English music 'tommyrock', do we? But I don't really give a shit, at the end of the day.

DIETER MOEBIUS For me, krautrock was more bands like Guru Guru or Kraan. They were at least doing rock in a classic line-up, with drums and guitars. Cluster now being classed as krautrock, retrospectively, and me being called a 'godfather of krautrock', that's a misunderstanding.

GABI DELGADO-LÓPEZ For us punks back then, krautrock was more like Grobschnitt, Jane or Birth Control, all music we weren't much into. We didn't include bands like NEU! or Kraftwerk. The problem was actually the word 'rock'. We liked everything that was a bit less 'rocky', stuff like NEU! or Tangerine Dream and Klaus Schulze. It was just newer and more interesting. Guru Guru or Grobschnitt were boring by comparison. Hippy music. The Brits meant krautrock as a term of abuse, and I wish the German bands they labelled with it had found a more confident musical response. I wish they'd said: we're the Krauts! Like African Americans in hip-hop did with the N-word: just annex the term of abuse and turn it around.

LÜÜL Everyone involved at the time had a kind of love–hate relation-ship with the word. But over the years it became more like a seal of approval, partly through accolades from people like Brian Eno and David Bowie. In France they called it 'cosmic music', which I liked a lot better.

LUTZ LUDWIG KRAMER I love my food, but we stood for something new and not for the sauerkraut our grannies used to make. We broke with structures – how could they give us such a backward-looking name?

JEAN-MICHEL JARRE There's something symbolic inherent to it too, though: the sense of affront because the Anglophones weren't involved in the phenomenon. Then again, they're distancing themselves, making it clear that their music is different. A lot of Americans and Brits didn't have the imagination for this kind of music. Of course there are interesting rock groups in France or Germany, but ultimately we only ever produce copies based on American and British templates. After World War Two, rock colonised the whole world. Krautrock was its own thing, with European roots, and that wasn't to everyone's taste.

LIMPE FUCHS I still make my own sauerkraut.

THE FIFTIES

POST-WAR YOUTH

'As a teenager, I daydreamed about shooting up my school
with a tank. But I couldn't afford it so I ditched the plan.'

HOLGER CZUKAY

ALEXANDER VON SCHLIPPENBACH When I started school we still
had to say *'Heil Hitler'* for two days – and all of a sudden it turned into
'Guten Morgen'.

HANS-JOACHIM ROEDELIUS I lived through the tough air-raid
nights and then the whole evacuation, escaping the bombs; it was
crazy. Now, looking back, none of it seems as grim as it felt to me at
the time. I can't even remember if I was really scared when bombs
were dropping on me, for example. My sister says I was scared shitless.
She sometimes had to take me down to the air-raid shelter because our
parents were in a different one.

ALEXANDER VON SCHLIPPENBACH We saw the Russian invasion.
I remember the Americans came to our village first, but unfortunately,
they left again a fortnight later. Then we had to move from comfortable lodgings to a bomb-damaged house with cracks in the walls. It
was pretty special in the winter. It's hard to say whether that childhood
has anything to do with the way I perceive music and express myself
musically. My father hadn't fought in the war because he had a lung
injury. I heard stories, of course, from friends' parents. I knew about
the destruction in the big cities and the massive air raids and I remember the drone of the engines when the American planes flew their
attacks at night. People didn't talk about the war much, especially at
school. They were all just too busy surviving, in those post-war years.

HANS-JOACHIM ROEDELIUS After the war ended in 1945 we were near Berlin, in the Spreewald area, which was Russian-occupied. My mother tried to get me piano lessons but the piano was out of tune. I didn't feel like reading notes and the out-of-tune piano annoyed me as well. Then when my father died of TB in 1948, my mother couldn't afford the lessons any more anyway. My father had been a medical orderly in World War One, had breathed in mustard gas and was left with damaged lungs. That's why he didn't have to go to war later on. No one fired a single bullet in my family, thank God!

JAKI LIEBEZEIT I'm ancient, born in 1938, old enough to have experienced the Third Reich. I didn't understand it at the time, though. Just that my father wasn't there, that puzzled me. And then when I got shot at, I thought it was normal. There were bullets flying around me a few times and I saw bombs hit. As a child, you don't think you might die at that moment. I was very lucky but the Nazis still damaged me – and plenty, at that. I first started asking questions during my schooldays. Up to the end of the sixties, there were a lot of Nazi ideas still going around in Germany. People acted accordingly, that authoritarian master-race behaviour. Most of the teachers in my schooldays had a Nazi past. They weren't really bad Nazis, but they were Nazis. You come across it even now, sometimes. By 1968 the war was only twenty years ago, and plenty of Third Reich mud had stuck. What we did then with Can had a lot to do with clearing away that past.

HOLGER CZUKAY I came to Germany from Poland in 1945, to Beetzendorf near Salzwedel, in the East. I was very young at the time, about six. There were five of us children. When the Russians started closing in, we fled to Limburg. My brother's a philosopher, he went to England and ended up as a philosopher with the Royal Air Force in the early sixties, he really did. Czukay wasn't a good name in the war. So my grandfather made a fake family tree and just claimed we were really called Schüring, to get round the whole Polish thing. Later, I played in a pub with two Polish women on vocals, and they asked me if I knew what *czukay* means. No, I didn't know. It means 'search'. That name suits me better than any other, I thought. Stockhausen advised me to re-adopt the name as well.

IRMIN SCHMIDT My school was a viper's nest of old Nazis. We had a history teacher, for example, who'd been head of training for the Nazis' Reich Labour Service. I found that out because I was reading more and more at the time. The teacher was actually all right as a person, but his past was still an issue for me. I started writing for the school magazine at fifteen, and I went public with every teacher's Nazi biography that I could prove. A man helped me, he was the director of the Amerikahaus. I'd met him at concerts there. He was Jewish, so I thought he was bound to know a lot about what happened back then. Anyway, this man got hold of documents for me; he must have been fascinated by this fifteen-year-old coming along and bombarding him with questions about those days. It must have been around 1952, a bloody long time before 1968. That was when my struggle with German history began.

BERND WITTHÜSER I was born in 1944 in Mülheim on the Ruhr, practically down a mine, the Rosenbogen Mine. The pregnant women and the women who'd just had babies, they were exported to the Sauerland for a while, back then. But after that they all had to go back to the mine, and that's where we got bombed by the Brits. My mother used to chuck me in a bag and run to the nearest bunker. Deep down, I still have that feeling that I only ever wanted to get away; I've always been on the run in my mind. But actually, as children, we liked playing on the bombsites. We had plenty of space; everything was flattened. I didn't know my father and my mother was far too busy to talk to me. So we never spoke about Hitler and the lost war or anything. But my family were miners, salt of the earth, they weren't interested in all that. They had enough on their plate just getting their kids through, there was no scope for deep thoughts.

HARALD GROSSKOPF My schooldays were pretty bad. Apart from a few young teachers, we were taught entirely by Nazi-infiltrated, authoritarian old men. We argued a lot, but less about the Nazi days than about their authoritarian ways. When we got bored we'd just ask the teachers what it was like in the war, and then they'd bluster on about their heroic adventures for hours on end. Later on I saw a few of them on my old school's website, three of them in photos from the late thirties, and if you looked carefully you could clearly see the Nazi party badges on their lapels. The teachers punished us with beatings and bad marks. I once saw a teacher break a boy's finger when he raised his arms in self-defence, and even that had no consequences. Or the school caretaker would come into our classroom if we were too noisy, put his hands on his hips and yell: 'It's like a Jews' school in here!' They got away with that kind of racist crap. No one got upset about it back then.

BERND WITTHÜSER We never talked about the war at school, either. The only thing that happened was more and more teachers came back from POW camps, and they were always crying. But we weren't easy kids, we used to torment them. We were young and we wanted to live – and all they ever did was weep. But you don't pick up on that as a child. When we started to understand it all, later, it was pretty terrible. One more reason for me to want out of there, away from that grey coal-mining country.

IRMIN SCHMIDT In the end I got thrown out of school for my Nazi research. There was our Latin teacher, for example, who I actually liked a lot and he liked me, but unfortunately, he'd been a major in Rommel's army and he didn't exactly stand out for acts of resistance. Another teacher, some Baron von something, had even been head of a Nazi party school in Hungary. I got on well with them but I still went public about their past, which didn't exactly endear me to them, of course. And they came to me and said: 'Schmidt, can't you just stop this?' And I said: 'No! I'm not going to stop. What I find out has to come out, has to be said, and I'll do the same with my father.' The fight with my father was especially painful, naturally, very painful. I asked him how he could live with guilt like that. With something like that on his conscience. And no surprise, he fought back against my accusations.

BERND WITTHÜSER My mother wanted two things: first, for me to get confirmed, as a Protestant – so I had to trudge through that. And secondly, for me to learn a trade, best of all mining. I thought of my grandad and my uncle and their sad black eyes and I knew: I'll do anything, but I'll never go down the pit! So then I trained as an electrician at Krupps. That wasn't all that bad, but I still thought it was shit. Where they'd been making cannons, now they were making little bells. Factory work was not for me, either. I started playing music back then, and soon got out.

GÜNTER SCHICKERT There weren't enough teachers after the war; lots of them had been wiped out. They took the survivors and asked them a quick couple of questions, and Bob's your uncle, they were de-Nazified and they could go back to work. It was exactly the same in the justice system, where the judges and prosecutors were often old Nazis as well. They'd all been officially de-Nazified, but they were pretty authoritarian and stiff. We had a teacher for *Heimatkunde*, which was like local history, Herr Brandt, and everyone had to stand up when he came into the classroom, stand to attention and chant: '*Guten Morgen, Herr Brandt!*' If anyone didn't do it, he'd throw his keys at him. Then one day Ronald, the oldest boy in the class, went to the front, slapped Herr Brandt in the face and said: 'If you throw things at me, I'll hit you.' He got sent to the headmaster and expelled.

JAKI LIEBEZEIT I remember a geography teacher who proudly proclaimed he'd been a U-boat captain. I thought that was interesting and didn't think any more about it. He was a good teacher too. There was

19

no arguing with the teachers. My school was completely conservative and authoritarian. If you said anything bad about a teacher you had to go to the headmaster and you got a warning, and if it happened again they threw you out. I got expelled because I didn't meet their expectations of subservience. So I had to move from the small town of Hannoversch Münden to Kassel, and I soon met the trumpeter Manfred Schoof there – free jazz, no more subservience.

MICHAEL HOENIG The school I went to was a totally reactionary place, Schiller Grammar School, the second school in Berlin to teach French as the first foreign language. All the teachers were men from the Third Reich who'd managed to get back into their old jobs, with a few rare exceptions, of course. In 1967 the headmaster called me in front of all the teaching staff. They wanted to make an example of me, after the [right-wing] Springer press had published a picture of me at a demonstration. It was to be made clear to me that something like that was not allowed, and they wanted to bully some sense into me with bad marks. Luckily, my father was clever enough to go to the school and make a complaint about my treatment. Him doing that for me made me very proud and gave me a lot of strength and emotional protection, but it didn't achieve anything else. I went on arguing with my parents every day. They both worked, worked their fingers to the bone; there was nothing left of their wealthy background after the war. How many women worked back in 1967? My mother went out to work every morning.

IRMIN SCHMIDT At seventeen, I met the photographer for the Dortmund Opera House, a Jewish man who'd come back to Germany. He'd got out of the country by hook or by crook at the last moment, before the war. He was a wonderful person, to whom I owe my love of literature. He was a kind of intellectual father figure for me, and one day he said: 'Everything you've done is good, but it's time to stop now. You have to think of yourself as well.' There's a story that says a lot about what he was like. We were once invited, he and I, to some rich people's house where I'd played chamber music as a student. There was a dinner, and there was this brash man there, perhaps forty at the time, but he didn't know my friend Kirchberg was Jewish. He felt the need to bring the topic up, which none of us really wanted. But this guy just couldn't stop talking, and he said no one could imagine the thing with the six million dead Jews, how was that supposed to work? And then Kirchberg gave him this kind look and said: 'No, I can't imagine it either, all I can imagine is sixteen dead Jews: my father, my mother, my two sisters . . .' – and he reeled off all his murdered relatives. Perfectly calm, listing every one of them by name. You could have heard a pin drop at the table. The man who couldn't stop talking left the room immediately.

HARALD GROSSKOPF We were far too young to stand up to all that, and we hadn't even had it explained to us what it meant to be a Nazi. I was twelve when we went to Bergen-Belsen, and I was shocked. We went along perfectly happily, completely clueless, but when we entered the camp we went quiet. We stood there facing long mass graves with gravestones saying 2,500, 5,000 or 15,000. And then the photos. That was the first time I was really shocked. After that I started asking my parents questions. But our parents wanted to suppress it all, there was suppression everywhere: in the justice system, the police, at school – and at home. The Third Reich cast a huge shadow over West Germany.

MANI NEUMEIER They didn't tell us what Uncle Adolf had done, at school in München. We'd hear stories from parents, friends and acquaintances about what had gone on, but we never covered it at school, neither in writing nor out loud.

GÜNTER SCHICKERT My mother walked out when I was twelve. But she came back, because of me and my sister. My father was severely disabled, often in terrible pain and on tablets. He'd sometimes lose his temper when he drank. At some point it got too much for my mother once and for all, and then she was gone. After that I was alone with my father. So at the time when I asked those kinds of questions, my mother wasn't there any more, and my father refused to talk about the war. When I asked, all he'd say was that he'd been a motorcycle marksman, with a gun in his hand in a sidecar, and always had to give reports. That was in France; I presume he killed a few people there as well, but he didn't like talking about it. But he'd only been there at the beginning, and then his illness meant he was soon unfit to fight. He spent the rest of the war in Berlin. That was bad enough. My mother told me how tough that was. But I didn't see how bad it really was until later, in pictures and films. At school, I was shown a film with footage from the concentration camps, twice. At primary school we all went to the school hall, lights down, roll the film. It was really the hardest things you can imagine, piling up the dead with bulldozers, horrific . . . The looks on their faces. Terrible. It's stayed with me all my life. That horror is still lodged deep inside me.

HOLGER CZUKAY I never really knew my father; he was definitely a Nazi. He used to tell people little things about the Russian campaign, but he never actually said anything. And my mother held back completely on the subject. She felt it was tasteless.

HELLMUT HATTLER They were all just programmed that way. My father always said he did have to go to Russia but he never shot at anyone, because he thought the war was shit. That's not necessarily the truth, but I still thought it was great. My father experienced bad things, of course, but he tried to keep out of it as best he could. I believed him as well. In retrospect it's clear they were traumatised and just wanted to be left in peace. All our parents cared about was owning a home and eating regular meals. I couldn't understand it at the time; I found it unbearable and I just wanted to do everything differently. Through the post-war economic boom, though, and with the new sexual liberation, my generation was in a comfortable position; it was an era of experiments. That freedom we young people had scared the older generations; they'd never known anything like it.

HARALD GROSSKOPF My father was a Nazi party member. There's a photo from 1944, not long before the war ended, where he's wearing his uniform with a blue mark on the lapel. And when we looked carefully, it turned out to be a party badge. So my father stuck with the party to the bitter end. My fight with him became the major conflict of my life. He thought war was terrible, and he even supported me to do community rather than military service, but he claimed the Nazis weren't all that bad. He said he'd had a good time in the Hitler Youth and my mother in the League of German Girls, but it was all long gone and why did we have to talk about politics so much? When I was doing my community service and went home for the weekend, it wasn't ten minutes before the two of us were at each other's throats, always on the same subject. My big brother hadn't asked those questions, but I was the rebel, which was probably what ended up taking me to krautrock.

KARL BARTOS The street where I grew up was full of late returners from POW camps and wounded old soldiers. Someone would knock on our door every day and ask if we could spare anything to eat. They weren't beggars; they'd lost their roots, they didn't know where to go. There were a lot of layers to post-war Germany. There were old Nazis who were now judges or policemen and had just slipped into the next system unnoticed. And there were the broken working people who had nothing, like my parents. My father wouldn't talk about the war; it was taboo. He'd been a Russian prisoner of war at the age of twenty, for more than two years, and he still had frostbite on his feet and severe malaria attacks – hard to imagine. I can even understand, in a way, that he didn't want to talk about all that; he'd handed over his future and his emotions in Russia. These days, Bundeswehr soldiers get a medical release for PTSD after three months in Afghanistan. That's a good thing, but back then a whole generation had post-traumatic stress disorder and psychoses, and never got any treatment. My father suffered from it all his life. I didn't understand his hostile reactions to my questions until much later. In my younger days, it ended up in absolute non-communication. My parents simply weren't capable of having these conversations with me. My father had been brainwashed in the Third Reich. He still functioned after the war, took good care of his family, but his emotions were shot. He thought Marlene Dietrich was a traitor. And then my sister married an occupying British soldier.

LUTZ LUDWIG KRAMER From the age of six to ten, I was at a convent school in the Allgäu, surrounded by nuns who maltreated us. You'd be forced to eat your own vomit for a day and a night, for example. I didn't do it. You'd sit there with your plate, everyone had gone to bed, they wouldn't even let me go to the toilet, I wet myself and was caned on my bare arse and my fingers. I was sent there at six and a half and they let me go home again four years later. After the war, my parents were more interested in their careers than in me. My father was in the film business and my mother was a soprano, worked with the opera singer Rudolf Schock and lots of others. I think they just wanted to get me out of the way. They sold it to me by saying they'd been advised to send me there, but I never believed them. My time with the nuns was traumatic, still is to this day. If you're beaten and maltreated like that at six and a half, you never get it out of your head.

PETER BRÖTZMANN My childhood was fine, actually. My father didn't come back from his Russian POW camp until late; that was in 1949. My mother, my sister and I were evacuated to Pomerania in the last years of the war. And then my mother got us out to the West somehow. For me, that meant I grew up relatively unattended. We spent a lot of time playing in the streets, and that wasn't a bad thing. I learned how to feel independent from a young age. We ran around in street gangs, stealing whatever we could get our hands on: fruit, coal and wood, turnips out of fields, and so on. Pretty much everyone was doing it. We were well organised, but the police would still pay us a visit now and then. At the end of the day, though, our youth was a good time, an adventure. My father had only been a private and he came back from the war at the same rank. His older brother was a high-ranking Wehrmacht officer, though, who'd come and see us once in a while. My father hated talking about his war experiences, but his brother loved telling us about the Wehrmacht's heroic achievements. Listening to him was interesting, at least. But my real conflicts with the Nazi era happened elsewhere. I remember them showing Alain Resnais' film *Night and Fog* at my grammar school one day. I must have been about fourteen. That was the experience that changed everything for me; my parents both came from what's now Poland. And then I read up about the Warsaw ghetto and stories like that, read everything I could find on the subject.

MICHAEL ROTHER The past wasn't talked about at home. My father suffered a lot during World War Two. He was desperately unhappy to be called up for military service, he said, and I believed him. He spent five years as a prisoner of war in Russia, didn't get back until 1949. I played in München recently, and before the gig I went for a walk around the neighbourhood where I first grew up. I took photos, went to the building where we used to live, stood in the doorway and looked out at the world, to compare my memories of the past with the present. From a child's perspective, all the war damage was exciting; a good deal was burned down and bombed out. We got to play in the ruins of the bombed houses. Secretly exploring blocked-off stairwells was an adventure. My parents created a perfect world for me. I was well looked-after and loved, shielded from anything that might have been upsetting. Painful war memories and things like that weren't discussed when I was around. So it was an advantage that I was still so young after the war. When I came back to Düsseldorf with my parents in 1963, after our years abroad, every trace of the war was gone and the economy was up and running again. But my father wouldn't have been willing to talk about it. Then again, I never thought of raising the subject either. After his time in Pakistan, and before that in London, the nice schoolboy Michael had four years of school to catch up on. That's a lot; you can imagine how many sleepless nights I had. I was even tutored in German for a year and a half. It was hard work. My father died before any tension could have come up between us. After that I took care of my mother. It never occurred to me to make trouble. And I never had to argue; I was even allowed to bring girlfriends home. My mother even put up with me practising guitar for six hours a day.

CHRISTIAN BURCHARD I saw hardly any war damage. There wasn't much bombing in Hof or Bayreuth, or not compared to München, at least. As a child, I was incredibly impressed to see tanks driven by Black soldiers. I have very clear memories of that. The soldiers would smile and wave at us kids. That was a big experience for me. I thought: cool, Black men are in charge of the world! I must have been about three or something. The Black soldiers were very friendly, but everyone ran away from them. We had a teacher at primary school who kept talking about how he'd shot Russians. He loved reminiscing and revelling in having wiped out piles of Russians with his machine gun, which ones he'd shot in the head and where he'd shot them all. That was part of our primary education. And it went on the same way at grammar school. On the day commemorating Stauffenberg's attempt on Hitler's life, the teacher came into the classroom and stared out of the window and then said he had to do this commemoration with us, but that the men we were commemorating were actually traitors. The headmaster was an SPD member by then, but he'd been a high-ranking Nazi party functionary before. We were well aware of that old Nazi stench. A lot of teachers still revelled in their acts of heroism, called the resistance in Germany a terrible disaster. Said we'd only lost the war because of all those traitors. Debates weren't possible; they could ruin your life if they wanted to – you didn't stand a chance as a schoolboy. We had to write an essay once about how we imagined German reunification. I suggested leaving NATO and joining the Warsaw Pact, and that would get reunification done pretty quickly. Of course, that got me an F and a whole lot of trouble. I even had to sign something saying that that had never been taught in class. No teacher I had was ever brought to justice for what he'd done in the Third Reich.

PETER BRÖTZMANN At grammar school, there were teachers with personal 'background issues', if you will, but I was lucky enough only to be taught by sensible people. We read Brecht, Kafka and [the humanist writer] Wolfgang Borchert at school. I had no reason to complain. I set up a jazz club at school when I was fourteen. I'd play the dozen records I owned in the music room in the afternoon. There was a school band with a good clarinettist. He finished school and his spot was free, so I picked up the clarinet and started playing along with my records. And that was how the entire drama started.

LUTZ LUDWIG KRAMER I never tried to fit in at school. Maybe that's why they picked me as class representative. All I did in the job was propaganda for the Beatles and the Stones, and I made sure all the important Merseybeat news made it to our noticeboard. I was constantly arguing with the teachers, who were really tough on the less well-off kids. And then I'd complain to the headmistress about that kind of thing, because it was so unjust. One of my school reports said I had an 'exaggerated sense of justice' – word for word. They claimed I was incapable of fitting in, so they decided to send me to the school psychiatrist. His name was Kaschinsky; he said I was 'not pliable' and recommended they take me out of grammar school and send me to a secondary modern, and then they wanted me to train as a bricklayer later on. So I got sent to a new school. The headmaster was an early Nazi party member who hadn't been allowed to work in the fifties, for that reason, but then got a job at this secondary modern school. The day I turned up, he tore the 'Make Love Not War' badge off my parka. West Berlin was still fascist in spirit, all over the place physically and mentally. My class teacher advised me to leave as soon as possible, persuaded me I was intelligent enough for grammar school. And later I did go back.

GÜNTER SCHICKERT I was conceived during the Soviet blockade. I didn't think post-war Berlin was that bad. My mother used to say: 'You were born when the first bananas came.' After the blockade, West Berlin was a great place to be, nice and quiet, hardly any cars, plenty of space everywhere, like one big adventure playground. There were bombsites on every street. We'd play in old garages where the concrete ceilings were slanting in, but we still went in there, of course. We'd go down to the cellars in the embassy district in Tiergarten; one of us got buried under rubble down there once.

PETER BAUMANN My first memories of Berlin start around ten years after the war. What's stuck with me is that there wasn't any fruit. When things were going well, my parents would get us an orange once a week, which we shared between the four of us. As a child, I thought it was normal that so much was destroyed. We didn't even notice all the bullet holes left in the walls. I only became aware of the political circumstances in 1961, when the Berlin Wall was built. I was away with my mother and brother, and my mother suddenly said we had to go straight back to Berlin because they were building a wall there. That didn't scare me much, but I was a bit shaken by how nervous my mother was.

LÜÜL I was born seven years after the war, in Berlin. But there were still ruins everywhere and lots of bombed-out buildings when I was little. I lived in Charlottenburg, though, where everything had been fixed up nicely again; we'd just discover an old bunker now and then. We were perhaps the first generation who didn't experience the war first-hand. My father had been a soldier, and my sister, who was on the far left, always started arguments with him. I was less interested in politics. It was much more important to me that my parents were loving and open. At some point, though, I did wonder how it had all been possible. Later on, I drove through East Germany a few times and got regularly stopped and searched, with my long hair. I felt kind of sorry for the guys who did it, because they were all just taking orders. But the intimidation still worked. For later generations, it's always easy to say: how could you let it happen? But when push comes to shove, only a few people are really brave.

MICHAEL HOENIG I was born in Hamburg, although both my parents were from Berlin. They had to get out of Berlin for a while, there was no other way to escape. We moved back in 1954, but the city was still in a state of destruction. We moved into social housing by the Lietzensee, a beautiful lake. My parents got a flat in a new building that belonged to [film director and mountain climber] Luis Trenker, who lived right at the top in a penthouse with a roof garden. I had an idyllic childhood in that neighbourhood: church and kindergarten, a perfect world. The war ruins were far away in other parts of town. But my father would take me walking around them and explain to me what had happened during the war and why. It was a really clever thing to do, sometimes taking me around town on a bus on the weekend and telling me about his younger days. Only I didn't understand how it was all connected for a long time. That didn't happen until I was twelve or thirteen.

LUTZ LUDWIG KRAMER We lived in this amazing flat in Berlin's Neu-Westend area. Every third mansion had been bombed because the Nazi generals used to live there during the war. And we'd play Cowboys and Indians in the ruins of these old Nazis' mansions. I remember the swimming pools full of shrapnel. That was the atmosphere I grew up in. My father had been classified as half Jewish by the Nazis and persecuted. He was in the Reich Theatre Chamber but he got hardly any acting jobs. He'd always black out his Jewish name on forms because our real name was Lazerus, which would be my name as well, in theory. But my parents took my grandmother's name instead, and that's what saved them, because she was from this elite Rhineland family, heritage white as snow. My mother was a singer. She went to the front in the war and sang there. My father tried to get acting jobs and set up a concert agency in Potsdam. I've got boxes and boxes of correspondence that proves my father was persecuted not just by the Nazis, but by the East German Socialist Unity Party as well, later on. My parents tried not to talk about the war. And they had very bad memories of it because they'd been bombed out twice and lost everything. In the GDR, they lost their land as well, by appropriation. All my father ever said was that there could never be anything like the Nazis ever again. He was left-leaning, while my mother was pretty conservative. She was pals with [the Bavarian arch-conservative] Franz Josef Strauss; she met him and got his autograph. I've got letters from [the conservative politicians] Ludwig Erhard, Strauss, Helmut Kohl and Edmund Stoiber to my mother. A very strange story.

LIMPE FUCHS My mother was a zither player from Innsbruck, and my father was a violinist in a silent-movie theatre in München. During the war they had to sell their instruments to buy food. Then they never went back to playing after the war, and the only music we heard was on the radio or, later, the TV. I grew up in München, and my father only ever wanted to listen to the Bayern 1 station, but I always loved the whistles and trills of shortwave radio. My father thought that was odd, of course, because the only music you get in München is German folk music and classical stuff. But we never argued over it; actually, we barely talked to each other. My father was a convinced communist. He was denounced, locked up in Stadelheim prison for three months, and then emigrated to South America. He really wanted to go to the US, but they wouldn't let Germans in.

RENATE KNAUP The war hadn't made a mark on the Allgäu region [in the mountainous deep south of Germany]. Here and there a town centre had been shot up, but I never saw any of that as a child. There'd been hardly any air raids, either. The British Army was stationed in our town, Sonthofen. It's a garrison town with three military barracks, and it's where Hitler had his horrific Ordensburg cadre school. As an attractive young woman, I'll just say it was a terrible place to live because there were always about forty pairs of eyes on you wherever you went. My best friend and I swore an oath never to go out with a soldier. We talked about the war at home, of course. My father was a pilot and a mechanic and got sent to Tunis and I don't know where else. He probably only survived because he'd behaved badly and they wouldn't let him fly any more. Everyone else from his squadron died. My father was a Nazi too, but not the really rigid kind, more like: 'We were men!' My grandfather, though, completely condemned National Socialism and often argued with my father about it. But I never talked to either of them much about the war. When my father got the blues, he'd cry. A lot of men came back from the war with their nerves shot. And they were never looked after. No one ever asked them how it had been for them. My father drowned his blues in alcohol, if he had to.

MANI NEUMEIER I didn't pick up on much of the war. Luckily, we didn't live in München; we were out by Lake Starnberg. But I did see the night sky light up above München from there. The droning of hundreds of American planes flying over us – I still have that sound in my head. The surrender was very liberating; the feeling of constant fear fell away.

RENATE KNAUP My father was a musician, played swing and that kind of thing. He did it professionally until I was six. Then he was in an American prisoner-of-war camp. He was an agile, worldly man, so he started a band in the camp, and that meant he got into the officers' mess and got hold of great things for trading and fabric my mother could make clothes out of. There was a lot of wheeling and dealing. I

31

only knew my father as a nice-smelling man in a black tuxedo, going out and coming back home with friends at four in the morning, and then my mother would conjure something up in the kitchen and we kids would sit on the musicians' laps. I thought that was great, even if my mother didn't. But we were a bit out of things because we weren't an average family. I've got three siblings, and we were always singing at home, four or five of us. We didn't get our presents at Christmas until we'd sung the whole litany, in six parts. My father was a very good singer, and so was my mother.

CHRISTIAN BURCHARD First there was nothing but football, and then music came along. No idea why. I had piano lessons as a kid and had to play Bach and that kind of thing. If I played a wrong note, the teacher would whack me so hard on the fingers that it hurt for a week. The first music I was into was on the radio; I can't remember exactly what it was. All I know is that my parents switched it off. Some sort of jazz, presumably. Then we went on a school trip for a week, and there was a piano, which they let you play. I plunked the keys a bit and my friend Dieter drummed along on saucepans. We were surprised to find people liked it. And it was so much fun that we got more and more into music.

RENATE KNAUP I liked learning things, but my parents didn't give us much support. When it came to school, we were on our own. Then when I did my O-levels [*mittlere Reife* in Germany] there was a teacher who didn't like me, and she failed me. They'd punish us at school by slamming our elbows on the edge of the desk. One girl who came from a difficult social background got washed with the blackboard sponge every morning, in front of the whole class. Pretty scary stuff. It was women who were mean to us like that. Because I had a good singing voice, I got sent to other classes to demonstrate: 'This is Renate, listen to her, this is how to do it!' That was a bit of a privilege. After I left school I did a commercial apprenticeship. I had to get out from under my parents' feet and earn my own money. I had no idea what I wanted to do, so my mother said: 'Come on, you've got to do something sensible, do an apprenticeship in a shop.' I just looked at her and said: 'Mum, I'll do it for three years, but afterwards I'll do something completely different.' And then I stuck it out for three years in an optician's, jewellery and china shop in the Allgäu. The boss wanted to keep me on and make me a department manager, but I said: 'No, thanks – I've got to go to England.' That was a big decision, obviously.

ASMUS TIETCHENS I grew up in Eimsbüttel in the north of Hamburg. At Hellkamp station and across the road, there were bombsites where we still played as little kids in the late forties and early fifties. There were no unexploded bombs left, though; they'd all been cleared. I have very clear memories of it. But we never asked what had happened there – we were kids. The rubble was just there. It's not like kids these days would ask: 'Where do the nice trees and pavements come from?' If the adults didn't explain of their own accord why the rubble was there, and as long as our building was all in one piece, we didn't ask. Of course, once I got older I did start asking questions at some point. I went to a conservative grammar school, so those questions were answered in a very particular way. Looking back, I have to say that some teachers misrepresented the facts. They taught us a hair-raising version of history, but hardly anyone questioned it. A few of my schoolmates knew more than me, reflected more on the matter and dug deeper. For a long time, I didn't understand their protests, and I was very late to start wondering: why are they arguing so hard with our history teacher?

JEAN-MICHEL JARRE There were discussions in France too. My mother fought in the French Resistance. Through her, I grew up with the attitude that we had to make a new start after World War Two – on all levels. My mother was also clear from an early age that you must never equate ideologies with people, and that a German isn't necessarily a Nazi. That was a rare standpoint in France at the time. Her message was: cast off all the ballast and seek your own path. That was how she pushed me into the future.

JEAN-HERVÉ PERON My mother came from the Basque country. She worked for a Spanish countess, and she loved singing. My father was from Brittany. He played the violin and built ships. I was born in 1949 in Casablanca, and my sister was born there too; it had something to do with the war. We played a lot of music together at home. My mother was always singing. She sang while I was still in the womb: Spanish, French and Basque. It must have influenced me, for sure. To this day, I have folk songs in my mind that my mother used to sing and schlager tunes by Gilbert Bécaud and that kind of thing. My sister and I were forced to go to music school. I was young and didn't want to make music. And music lessons at school were awful. But I still played the trumpet.

JEAN-MICHEL JARRE I always had a special relationship with Germany; that goes back to my mother. A cousin of mine was in charge of feeding the French troops in Berlin, and I spent a few summer holidays with him at the end of the fifties. That was a Berlin still scarred by the destruction of World War Two, a dark, unruly city where you'd see a lot of suffering. But, for me, the chaotic atmosphere was really exciting. You got the feeling anything you could possibly imagine might happen there, because nothing really worked properly any more. Berlin back then was full of people who wanted to try things out and experiment. There was this ludicrously creative atmosphere. I remember you could physically feel the city's huge energy. And that was reflected in new German film and in music like krautrock. It all has its roots in the time before the Wall was built.

MICHAEL HOENIG I never got any musical training and I wasn't interested in it either. Music was something my grandmother listened to, when I had lunch in her apartment on Richard-Wagner-Strasse twice a week, opposite the ruined German Opera House in Berlin. Once they rebuilt it, she immediately dragged me along to all the performances. All my friends and I tried things out back then, experimented with various forms of expression: I was doing photography, light projections, which were always fun and inspiring. I was sixteen or seventeen at the time. I started making music at eighteen. Not that people would call it music; it was more on a metaphysical level. My parents had always offered to get me piano or guitar lessons. All my friends had learned some instrument or other. I tried it for a while, but I couldn't stand being taught something in such strict arrangements. Music lessons seemed to me like some Nazi trying to force me to do things. So I never learned an instrument. It was just too boring. Luckily my parents were wise enough to say: 'If you don't want to, you don't have to.' So music wasn't on the agenda for me at all.

RENATE KNAUP I stayed in London for a year and a half. My parents didn't have a telephone back then, so I just used to write occasional letters home. My boyfriend was working at Ronnie Scott's, where I saw a lot of big acts. And then I'd often walk around Soho on my own at night – pretty dangerous. I lived on Wardour Street and used to take a short cut down Dean Street late at night. It was scary, but very exciting.

ALEXANDER VON SCHLIPPENBACH There wasn't a lot of music at home. There'd be Bavarian folk music and marches on the radio sometimes. My father wasn't bad on the accordion, and after the war people in Upper Bavaria would sometimes play music for food. The first strong, direct musical influence I remember was the Upper Bavarian Jakob Roider, known as 'Roider Jackl'. He was a very popular man, almost an icon of Bavarian folk. He played the guitar and sang. His performances were impressive experiences because it was clear he was at one with his music. I still remember that very well, to this day. I must have been seven or eight when I saw him; I was still at primary school in Törwang near Rosenheim. A village in the middle of nowhere.

JAKI LIEBEZEIT I wanted to be a musician even as a child, and I started young. I had accordion lessons at the age of seven. My mother sent me to an old man who taught me a good few things, simple folk songs and chords, basic musical knowledge. But I didn't like the accordion. Music was always important in my family. My father was a musician, but I didn't know him. Still, he cast a long shadow, a respected man as a musician; he played the organ and violin. Other than that, I know very little about him. Except perhaps at least that music wasn't a bad thing. My mother still tried to persuade me to learn a decent trade, but I always wanted to make music. I could have been a sound engineer, there was a job going on the radio. That's why I moved to Köln when I was twenty. Before that I'd ended up in Kassel, where Manfred Schoof introduced me to jazz. And then he went to Köln to study orchestral music at the conservatory.

HANS-JOACHIM ROEDELIUS I was born in the west of Berlin, and after the war and our evacuation, I stayed in the Russian zone. I went to school there until I was sixteen, and then I had to do military service in the East German army. One year in, I made an escape attempt, and it worked. Then I was in the West.

IRMIN SCHMIDT Even as a child, I had these moments when I felt totally out of place. I was sent to a home on the North Sea for a while when I was twelve. Lying in bed with the other twenty boys in the dorm, I heard the sniffling of homesickness. But even though I was very close to my sisters and parents, I could easily imagine never going back home. Thinking about it, I felt so heartless myself that it made *me* cry. My mother was very musical, with a ruthlessly good ear. When I was doing my piano practice, she'd come in after a while and say: 'You've just made the same mistake for the fourth time over.'

HOLGER CZUKAY I never rebelled against my parents; it didn't even occur to me. Partly because I never really got to know my father, because he got very ill quite early on – multiple sclerosis – and I had no reason to stand up to him. I was more likely to launch into teachers or the headmaster. And then I was a real rebel. I made sure I got made class representative. I was in all the newspapers, even when I was at school. My sister was the only one in our family who had a strong interest in music, and it was she who first discovered my musical talent. I'd started playing little things on the piano back in kindergarten. Our first radio, during the war, knocked me for six: the first time I heard Mozart's *Eine kleine Nachtmusik* I was transfixed. After the war, I discovered my love of electronics in a radio workshop, where I had a job repairing old radios.

JÜRGEN DOLLASE I grew up without any media. My father was a headmaster, there were five of us children, and we saw our first TV in 1962, when I was fourteen. Back then, not all the Nazis' pipelines had been capped. My father had trained as a teacher in the thirties. He was on the left, and directly after the war he had something to do with the communists. Laurel and Hardy and that kind of thing was too American for us. We didn't watch Hollywood movies in the cinema as kids. That was trashy American culture – my parents still had that attitude from before the war. My father didn't see my older brother for the first time until he was four years old. But I got a really good education from my father. Because we didn't watch or listen to any media, I barely experienced 1950s phenomena like schlager or rock 'n' roll. Oddly enough, my father did buy himself Bill Haley's 'Rock Around the Clock'.

GÜNTER SCHICKERT Schlager was so popular because there was no other German music left. A lot of people didn't like English stuff, called it 'Hottentot' music. My sister had to fight with my parents to listen to rock 'n' roll. And I only ever listened to Elvis secretly, when no one else was at home. I'd stand in front of the mirror and sing along.

HOLGER CZUKAY My father was a lawyer, so that meant I never wanted to be one. The job had a stench to it that I didn't like. I always knew I wanted to do something to do with music. When I discovered my passion for electronics, I thought for a while I'd be a radio engineer. But then I turned eighteen and had an awakening. I thought I was too late for a music career, I'd missed my chance for a career as a wunderkind. So I said to myself: 'You're not going to be a wunderkind now!' I joined a Dixieland band at school. I picked up a guitar; at first I only played one string, but then I learned a new string every week until I could play all six. I worked my way in slowly.

JÜRGEN DOLLASE One thing my father talked about more than the war was his time as a prisoner of war. He'd been deployed doing harvesting work in the French countryside for a while. I went to the place later, Chappes-sur-Allier, to compare what he'd told me with what I found there. I'll put it like this: he'd described everything a bit bigger than it really was. The chateau where he'd worked was a pretty measly place. It was strange: when I walked along the village streets, a couple of old women gave me some odd looks. I look quite a lot like my father. Anyway, my father always raved about French food, which made a lasting impression on me. The only thing he said about the war was that he'd once been demoted and interned after making rude remarks about the Führer when he was drunk. He was lucky they didn't put him up against a wall.

IRMIN SCHMIDT It wasn't a problem being German in New York in 1966. No one in the art scene cared where you came from. Steve Reich is Jewish, and he never made any comment on the subject. We only talked about music. John Cage and the others were all extremely tolerant. Our Can records came out on United Artists in the early seventies. A lot of the staff there were Jewish, and I never heard a bad word from them, either. Even though I made a big fuss on my first visit there – when I listened to the newly distributed pressing of our first album released in the US, *Ege Bamyası*, I noticed they'd mixed a whole load of reverb over the top. Our original was too awkward for them. I flipped out; it sounded terrible. They'd have had good reason to say: 'This German idiot's annoying! Not only does he make unsellable music, he's really hard work as well.' But they were still always really friendly.

ACHIM REICHEL What interests me is the cultural fracture that arose from the war. I never understood why we put a stop to our entire culture because of thirteen years of the Third Reich. All of a sudden, everything risky was suspicious, dangerous, because it might lead to fascism. But if you went on that basis, you might as well have just stopped straight away. What I wanted was to go to sea, like my father and grandfather, but then the guitar got in the way. It wasn't a conscious decision. That was just what you did. My father died when I was little, and my mother thought I'd be better off learning a trade.

IRMIN SCHMIDT Someone said the other day that there's always a certain darkness and melancholy to my sound worlds. I grew up in a time when Germany had been destroyed, and its entire culture along with it. I had to deal with a lot of unpleasant things, growing up. A lot of sadness came out of that. The centre of all my grief was my conflict with my father. At some point, though, we made a kind of peace with each other. In the end we found harmony, partly thanks to my mother. My parents lived very long lives, and from a certain point there were things we just stopped talking about. Making music has helped me to cope with a fair amount of anger and grief.

JAZZ

'We jazz men were as rejected back then as rock musicians.'
PETER BRÖTZMANN

SIEGFRIED SCHMIDT-JOOS The Nazis had left a cultural vacuum in their wake after World War Two. Left-wing and liberal artists and intellectuals had either emigrated or died in concentration camps. The lost Jewish creatives left a gap in popular and entertainment music as well. As ecstatic non-European music not rooted in English and Viennese operetta, jazz was more or less banned. But there were a lot of jazz men among the musicians, of course. They started right back again in May 1945 with improvised, swinging sounds – and faced a lot of resistance in the early post-war years from cultural bodies and local authorities.

JAKI LIEBEZEIT German jazz musicians were a protest movement to begin with. Jazz was the music of freedom; it had been banned by the Nazis. That's one reason why it got so big in Germany after the war.

PETER BRÖTZMANN We had to start over from zero. And my colleagues in rock were in the same boat. Jaki Liebezeit and I are the same generation and we both had quite a struggle with our unwanted 'heritage'. The feeling that I had to live with a sense of shame set in pretty early for me. Presumably back in my schooldays, the first time I came across it. I kept being confronted by German history, through talking to people in Holland, England, Scotland and wherever my music took me later on. Being German was a pretty strange thing at the time, and sometimes it wasn't easy.

40

MANI NEUMÉIER At home, all we listened to was endless schlager and oompah marches.

PETER BRÖTZMANN At home, my parents only listened to European classical music, which used to wind me up. Whenever my father came home, he was in charge of our listening. We only had a record player and one radio. I'd listen to my jazz programme on the Voice of America, at midnight. I had to tiptoe downstairs and put my ear to the radio, 'Take the "A" Train' and that kind of thing.

MANI NEUMEIER The first music I liked was a Louis Armstrong record I heard at fourteen. It was 'Skokiaan', a great track – it was so different, so effervescent, exotic and alive, just hotter than anything I'd heard before! From then on, I was a jazz fan, and I knew I wanted to do something in that direction myself.

PETER BRÖTZMANN I was fourteen when I saw Sidney Bechet in Wuppertal. The first time with an American band, and then a year later with a French one. There was this saxophonist on stage, he really let loose, even on ballads. A few years later I saw Coleman Hawkins, Bud Powell, Kenny Clarke and Oscar Pettiford in Essen, all milestones. Jazz offered me unique emotions.

MANI NEUMEIER Then I saw Louis Armstrong a few years later, live in Zürich, which knocked me right out. He came out on stage, and five thousand people went crazy! It was totally full on, from the very first note. You don't get that kind of thing in jazz these days. Back then, all the great jazz masters came to Zürich: Art Blakey, Duke Ellington, Miles Davis, Thelonious Monk, Charles Mingus and John Coltrane. Stockhausen played there later too. I learned my trade from those musicians, if you like, or at least I started to drum on anything and everything at the age of sixteen, and at seventeen I had my own Dixieland combo. I'd never heard a note of rock up till then. I had to learn another trade, though, as a plumber, because I was supposed to take over my uncle's business, but then I made it clear pretty quickly that that wasn't going to happen.

ALEXANDER VON SCHLIPPENBACH I went to boarding school at ten and started playing piano there. What attracted me to the piano was that you could play so many notes at the same time. And it was easy to make the sounds – you didn't have to make a huge effort to get a passable sound out in the first place, like with a wind instrument. Plus, there were pianos just standing around there for anyone to use. Then this kid from Berlin came to the school who could play boogie-woogie and motivated me to copy him. That's how I discovered jazz.

PETER BRÖTZMANN At some point I found this group of students from the Folkwang School, all a bit older than me, but I just went along with my clarinet and joined in. And they didn't send me home; they told me I could come back again. We played swing and that kind of thing. Later it got a bit more modern and they said I'd need a saxophone. So I sold my bike, my electric train set and all sorts of stuff to pay for my first saxophone. I was about sixteen at the time. Then I dropped out of grammar school and went to what they called a school of applied arts in Wuppertal, which also offered sculpture classes and those kinds of things. My parents were horrified that I didn't want to do A-levels [*Abitur* in Germany], of course, and they insisted I study advertising graphic design. But I was already taking painting classes on the side.

IRMIN SCHMIDT Jazz has been with me since I was fourteen. I've always had jazz records and really loved jazz. One crucial thing was certainly also that my parents called it 'Negro music' and thought it was 'terrible', 'horrific', especially my father. He was constantly trying to put me off jazz. He never forbade anything, mind you, even though we'd sometimes scream and shout at each other about it. So I had a close relationship to jazz early on, without ever making any myself. I first heard jazz on the radio and at friends' places, people who had less to do with classical music. There was a jazz club in Dortmund back then, and I think that was its name: Jazzclub. It was run by this guy who'd been horribly disfigured in the war. He had only half a jaw left, but he had incredible charisma and terrific energy to run this jazz club. He played piano and sang vocals. Things like Bessie Smith or Big Bill Broonzy just made me melt. I listened to an incredible amount of that kind of thing; I internalised it alongside my classical stuff and took both equally seriously.

GÜNTER SCHICKERT I started playing the trumpet in church, at thirteen. And then when I finished school at fifteen, I said: 'Dad, I'm going to study the trumpet!' 'Good idea,' my father said, 'but you can forget it; we can't afford it. You'll have to learn a proper trade first.' So I applied to a music shop, Musikhaus Simonowski near Zoo Station. And around that time, a friend of my sister's played me jazz records by Donald Byrd and people like that. I noticed it was pretty good stuff, if you played it fast enough. I soon got really into free jazz; you didn't need to learn any notes, just go for it, move your fingers quick and blow well. And I could do that! I carried on playing hymns in church, but only on the side. All that was just about the sheet music. It made me love the free-jazz sessions all the more – you were free, without notes. And that freedom fascinated me.

ALEXANDER VON SCHLIPPENBACH Jazz on the radio was very important. The *Voice of America Jazz Hour* was on the American Forces Network (AFN) every night from midnight until one, presented by Mr Willis Conover [now semi-forgotten, but a legendary name as a DJ in his time, especially in Eastern Europe]. It was a very good, informative show where they played all the new stuff: cool jazz, bebop and so on. I had to listen to it secretly, of course, on my little transistor radio. I'd set my alarm at boarding school, get up at night and sneak into the shower room to listen to jazz. I got my bearings by what was on the radio, and after the show I'd spend all my money in record shops. I'd take a train from my school to München, where they had the latest records from America, but I'd go to gigs there as well. My first live jazz was *Jazz at the Philharmonic* with Dizzy Gillespie and Oscar Peterson, the great masters. Impressions to last a lifetime.

JEAN-HERVÉ PERON I listened to jazz on the radio to begin with, and when I was twelve I joined a group that met regularly at a youth club to listen to records. First trad jazz, then cool jazz and Miles Davis, but always Louis Armstrong. They were my first heroes.

LUTZ LUDWIG KRAMER As a thirteen-year-old, I was really into Richard Wagner. That was the music my parents played. My father even once produced Stravinsky. I actually come from a bit of a culture-vulture background. From the age of thirteen, I practically grew up with John Coltrane, through my older brother – he was constantly playing Coltrane records. I'd listen to them secretly myself, because he was such an elitist that no one else was allowed to lay a finger on his holy relics.

HOLGER CZUKAY I entered a jazz competition when I was still at school. I was a complete amateur, but the jazz I played with a band I was in was really modern. Before my slot, a radio editor from WDR – his name was Schulz-Köhn – came into the dressing room and told me: 'Holger, the judges can't deal with you, they don't know what pigeonhole to put you in. But let me make a suggestion: you play here but don't enter the competition, and then later you come to me at Westdeutscher Rundfunk and I'll do some recordings with you where Kurt Edelhagen did his.' I'd just turned twenty and I didn't care about the competition, but that editor's offer – that was a big deal! The day before my appointment at WDR was my A-level music exam, and I failed. The music teacher came to see my mother and said: 'Your son's not mentally mature enough!' That made my mother go out and buy me a piano, thinking she had to give me some kind of encouragement and support. What I played at WDR was recorded; I've still got the tape. I listened to it recently and was surprised by how good I was at twenty. I'd already finished composing my first piece. After a few people heard it, it made the Duisburg newspapers. My teachers didn't like that one bit.

CHRISTIAN BURCHARD I started out studying in Erlangen, with digs in Nuremberg, but I soon realised uni wasn't the place for me. My choice was: either I throw myself into music or I find a place for myself in normal life. I picked music. My first stop along the way was Heidelberg; they had a jazz club there with sessions every night. A lot of musicians came along from the Eastern Bloc – they could still travel back then – and a lot of Black musicians as well. I met Jimmy Jackson there, the amazing organist who played on our first few Embryo records. People like Jan Hammer played at the club; later on, he moved to America and made it big there. But the Black musicians in particular were of a different school – when they kicked off it had groove and soul, people would stand on their chairs and scream and shout. Next up was München. There were two jazz clubs there just for Black people and three for white people, where they played more Dixieland stuff, which was in at the time. Bebop had a reputation as druggy music, and free-jazz players were seen as charlatans, but there were key things happening in modern jazz at that time. When world music came in later, I already knew the jazz pioneers, people like Yusef Lateef, who'd been working with Oriental scales and instruments like nose flutes since the mid-fifties.

IRMIN SCHMIDT There weren't any German jazz bands in our area to begin with. If jazz did come our way, it would be like in the Dortmund jazz club, where there was someone booking the British and American bands who were on tour. He usually brought them over from the Paris jazz clubs; it wasn't far away. But all the interesting stuff had to be imported, because there was nothing interesting left after the war. That was one of the reasons why I took such a vehement interest in Neue Musik and later staged John Cage and things like that – I wanted to be part of re-establishing German culture, to do my bit personally.

ALEXANDER VON SCHLIPPENBACH I'd played in amateur jazz bands before. Then my first proper job was when Gunter Hampel and I got an offer to accompany George Gershwin's musical *Girl Crazy* in a theatre for two months. After that we carried on independently, and I was in a quintet with Manfred Schoof. We were heavily featured on the radio by Joachim-Ernst Berendt, and that was how I started earning money out of music. Before that, I'd done a short stint studying composition in Köln in my early twenties, and I'd been interested in Neue Musik before that, specifically in the Schönberg school. In my composition degree, they taught us strict rules and basic music theory, which are very valuable if you want to make music. I never felt restricted by those rules, but I stuck with jazz in the end. At first, we made desperate attempts to play bebop and learn everything that came from jazz. Then I got hold of lots of free-jazz records and listened to them with friends. The idea, even then, was whether we could combine the atonal sound of Neue Musik, which had nothing in common with the pretty traditional bebop chord progressions, with the attitude of jazz – to invent our own new language. And at some point, what arose was a mental outline of that music, which we then filled in together. But not as a manifesto or out of wanting to do something absolutely different, more out of musical necessity, out of playing together.

PETER BRÖTZMANN The mid-sixties were the heyday of hard bop: Art Blakey, Horace Silver – wonderful music, but it wasn't enough. It was too formalistic for me, always theme–improvisation–theme, and all the instruments in a set order; I wanted to get away from that. I wanted to liberate the saxophone! And that liberation has always been a driving force for me. Others also wanted to liberate jazz back then, in Europe as well, but German free jazz always sounded different from the Dutch or British stuff, for example, because we had something to work through. The Brits focused on aesthetic and formal problems, and the Dutch had different resources, especially their links to folk. But we Germans had our gruesome history to deal with, which made our music sound much more aggressive than that of our neighbours. And they noticed it too. There were a lot of free-jazz fans who'd say: 'I'll listen to anything, except Brötzmann!' I was too aggressive for them, too wild, too lawless. That died down over the decades, but that's how it was back then.

ALEXANDER VON SCHLIPPENBACH Free jazz was in the air. My colleagues and I might have been among the first in Germany, but the music was developed in parallel in Holland, Scandinavia and Britain as well. In Germany, it wasn't freer than in the rest of the world, but it did have a different character. The Brits were all very abstract, and the Dutch had a good sense of humour and could work with traditional songs unselfconsciously. We soon had contacts with the Dutch and played with them, but free jazz was still something different for us, in our minds. For me and my friends, it was less out of protest or as an expression of some kind of dissatisfaction; we just had a different foundation, or none at all, at least at the very beginning.

PETER BRÖTZMANN I play my Wuppertal blues my own way. Copying American blues without understanding where it comes from and what it was about, and still is, that's a bit of a hot potato for us white Western Europeans. We have to be careful about it. In any case, I never really saw the point in recreating American music. I had to find my own voice, develop it, take it further. As much as I've learned from Americans – and I'm still learning from them – you just have to find your own path. Doing our own thing was the only right option back then. The same goes for the innovative German rock musicians as well.

47

WINFRID TRENKLER Brötzmann and the other free-jazz people blew up everything that had come before with their music. Brötzmann and other jazz men played gigs with the krautrock bands for a while too, because they were all counted as part of underground culture at the time. But at some point, they parted ways.

PETER BRÖTZMANN I was lucky enough to be invited to the Essener Songtage [Essen Song Days] festival. I remember drinking myself stupid with the Fugs. It was an interesting time because there were no pigeonholes; culture was completely open, and not just music. Thinking of the theatre in Wuppertal back then, that was very avant-garde too. Lots of directors who went on to make it big worked there. As a musician, you'd hang out in pubs with theatre and ballet people, and sometimes you'd work together. There was certainly a constant dialogue going on. It was a good experience. Starting in 1967, I had a lot to do with Brits like Evan Parker and Paul Rutherford. Whenever we met, the Germans were rioting like hell – in Frankfurt or Berlin, wherever. Things were tough in London too, though, with water cannons firing at demos and that kind of thing. Those experiences brought us together, even if lots of people took different musical routes later on. It was an incredibly important time.

ALEXANDER VON SCHLIPPENBACH At some point, it turned out you could make your own records; it was Brötzmann who set the ball rolling. That was what helped the movement to get established, even though it's still an underground movement these days; we're absolutely invisible in the media, on the radio and TV.

PETER BRÖTZMANN In 1968 I recorded the album *Machine Gun* – music with a different background to rock, but it still fitted like a glove.

MANI NEUMEIER I started in free jazz with Irène Schweizer and Uli Trepte. What we were doing back then was revolutionary. Then at twenty-four, I went on tour with Schweizer and Trepte. We all quit our day jobs before we left – the best and most important decision I've ever made! When I came back to Switzerland a few months later, I felt as free as a bird. We soon met Brötzmann, Gunter Hampel and Manfred Schoof, all the German free-jazz guys. But it was still a struggle, because naturally everyone said it wasn't the right thing for me and I'd never make a living out of it and I'd die of starvation. But I knew it was right for me, I knew I had talent, and I was completely addicted to the music. Without that addiction, you don't make it.

CHRISTIAN BURCHARD Free jazz was the real thing. The old jazz men didn't like it; apparently Thelonious Monk had heard Ornette Coleman and decided it was bullshit, which was printed in all the jazz papers. That was in the mid-sixties, and of course it was a crushing critique. The German jazz scene followed its idols. I went to see Dizzy Gillespie and John Coltrane play around then; the audience went crazy for Gillespie, but after that Coltrane emptied the auditorium in a couple of minutes. People were saying it was nothing but noise! Elvin Jones played the drums incredibly loud, as well; you could only hear Jones and Coltrane, and the pianist McCoy Tyner and poor Jimmy Garrison on bass got completely lost. But that gig was also an uprising against bar jazz, which was far removed from real jazz development. It's just that no one wants to admit it these days.

LIMPE FUCHS I was sixteen the first time I went to a jazz cellar, with a friend, in München. But we didn't just dance to jazz as teenagers, we'd also go for rock music like Bill Haley. You could hear it in München on AFN, because Bavaria was American-occupied.

MANI NEUMEIER I was the first free-jazz drummer in Germany. Free jazz came at just the right time for some, and shocked others because it was really new. From there to Guru Guru was another fracture, but even that was ultimately part of my path towards liberating music. The kick towards rock came from the experience of listening to Jimi Hendrix, because it showed me there were great musicians in rock as well. Apart from that, I wanted to play that electric rock sound, with amps. By some point we'd taken everything apart in jazz and there was no way forward. So I started the Guru Guru Groove Band with Uli Trepte, which became Guru Guru. The idea was not to do just free jazz, but free music – anything goes. We had two Marshall amps for the big sounds, and we knew that made us avant-garde; we wanted to expand music and break it wide open. And we were good; people wrote a lot about us.

CHRISTIAN BURCHARD The bookers always wanted us to play standards; that was the done thing. If you refused, you just didn't get the job. It must have been 1967 when I was invited to play a gig in Erlangen with the Mal Waldron Quartet. Waldron was one of my idols, and his band was one man short. He'd made records with Billie Holiday, John Coltrane, Eric Dolphy, Max Roach and other famous jazz people. Waldron must have written five or six hundred songs, including a good few standards. Anyway, they booked me for three days, and afterwards Waldron said to me: 'It's OK, what you're doing. Come along for the whole tour.' So I stayed in the band and shot straight from the third league to the first, if you like. Waldron's band was great training; I learned so much.

PETER BRÖTZMANN I started going abroad early on. For me, it was a whole different, free world, where I could breathe freely and get out of the dusty German backwater under Chancellor Adenauer at last. I had a Dutch girlfriend in Amsterdam, whose family owned a house in the Jewish quarter there. I lived in their attic for a while, but I had a few difficulties as a German in Amsterdam. My girlfriend had to come along with me when I went shopping to the baker or the greengrocer, as if to say: 'OK, he's German, but he's a good German!' I hardly spoke a word of English, and the Dutch noticed I was German the minute I opened my mouth. There were lots of shops that wouldn't serve me. That's how it was back then, and it was a bit of a struggle for me.

JÜRGEN DOLLASE Beat music was too hedonistic for me. The jazz faction was more into politics.

PETER BRÖTZMANN Now and then, I'd go to demonstrations in Berlin or talks by people like Angela Davis and Eldridge Cleaver. We put on gigs at the Free University there, but the funny thing was, none of them wanted to hear our music – the communards would throw beer cans at us. Sometimes there were even proper physical fights. They were happier dreaming of Bob Dylan.

ALEXANDER VON SCHLIPPENBACH For the Wuppertal people like Brötzmann, the political movement aspect played a much larger role. Just down the road, in our Köln circle – Manfred Schoof, Jaki Liebezeit, Gerd Dudek, Buschi Niebergall and me – it started out as a purely musical venture. As a group, we worked at the forefront, but then later we got together with the Wuppertal guys in the Globe Unity Orchestra and got workshops off the ground in Wuppertal. There was a lot going on in free jazz, if you want to call it that.

PETER BRÖTZMANN I noticed only sporadically what other musicians were doing. I had to earn money because I had a family with two kids. I was helping out my father-in-law in his forge, as well as my job as a musician. There wasn't time for me to look around. But I still got an idea of what kind of music was coming up.

ALEXANDER VON SCHLIPPENBACH When it comes to musical articulation, the krautrock movement picked up on a lot of things we'd been developing in free jazz since the early sixties.

PETER BRÖTZMANN We Wuppertalers in particular were just as rejected back then as nonconformist rock musicians. It took a long time for us to be accepted in Germany. Even with great guys like Manfred Schoof or Alexander von Schlippenbach, I first had to take a detour

51

by working with Carla Bley, Steve Lacy or Don Cherry to convince them my thing might be worth taking seriously. What was always a positive feeling was the reactions from American musicians. I remember a big festival appearance in Frankfurt early on, which the German press wrote about as usual – nothing to do with jazz, not proper music, etc. – but right after the gig, this older gentleman with an alto sax case came up to me and said: 'Don't get mad, just do your thing.' And that was Lee Konitz! That did me a whole lot of good, obviously. And over the years, I kept noticing that the Americans were much more open-minded than a lot of European musicians.

IRMIN SCHMIDT We experienced jazz in all its diversity and history, as a genuine twentieth-century artform. That was really important for Can's conception, partly because it meant something already existed, where no one could say – like they always say in Germany – this thing is great art and that thing is light entertainment. For me, jazz was part of what was new in the twentieth century, just like Neue Musik. In a way, jazz was a newer kind of music than Stockhausen. With Stockhausen's works, you can trace the family tree back to the Tristan chord. It's a European tradition, and it leads to Stockhausen or Boulez. The incursion of jazz was very different; it didn't come out of our history in Western culture. The only link was the slave trade, through which African music was transported to America. And the result was entirely new forms of music: jazz, rock and blues – all that was entirely new in the Western world. I had a deeply held feeling that I wanted to integrate these genres into my musical consciousness. And the same way as I'd internalised it, I wanted to experience it for real in music, to do it myself, start a band where it all played a role. The idea of the spontaneous and everything together was more of an ideological aspect that I added to it all.

PETER BRÖTZMANN Back when Jaki Liebezeit was still a jazz drum-mer with Schlippenbach and Schoof, we used to run into each other regularly. I could totally understand why he switched to Can. Jaki was never a jazz percussionist, to my mind, and I don't mean that in a bad way. Because Jaki as a drummer was far too much on the one, two, three, four. Swinging rhythms just weren't his thing. And then when he started with Can and moved away from his buddies Schoof and Schlippenbach, I saw what it was that drove him, because Can was much closer to his feel for metre than jazz. Of course, there were points in free jazz where things stagnated, later as well. You just have to fight back and go on with the show. I'm much too much of a jazz man and I need that swing, somehow, but Jaki didn't need it. Drummers have always been important to me, though; one of the first words a young drummer said to me when I played with him in Italy recently was 'krautrock'.

JAKI LIEBEZEIT I played jazz for a long time, then I wound up in free jazz, and that was like an end point. What comes after free jazz? At some point, with free jazz, I lost the conviction to keep playing that way. The only option left was to pivot to rhythm, because rhythm had got completely lost in free jazz. And rhythm is a pretty important factor in jazz. I've never managed to play percussion from sheet music, either. There are people who do it, but you can tell by listening. Real drummers can't sight-read – they think differently, they have a different idea of rhythm. You can tell the minute you look up the rhythm chapter in classical textbooks – it's all over in two pages. The European musical notation system makes rhythm really rudimentary. No one in Africa thinks about notation, they just let loose! That's freedom.

IRMIN SCHMIDT I'd learned a lot of jazz; I was a huge fan of Max Roach, especially because he did this polyrhythmic stuff I recognised, because I'd listened to African music at university. But a lot of what you heard as analysis of it, at uni, sounded like a joke to me later on. I felt the need for that kind of rhythm, but I couldn't play it. I only learned what 'groove' is from Jaki.

ALEXANDER VON SCHLIPPENBACH Liebezeit went into the rock scene – a decisive step, but one that we jazz men didn't take. We stayed good friends but we were in two different worlds. I have to admit I've never listened to a Can record or seen them play.

THE SIXTIES

BEAT

'I was actually a very un-musical person.'
ASMUS TIETCHENS

ACHIM REICHEL In the early sixties anyone with a guitar was a bit like a Martian: 'Can you make a living playing the guitar?' Forget it!

JÜRGEN DOLLASE The beat wave hit my school at the start of the sixties. I took dancing classes when I was fifteen and I picked up on beat mainly because of the girls, because I was more into the jazz scene at the time. But around 1966 we'd play 'Beat Meets Jazz' gigs. There'd be three beat bands and three jazz bands all on one night. I got into jazz as a double bassist. A skiffle band at my school needed a bassist. Later I ended up in a few old-time jazz bands, and after a while we did a bit of modern jazz. But then rock 'n' roll came along, and it exercised a huge fascination on me in my early days as a musician. Everything about it was new, the whole lifestyle was attractive – this beat music really promised a different life.

ASMUS TIETCHENS If you wanted to make music in Hamburg around 1965 you played either skiffle and Dixieland or Beatles and Rolling Stones covers – as best you could! Beat bands were ten-a-penny in Hamburg. That wasn't an option for me, though, because I couldn't play guitar. And I couldn't sing either.

MICHAEL ROTHER As a child, I listened to classical music. My father worked for British European Airways in Hamburg and München, and then he went on to Lufthansa, where they put him in charge of the territory that's now Pakistan and Bangladesh. I came back to Germany

57

from Karachi in 1963. We moved to Düsseldorf, and the first few times I went ice skating there, this whole range of new music came blaring out of the speakers: the Rolling Stones, the Beatles and the Kinks. I was crazy about them. After that, all I wanted was to get closer to that music. But people like that were miles away from everyday role models for a good schoolboy like me, obviously. I'd always been the friendly and respectful Michael; they'd even elected me onto the school council. Those musicians led a completely different life, all about freedom, rebellion and art.

ASMUS TIETCHENS The only music at our house was cheesy German songs. My father was at sea, so my mother practically raised me on her own, and she listened to schlager. My parents gave me a reel-to-reel machine at quite a young age; I must have been about twelve. At that time, NDR had a monthly radio show presented by Chris Howland. He'd give well-informed updates on the latest developments in British pop music. He was also a DJ on British forces radio, BFBS, which you could pick up in Germany. BFBS and Radio Luxembourg were the most important sources of information on English pop music, for me and everyone else my age. It was music I was really interested in, especially the Shadows. A guitar band I'd still bow down to today. They made me want to learn guitar – as a twelve-year-old, I immediately understood their music was made on guitars, although I didn't even know the difference between electric and acoustic. But I still begged my parents to get me a guitar, and one fine Christmas, they did. I plucked at the strings and noticed: that doesn't sound anything like the Shadows! Incredibly disappointing. Part of the present was twelve guitar lessons. I went along, but the lessons didn't work out because I'm left-handed and the teacher couldn't deal with that. He never thought of restringing my guitar, like Paul McCartney and Jimi Hendrix had. Not that I'd heard of them yet, so I couldn't ask him to, either. So me and my teacher ended up sitting there, clueless. And then he brought sheet music into it, and that was always a closed book to me. The circle of fifths and that kind of thing – they'd tried to teach me that at school, and failed. All that was too much for me: higher mathematics! And it didn't sound remotely like the Shadows! My parents sold off the guitar at a loss, and that was that. The end of the only attempt I ever made to learn an instrument.

MICHAEL ROTHER While I was living in Pakistan with my parents, my brother was training at a bank in München. Sometimes he'd come to visit us in Karachi and bring along a few singles. One of them was a recording of the Shadows song 'Apache', a cover version by Jørgen Ingmann, which really impressed me. That single was in my childhood bedroom in Düsseldorf up to my mother's death, in an old radiogram my parents treated themselves to after the war, which I've still got in my studio. I'd listen to stations like Radio Luxembourg on the radio part of the set. In Pakistan I wanted a sitar, but they were too expensive, I suppose. Instead, I got a wooden box with lots of strings and a typewriter keyboard. It's an instrument like Klaus Dinger used later on the first NEU! record, on the track 'Negativland'. You play tunes on it by pressing the typewriter keys. I didn't think that was exciting enough, back then in Karachi, and I wanted to make it into a guitar, presumably due to 'Apache'. But of course I didn't manage it.

IRMIN SCHMIDT At university in Essen, I listened to a lot of British beat bands, but I've forgotten what most of them were called. The only one I remember is the Pretty Things. The sound impressed me enormously, though. Beat was simple stuff, obviously, in terms of composition. If you wrote it on paper, you'd end up with three chords, maybe – but it had this impressive power. And thanks to minimal music as well, I gradually got to like simple chords. It was fine to be uncomplicated now and then if you had something else instead, and that [something else] was that power.

MICHAEL ROTHER There wasn't much music in Karachi and most of the radio stations played Arabic [meaning Eastern-sounding] songs.

So I listened to a lot of that, which certainly influenced me, in retro-spect. Obviously I didn't understand the music at all; it seemed to have neither beginning nor end, and I didn't understand the scales or the figurations, but it did touch my emotions and made its mark, flowed deeply through me; it went on and on and on forever. You'd come across musical groups playing it on the street, sometimes with snake charmers. The emotional impact was huge. And in 1963 I came back from that world to Germany and discovered the exciting new music of the British beat explosion, embodied by bands like the Beatles, the Rolling Stones, the Kinks and so on. Out of all that, the idea of tak-ing a musical step further developed over the years, coupled with the question of 'What makes me myself?' As a teenager, you're happy to imitate your idols as best you can: 'I wanna learn to play guitar like Jimi Hendrix, Eric Clapton and George Harrison.' That dream was never going to come true, but it was a great plan anyway. In Düsseldorf in those days there were at least two guitarists, pretty bad boys, who could imitate Hendrix fairly well. But they weren't Hendrix. And I was never a bad boy, I was always a nice guy – that's what I'm all about. Just after I joined Kraftwerk, the guitarist Houschäng Nejadépour played a couple of gigs with us. He was half Iranian with long black hair and an ascetic face – and such a great Hendrix impersonator that it might actually have held him back from doing his own thing. I learned by imitation as well, soaking up my heroes' techniques, but I think I already had a feel for melody. When I joined the Spirit of Sound, they confirmed that straight away: 'Michael, you're the solo guitarist. You play the tunes. Makes sense, right?'

LUTZ LUDWIG KRAMER We were the Ugly Things – after the Pretty Things. I'd seen them live and even met them. They were nice guys who liked talking to us kids. They told us everything we wanted to know, and they showed us their guitars. Phil May with his big long hair was a real dream guy. My best mate at the time was called Pretty, and then there was Fame, who was the Agitation Free bassist later on, and me. The three of us scraped all our money together – it wasn't much – and got ourselves instruments. We made our drumkit out of old Omo washing powder drums. And stuff like a washboard as well. We had our first rehearsal not much later, in my garden shed on Kastanienallee. The aim was to get at least as good as the Pretty Things.

MICHAEL ROTHER Bands like the Beatles and the Pretty Things had an incredible effect on us. It was their sound that made me pick up a guitar. There was music back then that really shook me up. Hearing a track like Cream's 'I Feel Free' for the first time was unbelievable. I was electrified. The structures were completely new, which confused me and got me all fired up.

PETER BAUMANN I played in a beat band when I was fourteen, started up by an American; we covered mainly American songs like 'Green, Green Grass of Home'. After that I was in a band that played covers of Led Zeppelin, the Rolling Stones and that kind of thing. I was eighteen when I started in Tangerine Dream, and I already found it odd that there were so many rock bands from the UK and America, but only very few from Germany.

GÜNTER SCHICKERT My parents listened to schlager. Heidi Brühl, Freddy Quinn and stuff like that. Berlin's big KaDeWe department store had a huge record department in those days, and I'd go in and listen to all sorts of things. When I got my first pay packet as an apprentice, I bought myself a Bingo record player for thirty marks and an old radio, and connected them up. Then I took the last of my money to the KaDeWe record department and went home in the end with the Rolling Stones' *Between the Buttons*.

HARALD GROSSKOPF I was in a band called the Stuntmen at fifteen. I was a massive fan of the Beatles and the Rolling Stones. I had a Philips reel-to-reel tape recorder, which I used to record a few records I didn't have, at a mate's place with a microphone, in mono. And while I was taping I drummed on the table, more or less unconsciously. After that we went to the public baths and listened to it – you could hear my drumming quite clearly. The bassist of a local beat band was standing near us, and he soon asked: 'Who's that doing the drumming?' It was great, he said, and he told me to start playing proper drums. Obviously, I thought that was a brilliant idea, and I started drumming. The Stuntmen were a pretty sophisticated beat band. We covered the more difficult Beatles songs like 'Paperback Writer' and Kinks tracks. People were into us. I had a bowl cut at the time, which looked terrible, and a Beatles-style jacket and high-heeled Beatle boots, plus 'Lords trousers' – the Lords had invented a cut with the seam at the front. The legs had a split at the bottom and fell open into big flares. That was how we ran around, getting plenty of attention and regular heckling. I kept hearing things like 'They should put you in a labour camp,' or 'In the old days they'd have picked you up long ago.' The most harmless was 'Go and get a haircut.' When it came to insulting strangers in the street, the good old Germans had no inhibitions. I was used to that from my teachers at school, though.

MICHAEL ROTHER Looking at photos of bands like the Pretty Things these days, it's obvious they looked very different to me back in the mid-sixties. They were 'bad boys' with long hair and leather outfits. A lot of those musicians were working-class lads, leading robust lives. They all looked much older than they were. Subliminally that must have fascinated me.

HOLGER CZUKAY The first tune I got really into was a single by Caterina Valente. The A-side was 'Ganz Paris träumt von der Liebe', which I didn't like that much, but the B-side really grabbed me: 'Dreh dich nicht um nach fremden Schatten' – it was amazing! I listened to it again recently and I still think it's great. Really dark. It immediately fascinated me back then.

GÜNTER SCHICKERT I started playing guitar after I'd seen Jimi Hendrix on TV. There was a church hall on Lietzenburger Strasse, and they had a youth club. There was always someone from the church there keeping an eye on things, you could play table tennis, and bands would play there now and then. I tried out drumming there, and at some point I decided: the guitar's my thing! What I liked most was the volume. You'd hear guitars in all the clubs, and there were about two thousand beat bands in Berlin in those days. I'd seen the first gigs by bands like the Lords, and they made a big impression on me. I couldn't play guitar yet, though. So I went to see Frau Abendroth at the insurance company where I was an apprentice, and I said: 'Frau Abendroth, I really need a guitar, haven't you got an old one lying around somewhere?' And she did, and she gave me an old Italian one. And that's what I started out on. I was seventeen. At first I used a valve radio as an amp, and then I got a proper one at a second-hand shop. I played things I knew from the radio, Blue Cheer, 'Summertime Blues' and so on, all very rocky and punky. We had to cover English and American stuff to start with because there weren't any role models in Germany. When I started making more and more music, I decided to change the way I worked, to have more time for it. I would have turned into a Kafka character at the insurance company, in the long run. You couldn't work half-days in the office. I handed in my notice and just did odd jobs here and there. If you want to do something new, you have to get out of the old. You can't stay in your old existence and wait for something to happen. You have to jump in at the deep end, I'm afraid.

MICHAEL HOENIG The Beatles and the Rolling Stones were omnipresent. After the war my mother had worked for the Americans, and then in Berlin she worked in a shop for US Army officers, so it was in 1963, I think, that I got one of the first Beatles singles: 'Love Me Do' on Odeon.

MICHAEL ROTHER I even had a run-in with the Rolling Stones. Because of my father's job, I was allowed onto the runway when the band arrived in Düsseldorf in 1965. There were screaming crowds waiting at the barriers behind me, and I got to go right up to the plane. I was fifteen and I'd thought up some questions to ask Bill Wyman. That didn't work out, sadly, because the Stones just came down the steps and headed straight off. I remember how surprised I was that Bill Wyman was so short. Then the fans broke through the barriers and ran screaming onto the runway, and the security forces turned water cannons on them. There was a machine behind me used for towing planes, with big wheels and a long arm, and various fans installed themselves on it. When they were hit by jets of water they let go of the metal arm, which clanged down on my foot – so I ended up in hospital with a broken toe. That was my run-in with the Rolling Stones.

MICHAEL HOENIG I listened to English pop until around 1967–68, and from then on more West Coast psychedelic or British progressive rock stuff. I had a group of friends back then and we'd buy new LPs every week when we got our pocket money. Whenever one of us had something new, the ten of us would sit down together and listen to the record five times over. It went from Cream to Jefferson Airplane and the Grateful Dead to Soft Machine. The whole psychedelic sound was overwhelming; it turned everything on its head because our perception changed so much – through drugs – that language became a very poor, insufficient means of communication. Everyone was taking acid and smoking marihuana. I studied the American hippy subculture and its art and literature because I helped a friend for a while with one of the first German hippy mags: *Love*. It was inspired by the US underground press. And that shifted interest from political problems, which could be put into words clearly, to problems and issues you couldn't grasp as precisely, more like life and survival in general, or life after death. Eastern philosophies came into play.

IRMIN SCHMIDT If Can were influenced at all by pop and rock music, then it was the American stuff – although there was a clear separation between the American government and politics, the war they were waging, on the one hand, and the young people who were against all that, on the other. Anti-Americanism was never on the table, as far as I can say. The idea of judging an entire country is absurd, anyway.

HARALD GROSSKOPF I went to kindergarten with Rudolf Schenker from the Scorpions, and we were both at Schiller Secondary Modern for a while as well. He comes from Sarstedt near Hannover, like me. Anyway, he left school after two years to start an apprenticeship. He already had the Scorpions in Sarstedt, and my band was the Stuntmen. We were the local beat heroes. Rudolf's father supported him and his brother Michael through thick and thin; he got them gigs and drove them around. Our parents weren't like that. We had old radios for amps and when we asked our parents to lend us money for proper amps, they said no. Rudolf Schenker's dad guaranteed for us instead; we were fifteen at the time. That was great. When the Scorpions' drummer couldn't play, I'd help out and play with them at youth clubs around Hannover. After I did my compulsory community service – I didn't want to go into the military – I wanted to join the band, but we had three dates in Hildesheim and they never turned up to any of them. So I thought: forget it!

KARL BARTOS My parents had a different career planned out for me. I was supposed to do an apprenticeship as a signals worker at the post office. I went along to the job, but there were two or three people there just as music-obsessed as I was. And before I knew it we were a beat band and did nothing but music. We didn't have a name but we still got passed round all of North Rhine-Westphalia. The only thing I really learned in my signals worker apprenticeship was music. We played everything and anything that was in the hit parade. I was a total Beatles fan and was lucky enough to grow up in a world where the biggest-selling records actually represented youth culture. The music back then had substance; it still stands the test of time. Jimi Hendrix's recording of 'All Along the Watchtower' still sounds amazing. Anyway, all that music had been speaking to me since I was fourteen. Instruments were like fetishes for me. They looked pretty sexy, to start with. But most of all, instruments helped me to express myself. Music had a magical attraction for me that I couldn't articulate precisely. But at some point, I made out a path for myself. It was the only thing I was interested in, apart from playing football. I grew up in Düsseldorf, which was occupied by the British Army at the time. The Americans and the Brits were the best thing that could have happened to us after the war. And my sister married an English lance corporal. He brought me my first two records: one by the Beatles and one by the Rolling Stones. That was in 1964, the luckiest day of my life. I was twelve, and the Beatles' first film *A Hard Day's Night* had just come out in our cinemas. The first chord of 'A Hard Day's Night' was the start of my musical identification; the music hypnotised me. I took my sister's guitar down from the wall; she'd never played it, and that guitar had been waiting just for me.

LÜÜL We took our orientation mainly from the Stones; the Beatles were a bit too difficult for us, in terms of chords and vocals. But around 1968 or so, we worked out we had to find our own path; there was a massive feeling of a new beginning on the air. The student rebellion brought a revolutionary impetus, the vision of a better society without squares or authorities. That made it clear to us, too, that we had to invent our own music and dare to make new sounds. Our guitarist at the time, Lutz Ludwig Kramer, had been to England and brought records back with him. You couldn't get that quality in Germany. He'd seen Pink Floyd live at the Roundhouse and came back really impressed; the rest of us didn't know them yet. He announced: 'My friends, it's a whole new musical direction!' I listened to their album *The Piper at the Gates of Dawn*, but it was too hard for me to digest at the time, too many new sounds.

STEVE SCHROYDER I went to Sweden with friends in 1968, and met a woman who first played me the Pink Floyd records *The Piper at the*

Gates of Dawn and *A Saucerful of Secrets*. She put them on back to back, and I thought: 'This is insane!' It was a trance experience, comparable to the first times I smoked hash, but in this case it was caused entirely by music. It really turned my head. I saw Pink Floyd back then. It was amazing: the gong! The light show!

LÜÜL My sister had brought the Beatles' *Revolver* back from England for me, which already had a lot of psychedelic moments; I liked it far better than *The Piper at the Gates* . . . But then my sister listened to so much Pink Floyd that at some point I got to like them after all – and the Doors, Allman Brothers, Velvet Underground, Grateful Dead and the Byrds. I have really clear memories of a very free live version of 'Eight Miles High'. At one point I wore a kaftan and a bell round my neck, which jangled with every step I took. I thought it was great, but it got pretty annoying after a while.

ACHIM REICHEL The Brits were just closer to the music, through their language alone. And rock 'n' roll was invented in America, after all. For us in Hamburg, all the clubs were great places to study beat music. There was an interesting band playing at every one. I often saw the Beatles at Indra, Top Ten and the Star-Club. And Ringo Starr at the Kaiserkeller, when he was still playing with Rory Storm and the Hurricanes. The Star-Club was always open until four in the morning. I'll never forget John Lennon coming on stage one night completely naked, guitar in front of his parts, with a toilet seat around his neck. He must have just ripped it straight off the toilet. I just thought: 'Who are these people?' It got me pretty fired up, I have to say. Only then he went and did a Hitler salute. We thought: 'Well, never mind what they say about the English sense of humour – that's a step too far.' Lennon obviously thought it was funny, but we didn't. But the fact that there were so many live music clubs in Hamburg in the sixties was a good reason to go there, for people who didn't live there. It made Hamburg something special.

BERND WITTHÜSER We started out playing covers of all the English and American bands. My aunt had married a miner from the British forces and moved to England. She invited me over and said, 'Come to England, everything's far better here.' I went over, and the mining town looked exactly the same as ours in the Ruhrpott, but there was a jukebox in the pub and I flipped right out. First it played 'The Last Time' by the Rolling Stones and then Bob Dylan's 'The Times They Are A-Changin''. I thought I'd lost my mind! It triggered off a whole lot for me. Once I got back to Essen, the first thing I did was get myself a mouth organ. Discovering Dylan was such a liberation. After that I only ever listened to the British forces radio BFBS.

JEAN-HERVÉ PERON After my parents moved to France, I had no choice but to listen to a lot of French rock 'n' roll, people like Johnny Hallyday and Eddy Mitchell, and pop like [the Belgian] Adamo and Sylvie Vartan. That kind of music was on the radio non-stop, and most of my friends listened to it, too. But actually, it wasn't that bad. All right, the lyrics were terrible, but it was the music we danced to with girls. But then there was Radio Caroline, the pirate station on a ship near us, and the things they played made me vibrate with happiness. You'd hear bands like the Troggs, the Pretty Things and the Who. All really fuzzy because you'd never pick up the station properly, but that just made the sound even more exciting. Who knows how much those atmospheric disturbances influenced me later on.

LÜÜL There were a couple of Stones songs with not many chords, like 'Everybody Needs Somebody to Love' or '2120 South Michigan Avenue', that you could play long versions of. Our road manager used to use a stopwatch: ten minutes, fifteen minutes, and so on. Cream's 'Spoonful' was very good for that as well. We used them to practise improvisation, we got better and the versions got longer and longer, until one day we reached the point where we weren't doing covers any more, we were coming up with our own songs. First we'd smoke a joint, then someone would just kick off, and the others would join in when they were ready. We had some wild jam sessions. Sometimes they were good, sometimes not so great, depending on how we came together. It was an adventurous way of making music, because it was never clear what was actually happening. For us, though, it was mainly a huge musical liberation. And the audience loved it because everyone was starting something new, in some way.

HAIR

'We were the counter-model to white shirts and ties.'
JAKI LIEBEZEIT

RENATE KNAUP We were just rebellious, absolutely against the whole bloody system. That's why we dressed in a way that made people's hair stand on end. I wore the world's shortest mini-skirt and then I back-combed my hair, which was very long, so it looked like a lion's mane. There were men like Rainer Bauer and Chris Karrer who had more of a Native American look, with decorated jackets. The others wore leather jackets with cowboy boots, beards and long hair. When we went out in the street we'd get threatened by taxi drivers right there at the taxi rank: 'You long-haired dogs'; 'Filthy rubbish.' We loved it, of course.

BERND WITTHÜSER Long hair meant trouble. You couldn't possibly work in an office with a long mane like that. I kept trying it for a while, whenever I felt something like regret [at cutting my hair off]. Then I'd call up firms and ask if I could work there, and it'd go all right for one or two days, maybe, and then I'd be out on my ear. At some point I was a lost cause for the normal working world.

BERND DOPP In the early seventies, long hair was still a statement: a mane made you anti-establishment! It meant you'd fought and won, against your parents, your teachers, most of your classmates and the mainstream as a whole. But when you ran into the wrong people on the bus or the street, long hair could be dangerous. Rockers were the most aggressive: 'Oi, mate, you a girl, or what?' That could get unpleasant, so you'd keep your eyes down and hope for the best.

HAIR

MICHAEL ROTHER I did my A-levels in 1969; I was eighteen, younger than most. My hair got longer in sixth form, and I developed my own political convictions and defiance. At some point I stopped accepting everything the teachers set before me, and started asking more and more questions. Most of the teachers at my school were conservative, some of them downright reactionary, and presumably they didn't enjoy me leaving behind my former cheerful, enthusiastic student self, under the influence of beat music and political upheaval. There were wild discussions; a lot of teachers didn't understand why we were questioning everything: 'Why, Michael? Why?' To my form teacher's dismay, I picked up my A-level certificate in an anorak, not a suit as was expected at the time and as tradition demanded. My hair was shoulder-length by then. Then I did my community service and my hair got longer. In Düsseldorf, I had to take the tram every day and change at the main station. One day, I was waiting for a tram and I felt a hand on my bum – it was obviously a sexual misunderstanding because it belonged to a man, probably confused by my long hair.

STEVE SCHROYDER The first boy at my school to grow his hair long – he was in the year above me – got expelled. That was in 1966. The rest of us were obviously very impressed, especially since he was also in a beat band and played gigs in pubs at night. He wasn't yet eighteen, and you needed special permission to play on licensed premises under the age of sixteen. I had to hide before I went on stage at my first gigs, or my brother-in-law had to come with me. I didn't get in trouble at home, though. My father had died young and I lived in a household of women with my mother, gran and sister. I could stay out late and had a lot of freedom in general. My long hair was more a cause of amusement at school. But it wasn't really long, more like Beatles-length. When the headmaster handed me my leaving certificate in the packed school hall, everyone laughed. My form teacher laughed and even the headmaster – they were all pleased I'd made it, despite my long hair.

71

ACHIM REICHEL We came back to Hamburg from our English tour by plane, and we were welcomed with stupid remarks like 'Boy or girl?' 'Are you a boy or a girl, or what?' You always wondered what was going on in those people's heads, but in the end you took no notice.

LUTZ LUDWIG KRAMER I was thirteen, the first kid in my neighbourhood with a Beatles haircut and a denim suit ten times too big for me. That got me not only stares from old Nazis all around town, but also really bad comments. I once walked around the neighbourhood in Berlin where the Nazi generals used to live, with my long hair. Some of them were still around, and they came up to me in the street and said: 'You look like a girl. A boy with hair like that belongs in the crematorium.' I went to my mother, all confused, and said: 'They want to put me in a crematorium. What do they mean?' I hadn't got it at all. My mother was embarrassed by it all. But still my parents wanted to confront them about it. I doubt they really did, because their quiet life was much more important to them than making a scene. My father preferred to go and make a film far away. That denim suit got onto German TV, by the way. I played a newspaper boy, in 1966, in a television play called *Weiss gibt auf*. With a young Siegfried Lowitz and Rudolf Platte. It was directed by the former resistance fighter Falk Harnack, and I made a few more TV appearances after that.

MANI NEUMEIER No other krautrocker looked as extreme as I did. I had really long hair and a Pedro moustache. A woman on the street in Wuppertal almost had a heart attack when she saw me. She screamed at me: 'What do you look like?' All I had on was these lovely velvet trousers and a blue silk shirt . . . I wasn't dirty or freaky in any other way, just a bit colourful. Children don't get shouted at when they run around in colourful clothes. But I'd reckoned with making enemies like that, it was almost preordained. We wanted people to notice us, otherwise they wouldn't have come to see us play. If you looked like we did, you reached the people who thought differently – our audience.

MICHAEL HOENIG We all had long hair and looked like Berlin hippies, pretty grey, a bit tatty and not all that colourful to begin with, but what brought us together wasn't our clothes; it was the feeling that things had to change.

LÜÜL My long hair was down to the Beatles as well. It started with a mop-top in the early sixties. My parents knew no mercy and I often had to get a haircut against my will. It was a long process before my hair got really long. By 1974 it came down to my belt. In the sixties I looked more like Brian Jones. In 1972 I had shoulder-length hair and wanted to hitchhike back from Basel to Berlin. After four hours, a car stopped at last. The guy wound his window down, gave me an evil look, spat at my feet and drove off again. After that I hid my hair inside my collar, and not fifteen minutes later someone stopped and gave me a lift. But we usually wore our long hair with pride; it was a kind of protest against the squares. We were happy to put up with the occasional problems it caused.

MANI NEUMEIER The police turned up at about every other gig we played. We were unusually loud, and the neighbours would always reach straight for the telephone to complain. The fact the sound was so unusual just confused people even more. That was normal for us, though. Because we had such long hair and didn't look exactly respectable in other ways, we were often ostracised. If we went out for a meal, some landlords would throw us straight out the moment we set foot in the place: 'We don't serve the likes of you in here!' they'd say. We'd make a few juicy comments back and then leave.

HELLMUT HATTLER During the Red Army Faction days, you got into a lot of trouble for looking different. The first time I heard the words 'labour camp' was in insults from builders: 'The likes of you belong in a labour camp!' It didn't hurt me. I just kept on walking, and thought: 'Poor bastards, having to work like crazy on their building site.' Our guitarist Peter Wolbrandt got ordered out of his car at gun-point by police, a few times. When we had an interview at WDR, a policeman came along with a gun and said he was looking for the ter-rorist Adelheid Schulz. Peter looked a little bit feminine; someone must have taken him for her and shopped him to the police when we'd got out of the car at the TV station – a pretty bad case of mistaken identity.

PETER BAUMANN I was fifteen, and I noticed that something was in motion, that something was going on in Germany. In Berlin, it started with little things like a red circle some people used to mark their cars with, which meant the drivers would pick up hitchhikers. And every-one grew their hair long. I was the first boy in my school to grow my hair. Some of the teachers and the headmaster asked me when I'd be getting a haircut. I didn't let that bother me, though. Everything was very laid-back in Berlin, you didn't get in trouble quickly. My father was a musician as well, and my mother was an actress; they didn't take it all too seriously.

MANFRED GILLIG I had a red circle on my old VW as well. It was a good campaign. You could stop by the side of the road anywhere in Berlin, stick your thumb out, and it was never more than fifteen min-utes before a car with a red circle stopped. The hitchhiker campaign with the red circle was really visible in Berlin. But the transit roads through East Germany were a challenge if you had long hair and a beard. 'Why don't you go and join the socialists with your long hair!' was a typical comment. You got a lot of abuse, with long hair. The dyed-in-the-wool Berliners were difficult; the Turkish migrant work-ers were nicer.

HARALD GROSSKOPF All my parents said was: 'We don't mind long hair, but you've got to keep it clean.' But I just went my own way and ignored all the remarks. Of course, my clothes and hair were meant to be provocative. There was this yearning for freedom and independence, for transgression, in everyday life. We were against the uptight world and all the Nazi crap. People wanted to use their authority to keep us down. I got abuse every day, in shops and on the street.

JAKI LIEBEZEIT We were the post-war generation who wanted to deliberately distance ourselves from the old Germany, and we dressed the way it suited that new movement. That's why we had long hair and dressed differently. Everything about our appearance was ultimately a protest against the establishment. Long hair was a protest against the widespread idea of a decent haircut. Even wearing trainers was a protest. These days that fuss about appearances is all over. When we crossed the border to Belgium or France, we'd get searched just because of the way we looked, and they'd search our car because they always suspected long-haired men of having drugs on us. The customs men were just as bad, wherever they worked. As a potential freak, you were always under suspicion. But in Germany, too, you'd get all kinds of stupid treatment with long hair. I never really cared, though. I wore it all out of conviction; what did it matter what other people thought?

JÜRGEN DOLLASE My hair was long and my fingernails were painted black for a while. Sometimes they wouldn't serve me at snack bars because of how I looked. They'd just say: 'We don't serve your sort.' It wasn't funny. You were a real outsider with long hair, back then. And we had really long hair in Wallenstein, at the start; but as musicians, we also felt we weren't dependent on society, even if we didn't have much money. Being in an outsider position was just too exciting. Other people's lives were dull and boring.

HANS LAMPE I was training as a clerk, and my superiors kept pressuring me to get my hair cut, which I never did, of course. I passed the exam and got my certificate, but the report that went with it read like a warning against employing me.

PETER BURSCH Long hair was an outrage. I grew my hair in the mid-sixties. My parents were appalled, unsurprisingly. And then I moved out in protest, after a huge row. When my mother saw me walking around town she'd stick my hair down the back of my jacket so no one would see it. But for all of us, it was a conscious attitude: we wanted to look different, as different as we felt and behaved. I never let it get to me.

ASMUS TIETCHENS I liked the idea of long hair, although I wasn't a hippy. Wanting to have long hair radiated to hippy-free circles. Of course, your father's and grandfathers' generation looked askance at you and watched you warily, but they let you be in Hamburg, there weren't any attacks. Mind you, a young man with long hair was excluded from a whole lot of jobs, even if you wore a thousand suits and ties. The Bundeswehr introduced hair nets – pretty absurd, but I didn't have to join the army anyway.

HARALD GROSSKOPF We called ourselves Blitzkrieg at first – meant purely as provocation. We didn't exactly look like Blitzkrieg warriors; we had hair down to our shoulders and we smoked joints. Our practice room was paid for by our manager, who had a hostess bar next door, a place with striptease acts where women picked up men. The footballers Günter Netzer and Berti Vogts would come to our gigs. I wasn't remotely interested in football, so I was confused about why everyone used to stare at them and hardly pay us any attention. Netzer and Vogts knew who I was, though, and they'd give me a nod for years afterwards, whenever I ran into them somewhere. I had long hair until I discovered Transcendental Meditation, where everyone had short hair and wore suits.

COMMUNE

'Who's shagging who today? Or shall we all shag together?'
LUTZ LUDWIG KRAMER

HELLMUT HATTLER For me, living in a community with others was important. We spent a long time looking around for a place where that would work. It was a political decision. I wanted us to take a different approach to private property and money, I wanted there to be no more private property at all. 'Own nothing that won't fit in the rubbish bin,' we used to say. In my naivety, I wanted to try it, at least. We had this enthusiasm for trying things out, just because they were possible. These days, if you moved in together with a few people and suggested sharing everything you owned, they'd die laughing. But back then we had this great idealism. At our place, we took all the doors off the hinges because we didn't want any private sphere – we were experimenting. We tried not to have private money either, only shared funds, which of course led to plenty of heated discussions. One guy wanted to buy dope, another guy complained because he didn't smoke dope and wanted fancy food instead. There was a lot of arguing, but that was all part of the experiment.

GÜNTER SCHICKERT At the beginning of the seventies I was living on Kottbusser Damm in Berlin. There were ten of us sharing 100 square metres, and we slept in loft beds that we'd made and attached to the walls. Rent in Berlin was really cheap in those days. If you worked for three months, you could spend the next six months making music. I once lived in a former factory building in the Wedding district, 180 square metres for DM175 a month. If you ran out of money, you'd find a new job at the drop of a hat. There were signs up everywhere, like

'Warehouse workers wanted', and then you'd work until you'd put a bit of money aside again.

STEVE SCHROYDER There were six people living in my room at one point. When I came back from a trip to Hamburg, my roommates were gone, and all my stuff as well. The rest of my flatmates sat down to tell me I'd been chucked out, and I had to move out by the next day.

RENATE KNAUP My parents were never bothered about me living communally; they trusted me. We trusted each other.

GIL FUNCCIUS We wanted to change everything, so we tried out plenty of things and put up with all sorts of things in communal houses, cried secret tears sometimes. But we had to try everything out.

HARALD GROSSKOPF I shared a place with four others back then. Some of them were other members of the Stuntmen. One day Jürgen Dollase turned up on our doorstep. He was looking for a drummer for his band; someone had let him down and then someone else sent him to me. That was how I ended up in Wallenstein and got stuck there for four years.

JÜRGEN DOLLASE I was in contact with a kind of commune and I often went over there, but I never really moved in. That's where I had my best LSD experiences, though. I was the youngest at twenty-one – a few of them were more than ten years older. They'd drive over from Düsseldorf, work a regular job during the week and indulge in psychedelics at the weekend.

PETER BURSCH We set up our commune in the second half of 1968. We moved in together at the end of that summer. Then the Essener Songtage happened that September. To get the rental contract in the first place, we sent a friend with a proper job to the landlord. We'd never have got the place otherwise – there were fourteen of us with no fixed monthly income, plus girlfriends and other band hangers-on. There were rules about who was responsible for what and when. We had a common room where we had discussions every Monday. We discussed political things, music or our plans for the coming week. There were often a lot of guests, and sometimes we'd invite people over for certain discussion topics. It was all pretty well organised. It sounds good, but there was a lot of stress as well, of course. There'd be arguments if someone hadn't cleaned the toilet. Sometimes people got so angry they moved out. And then the next person would move in. It worked for five or six years and then we went our separate ways. Some of them wanted to go to India; Embryo had invited us on tour there with them. But me and my girlfriend were having our first baby, and that was too much for us. [My band Bröselmaschine] split up in 1974, and the drummer and the singer went along to India. The bassist wanted to move to the countryside and become a shepherd – he's still got a pretty big sheep farm in southern Germany. The other guitarist Willi Kissmer and I were the only ones left. We reanimated the band later, but we didn't live together any more. The mood had changed by then.

BERND WITTHÜSER We lived a very relaxed communal life. It was fun, but we weren't an agit-prop machine like Berlin's Kommune 1; there were only five of us. Our flatmates only came and went occasionally. I never liked the idea of Kommune 1. Fritz Teufel was nice enough, but Rainer Langhans was a terrible bloke – a complete idiot, I couldn't stand the guy.

LUTZ LUDWIG KRAMER Rainer Langhans, Fritz Teufel and Dieter Kunzelmann were part of it as well; they came to a gig by my band Agitation Free at the Technical University, and Langhans thought it was amazing. Afterwards he said the communards wanted to do a session with us. They thought they could do anything in those days: make music or have a personal relationship with Mao. They saw themselves as geniuses, every one of them, and that made them a whole group of geniuses! Anyway, Agitation Free got invited to a session at the commune on Stephanstrasse in Moabit. It was a bit of a hassle, actually, because we didn't have a car to take all our equipment back and forth. But then Holger Meins offered to pick us up in the Kommune 1 VW bus. One floor at Stephanstrasse was painted jet-black; that became our rehearsal room. Then we met the people from Amon Düül and we'd have crazy sessions with them. They stole a clarinet from me, and they messed up our eardrums as well. Later on, I moved into a flat with Karl-Heinz Hausmann, Düül's organist, in the annexe at Stephanstrasse.

CHRIS KARRER In München we had political communes, sex communes and musical communes – everything you can think of. Kommune 1 is a good example of how political communes were completely un-musical; all they cared about was ideology. That wasn't what Amon Düül were about.

LUTZ LUDWIG KRAMER Once I'd decided to break with the establishment, I moved into Kommune 1. The very thought of having to go to school was a farce, one big circle-jerk to keep capitalism alive. And school stood for my parents as well. I was against them both! At sixteen, I was the youngest in the commune, and one of the freest. But they didn't take just anyone; they were pretty elitist.

CHRISTIAN BURCHARD This new trend suddenly started of everyone living together. Because it's cheaper, to start with. And you don't mind sleeping ten to a room when you're young. There were never any rules in my communes, thank God. They were always laid-back communities. Of course, there were always fights because someone or other wanted to be cock of the walk. But the music communes that were set up in those days all survived fairly well. We met the [hippy band] Checkpoint Charlie and had fantastic communes with them, first in Karlsruhe and then in the countryside. There was the Exmagmacommune near Stuttgart; they were [a fusion band] like us, not just covering the Beatles and the Stones – breaking new ground. And I still meet young people who listen to their records. Then there was the Missus Beastly commune, a cult band from Herford in Westphalia. There was a rumour going around about them; we heard they lived deep in the forest and did crazy stuff.

HANS-JOACHIM ROEDELIUS As a commune member, I only ever listened in to the discussions. I think I was in Kommune 2. Whatever it was called, it was the never-ending-discussions commune. I'd look after the kids while the others discussed themselves to death.

LUTZ LUDWIG KRAMER Life in Kommune 1 was ruled by questions like 'Who's going to clean?' 'Have we got anything to eat?' 'Who's going to get the dope?' And 'Who's shagging who today? Or shall we all shag together?' Sleeping around like crazy was part of everyday life for me at sixteen. They called me the Jim Morrison of West Berlin, because I always had plenty of girls. But the Kommune 1 orgies were fun. We had them in this big room full of mattresses. Separating off was frowned upon; the only ones who did were Rainer Langhans and Uschi Obermaier. Obermaier wouldn't even let anyone touch her tits; they were reserved for Langhans, Jimi Hendrix, Keith Richards and Jackie Stewart. Hendrix came for a smoke at Kommune 1 after his gig at the Sportpalast, had a go on my amazing bong, and then Langhans drove him to the Hotel Kempinski with Obermaier. Cue the nasty article in *Stern* magazine: 'Commune Love'. And the advertising poster for it: Uschi with bare breasts and Rainer with my bong in his hand. They went and broke it, and they never got me a new one.

RENATE KNAUP We made music everywhere, sometimes at home, sometimes in our rehearsal room. We played in our own rooms, but we also went to the rehearsal room every day. I was still having to work, but all the men in the commune had rich parents. Their dads had PhDs and their own companies, so they never had to do a day's work. Only Auntie Renate had to toil and slog. I was a translator and a telephonist for the media mogul Leo Kirch. It was great – really interesting people out looking for films all over the world. I worked until five o'clock and by the time I got back to the commune, the others had already done all sorts of things together. There were days when they wanted to use that against me, but I didn't let them get to me. And then music gradually took over. Once we started playing more and more paid gigs, I handed in my notice at work. But it was unthinkable for the financially independent men to pass the hat round for Renate now and then. Their solidarity didn't extend to money.

LUTZ LUDWIG KRAMER There was a two-tier society at Kommune 1, definitely. [Uschi] Obermaier had money coming out of her ears, earned a thousand marks a day. The rest of us had nothing at all; we used to steal cake by the yard from the Paech factory at night because we had nothing to eat. Obermaier came back from that fashion shoot for *Stern* – 'Commune Love' – and discovered five hundred marks tumbling out of her blouse. 'Oh, I didn't know I still had that,' she said. I said: 'Uschi, there's people here who need it!' And she replied: 'You need to take care of yourselves. Sell a bit of dope, Ludwig!' I remember the lawyer and activist Horst Mahler giving us hell about that *Stern* story, asking why we'd sold out to such a bourgeois rag. Those were extremely strange times.

RENATE KNAUP Later, when we had our own house, we had a treasurer to take care of our finances. I had to submit an application to him for every pair of tights I bought. We'd end up discussing whether they were necessary or not; it was pretty out there.

LUTZ LUDWIG KRAMER At some point, Kommune 1 got radicalised. I remember Holger Meins not eating for three days because of internal politics, and crying every night, or more like sobbing. That was a tipping point. All the radical stuff upset the balance. I still joined in with the fun happenings. We'd get sent propaganda material from China. That must have been around 1968. Six thousand copies of Mao's *Little Red Book*, and other stuff. They were delivered in enormous boxes and we'd load them into our VW bus, drive to the Kaiser Wilhelm Memorial Church, run up the tower and throw down the red books until the whole square by the church was polka-dotted. Once I went along with [the anarchist group] the Hash Rebels and we gatecrashed an event held by the drugs police. It was called something like 'The Dangers of Drugs' . . . It was in some uni building and they had plenty of material for show and tell: hash, grass and LSD. There were about a dozen of us, and we sat separately around the auditorium. On a signal, we all got up and headed straight for the podium, pocketed the drugs and cleared off out of there.

MANI NEUMEIER We lived as a community, like the Native Americans – we weren't just a band, we were a clan; for most of us, it was a replacement family. We tried out new ways of living but we had to watch the money because we didn't make a lot out of our music. Sometimes we had only one or two gigs a month, and then it was a good thing we didn't have to spend DM800 a month each in rent. We spent two years with four of us living on our tour bus, the three of us from the band and our road manager. I mean, obviously it was a bit crowded, so we made sure we stayed with friends and girlfriends as often as we could. Things were very laid-back around Heidelberg, we knew a lot of people there. If someone had a house, we'd arrange to rehearse there. Then in 1971 we got our own house in the Odenwald hills – not in the city, up a mountain. We're still there now.

SUZANNE DOUCET I've always been a loner; I prefer to go home alone, write alone and make music on my own as well. I wasn't the type for communes. I never did all those communal trips. A lot of my friends were looking for a community, but I never wanted that.

IRMIN SCHMIDT The idea of a commune horrified me. Can never lived together. Inconceivable! Hildegard and I had been together for a few years and were living together. All right, Jon Hassell stayed with us for a few weeks, that was fine. And Malcolm Mooney had a room in our flat for a couple of months. But it wasn't communal.

HOLGER CZUKAY We weren't hippies and we didn't want to live together. We were constantly making music together, so we spent a lot of time together anyway. I was really glad to go home alone after our sessions and get a bit of peace and quiet.

JAKI LIEBEZEIT A communal set-up wouldn't have worked for us. Our commune was our studio that we'd set up together.

ACHIM REICHEL My wife and I met some nice people from Kassel, on holiday in Greece. After a while the man told me his commune back in the day was named after my record *Die grüne Reise*. I never lived in a commune, though.

1968

'When you're right at the heart of things, you don't
really notice major events happening.'
KLAUS SCHULZE

HELLMUT HATTLER Come 1968, everyone was suddenly a leftie. The
only thing they talked about in cafés was revolution, that was the vibe.
It didn't influence the way I thought, though. Our generation always
had enough to eat and had an unprecedented level of freedom. It was
a freedom we weren't aware of, we just used it. And then they said the
revolution was everywhere – not just political; psychological, sexual
and spiritual as well. And they said you had to take drugs to make
progress in life.

NIKEL PALLAT The feeling of freedom was everywhere in 1968. It
gave you more courage to question the demands on you. Berlin was in
a state of flux, but the revolts were happening all over West Germany.
It's just that people lived it a bit more in Berlin and it escalated more,
partly due to the city's special situation: on one side the Extra-
Parliamentary Opposition with Rudi Dutschke, and on the other the
arch-conservative Berliners. 'Go over to East Berlin if you don't like it
here!' they'd say to me in those days. Then again, Berlin was also more
tolerant than West Germany; we've always had our fair share of crazy
people here.

PETER BURSCH We were itching for change. We didn't want to be
like our parents. We ate a vegan diet, for instance, except we called it by
a different name back then: *macrobiotic*. We didn't eat meat for a year
because we'd worked out it might be good for the planet. Then came
Buddhism and other spiritual things, then a campaign against alcohol.

We were always sliding from one thing into the next, and we thought every one of them would change the world. The one true way of life!

MICHAEL HOENIG 1968 was a time when everything seemed possible. Everything was in turmoil, you could just feel it. You could change teachers or get them kicked right out of their jobs. At the university in Berlin, we really managed to completely wipe out our professors. A lot of questions came up that we had no answers for, though. I had nothing to do with music yet – music was something overly structured, from the past. I'd been arguing with my father about politics for years. He read [the conservative paper] *Die Welt*, and my aunt had got me a subscription to the [leftist] *Frankfurter Rundschau* for my birthday. From the time I turned thirteen, all I did with my family was argue: about what was going on in Germany, about Germany's relations with America, and so on. And then Benno Ohnesorg's death [on 2 June 1967] changed everything. I remember I'd been standing about a hundred metres away from him when the shot sounded; I even heard it. The demonstration was in the morning and I'd bunked off school to go along. The next day my father read the *Frankfurter Rundschau* for once, and our family harmony was briefly restored.

BERND WITTHÜSER 1968 changed absolutely everything. The only students who didn't want change were in Essen; they certainly didn't want to change their lives. They joined in the protests to begin with, but after a while they all went back to their studies and became engineers or whatever. It was only me and a few friends there, who were a bit like the Freak Brothers. We started living and destroying things, chucked eggs at Franz Josef Strauss, etcetera. I demonstrated against anything and everything, against the [right-wing] tabloid *BILD*, whatever you had going.

GERD KRAUS It was an incredibly intense time of rethinking and rejecting fossilised structures in society, and forms of music as well. We

Germans had the toughest material to get our teeth into, because the Nazi catastrophe had inescapably wormed its way into lots of people's heads, sometimes as guilt complexes that people covered up with bourgeois trappings. It was all the more urgent for us to ask questions of the generations before us, and that was something a lot of our musician friends had in common.

LIMPE FUCHS I knew I had to go to university to find some way out of the strict corset of working-class Catholic life.

SUZANNE DOUCET I was at the first student riots in München. I was sitting on the road with the students when the police turned up. That was an important experience for me, but it wasn't yet political activism. But still, we young people felt at the time that the world had to change. We wanted to change the political rules, make the social system more just. What we all shared was the feeling that something wasn't right with the world. I'd been writing my own songs since 1964 and I produced my own record in 1966, the first one. I was doing poetic and philosophical chansons, which didn't get a lot of listeners, but the critics paid attention to me. Then in 1968 I picked up on the insanity of war in the song 'Kleine Kinder'.

CHRISTIAN BURCHARD The riots in München's Schwabing district were way back in 1962, but they were part of it because protests were taken openly to the streets.

STEFAN MICHEL The Schwabing riots started everything off, for me. That was when we realised there was something else out there other than our old parents. There was a café on Leopoldstrasse, where two people sat outside one summer evening and started playing guitar. Some idiots complained about it, and that kicked it all off. There was a riot – the police came in with their truncheons swinging, even at innocent bystanders. And by the next day, all of Leopoldstrasse was occupied.

People dug up the cobblestones and threw them at the police. It went on for three or four days, and I was part of it. That's how I learned that another way of life exists.

CHRISTIAN BURCHARD München has always been a bit conservative, but in 1968 things hotted up even there. The art academy students occupied their building and the whole street was flooded with police, ready and waiting for orders to take the place back. The students didn't do much more inside than paint wonderful pictures on the corridor walls. Later, once they'd been chased out, it was all whitewashed over – those pictures would be cultural artefacts, these days. It was a problem for us too, because we stored all our equipment at the art academy, and after the police had cleared the building we couldn't get at our instruments. All of a sudden, they were saying we were accomplices to the crime and it was trespassing. They practically threatened to take us to court. Then the director of the art academy came to see me and said: 'I'll open the back door tomorrow – you guys come and collect your stuff.' He didn't approve of how we were treated either. The political climate in München was ruthless. Franz Josef Strauss was already in power. We did a gig with Checkpoint Charlie in the München Art Zone. They started off, and the first thing the singer yelled into the mic was: 'Where's that swine Franz Josef?' Five minutes later they were banged up in jail. Checkpoint Charlie got reported to the police by the local mayor when they played in Kempten, for having a papier-mâché pig on stage that they called 'Franz Josef'. After that they argued over whether they'd mentioned the name Strauss or not. Why should anyone be banned from calling their papier-mâché pig Franz Josef? Anyway, Checkpoint Charlie ended up with a DM60,000 fine. Strauss had all the Bavarian courts on his side, and the police as well, obviously. So the director of the art academy standing up to him was great, because he showed the courage of his convictions. We went on a lot of demonstrations – logically enough. Embryo played on a lot of marches too. The lefties used to rope us in as musical entertainment. Later on, we played for the Socialist German Workers Youth [SDAJ] group once. They'd booked us for two days, but at the end of the first day the boss came along and said: 'You can have your money, but please leave tomorrow.' They were angry because we'd worked with a company that had dealings with the East German dissident Wolf Biermann, but they hadn't realised that until we got there.

GÜNTER SCHICKERT The atmosphere in West Berlin was really open at the time. I was nineteen in 1968 and I'd just taken my exams to be an insurance clerk at a private health insurance company. That meant I'd leapt through all the bourgeois hoops I had to. My parents got divorced that year as well. And I was sleeping with men in those days, for two or three years from eighteen to twenty. I thought at first it was freer to be with men, that gay men lived outside all the norms. I was wrong, of course; you get the same jealousies as everyone else. Then I fell in love with a woman again and that was the end of that.

LUTZ LUDWIG KRAMER I was the only political person in Agitation Free. The others were more into smoking dope, which was political as well, in its way, and another form of liberation.

RENATE KNAUP You could tell there was something on the air, in 1968. There were all these cafés on Leopoldstrasse where we'd meet up. Then there was the Domicile, a big jazz place where Mal Waldron played chess every day after breakfast. But the main nerve centre was the Europa. People came back there from their trips to Nepal with fresh deliveries, and you could always go there to meet someone. There were certain places on Leopoldstrasse where you knew who you'd run into as the day went by. You'd find your people either in the Schwabinger Nest, the Capri Ice Bar, Café Europa – BOOM – there they are. We didn't have mobile phones, obviously. The film people went to one place, the jazz people hung out at a different one, the freaks somewhere else, but it was still a good mix.

ACHIM REICHEL The late sixties were wild days in Hamburg. There were these legendary dealer mansions out at the Rondeel lake in Winterhude, great big houses where the drug packages were piled up to the ceiling. You'd think: 'Jesus, what's going on here? It's absolutely insane.' And that scene was part of the music, those Hamburg apartments and houses where there was always something going on. You could turn up any time and someone would have rolled a joint and there'd be people playing music. If you got bored in one place, you'd just move on to the next one.

ASMUS TIETCHENS In 1968 I'd just finished training as a commercial clerk and there were two things I wanted: money and long hair! That wasn't possible in a normal job – you couldn't have long hair in an office. There was only one place where you could make a lot of money and still have long hair: advertising. All right, in music as well, but I wasn't a musician. And anyway I'd have had to work hard to make it, and that wasn't my style. I was already experimenting with tapes in 1968 but I had no ambitions to take that anywhere. So advertising it was. And once I started working there, it turned out I was right: I had long hair and plenty of money! But then four years later, a good friend got me out of advertising; she tore me off a strip and convinced me what I was doing was inhuman. She even blackmailed me: either you come on this demo, or it's over between us. I had no awareness of politics before 1968. But then a lot of people I knew and a bit of thinking made me a very political person and I went on a good few demonstrations. Not just as a foot soldier; out of conviction. So I dropped advertising like a hot potato after four years. And since then I've never had what you might call a proper job.

ACHIM REICHEL There was the Ho Chi Minh faction in Hamburg as well. Our political content was our music, though – our music was a statement in itself. I just didn't see much point to protest songs like the ones we knew from the US. It was clear, if you do something like that in Germany, no one will ever play you again. But that was never my thing, anyway. Our lyricist Frank Dostal was more into that, he was more au fait with politics. But I'd always say to him: 'Hey, man, we're musicians, not singer-songwriters where you don't even need to strum along to the lyrics.' There was the Burg Waldeck Festival [Germany's first open-air festival] for 'political content' – you could forget the music there. I thought specific political statements in music were out of line. All I was interested in was the music. I never pretended otherwise, which is honest enough, isn't it? But it wasn't ever just about making a living out of it; I wanted it to be something I could stand by. I knew that early on. We had fun without regurgitating a manifesto. I didn't need a lot of words to feel that it was great music.

HARALD GROSSKOPF In 1968 I was nineteen, and certainly not a '68er'. I was a painter and decorator in Hannover, but I sensed that things were changing. I didn't have A-levels and I wasn't political, but I did wonder what the students were getting up to. Why are they ripping up the roads and scrapping with the police? The first time I had any contact with educated people on the left was when I did my community service. I spent a lot of time talking to them, and it was only then that I developed any political awareness. I didn't vote until I was in my late twenties. But some of the election letters didn't get to me because I had no fixed address for a while, just stayed where I could.

KLAUS SCHULZE 1968 was political, and after that it was interesting, of course, but it got more and more volatile because of the Red Army Faction. We weren't consciously aware of it in the heart of Berlin; it was just our everyday life. We picked up on the Rudi Dutschke thing, obviously, and what was happening at the universities [Dutschke was a popular extra-parliamentary student leader who would survive an assassination attempt in 1968]. I was doing German studies at the Technical University. I didn't demonstrate much because I wasn't interested in any of it. The marches were always about things that weren't important to me. I paid attention to what was going on around me but I didn't join in. I was never in the Republican Club, where Dutschke always went, and I never joined a demo outside the Amerika-Haus.

LUTZ LUDWIG KRAMER 1968 was a really hyper-speedy time, like being permanently on amphetamines. I left home in 1968 and moved into Kommune 1. My father didn't give a shit, he was high up at the Sender Freies Berlin [Radio Free Berlin] TV station and travelled a lot on film business. But my mother came looking for me, with a family friend. I was moving from one commune to the next, at the time. I was only going to school in Charlottenburg every now and then, and after a while I dropped out. It was just too far from Moabit to Charlottenburg. My parents had no influence on me by then, hadn't for a long time.

GÜNTER SCHICKERT I lived in the middle of West Berlin, on Passauer Strasse, where there was always something going on. You'd pick up on everything that happened in the city. I was always interested in politics. When the Russians occupied Czechoslovakia in 1968, I went to the Technical University the next day, of course, and watched [the students] preparing for their demos. They talked about the black bloc [the most radical protesters] and who was allowed to march at the front and who didn't want to walk behind who. Anyway, I got the feeling they were all beating about the bush, and it was all about something that didn't interest me at all. I still went to the demo, the next day. And then along came the mounted police and scattered the crowd. A few frightened demonstrators climbed up the concrete honeycombs of the Memorial Church at Zoo, the ones that look like powder boxes, and the police went after them with rubber truncheons and battered their feet and hands – knocking the demonstrators down from twelve feet above. I just thought: 'You don't belong here, Günter!' So I turned off onto Joachimsthaler Strasse, stood in a doorway, watched all the goings-on and said to myself: 'Nope, this isn't for you!' I wanted to demonstrate and share my opinions, but I didn't want to get into fights with the police. Any form of violence is anathema to me. After that, I usually kept away from demonstrations, but I was still interested in politics, of course. And when Benno Ohnesorg got killed on 2 June, I was actually at that same demo. I even heard the shot go bang. That sent me home right then and there; it was frightening. I was scared! It had all got too big for me. And apart from that, I felt like we didn't stand a chance against that kind of state authority. I shared the demonstrators' political aims, but my route to them was different to theirs.

PETER BURSCH We played at the Easter Peace March in Duisburg every year. And we marched with them. I played with Joan Baez there once – it was amazing. That was before Bröselmaschine. When things really heated up, the band went to Essen and tried to stop deliveries of *BILD*. We sat on the street with a big crowd of people, until the police started dragging us away a few hours later. We often did things like that together as a band; we did a tour of Germany where we only played in squats.

MICHAEL HOENIG I bunked off school early to go to the demo against the Shah of Persia at the opera house. I could afford to because I was pretty good in class, always got top marks. Benno Ohnesorg was shot that evening. There was a huge crush. First of all, no one knew what had happened. It was a sound no one knew in Germany any more, because nobody had firearms. The police never used guns. I remember it clearly; that sound went right through me. The experience was very strange, frightening and confusing. Four weeks later, I was exposed as having been there by a photo in the newspaper and told that the school didn't want any ringleaders. That shot at Ohnesorg altered our reality, because it suddenly exposed the violence of the people at the top. My father understood me better after that, at least. But I didn't realise it until later; we just went on arguing at the time.

STEVE SCHROYDER Before, I'd been a singer in school bands doing beat music. I'd come to Berlin in 1968 because you didn't have to do military service if you lived there, and to look for a new band. Berlin was a turbulent place. First I wanted to do theatre studies, but the first time I got to the theatre studies institute at the Free University, it had just been occupied. It was impossible to study, from the very beginning. If there wasn't an occupation going on, there was a demonstration. I got sucked straight into the student movement, the 68ers, and the police took down my details straight away as well, after I threw paint at the wall of the institute. They accused me of damaging a police officer's uniform. Two days later, I was arrested out of the blue at the uni canteen. They let me go after a night in a cell, but they fined me DM100 for the dry-cleaning costs.

HELLMUT HATTLER In Berlin I ended up in jail because I was suspected of doing something or other at a demo. I was inside for a night, and I was charged with breaching the peace, but since all I'd done was take part in a demonstration, they let me go again pretty quickly.

LUTZ LUDWIG KRAMER I was charged with grievous bodily harm because I was a really radical protester. I'd run between the police horses holding a wooden fence post and knocked them over, but the horses had trampled over us demonstrators. Then I chased after the police and beat them up. Anyway, I was arrested and the pigs dragged me away by the hair. But then this young man popped up and said he was a lawyer and on my side and wanted to take care of things for me. I called out my name to him. It was Klaus Eschen from the Socialist Lawyers Collective, which Hans-Christian Ströbele and Horst Mahler were part of as well. And Eschen defended me. I was only seventeen, so they could only put me on remand. The judge saw that I came from a 'good family', called me up to the bench, gave me a good talking-to, and then sent me to the Forest School. A friend of mine from the wrong class did time for way less than that. The mild sentence achieved the opposite with me, though; it only intensified my hate for the fascist justice system. For me, that judge was the epitome of all that was wrong with Germany. I had no money to pay the court fees, of course, so I sent the law to my father. The trial cost him a shitload of money but he paid up without a word of complaint. He got me out of jail in Morocco later on, as well, without a word. I was still in there for seven months, though, for seven kilos of hash. That long in a Moroccan jail is not a nice experience for a nineteen-year-old. But I saw the thing in Berlin as self-defence, that was all; I'd hardly done anything. It was the state that was wielding the violence, back then. I'm not a radical leftist any more, I'm not dogmatic about it, but back then the state wanted things to escalate. They wanted to pass their Emergencies Act and they wanted the minorities to be radicalised, with help from the press. It was a set-up.

STEVE SCHROYDER The Battle of Tegeler Weg was wild. It was all about Horst Mahler, who was in court at Tegeler Weg for demonstrating against the [right-wing] Springer newspapers. He was defended by his lawyer buddies Otto Schily and Hans-Christian Ströbele. Anyway, everyone on the left had been called up to demonstrate outside the court. The word 'battle' is appropriate, because it was a military occasion. The police had driven up these huge water cannons, and the demonstrators were throwing bricks and stones – it really was a battle. I'd got hold of a helmet so I didn't get a truncheon on the head, and then I locked arms with the others to hold off the police. We didn't have official permission for the demo, so the police started breaking it up right away. After two orders to clear the way, they immediately turned their water cannons on us. Chaos broke out and I ended up in a cell, spent the night at the Friesenstrasse station with ten others.

KLAUS BRIEST There were times when we just wanted to be provocative – we looked at it as a 'moon-rising'. If we were driving back from a gig through posh areas, we'd press our bare arses up against the car windows. Just to show them what's what. Our message was: 'Fuck you!' But it always went so fast, they couldn't call the police; we'd be miles away by the time they got there.

STEVE SCHROYDER I was never scared. I used to get euphoric about it. Around Christmas one time, we burned the Stars and Stripes outside the Amerika-Haus in Berlin and then we ran down the middle of the big Kurfürstendamm shopping street, totally euphoric, and I really thought: 'The revolution is victorious!' Just because we'd set fire to an American flag outside the Amerika-Haus . . . Well, our idealism caused a lot of euphoria in those days.

JÜRGEN DOLLASE The first book I bought myself, at fourteen, was a political paperback, something about the Nazi era. When my father came home from school for lunch, we'd always have major political discussions and arguments. Over the course of the afternoon, we'd creep out of our holes and go back to normal. I've been reading *Der Spiegel* magazine every week since I was fourteen. We'd argue about the typical Extra-Parliamentary Opposition subjects. Before the Extra-Parliamentary Opposition there was a subculture called the *Gammler* [not unlike the beatniks], and that was a springboard into politics. It was like a mix of French existentialism and nonconformism. The word 'nonconformist' was a key term.

STEVE SCHROYDER Our generation was distancing itself from our parents' generation, and that atmosphere was very obvious, but we didn't know where we wanted to go. I went to the International Vietnam Congress but I never understood why people had posters on their walls with Chinese Mao quotes, for example. In the commune I soon moved into, this friend of mine had the back room; he was a great proponent of the Chinese direction and he wallpapered his room with Chinese posters. Still, it all influenced me so strongly that I thought, after two semesters: 'Why should I go on with German and theatre studies? It's ancient old crap – I'm switching to sociology, psychology and politics.' But the political students in Berlin horrified me. When Zappa and his Mothers of Invention played in Berlin, the place was full of political students who demanded Zappa make a commitment to the revolution and all that. Zappa didn't want to, and after a while he lost his temper, wagged his finger and said, a bit patronising: 'It is the evolution, not the revolution!' And then this scream went around the whole venue, followed by utter chaos. People rushed the stage, raging with anger, and smashed everything up. I thought it was appalling, not least because the Mothers had all this great stuff with them, puppets and things. The political students were violent and only wanted to destroy everything. That was definitely not my politics.

LUTZ LUDWIG KRAMER Zappa played at the Sportpalast back then, and he started insulting us. He said we Germans were all evil: Nazis, or at least the children of Nazis. That was out of order. We might have been the children of Nazis, but we weren't Nazis! He and his band, the Mothers, said us West Berliners were all crazy and our 'revolution' was stupid trash! It wasn't revolution they wanted, it was evolution. And then he said, 'Bastards.' We didn't like that at all. 'Smash it all up!' was our response. No one comes from America to Berlin to tell us what's what. The political scene in Berlin was very organic and interwoven. There were only a few big egos, because we all added up to one huge ego. We were just right there in the here and now. Anyway, we ran Zappa off the stage and smashed all his equipment. Later on, I saw him standing by the stage door, cursing and shaking and playing nervously with his plectrum. I went up to him and said: 'Frank, wrong words! Don't talk with us about revolution and evolution. Just play your music!' And he answered: 'You motherfuckers! You motherfuckers!' The musician in me felt for him, though; I asked him about his plectrum, paid him a few compliments, said he was a really great guitarist and I could tell because I was too. He gave me the pick.

JÜRGEN DOLLASE I wasn't a 68er, more of a 69er. The 68ers were uptight – we 69ers were hedonists. I'd never have become a restaurant critic as a 68er, but I did as a 69er. I've always been an individualist. I was involved with a jazz community in Viersen/Mönchengladbach, but I was never fully part of it. I never felt a need to join committees. Strangely enough, though, I did end up back in the political scene at the art academy because we had there what we called the Basisgruppe Kunst [literally Basis-Group Art], a radical left-wing group. The boss was a Spartakus member, and we'd read up on our Marx, Engels, Lenin every week [Spartakus was a small revolutionary anti-war movement]. 'First we read, then we discuss it!' Horrific. But I joined the student council in my second semester, and from there the art academy's governing board.

KLAUS BRIEST Our band Xhol's music was intense and vivid and had its ecstatic moments. It often got the audience worked up into a frenzy. There was one gig at Mainz University where the venue was packed to the rafters. The police should have intervened for overcrowding. We put on a decent show on the stage; we had two singers, and they were both great entertainers. It was boiling hot. At some point a couple from the front row came up on stage and started groping each other. We watched them and thought, 'What's next?' Then they ripped off their clothing and adopted an unambiguous position. We laughed and just went on playing. It was completely crazy. But it's always amazing, as a musician, if you can get your audience so worked up that they lose all their inhibitions.

LUTZ LUDWIG KRAMER At some point I got too radical for the rest of Agitation Free. The happenings and political activities were more important to me than discipline within the band. Sometimes it helped, though: there was one time when a can of Coke tipped over the amp and it gave up the ghost. I just picked up the guitar, improvised and chanted, 'Ho Ho Ho Chi Minh!', and the whole audience yelled back:

'Ho Ho Ho Chi Minh!' It turned into a gigantic session, and it went on until the amp was repaired. Later on, Lüül said it had saved our arses. But Lüül was never political himself, or Christopher Franke either. Michael 'Fame' Günther flirted with the left a bit but didn't want to get his arse kicked. They were all bourgeois boys, in the end. I was too, but I left it behind me, and that's why I didn't want to make records and let any nasty producers get their hands on our music. What I wanted was to get out the sitars, eat macrobiotic food and sleep on the floor. So it couldn't last. Looking back, it's a shame, of course, that I never made a record with them. Publishing companies are always asking if we've got any material from those days. They offer a thousand euros, sight unseen, for any old crap. It's a pity, but what can you do?

STEVE SCHROYDER I tried my best to be a student for a while, but in the end the revolution was all that mattered. It was interrupted, though, when I went on a trip to India with an old schoolfriend in 1969. We set off in February, in an old 2CV with 'Berlin–Delhi–Kathmandu' painted on the back. That trip changed everything. The car conked out in Iran, and these Persians helped us repair it, and they were fantastically friendly. I'll remember that forever. Along the way, I smoked my first hashish in Afghanistan. This guy came out of the desert in a caravan, walked straight past the camels over to me and foisted a hunk of hash on me. I thought: 'What's this all about?' There was this room where people went in and then came out again coughing. My mate didn't have the guts, he thought it was all too much. I had no inhibitions, and I had the most amazing experiences on that trip. After I got back, I wanted to either be a farmer in India or make music in Berlin. It ended up being music, obviously.

MICHAEL ROTHER Around 1968 a new chapter opened up and an alternative approach was sought, in art, film and music – a climate that had a major influence on me. Two years before my A-levels, I'd said I wanted to be a lawyer. I was attracted to the basic idea of helping people to get justice. Friedrich Schiller's *Sturm und Drang* [meaning 'storm and stress'] plays and poems from the 1770s had given me a sense of freedom and justice, which affected me at the end of my schooldays, as did an interest in psychology. It was that interest that made me choose a psychiatric hospital in Neuss for my compulsory community service. Joining the Bundeswehr, any type of military service, was out of the question for me, against all my convictions. Of course, I developed a political consciousness during those years. I was horrified when a police officer killed Benno Ohnesorg, and like a lot of people I knew I vehemently rejected the Vietnam War. But political debates at my school were usually too orthodox for me. The Marxist–Leninist faction seemed too narrow-minded, but I definitely wanted to break out of the conservative climate of the time. The eighteen months I spent doing my community service meant a lot to me. By choosing community rather than military service, you automatically became a political person, because you saw some untenable circumstances on the psychiatric wards and fought back against them and stood up for patients.

PETER BRÖTZMANN People didn't think in little boxes at the end of the sixties, like they do again now. Our generation all pulled together back then, whether you were doing jazz or rock. We all had dealings with each other because we wanted the same thing: to change not only music, but society as well. That's why I got on with the rock musicians; we shared the same inheritance that we had to face, the shame at what had happened in World War Two. We wanted to understand and compensate for it with our music.

ALEXANDER VON SCHLIPPENBACH In 1968 I was living as a kind of farmer, or maybe a hippy, in an old farmhouse built in 1653 near Köln, with my family. It was beautiful there, and we could rehearse outside. Whatever else happened, all the demonstrations and so on, we only got wind of on the radio or TV. I never went to a demonstration. Politics in the strictest sense was never a driving force for me, I have to admit. Instead, we did the Anti-Festival in 1968, in an underground garage in Köln. It was an event to push back against the established Jazz on the Rhine festival, where the traditional and established jazz stars performed. So we free-jazz men, Schoof, Brötzmann and I, we decided to do something that opposed it, and we did a pretty good job of it. There were artists and writers involved as well. It was the first action campaign organised by musicians that I can remember. We played with our group, and then came Brötzmann with his people, and then Amon Düül from southern Germany. Jazz and rock came together in a totally natural way in that garage – it was literally and figuratively underground.

HOLGER CZUKAY The politics of 1968 hardly affected me. I've always said, even back then: politics swallows music whole. That was how Stockhausen saw it too. Music has a life of its own. All that guitar-strumming with political lyrics is a misunderstanding; music is actually something cosmic.

IRMIN SCHMIDT I wasn't very politically active any more in 1968. I'd fought my battles with my father as a teenager in Dortmund. He'd been a high-ranking functionary for the Ruhr region in the Reich Labour Service under the Nazis, and I accused him of having known everything. I was interested in what happened in 1968, but the student uprising didn't really affect me; I was a bit older by then. Naturally, the DKP [the German Communist Party] guys were always coming over to my place and trying to persuade me to join the Communist Party, presumably partly because I'd read all the Marx and Lenin stuff; I was incredibly left-wing, eloquent and blazing with enthusiasm. But they lived in a different world to me because I wanted to know exactly how all the theory would be put into practice, or had been put into practice. I was pretty sensitive since I'd got so immersed in researching the Third Reich. Any form of dictatorship horrified me. I wasn't dis-illusioned in 1968, but I had no faith in any violently imposed healings and upheavals of society, and although I did understand the 68ers' critique of the existing conditions, I thought they were exaggerating how bad it was here. Of course, I also saw that there was a lot we had to change and I admired and liked Rudi Dutschke a great deal, but I was just against all forms of violence. And when the Baader–Meinhof gang came onto the scene, my sympathies were over; that was clear-cut. I remember, it was in spring, beautiful weather, we were sitting in an ice-cream café on Ludwigstrasse, and this girl came along from one of the communes and she was wailing and lamenting – 'They've been caught!' – and then she told us about the arson attacks on the department stores in Frankfurt. I was appalled and I said: 'I'm sorry, but you almost killed a nightwatchman.' For her, though, that was the price to be paid for a better world. That was one of the moments when the curtain fell for me, that was the end of it for me. Then again, founding Can in 1968 was also a real 68er thing to do. Because I was actually on my way to a career as a conductor. Just chucking it all in and starting a rock group, in which the music is spontaneously invented together, was also a radical break with what came before. For me personally, founding Can was a political manifesto.

HOLGER CZUKAY I never demonstrated – I don't go chasing after ideologies. All those demos back then put me off. And I didn't get any of it, intellectually. The one time I voted I picked the liberals, the FDP, because that was my mother's party. After that I never voted again. I'd lost interest in politics, and I knew my heart's not in the right place for political engagement. I was never anti-American either; I liked Americans even as a kid. Back then, I'd ended up in Limburg an der Lahn, and the Americans were right next door. I sang chorales for them, in my usual singing voice, and I mouthed the counterpoints in between. The Americans listened and gave me money. Apart from that, I was addicted to Coca-Cola. Every penny I laid my hands on, I immediately invested in Coca-Cola. One time an American guy put me under the shower. But the water was warm, and afterwards he gave me a whole jar of sweets. Americans were very different to the Germans, and I liked that a lot.

IRMIN SCHMIDT People had political expectations of us; sometimes they'd come along and tell us what campaigns and demos we ought to join in with. We almost always ignored them. The one or two times we did go along with it, at some rally or other, it was always supposed to lead to communisation, which was not at all our thing. And what they said at their events almost never went along with what we stood for. We never talked politics among ourselves. Never! It was always about music for us. We talked about interpersonal politics – you know, how we work together – but we always agreed on that kind of thing. So you can say, all right, you guys were unpolitical, but our political feelings started at our own front door. That was Can. And we wanted to do it in a way that hadn't been done before. Our political act was Can. But that wasn't a whole new society. And despite all our criticism of the existing society we lived in, we did know that we only had the freedom to do something like Can in that society. We couldn't have done it in East Germany.

PETER BAUMANN Politics never played a major role for me. A friend and I went to Kommune 2 for a night, when I was about sixteen. They'd just got new flyers in, but it was all way too serious for me.

HELLMUT HATTLER Kraan never made direct statements, but that doesn't mean we didn't have a political effect. We encouraged people to change the way they thought. I just always hated it when people pushed on you how society ought to work. That's the opposite of freedom, for me. Freedom is when you decide for yourself what's good for you, and you don't take anything away from other people's freedom.

MICHAEL HOENIG Voting was never on my agenda. I always abstained. OK, it was stupid, but it was a conscious decision back then. There was no political party for us. The Greens didn't yet exist. Everyone I knew didn't vote, out of protest. My first sympathies for politics only came with Willy Brandt from the SPD, in the very late sixties.

IRMIN SCHMIDT I think it's dumb not to vote. I've always cast my vote. Despite all the inadequacies of the existing form of democracy, all you have to do is look around the world, our direct neighbours, in fact, to see that we're not all that badly off. Not voting is a pretty stupid form of protest. What does it ever change?

KARL BARTOS I was sixteen in 1968, doing an apprenticeship, and already working nights as a musician. I moved in with my grandparents that year, when things weren't going too well between my parents and me. But I wasn't unruly. I was never a rebel. It was just difficult with my parents when I switched to wearing jeans, but actually they were cool people. I never went on a demo and I wasn't against nuclear power either. I didn't become aware of how things tied in together until much later.

JÜRGEN DOLLASE In 1968 I was in the Federal Border Guard, and I somehow got my mitts on Jimi Hendrix's *Electric Ladyland*. That left a lasting impression on me, spurred my interest in rock music. Then I was briefly in a local band called Speed Kills, where we didn't play any songs less than an hour long. We played until our fingers bled. People who listened to it on drugs told us later that they'd never experienced anything that intense – a complete high. I'd signed up for two years with the army because they paid well, but then I did rebel and get in trouble there. I had this illustration of the songwriter Franz Josef Degenhardt pinned up in my room, this anti-war thing, which some of the officers didn't like. One important reason for me to join the army was that if you signed up to the Federal Border Guard for two years, you'd get much more money than the standard service pay. My family was on the lower end of the financial scale, let's say. But I still left after a year and a half; I was in the Federal Border Guard from the autumn of 1967 until 1969 and then started studying biology. I don't know why. I think my father pushed me in that direction, but anyway, I dropped out of my degree as well. My music was really kicking off at the time, and I was also doing hallucinogens.

JEAN-MICHEL JARRE The Paris students revolted in 1968, and so did I. We rebelled against the establishment, in society and in culture. In music, we'd had enough of dusty old classical stuff and American rock. For me, electronic music was a form of rebellion, like some German krautrock records.

MICHAEL ROTHER It was a demo that led me down my later musical path. But that wasn't until 1971, in Düsseldorf. At the end of the demonstration a guitarist friend asked me if I fancied coming along to a studio with him, where they were recording a film soundtrack. I asked him what exactly was going on there, and he said a band called Kraftwerk was working there. That was the first time I'd heard the name, and I thought it was a bit odd – I think I even said the name sounded really stupid. But I went along anyway, which was my first introduction to Ralf Hütter, Florian Schneider and Klaus Dinger. So that demo changed my life, ultimately. But then I never had political debates with either Klaus Dinger, Kraftwerk or Harmonia, even though I was a great admirer of Willy Brandt. He embodied the slogan he announced when he became chancellor in 1969: 'Dare more democracy' gave me hope for a new political departure to modern times. NEU! even played for him once in 1972, in Düsseldorf. My later tax advisor was chairman of the Young Social Democrats at the time, I already knew him back then, and he asked if NEU! would play at one of their events to support Willy Brandt. Brandt even came up on stage with us.

NEW BEGINNINGS

'I stopped listening to music in 1970. I wanted to
forget everything that had gone before.'

MICHAEL ROTHER

IRMIN SCHMIDT There was this general feeling that we wanted to
start over at zero. It was a new beginning for me personally as well. For
Michael Karoli it was just a beginning plain and simple, because he'd
only just done his A-levels. He wanted to go to law school and he'd
done one semester already, but he hated it. For Jaki, Holger and me,
though, Can really was a new beginning. We all saw it that way. And
it's no coincidence that bands like Amon Düül, Tangerine Dream and
the forerunners of Kraftwerk started around the same time.

JEAN-MICHEL JARRE New music always illustrates the society it's
made in. Electronic music came out of that wish for change. It often
works for purely hedonistic purposes, but it also reflects its social
environment. As musicians, we wanted to get away from what had
come before, and we wanted to experiment: with melodies, with classical music, with rock. We were only a small group at the time but we
wanted change, wanted to shake off the ballast of our forefathers. It
was an instinct that we had in common. The krautrock band Can and
I found our way to very different music, but I suspect we had similar
motivations driving us. It was strange that we hardly knew anything
about each other back then; it was a pre-internet era. Everyone experimenting with electronic music did it on their own, in their garrets.

NIKEL PALLAT Ton Steine Scherben [literally Clay Stones Shards or
Sound Stones Shards] weren't on the innovative instrumental electronic scene; our focus was on our songs. But our paths crossed all the

time in Kreuzberg. We took over Tangerine Dream's rehearsal room once. A lot of people took advantage of the first synthesizers that came to Germany, opened up new possibilities for themselves. Bazon Brock had a completely barmy music series on the radio in 1969, where he played stuff that was neither beat nor the usual mainstream rock. Up until then, music had come out on singles and the albums were basically singles compilations, but it was then that songs started taking up a whole side of an LP, sometimes, and the album format was really used to the full. Even the Doors had had a few songs that went over eleven minutes.

PETER BURSCH Rock music changed. More and more bands started improvising. You could play one piece for half an hour, if you wanted. In the mid-sixties the songs were still fixed, but by 1968 the mood was much freer.

MANI NEUMEIER The idea at the time was just: anything's possible. If you've listened to Louis Armstrong and John Coltrane and Karlheinz Stockhausen, you realise a whole lot is possible.

IRMIN SCHMIDT Understandably, after twelve years of utter destruction of all culture in Germany, everything interesting was coming out of Britain and America, even in classical music. It made sense; a lot of German intellectuals, including the painters and artists, had emigrated. They came back only slowly – or not at all. I wanted to link up all the more to Germany's musical culture from before 1933. That's why you can hear a clear influence of Kurt Weill in Can, and in what I did after that as well. His music walked the tightrope between high art and entertainment too, to get a bit German about it all. And it really took more than twenty years before we started getting familiar with modernism again, thanks to influences from other countries. The only pioneering German composer, for me at the time, was Karlheinz Stockhausen. All the others came from elsewhere, America or Italy. And then around

1968, the need for a new start germinated in several minds in various German cities, the need to reclaim our own history.

JEAN-MICHEL JARRE I heard of Can early on, and kept an eye on what they were doing. In Germany, the krautrock musicians were at least aware of each other; I was completely isolated in France. All I had was a small group of people to exchange ideas with, with Pierre Schaeffer at its heart. But even within that group we were very French, working in isolation, every man for himself – a pretty arrogant way to work. We had no idea of what was happening out on the streets outside our own front doors, let alone in the rest of the world. The message was: we know the truth; everyone else is ignorant, just churning out rubbish. After two or three years, I wanted out. Pierre Schaeffer told me: 'Stop wasting your valuable time on this nonsense.' I was constantly arguing with those elitist types, saying to them: 'Take a look outside! They're making exciting new music in Germany, and Soft Machine and Pink Floyd are working on amazing sounds in the UK. They're all looking at things you guys just intellectually romanticise. And I want to bring it all together!' But they weren't interested. That was why I went out on my own in the end, after three years, to bridge that gap between experimental music and pop.

MICHAEL ROTHER In my enthusiasm for Cream, Jimi Hendrix and the Beatles, I listened to a whole lot of music as a teenager. But by 1970 at the latest, I said to myself: 'You have to let it all go, forget it all to develop something of your own.' I really didn't want to hear anyone else's music. The less, the better. In 1973 I was on WDR with Harmonia and they played something by Tangerine Dream – but their path wasn't an inspiration for me either. My visions were very different.

BERND DOPP We knew the new German bands didn't have Anglo-American roots, and that was important to us. A certain cultural imperialist situation came about at the time, and we weren't into it. There was a tendency for anti-American politics in those days that influenced pop culture as well, and even my consumer behaviour, like with many people my age. The German experimental bands made us feel superior to people who only listened to international rock.

PETER BURSCH The Essener Songtage were incredible. Before that, we only knew a few bands that were on our wavelength, since Bröselmaschine had got out of the folk niche. In the band before that, we'd still been playing Bob Dylan covers. The folk fans had their discussions too, of course, especially at the annual Burg Waldeck festivals starting in 1964. There were arguments right there on the stage, like between Hannes Wader and Reinhard Mey. Wader accused Mey: 'If you go on like this, you'll end up a schlager singer!' And Mey shot back: 'If *you* go on like this, you might as well convert to communism right here and now!' There was a lot of debating and arguing at the Essener Songtage as well, but the atmosphere there was really different, really great. Bernd Witthüser invited us; he was part of the team. We'd played a couple of gigs with him before. We even bedded down in our sleeping bags in the venue, the Grugahalle. We didn't want to leave – there was an incredible feeling of community. We met Amon Düül and Guru Guru there; they were still called Guru Guru Groove at the time. They were the two German bands that had moved us the most, and then we were directly in touch with them, arranged to play together. We invited them to Duisburg, and then they invited us to their towns. That was actually where it all started. We noticed that there were lots of others on the same wavelength as us, people who wanted to do their own thing like us.

MICHAEL HOENIG It was obvious we wanted to move away from the sound of previous generations. The only music in German back then was schlager; there was nothing else. We thought the German beat bands like the Rattles were kind of embarrassing. What we didn't want was to follow the blues scheme, for the simple reason that we just didn't feel the pain of the blues, its history and the endless suffering of it. We weren't into pain; we were interested in projection.

KLAUS BRIEST Xhol Caravan were originally called Soul Caravan; we started out as a soul cover band. But that sound was too predictable in the long run, too much painting by numbers. Mind you, even as a soul band we didn't just play cover versions; we had our own material. And that was where the development began towards more improvisations, and longer ones. We did pieces by John Coltrane and Cannonball Adderley. Smoking dope meant we were more daring about trying out crazy things. Not accepting any more templates, just letting everything flow and develop of its own accord, acting in the moment and following spontaneous inspiration.

GERD KRAUS All of us came from a scene where we said: 'For God's sake, get me out of here!' And that's why we smashed up all the old structures, in music as we did elsewhere, to find our own sound. There were undercurrents that moved us, needs floating along with us, without us ever having talked consciously about them.

WINFRID TRENKLER With all due respect, bands like Achim Reichel's Rattles were epigones [unoriginal imitators]. Then again, they'd been on UK tours early on, even toured with Little Richard. But it wasn't until later that something autonomous came out of Germany.

ACHIM REICHEL Every trace of musical culture that had once existed in Germany was wiped out after the war. And at some point, the musical fodder they gave us made you feel you knew it all, you'd heard it a thousand times before. So A.R. & Machines was a liberating experience for me, at the start of the seventies. The time was ripe.

HARALD GROSSKOPF I had a bit of an inferiority complex, as a German musician. I was always worried I'd never be as good as my role models.

KLAUS SCHULZE We were pretty battered from all the British and American music. If you wanted to be a success in Germany, you had to copy them. But we wanted to make something of our own. That's why we did so much experimenting, as you can hear on the first Tangerine Dream record, *Electronic Meditation*. That was our bid for musical freedom, almost a kind of punk. The real electronic music came later; at first, we just ran off in any old new direction.

LUTZ LUDWIG KRAMER I knew at sixteen that I didn't want to make music like the Stones or the Beatles. I didn't need a 'Hey Jude' or Mick Jagger's sex appeal. It was obvious to me that we had all that ourselves, just different. But it wasn't an intellectual approach, more an anarchic one: just starting over at zero – but with the feel of the times, moving forward somehow. They were hot times, what can I say? Even in winter it was 'Summer in the City' – you could burn yourself on any street corner, and we were looking for just that; it was OK to get burnt. And sure, being German was a burden on our shoulders, and the past was nothing but ballast. I was insulted as a German boy in London once, and in Mallorca I was branded a child of Nazis at the age of seventeen – I'd always try to apologise. It still takes my breath away when I think about it, even now. Making music was liberating and cleansing, though. As a musician, I felt like a phoenix rising from the ashes.

HELLMUT HATTLER I read Eric Clapton's biography a few years ago, and it hit me: Clapton and the people around him looked to Black blues musicians for inspiration, practised their riffs and wanted to do everything like them – continue a tradition. As a German, that was exactly what I couldn't and wouldn't do. And it was on that basis that so many experiments came about, that so much was tried out that didn't look to the past. Like me digging out my violin and electrifying it. A lot of Americans I met later said things like: 'I want to compose things my mother will like too.' I'd never have thought that way. Of course, like a lot of people I started out covering old songs, but once we started

111

the band it was clear we'd be doing our own stuff. And a lot of people in Germany felt exactly the same way. The Brits soon worked out that things were happening in Germany that had never happened before. You could call it a minor cultural revolution.

KARL BARTOS Going to the States really opened my eyes. We were in San Francisco, and Muddy Waters played in a club there in front of ten people. That's when I first felt we had our own thing going. It wasn't like Klaus Doldinger, who got to the US, parped out his sax solos and still wouldn't ever be as good as Charlie Parker. The major chords we played matched our view of the world, not someone else's. When we took *The Man Machine* to the US later on, Neil Young came to our Los Angeles show. Afterwards I went back to his ranch with him. Just me and the roadies; the others didn't want to hang out with him.

PETER BAUMANN I soon got bored of covering British and American tracks, and I always wanted to do my own stuff. When that got more and more obvious, my band at the time wasn't much impressed; the rest of them just wanted to make a bit of money. There was just one guy who we used to do experimental things with, weird stuff like recording smashing glass or breaking plates. That was in 1970, when I was seventeen.

RENATE KNAUP Amon Düül were never going to sound like the Rolling Stones, that much was clear. First of all, we were 'German', and secondly, we came from classical music and folk contexts; we didn't have that Anglo-rhythmic background. John Weinzierl had Mersey Beat ambitions, wanted to show off on the rhythm guitar – but sorry, no chance, it's not in our blood. We didn't have to discuss the matter, it just came about naturally, like when we were composing: one of us had a guitar riff that sounded a bit Oriental or Spanish maybe, then John played something else to go with it, and Peter made it even wilder with his crazy percussion. It was part ineptitude and naivety, but it was always part inspiration and a whole lot of intention. We put it all together and got this amazing, insane stuff. We could tell what we were doing was interesting, and we felt it when it flowed just right.

MICHAEL HOENIG I never took music lessons, it was all totally autodidactic. That's why I still find some things really hard, even now, and some things take a long time. But, of course, there's a certain freedom in autodidactic playing, because you've never learned any conventions and you don't have any limits. The great thing about the new electronic music was exactly that: there were no teachers or set structures you had to follow. There just wasn't yet any tradition to slow you down.

STEVE SCHROYDER For me, it really started in 1970, when I shut myself away with a little electronic organ, a Farfisa Compact Duo, thinking I had to create a new kind of music. I was convinced I was the one who could make it. To be specific, I wanted to use the standard organ keys to somehow create entirely new sounds. I had a Dynacord tape echo, which I used to alter the sounds. Later on, that became my main occupation in Tangerine Dream, where I tried not to sound like an organ on my organ.

SIGGI LOCH It was important that these musicians became aware of their own musical origins, detached themselves from the American role models. The more autonomy you have, the more future you get. No one actually thought that out loud, but they acted intuitively on that principle. And that's the only way Can, Amon Düül, Tangerine Dream or Kraftwerk managed to make their own contributions to modern rock and pop music. The Scorpions were incredibly successful but they don't have their own sound. They just played American rock music as effectively as the Americans, gave us German Coca-Cola, if you like, which isn't something you could ever say about most of the people around Rolf-Ulrich Kaiser and his labels Ohr and Pilz, neither Guru Guru nor Popol Vuh, Klaus Schulze nor Tangerine Dream. What annoyed me, of course, was that the so-called Berlin School of musicians all went and signed contracts in the UK and not in Germany – with me, for example.

MICHAEL ROTHER Around 1968, a more complex need developed: OK, we'll take these set ideas as a starting point, but then let's start to improvise and add parts of our own. It was a very gradual process, from slavish covers to embellishing the original. But at some point, I felt like even that had got me into a dead end. There was nowhere left to go, it wasn't enough any more. That was around 1970, when I was doing my community service. Another guy doing community service with me played me all kinds of jazz, which was interesting, but it didn't really suit my musical taste. And then in the Kraftwerk studio someone put a bass in my hands, and during the session I thought: 'Right, I'm not the only one, these people feel the same way as I do.' I never cared about a 'German perspective', though. One of the lessons of World War Two, for me, was that nationalist thinking had to be overcome and we really have to think internationally; that was the vision. Obviously, we have regional musical traditions and differences, but still. The first time I jammed with Ralf Hütter I noticed we had the same understanding of melody. In those days it turned my stomach when someone played a blue note. Almost everyone was doing it, but I knew I had to steer clear of it. I felt a more central European understanding of melody and harmony, a basic emotion that might have been implanted in me at a pre-conscious age by my mother playing the piano; her favourite composer was Chopin. And then my later experiences were embedded into that basic feeling: the endless music in Karachi, and Little Richard as well, the whole 'let's get out of here, let's break down the walls' ecstasy of rock 'n' roll, that's really important to me too, still gives me goosebumps. But they're not opposites for me, certainly not national contrasts; they're more like inner layers.

WINFRID TRENKLER In Germany, the krautrock bands were left on the shelf to begin with. That's why I stood out, with my radio show and my magazine articles, because I tried to report about the new German groups as much as I could. That put me in touch with a good few of the musicians, and then I went along with Amon Düül, Can and Atlantis on their first British tours.

MANFRED GILLIG I'd left Berlin to go to uni in Freiburg, and I put on bands like Bröselmaschine and Kraan at the students' union. Before that, I'd asked my favourite music mag *Sounds* if they needed anyone in the southwest – and the first thing they sent me was Wallenstein's debut album [this is the German monthly called *Sounds*, not the British weekly of the same name]. From then on, I was their krautrock man. Jörg Gülden and his Hamburg guys wouldn't touch it with a barge pole, they couldn't stand it. From the start of 1972 I'd get a parcel once a month with about twenty records to work my way through. Either I'd write a round-up, or if the records were good I'd do a longer review. I dutifully did it for a few years – it was always interesting. *Sounds* was still based in Köln when I started writing for them, but they'd already changed direction. Shortly afterwards they moved to Hamburg and Jürgen Legath took over. Back in the early days in Köln, they took their orientation mainly from jazz. The founder Rainer Blome was still with them, a really interesting guy: first a free-jazz man, then he veered off to prog rock, and later he went all around the place as a reggae DJ. In Hamburg, though, the West Coast faction set the tone, from Gram Parsons to the Eagles, and German music almost got left behind.

WINFRID TRENKLER NDR radio were so narrow-minded back then that they sent the first review copies from Sky Records back to the label: 'Not interested, thanks.'

MANFRED GILLIG At some point, I became the magazine's go-to guy for German music, and word soon got around in the scene. From then on, a lot of people just contacted me directly.

WINFRID TRENKLER I talked my way onto WDR radio. Up until then they'd only had top-twenty shows. So one day I walked in there and said, 'I'd like to do a show here,' and I explained that there was so much more music than the top twenty and asked who I had to talk to. They sent me to the dance music editor, and I managed to convince him. I was granted an hour-long audience with him, and I explained what exciting music was out there and told him I knew all about it. And then he gave me four weeks to work out a concept. 'Don't get me in trouble!' he said, and he gave me the green light. I interpreted that to mean: play whatever you like, as long as there's no repercussions. It was a good deal for me because I had free rein. I was still enrolled as a student, so if any problems did come up, I could always go back to uni. So I had an hour on air every other Friday. On my first show I played Love, Kevin Ayers and Kraftwerk. My slot was at the same time as the TV detective show *Der Kommissar*, which everyone in the country watched. No one was actually listening to the radio, and that was my big chance! I could play my weird stuff because no one tuned in anyway. I got to run wild while the cat was away. Later on, one editor did want to stick his oar in. He made me show him my playlist in advance, but since he never knew any of the names he only complained when something was longer than six minutes. But he soon gave up, and that was the only attempt to intervene, which meant I could pull off my progressive programme undisturbed: jazz rock and electronic music. The electronic stuff went down especially well. I got lots of encouraging letters from listeners. One time, though, I played a half-hour track by Wendy Carlos and a woman called in, up in arms over the sheer impertinence, and complaining that electronic music didn't belong on a rock show. She had to get it off her chest, but actually that was the only complaint I ever got from listeners.

JÜRGEN DOLLASE Journalists like Winfrid Trenkler made a lot of these so-called careers possible, fostered them because it was on their journalistic level: going *beep, beep, beep* on the keyboard and a bit of chirruping on top was enough for a lot of people. They couldn't cope with anything more than that, they didn't understand anything about music, and that's why they got excited about that stuff.

WINFRID TRENKLER I also wrote a weekly music column in the *Kölner Stadt-Anzeiger*, a local paper in Köln, preferably about German groups like Amon Düül, Can and so on. Kraftwerk soon picked up on it and contacted me. I'd seen them at gigs, like at Photokina. When they were mixing the first Kraftwerk record, Ralf Hütter took me along to the studio where Conny Plank was working. I had to cancel an interview with Wallenstein at short notice once, not enough time. In my next interview with Wallenstein, Jürgen Dollase told me it had been the first time a German journalist had apologised to him for not keeping an interview appointment. Rolf-Ulrich Kaiser was sitting next to us; he was still the middleman in those days.

HANS-JOACHIM ROEDELIUS The only lobby we had in Germany was Winfrid Trenkler at WDR.

MICHAEL ROTHER It was journalists like Trenkler who first reported on NEU!.

DRUGS

'LSD kicked reality out from under me.'
HARALD GROSSKOPF

BERND WITTHÜSER The first joint I smoked, it went 'BOOM!' and then it kicked off. No idea when it was exactly; it was followed by many, many more joints. All I know is that it got more and more fun. It was a very, very good experience, definitely. Booze and pills did the trick before, but a joint was better.

PETER BURSCH People smoked marihuana and hash in our commune. We did it out of a sense of community, because all our friends did it too. Whenever we sat down together, someone would pass round a joint. It just had a different meaning back then. Joints stood for togetherness and a good atmosphere. Then one day, one of our band made a little machine where the slab of resin went in one side, and the cigarette paper on the other side, and then you cranked a handle like a laundry mangle and the crumbs – the *Brösel* – would fall straight into the paper and hey presto, your joint was done. But naturally we were never allowed to explain our band name like that to anyone else. Luckily, our singer had a boyfriend with a motorbike with '*Bröselmaschine*' painted on it. A photo of it did the rounds, and that became our official explanation for the name.

LUTZ LUDWIG KRAMER Drugs were very important, they were the main element of our music. Or actually, sex and drugs were probably the most important.

MANI NEUMEIER Our Guru Guru bus was easy to spot because it was so colourful. It was a Ford; we'd spray-painted it in eight different colours. We'd installed a long palm leaf on the roof rack, brought back from Italy, and a banner flew at the back that mixed the Swiss and American national flags, with 'LSD' printed on it in eighty-centimetre letters. That was probably the main reason why we kept getting stopped by the police; we did stand out. We got searched the most on the way to Berlin, of course.

MICHAEL HOENIG People didn't talk about it much, we just took the drugs. They opened up a world previously closed to us, which wasn't accessible any other way. The music we made afterwards was partly an attempt to express those consciousness-expanding experiences, in nonconformist ways. It seemed completely clear that they couldn't be expressed using the old methods. Sometimes it was bungling and awkward, but it was also new and interesting. We all agreed we had to give it a try, at least.

ULRICH RÜTZEL In those days, if you didn't take anything, you didn't belong.

HANS-JOACHIM ROEDELIUS I presume drugs changed a lot of things for me. You can never be sure of it, but I think they did.

KLAUS BRIEST The drugs were part of what changed our perception. And the abandon that came with them made us aware of our formulaic ideas, and made us come up with new, spontaneous ways of thinking to counter that. The concept of the song was already restrictive. We'd do a quick hour of improvising, taking the audience along on a trip – they weren't songs, they were more like 'segments'. Communication and anticipation were completely different under the influence of drugs, more intense. And listening to other bands play live, like Amon Düül and Guru Guru, that changed too. When it came to sound alterations, we were very creative as well: we used the sound of a toilet flush at the start of the *Electrip* LP. The people who came to our gigs were high too. A lot of them had taken something, as well as us, of course they had. They'd have loved it if we'd just played all night long.

HARALD GROSSKOPF Drugs were important. I played high, and at some point I realised I was only imitating other drummers – and suddenly there was this voice, telling me: 'Listen to what the others are doing! Don't think about wanting to be Billy Cobham or Ginger Baker.' And then it just clicked! From then on, I drummed as myself, I was liberated. That's how I arrived at my own musical language, and the electronic guys in Berlin thought it was great. At the same time, a huge musical discrepancy developed between me and Wallenstein, as I realised I couldn't play rock music any more. I left Wallenstein soon after that.

LÜÜL In Agitation Free, things mostly went the same way: we'd roll a joint and then start making music. That was just how it was. We recorded a lot of music in that state, which we thought was incredible in the moment. But when we listened to it sober, we were usually really disappointed. The problem with drugs was that a lot of musical stuff only went on in our heads, which obviously you couldn't hear on tape. Then again, the LSD experience took us to very different places that we couldn't have imagined before, major influences: pushing boundaries, questioning things and just working in unconventional ways. That's why the synthesizer was such a gift from the gods, because it really enabled us to create something new, with no set paths to follow.

MICHAEL ROTHER With my passion for psychology, my interest in our perceptions and exploring our consciousness, drugs were of scientific interest for me as well; well, OK, let's put 'scientific' in quotation marks. But anyway, I tried LSD a few times, of course. A guy who worked on the psychiatric ward got some good stuff for me. And it was a life-defining experience – especially finding out you can taste sounds and music, and every sense overlaps with the others: synaesthesia, in other words. That was a fascinating thing for me to learn. But it wasn't only positive, all in all; I did see both sides, including the darker side. So it never became a habit, and I've kept a safe distance from drugs of all kinds since then.

HARALD GROSSKOPF I missed the deadline to declare myself a conscientious objector and do community service, so I had to join the army for three months, but at least I had my first experiences with drugs there, when someone rolled me a joint. Before that, I only knew drugs from pulp fiction, things like Jerry Cotton detective stories, such as *Zum Frühstück eine Prise Hasch* [*A Pinch of Hash for Breakfast*]. I had wild fantasies about drugs because I got all my information from the most abstruse horror stories in trashy magazines. I thought you'd get addicted to hash the first time, and then when I tried it and didn't feel anything at all, I was really disappointed. A bit later, I tried it again in Köln, and then I did end up in a kind of drug swamp. I woke up one morning draped over a rubbish bag, with a head like a month of Sundays. Then we smoked like crazy for a while. One of the guys I lived with even injected opium. I was horrified by that, though, seeing how careless he was with his dirty needles. It cost him his life, a few years later. Heroin was always off limits, for me.

MICHAEL ROTHER Whether my music would have turned out the way it did without my drug experiences, I don't know. I never wanted to just drift in a fug; I wanted to make and listen to experimental music consciously, with a clear mind. That was always my aim. Drugs weren't my way to do that, even though a lot of my colleagues saw that differently and occasionally laughed at me for not doing drugs. But my conviction was always more important to me than substances, for inspiration. Klaus Dinger, an avowed drug fan, had a completely different way of life. He once wrote on his website that he'd taken more than a thousand LSD trips, which meant the ratio of his drug consumption to mine was a thousand to zero. He was wrong about my side of the equation, but perhaps he was telling the truth about himself.

JEAN-HERVÉ PERON We always had plenty to smoke in Wümme. It was very good stuff, inspiring, but we'll never know whether Faust would have sounded different without drugs. I don't think we necessarily needed drugs for our music. I'd even go as far as saying that the drugs actually held us back. There's no one truth about it. We didn't always take drugs when we made music; only when we felt like it. When we'd smoked a whole lot, we tended to lie around happily and tinker away at things, but not record anything. Faust's music was too complex to make it on drugs. Our craziest ideas came from completely clear heads.

HOLGER CZUKAY I could well imagine that Can would have sounded different without drugs. Hashish fills up your ears, first of all. You had to adjust yourself to listening, not to playing. Playing on drugs wasn't important, it was part of the discipline. But listening on drugs, if you switched on to it properly, was something really important.

IRMIN SCHMIDT We wouldn't have sounded much different without drugs. Can isn't druggy music, and getting all nostalgic like that is rubbish. Of course we got stoned sometimes and smoked dope, but the music didn't depend on it in the slightest. I had my LSD experiences primarily before Can, in the Stockhausen time at uni. Stockhausen himself had nothing to do with drugs, of course, but a couple of American students had brought some over with them. There was coke as well, but none of us found it helpful for our music, because it takes you straight off on an ego trip. Plus, you get really talkative, so it was frowned upon. It was only useful for getting out of bed in the morning on gruelling tours. You'd sleep until quarter to twelve, then have a quick toot, and at five past twelve you'd be down in the hotel lobby with your bags packed: 'Are we off, lads?' Or drugs were something we did at parties now and then. But none of us needed them, certainly not for the music, because that didn't need anything. The opposite, actually: if someone just never got to the end of his solo, you'd start asking yourself if he might have a nose full of coke.

JAKI LIEBEZEIT There weren't many drugs involved in Can. People always said there were, because we sounded so strange, and a lot of people put that down to LSD, but that was a misunderstanding. All right, occasionally something did happen, but drugs weren't really big for us, and never hard drugs. Now and then we'd smoke a joint, maybe take a trip, but everyone was doing it back then, really. It didn't influence the music. I don't think drugs can influence music, anyway. They can't create anything that's not in you. Of course we tried things out to get an idea of them, as you did in the hippy era. To have a critical consciousness, you had to test out the effect of drugs. So we recorded music on drugs once or twice, and asked ourselves if it was usable or not. And it was always completely unusable.

HELLMUT HATTLER Of course we all experimented: 'We'll give this a try and wait and see what happens.' When you recorded something in that state and then listened to the tape later on, the results were usually dubious. It was better to play straight and get stoned later; listening to music stoned was amazing. And it goes without saying that most of the people at our gigs were off their faces. They'd lie down on their parkas with a bottle of Lambrusco and smoke a big fat joint. Sometimes they'd get shook up if we suddenly played too fast; they wanted everything really laid-back.

RENATE KNAUP Everyone at the gigs was always stoned and tripping. It was all the rage in those days. The gigs were sensational, especially in the UK, France and Italy. Everyone was so happy and felt at one with the whole world.

HARALD GROSSKOPF Perhaps my music with Ash Ra Tempel would have sounded different without drugs, but it's hard to tell.

Manuel Göttsching was a very calm guy from a healthy, laid-back family. He never had time for any Nazi crap. He'd have made the same music without drugs.

ACHIM REICHEL My album *Die grüne Reise* wouldn't exist without drugs, or not as an LP, because then my rational mind would have got a word in edgewise and said: 'Get a grip. It might be interesting, but you'll get a much better deal with a rock album.'

HARALD GROSSKOPF LSD can easily pull the rug out from under you; I underestimated it at the time. We dropped acid willy-nilly, without knowing anything about it. I had good and bad experiences with LSD and I'm lucky to have coped with it mentally. But I'd never take it again. I'd stopped taking trips by the time I made my solo records; all I did was drink coffee. Very bad things can come to the surface on LSD if your psyche's not intact. I saw it often enough in people around me, like Jerry Berkers, the Dutch singer with Wallenstein, who ended up dying of an overdose in a park. He was a very sensitive type who'd been to Vietnam with a Dutch showband and had traumatic experiences there. He'd seen a Vietnamese dancer get shot off the stage by a sniper, for instance. LSD kept bringing up memories like that for him, so strongly that we couldn't work with him any more. And we were too young and inexperienced to offer him any serious help. It certainly put me off, and I could never stand the heroin guys either.

JÜRGEN DOLLASE Some people took LSD just for entertainment. It was different in our commune; we took it seriously. We mixed LSD with philosophy, made it highly political. We did some proper deep thinking, all about mysticism and Far Eastern wisdom; thankfully, I never had a bad trip. Of course, we tried to play the Wallenstein stuff on acid, but it was utterly pointless, way too complicated. But the audio effect of our tracks was very good on drugs: long and intense. There was a certain druggy dynamic to the music. I'd heard it before on David Bowie's *The Rise and Fall of Ziggy Stardust* – that was really the perfect druggy timing. And it was pop, not the usual dirges, just that drug groove. Spooky Tooth had it too, especially on *Spooky Two*. They played it in Amsterdam in places like Fantasio, where you could take a trip under supervision.

PETER BRÖTZMANN Our jazz drug was alcohol. In moderation it's a social drug, but there were people who took it to excess. The good thing was, you could get alcohol anytime and anywhere. It wasn't that easy to get hold of good grass in Germany in those days. I remember when I'd visit Jaki Liebezeit in Köln back then, there was always a little table in his flat covered in 'slabs' from Morocco. For me, only alcohol came into it; none of the other drugs were my thing. But I don't think it influenced my music. When my body started sending me clear signals about my alcohol consumption a few years back, I gave that up as well. I'd had enough by then. A lot of jazz musicians didn't manage to kick the habit, and some of them died of it.

JAKI LIEBEZEIT Alcohol is a drug that prohibits you from making music.

MANI NEUMEIER Plenty of people have died from alcohol, but no one's died from hash. And that's official statistics, we didn't make it up. We played a couple of gigs and made a few records on LSD – otherwise it would have sounded way more normal. But I don't need it any more, it's enough to have had that experience of going beyond all the normal schemata; it gave us a lot of freedom at the time. I started on drugs fairly late. I took my first trip in 1969, at the ripe old age of twenty-nine. And I only started smoking at twenty-four. But it's bad for your brain if you start smoking dope at fifteen, and of course it's all down to the dose, ultimately. It's like cheese: it's not good to have too much of that either. My experiences made me more confident, relaxed, free and open, though – definitely not lazier.

MICHAEL HOENIG No one in my social circle drank alcohol, neither beer nor wine. We drank Coca-Cola, fruit juice or water. We smoked marihuana.

MICHAEL ROTHER There was a Harmonia gig, at Melkweg in Amsterdam in 1973, where I'd been foolish enough to eat hash cookies beforehand. The effect kicked in with a delay, mid-gig. I suddenly couldn't play any more, on stage. Everyone thought it was hilarious, even Achim and Moebi later, who'd had more experience with that kind of cookie. But no one at the gig cared; the whole audience was completely stoned anyway.

LUTZ LUDWIG KRAMER I took drugs for far too long, and then I went off the rails. I had to leave Berlin, my innocence was lost, everything went downhill. And then I was a victim of hard drugs for eight years, while I was living in Thailand.

HANS-JOACHIM ROEDELIUS Without drugs, my life would have taken a completely different course. Who knows, maybe I'd be a big fat masseur in a wellness spa by now.

ZODIAK (IN BERLIN)

'Beautiful women and creepy guys.'
THOMAS KESSLER

KLAUS SCHULZE Back then, Berlin was kaput in the best sense of the word; it had an excitingly destructive sense of romance about it. You knew about the history and you felt kind of special somehow, partly because of the island situation, with all the complicated border checks around West Berlin and so on. And we all knew each other: Ash Ra Tempel, Tangerine Dream, Conny Schnitzler and all the rest; everyone played with everyone at some point.

LUTZ LUDWIG KRAMER In other cities at the time, you could tell how much young people wanted to live like we did in West Berlin. The rest of West Germany was still square and strait-laced. If you moved to Berlin, the place quickly knocked that out of you.

PETER BAUMANN Berlin was different because we didn't have to join the army there. You were kind of proud of being a Berliner and not being part of the rest of the country. There was a bit of arrogance behind it too, of course.

THOMAS KESSLER It was typical of Berlin to want to be different, and that was reflected in the music.

GÜNTER SCHICKERT Something like the Zodiak [Free Arts Lab] worked so well in Berlin because the city's so big. If you were a freak in Lüneburg or an outsider in some other way, you had nowhere to go. That's why so many of them came to Berlin. I once went to a gig at the Sportpalast where Ravi Shankar appeared with Yehudi Menuhin and Jimi Hendrix. All three on one bill! You'd never get that range of acts today.

GIL FUNCCIUS That was the most exciting time in Berlin. And there was a steady stream of young men turning up from all over the country to get out of military service.

MICHAEL ROTHER Even driving to West Berlin was frightening; the East German border guards were not to be messed with.

HELLMUT HATTLER Six weeks before my A-levels, when I was nineteen, I chucked it all in and went to Berlin; all I wanted to do was make music. If you wanted to play gigs outside Berlin and you had your own PA, you had to fill in forms at the customs office every time. And if the slightest detail was out of place, if you were missing one stamp, the officers at the border would send you back. The border guards weren't exactly friendly at the best of times: 'Where did you get this PA? I bet it's stolen, isn't it? Admit it!'

HANS-JOACHIM ROEDELIUS I was born in the western part of Berlin and I ended up in the Russian zone after the war and my evacuation. I went to school there until the age of sixteen, and then I had to join the National People's Army. After a year I tried to escape to the West, and I made it. But my mother begged me to come back, which I did, and they put me straight into prison. They let me out early on condition that I never leave the country again. I trained as a physiotherapist, but I also worked as a palliative therapist in various hospitals. I took my state exam at the Charité Hospital, under the communists, but I wasn't very careful and I had a lot to do with dissidents. I met the actor Manfred Krug and the singer-songwriter Wolf Biermann, for example, or the Stalinallee architect Hermann Henselmann. The Stasi didn't like me; I had to report to them every four weeks because I was on probation. At some point I got scared and skipped off to the West for good. That was in 1960, a year before they built the Berlin Wall. They wouldn't accept my qualifications in the West, so I had to earn a crust with all sorts of odd jobs – such as detective, delivering payment summons or spying on adulterers, but I also did roofing jobs, advertised newspapers on the street and worked as a butler and maid-of-all-work for a factory-owner's family. One job took me to a nudist camp on Corsica. Just after I started making music I gave up all my odd jobs; I'd been working as a masseur.

DIETER MOEBIUS Berlin was unusual just because of its location, like a cosy little island where the conscientious objectors and loads of other young people had gone to hide away. The only thing was, you were at risk of missing out on world events in the whole idyllic place.

HANS-JOACHIM ROEDELIUS Because I was always the oldest, I didn't go to the demonstrations. I'd been once bitten by my East German experiences, so I was more than twice shy of being ordered to march in the streets for some cause or other. Instead, we started the Zodiak in Berlin in 1968. We'd been talking for a long time about coming together and doing something. I'd met Conrad Schnitzler doing roofing jobs in the Corsican mountains. And then I was also in the group that later became the Zodiak house band Human Being; it was actually a working commune. The experience that set the ball rolling came before that, though, on Corsica with Conrad, in a river by an old mill next to the camp where we were mending the roofs. I spent a night there drumming on an empty petrol drum until my fingers bled. Everything developed from there. That drumming was my way in. Later at the Zodiak I had my own drum, a bush drum. We saw the Zodiak as a living space and ran it that way. A lot of people were glad the place existed. We spent all our time there. The only thing we did in our own communes was sleep; at that time I was still living with Conrad, his family had taken me in. We made the Zodiak what it is to this day: a legend.

NIKEL PALLAT In Berlin, the Zodiak Club was ground-breaking at the time – the most important thing of all, a place where there were no artistic boundaries. The music went from free jazz to rock to electronic. Whoever happened to come by played the music they felt like playing. And for as long as they wanted. You'd hear things there you'd never heard anywhere, things you couldn't get on records, always surprising. People played there who were looking for something.

GÜNTER SCHICKERT It was basically a big black room run by Conrad Schnitzler and Roedelius. I often hung out there and also played the trumpet there; everyone played with everyone. You did have to sign up beforehand if you wanted to play, but there was always someone you knew there: 'Hey, shall we do a session?' 'What do you play?' 'Trumpet.' 'Great!' 'Let's do it!' Every ensemble had thirty minutes. You had to put your name down at the bar at 7:30 and you'd get a slot and two drinks – Coke, beer, whatever you wanted – and ten marks for playing. That was once a week. There was a theatre upstairs; it's still there now.

KLAUS SCHULZE The whole cultural scene around the Zodiak was very avant-garde. Downstairs from the theatre, there was a small artists' bar, and when you went through there to the back you got to a big hall that was never used at the beginning, until all the underground bands in Berlin discovered it as an event and practice space. One day they just started charging to get in, and then we played there as well.

GÜNTER SCHICKERT The Zodiak started at ten because that was when the performance was over upstairs, and after that you could make as much noise as you wanted. The sound at the Zodiak was free jazz and rock, and in essence that was the root of the music that grew into krautrock.

PETER BRÖTZMANN I was a frequent visitor to the Zodiak. And I played there once as well, as a trio with Mani Neumeier and Uli Trepte.

GÜNTER SCHICKERT You'd just start playing spontaneously and see what happened. It was a totally free approach to music, we didn't usually have any real 'themes' to the sessions. But then if you found yourself having a lot of fun with someone, something would come up. You'd arrange to play again the next week or whatever, and little combinations came together. Edgar Froese was still playing the guitar in those days, and Klaus Schulze was on drums. His band was called Psy Free, with Alex Conti on guitar – they played like crazy, Schulze's fingers would bleed after a gig.

KLAUS SCHULZE After Psy Free I played with Tangerine Dream in the Zodiak, and with Conrad Schnitzler in Plus/Minus. The whole of West Berlin's underground scene met up there. It was interesting and productive, because you'd be in there together in a fairly small space, like a pressure cooker.

GÜNTER SCHICKERT If you'd heard it once, you knew what direction things could take. Blues was off the table by that point because no one could play it anyway, and nobody wanted to.

MICHAEL HOENIG Blues was just a different tradition. Those chord progressions didn't come into it in Berlin – it wasn't a conscious decision but it was very important, because letting go led to something new. I think Berlin was different to a lot of other places in that respect. True, in München you had Florian Fricke from Popol Vuh, and of course Amon Düül, but with them you never knew exactly what they wanted. In Düsseldorf there was [Florian] Schneider-Esleben, who definitely had something different in mind as well. But in Berlin, I think, improvising was much more standard practice.

GÜNTER SCHICKERT Everyone there was a total free spirit. And the audience often wanted to join in.

LUTZ LUDWIG KRAMER There was hardly any boundary in the Zodiak between the audience and the musicians – we were all one and the same. I always thought it was important to remove the distance between the stage and the audience. Sure, we wanted everyone to see us on stage, but the idea was to hand out instruments to the audience so they could make music with us. I also objected to any recording; I wanted music just for the here and now. Nothing out of a can! I regret now, of course, that there aren't any records. But we did do recordings in Kessler's Electronic Beat Studio, the famous lost tapes.

MICHAEL HOENIG The Schaubühne am Halleschen Ufer was on the first floor, the theatre where Peter Stein worked at the time. I used to go to every premiere there, as a teenager. And downstairs in the new-build was the Zodiak, run by Conrad Schnitzler, Achim Roedelius and Boris Schaak. The Zodiak had a white room at the front and a black room at the back, where completely off-the-wall types stood on pedestals and made extremely amplified sounds: Human Being, with a changing cast of musicians back then, Tangerine Dream and Agitation Free.

DIETER MOEBIUS There were three or four podiums dotted around the room, with musicians on them who played to each other from these different stages, just started off improvising. There wasn't usually a lot going on in the Zodiak, it wasn't always packed. The music there wasn't necessarily to everyone's taste. But I liked the idea of improvising freely, following new paths, trying things out. That's the only way for autodidacts, anyway.

HANS-JOACHIM ROEDELIUS The point of the Zodiak was finding joy in music. We always drew up the programme on the spur of the moment, there was never much planning ahead. If someone said, 'I'll come by on Thursday,' then we'd put him on Thursday's programme. And we used every gap to make noise of our own. The place was great. And we had the drugs as well. But most of all it was about working together, about getting like-minded groups off the ground. People came from all over Europe to make music and talk to each other. Conrad Schnitzler pulled the strings; for the Zodiak, he was a bit like Andy Warhol for the Factory. Unfortunately, he never stuck to anything long enough; he always pulled out of the many projects and ideas he put out into the world. Maybe it was laziness; otherwise he'd have had to do something. He left the Zodiak pretty soon as well. He was always a solo player, in the end, but he often gave things the momentum they needed. If it wasn't for him, I'd be doing something different now.

THOMAS KESSLER I'd get invited to the Zodiak Club by the bands at the Electronic Beat Studio, and I went along a few times. And the bands would ask me where I'd usually go, so I'd tell them about the Sender Freies Berlin radio and TV station on Masurenallee. They often had very nice concerts there, joint events by WDR and SFB. 'What are they playing tonight?' 'Xenakis and Varèse!' 'Is it any good?' 'It's incredible!' Then they'd go along and be bowled over by it all. They'd never heard anything like it, and it was great. For me, their Zodiak Club was pretty impressive as well. You'd go in and you'd be surrounded by incredible amounts of smoke and dim light, beautiful women and creepy guys, and good friends.

KLAUS SCHULZE The people who ran around in the Zodiak Club were definitely different. They looked different, and most of all they thought differently, in political and cultural terms. The audience was much more political than us. Our music was only political in the sense that it was free from all norms. But were Warhol or Lichtenstein more political? That's debatable.

THOMAS KESSLER There was music booming and blasting all around the rooms. I never played there myself, sadly. But I went along when Tangerine Dream or other people from my studio performed there, of course.

LUTZ LUDWIG KRAMER Our pal and band member Tricky died of heroin at seventeen. Fame and I were the remains of the beat band the Ugly Things, and then we met Lüül and Christopher Franke and fell in love with each other. Initially we were called the Agitation – the Free part came later. It all started at Christopher Franke's parents' place in Eichkamp. His father was a violin teacher, and his mother was a pianist and a schoolteacher. The Agitation were supposed to copy the Beatles, at first. I'd just got back from London, highly motivated; I'd taken my first trips and had my first sex, so I was far ahead – and because I kept mouthing off about it, I soon became the frontman. We ended up being the house band at the Zodiak pretty quickly. The place was pitch black and the nights went on until the morning. They had an open stage, but you did have to put your name down in advance. Anyway, Agitation Free soon had a permanent booking, and we played there non-stop one summer, and the odd night with Tangerine Dream or Amon Düül. You could meet Guru Guru and Can at the Zodiak too.

GÜNTER SCHICKERT All the musicians in West Berlin who had a bit of a 'whiff' to them went to the Zodiak – the tokers. In those days there'd be VW Beetles driving around Berlin with 'Drive carefully – maybe the driver has *kifft*' on the back – all in English except for that one word, which means 'has smoked dope'. Nobody got it. You could stroll around Berlin with a joint; it might have smelled a bit funny, but no one really knew what it was. There was no closing time for bars, either. So from the mid-sixties to the early seventies it was a really free city, but at some point some bureaucrats decided to put a stop to that freedom. They closed down the Zodiak because it was too noisy and too many people took drugs there. Even before, the police kept paying visits to see what was what. The end made me sad, naturally, because there was never anywhere else like the Zodiak. I mean, there were plenty of other clubs in Berlin after that, but none of them were as progressive and avant-garde. They never had sessions there; the best you could do was lie down and just listen. All my life, I've tried to initiate something like the Zodiak again somewhere, with open music nights and all that.

HANS-JOACHIM ROEDELIUS The Zodiak got closed down because we smoked too much weed, especially on the grass outside. There were a lot of complaints from the public. And of course we were loud as well. The Schaubühne theatre upstairs was really hip, with the top director Peter Stein, and the smartly dressed audience would come out after the show and pass by the Zodiak, and there we'd be, smoking our joints. Underground, what can I say? It actually went together really well, and I think Stein himself liked the combination. But there were just too many of the people who got called *Gammlers* at the time: hippies, people thought they were lazy. After a while there was a bit of a bust-up between drug dealers, and a car got set alight. It all came to a head, and the city council closed the place down. But something really happened down there: Tangerine Dream invented themselves there, and Ash Ra Tempel and Michael Hoenig as well. A lot of big names started off in the Zodiak.

KLAUS SCHULZE At the time of the Zodiak, when the Berlin Wall was up, Berlin was an artists' ghetto, a pool for creativity. Rent was cheap and you could afford big lofts. Those days are long gone. I left Berlin years ago too, moved to the country.

DIETER MOEBIUS We had good reason to move to West Germany right after setting up Kluster. We wanted to try our luck there and not wither and die in Berlin.

KLUSTER

'We could never play any piece twice.'
DIETER MOEBIUS

HANS-JOACHIM ROEDELIUS After the end of the Zodiak Club, we decided – the Human Being group, which had run the Zodiak since Schnitzler left – to set off for Africa in two yellow post office buses. We wanted to smoke our brains out together! That was in 1969. We were interested in African culture as well, obviously, but a lot of it was pure lust for adventure. We wanted to go somewhere, and in those days everyone wanted to go to Africa. It was more popular in our circles than India, for example. On the way there we stopped in all these towns and cities to go busking. I played the flute and a drum. We made it all the way to Casablanca, where we all got dysentery – diarrhoea and fever. Then we made a decision in a car park in Casablanca: one lot's staying here, the others are going back home. My girlfriend and I drove back in one of the yellow buses. We had a PA for busking, in the south of France and so on, occasionally even by invitation – the high point was getting stopped on a road somewhere by a local thug and his gang, who dragged us out of the bus and beat us up. We didn't fight back – we were peace-loving pacifists, after all. What a stupid thing to do! All the police said was: 'Tough luck! He hasn't got a problem with you, he just has to beat people up now and then, he can't help it.' We took a break then until our injuries healed. We went back via Corsica because I knew I'd get a job again there, and I did, in a restaurant kitchen. Plus I played gigs on Sundays. But we did head back to Berlin in the end. I had no idea what to do with myself to begin with. I was living back at Conrad Schnitzler's flat, and we painted houses and flats for a while to make a living. But Conny soon decided to start a

136

band. Our first group was called Geräusche, and that turned into Plus/ Minus. We made our first tentative public appearances at the Galerie Block. Then Schnitzler brought Moebius into the band for our first gig at the Galerie der Künste, and the second was a twelve-hour all-night show at Galerie Hammer, which was also our farewell gig in Berlin. After that the three of us got in a van – another yellow post office bus, by the way – and drove through East Germany, as it was then, first to Hannover and then to Düsseldorf. We stayed with friends there for a few months, going round the museums and galleries and introducing ourselves. Schnitzler had studied fine art under Joseph Beuys, and of course he was the band's conceptualist. It was him who created Kluster. But then we continued it with a very different drive.

DIETER MOEBIUS We weren't aware we were playing a new sound. We didn't take an intellectual approach to it. We tried to improvise, like making sounds you wouldn't expect from normal organs. And it worked pretty well. Because of the pieces' monotony and length – often a good eighteen minutes or more – it was clear they weren't suitable for the radio, or hit-single material. We could never play them the same way twice. We'd tried out at the Galerie Hammer what it would be like to play for twelve hours and really see if we were on the same wavelength. But that was pretty clear, actually, because we'd often met at the Zodiak, so we were optimistic enough to impose our sounds on other people.

HANS-JOACHIM ROEDELIUS We just wanted to see what was slumbering within us, what we didn't yet know. After our first musical undertakings, I saw it was the right path for me and I put my money where my mouth was, took out loans and bought equipment, an organ and all sorts of things, and then the three of us worked our way into our sound-painting step by step. Schnitzler was just great at seeking things. And finding things.

LÜÜL Conrad Schnitzler started this great initiative in 1970, after he'd left Tangerine Dream. He wanted to try out new ways of making music. He called it Eruption, and he'd invited Klaus Schulze as a drummer and Hartmut Enke from Ash Ra Tempel, actually all of Ash Ra Tempel with Manuel Göttsching, then Michael Günther and me from Agitation Free, and Klaus Freudigmann as well, who later joined Ton Steine Scherben. It all added up to a kind of giant Berlin supergroup, and we played a couple of pretty impressive gigs. When we played in the Quartier Latin venue, we set up in a circle along the walls instead of on stage. We all got into a certain position around the audience, who gathered in the middle of the space, and then we played at them from all sides. It was a huge inferno, literally an eruption of sound, pure ecstasy. I played near to Klaus Schulze, and we had a good groove together. The audience were amazed.

HANS-JOACHIM ROEDELIUS Schnitzler was great at motivating people who probably wouldn't have got involved in art otherwise – like Moebius, for example: he was a chef, he wasn't interested in making art. Schnitzler saw him and said: 'You're a good drummer, come and join us. Just do it, I'll get you everything you need, just give it a try! You've got nothing to lose.' He worked on Moebius like that for six months before he said yes. At the first show in the Akademie der Künste, there was this huge percussion kit waiting for him, even though he'd never worked with anything like that. Tin trays with microphones, drums, timpani, a viola da gamba. From that point on, Moebius was an artist – there was no other option. That was in 1969; so much was going on around then.

DIETER MOEBIUS We recorded the first two Kluster albums in one night, mainly for money reasons. The organist at the church in Düsseldorf had arranged for a bit of money for the session from the publishers, Schwann. The reason we made two albums is that we just didn't stop playing.

HANS-JOACHIM ROEDELIUS Before my Zodiak days, I used to listen to Frank Sinatra and other American popular music. I didn't have any records of my own; I only ever stayed at other people's places. And then when I started making my own music I had no time to listen to anything else, I was always way too busy finding my own sound. It took years for my music to take on contours. It started as pure action for action's sake, as the times demanded. But anyone with a gift for making more out of it still has a name for themselves today, no matter how far apart things ended up. Edgar Froese gave me a Mellotron back then, just because he saw I could make good use of it. And I'm still grateful to him for that, even though I had to sell it at some point when I ran out of money.

ASMUS TIETCHENS The first time they came to Hamburg there were three of them, still with Conrad Schnitzler in those days, and they still spelled their name with a K: Kluster. Not that many people turned up to their gig at the Fabrik, but the ones who were there were stoned out of their minds. The band must have been too, because what they did wasn't much good. You can't make music stoned, or not anything that works for people who aren't stoned or that still works the next day. Six months later, Cluster came back again, this time with a C, and we met personally that time. You could just go up to bands and tell them you liked their music and you did something similar, and that's how you'd get talking.

DIETER MOEBIUS All different people came to our gigs, from anarchists to art fans. It always depended on the location. We didn't have much of an audience to begin with anyway. Then, when Achim and I carried on without Conrad, we ended up in the art scene, by coincidence – which was a stroke of luck for us because you could make good money there. We got to play in galleries, museums, art spaces all over Europe. We served the art audience, which was very rewarding because they're people who like experiencing things they don't understand. They couldn't get enough of our strange stuff. But we would have made the same music anyway.

THE SEVENTIES

KESSLER

'Notes were too square for us.'
LÜÜL

WINFRID TRENKLER The Berlin School started with what Thomas Kessler showed his students at his Electronic Beat Studio.

THOMAS KESSLER I'm actually Swiss, but I wanted to study music in Berlin because the conservatory had a good reputation. When I got to Berlin I lived in a building that belonged to an uncle of my wife's, but he was never there. One of the people I shared the flat with was Nike Wagner; I didn't realise she was Richard Wagner's great-granddaughter, she was just Nike with her husband. We had our own kindergarten on the ground floor. I set up my first studio in Berlin in 1965. The equipment was ridiculous; I didn't even have a mixing desk. What I did have was three lovely Revox tape machines with a studio speed of thirty-eight centimetres per second and a couple of simple microphones, and with professional tape material I could get very good sound quality out of them. I spliced together fascinating sounds by hand back then. And that was where I made my first tracks; actually, it was *musique concrète*. The only other studio in Berlin at that time was at the Technical University, but it was totally inaccessible for outsiders. No one was allowed in there apart from Boris Blacher. Why? Heaven knows! I was one of Blacher's students at the conservatory myself, he gave me a lot of encouragement and support – but no one was allowed in the sacred studio. I couldn't understand it – it wasn't like you could just work on your computer in your bedroom in those days, like you can now. At that time, a studio was a monopoly.

MICHAEL HOENIG The first time I went into a studio was through Thomas Kessler, who'd started the Electronic Beat Studio with Agitation Free.

THOMAS KESSLER I knew about Stockhausen in Köln and Pierre Schaeffer in Paris. The stuff you could get your hands on sounded amazing and was a major influence on me. What took me to electronic music specifically was musicians from the New Phonic Art Ensemble, great people like Vinko Globokar, who said to me: 'If you push a chair around the stage, it makes wonderful music. It whistles and sings. But it's too quiet. Can't you amplify that sound?' And then I was in. That was at the Akademie der Künste [Academy of the Arts] in the early seventies, I think. I just fell into it because I knew about electronics and soon understood them as an instrument. That's not unimportant for the Electronic Beat Studio, because that's why I had the openness and willingness to understand people who were not only much younger, like Edgar Froese, Agitation Free and Michael Hoenig, but also had a very different background.

MICHAEL HOENIG At the time, Agitation Free consisted of Christopher Franke, Michael Günther and Lüül, who had kitted out two semi-basement rooms with Thomas Kessler, provided by Schöneberg borough council for an experiment.

LÜÜL I was ten years old when I told my father I wanted to be a musician and absolutely had to have a guitar. So he bought me an acoustic guitar, and that was how it all kicked off. We set up a band at school pretty soon after that. My very old friend Christopher Franke was in it too. He'd taken his parents' telephone apart and made the mouthpiece into a microphone. Then in 1967 we set up Agitation, as the band was called to begin with, and we learned to play a handful of songs. First we practised at Christopher's parents' place, but that stopped working, so his mother put us in touch with a music school in Wilmersdorf.

The head was very dedicated, and Christopher's mother persuaded him to set up rehearsal rooms in the school for beat bands. Once the financial and organisational structures were clarified, it became the now-legendary Beat Studio at 32 Pfalzburger Strasse. And Agitation Free was the first band that cleared out two basement rooms there, stuck egg boxes all over the walls and ceilings and moved in.

THOMAS KESSLER Konrad Latte, who was the head of the Wilmersdorf Music School at the time, called me and said they had a bit of money and he'd heard I was familiar with electronic music. He asked if I had an idea for a studio where young musicians who weren't pursuing an academic career or studying at a conservatory could meet. It was a great idea. Christopher Franke, an acquaintance of Konrad Latte's, piloted all the young experimental bands into the studio, and they all stuck egg cartons on the walls as soundproofing. In the end we had two nice big studio rooms in a Wilmersdorf school building. The bands didn't just need rehearsal rooms back then; what they needed most was a studio. To start with, we got reel-to-reel machines and a small mixing desk. The equipment grew from year to year. My Revox tape recorders were there too, and a couple of brand-new machines. You could make noise any night of the week – I mean: music. As loud as you wanted.

LÜÜL We made a giant musical leap with Thomas. He taught us to make music consciously, to listen and develop our own techniques. From Mondays to Fridays, from the afternoon until very late at night, interested young bands could rehearse there, record and learn music.

THOMAS KESSLER I only became the studio manager because there was no other alternative. People had often asked me to help them out before that, like Luc Ferrari, and I'd always enjoyed it. Composing is very lonely work, but being part of a concert is great. I've always preferred working hands-on with other people to theoretical work at my desk.

LÜÜL We did these great improvisation exercises with tape recordings, but we also learned the basics of harmony and rhythm. Thomas introduced us to lots of new avant-garde composers who were playing in Berlin or otherwise making a name for themselves, people like Peter Michael Hamel, Steve Reich and Terry Riley. The electronic sounds produced in the Electronic Beat Studio were a huge influence for all of us, opened up a completely new horizon. We were soon sharing sessions there with Tangerine Dream, Ash Ra Tempel and [the blues band] Curly Curve.

MICHAEL HOENIG One day, a friend of mine said there was a guy with an orchestra where people without musical training were making interesting sounds. That guy was Thomas Kessler, who was doing something in Berlin modelled on Cornelius Cardew's Scratch Orchestra, generating sounds according to purely metaphysical prompts: 'Right, all of you sit down under a tree and play what the tree feels like to you.'

THOMAS KESSLER I'd met Cornelius Cardew in London and went to a Scratch Orchestra rehearsal. It was a fantastic idea and I thought it had to be taken to Berlin, so I started doing it there. Lots of other people from the Electronic Beat Studio were part of it. I never told them what to do, though, just made suggestions about what could be done.

MICHAEL HOENIG We liked working with found instruments. I turned up one day with a zither, for example, that I'd bought at the flea market the previous Saturday. But I had no idea how to play it or even tune it. I just wanted to make sounds, to express something I couldn't formulate verbally. Music was like a gateway for letting out emotions. It went wonderfully with the zither. And that was the first group experience that made an impression on me. There were a lot of people in Kessler's Scratch Orchestra who found their way to each other musically, all differently. It was a daring mix of traditional musicians looking for something new and complete amateurs. Some people just muttered away to themselves, one woman bashed away at saucepans all the time, someone else abused a clarinet. It was all incredibly abstract but totally fun, liberated from any and all conventions. Starting from that freedom, the electronic and technical side began to make sense.

THOMAS KESSLER I had a brother who was a tape freak. He had a good job in Berlin, and money, and a flat full of expensive Revox tape machines from Switzerland. I told him it would be great if I could use them for the recordings.

MICHAEL HOENIG Kessler had three Revox stereo tape recorders in his studio to begin with, which he recorded everything on. So we could almost always listen to what we'd just played, and permanent reflection became a normal part of the process. Everything was improvised; we very rarely wanted to repeat anything. What we wanted was to play what moved us in the moment when we made it, to express how we felt, individually and as a group. Agitation Free didn't have any set pieces at that time, and nor did Tangerine Dream. We played whatever was inspiring us right then. That was the liberating thing, that we weren't just playing some pop song. Tommy showed us in his studio what was interesting, and why. He motivated us and pushed us through one paper wall after another, in his own way. All the other musicians in Berlin were covering the Stones, the Beatles, the Dave Clark Five or whoever else was in the charts. We consciously avoided doing exactly that; instead, we played our own thing, or actually our own selves. The musical outcome was never predictable and varied hugely, but it was always extremely exciting.

LÜÜL When I was twelve my father sent me to music classes, where I met Manuel Göttsching. We'd practise Bach études and stuff, when what we really wanted to do was play so-called beat music. We didn't learn any chords there at all, only scales, harmonies, fingerpicking and classical music, but not what interested us: rock 'n' roll, blues and beat. The lessons were dull, of course, but I'm grateful now that I learned the basics there and can read notes. In Agitation Free, though, it all had to go – you couldn't write down the ideas we had back then on staff paper. And that total rejection of conventional music-making was part of our antagonistic attitude.

THOMAS KESSLER As soon as you study music at a conservatory, the blockades come along. Back in Darmstadt on the summer courses, I wasn't allowed to write an octave, as a composer. I had to get over that again later. Which is a good thing. Composers always need something to rebel against, to overcome. A lot of the musicians from the Electronic Beat Studio had to overcome their non-academic backgrounds, and I had to overcome my academic learning. Ultimately, it ended up the same: we all had to make a leap.

MICHAEL HOENIG The Electronic Beat Studio was a fantastic catalyst for the people later called the 'Berlin School'. We couldn't even remotely formulate what we wanted back then, even though we did a whole lot of talking. We had this huge urge to express our psychedelic experiences in music, things impossible to formulate in language. Thomas was very subtle about performing great didactic feats, showing us ways to do that. It was an experience you'd only get these days from private 'coaches'.

THOMAS KESSLER I once had a formative experience with Earle Brown: he'd given me notes by Steve Reich, at a time when only handwritten notes were doing the rounds. They included *Pendulum Music*, a piece where you suspend four microphones above four speakers and set them swaying, resulting in feedback at regular intervals. I staged it at the Akademie der Künste in Berlin, but I found it a bit boring so I wanted to use a filter to vary the sounds. When I suggested it, Brown got really angry – I'd never seen anything like it! He started complaining that we Europeans always wanted to keep changing things when something was already finished! That accusation weighed on my mind at the time. And he was right, it's a European mania not to leave things the way they are. In this case, there were just four microphones swaying above four speakers, no more than that. If Mark Rothko painted a picture red, then it's red and that's that. Still, I went all out for us to stage Reich's *Pendulum Music*. What I mean to say is that I'd learned to support things that I didn't necessarily warm to entirely myself. In the Beat Studio as well, I found a lot of what the people did there a bit pointless, but I'd never have put it down or prevented it. And it was definitely a good thing for everyone involved that I played the friendly electro-professor and not the unerring maestro.

MICHAEL HOENIG At some point, Thomas recommended me to Agitation Free, whose guitarist Axel Genrich had just moved on to Guru Guru. Two weeks later, the drummer Christopher Franke switched to Tangerine Dream. When I arrived, Lüül and Fame were facing a brand-new start.

THOMAS KESSLER Of course the music in the studio often bored me, but they probably said the same of my music. The only thing I told them off about was never singing. I remember saying to Edgar Froese: 'Why do none of you sing?' No answer. But at the time, I really thought the human voice could open up a new dimension to their music.

LÜÜL For Agitation Free, Thomas Kessler was what George Martin was for the Beatles. We'd run into other bands at the Electronic Beat Studio and end up playing sessions with them.

THOMAS KESSLER We always started in the studio at about six in the evening, and then we'd go on until late at night. There were no rules and anyone could bring along new musicians whenever they liked. I recorded all the music made there. Later, we'd listen back to it together and talk about it. I offered music theory there as well. I even gave counterpoint lessons to Tangerine Dream. They just wanted to learn the theoretical side. It was only a couple of hours every time, but it was a kind of introduction, at least. We discussed music a lot in the studio, talked about concerts we'd been to together, classical or modern. Or about the time Jimi Hendrix played in Berlin, at the Sportpalast. It was down to them that I went and saw him in the first place.

LÜÜL Kessler was a major influence on us and introduced us to a lot of new sounds; he opened up new horizons for us.

THOMAS KESSLER One day, Earle Brown came to the Electronic Beat Studio with John Cage, because Cage couldn't find anyone in the whole of Berlin who'd copy him a tape at thirty-eight-centimetres-per-second speed. The radio had said no, so Brown said to Cage: 'Come on, we'll go to the Electronic Beat Studio.' Cage came along and thought it was all very interesting what we were doing there, but he didn't join in. Maybe he was waiting for me to ask him. But for some reason, it didn't occur to me. Stupid. I certainly didn't have any aesthetic barriers. Earle Brown had let me have test pressings of Steve Reich's and Terry Riley's first records. He said Steve Reich wasn't his style, but I'd probably like it because there was electronic stuff on there. A compliment, right? Those vinyl records went round Berlin like wildfire, ending up with people like Tangerine Dream and Agitation Free and a few Berlin composers; they'd never heard anything like it.

MICHAEL HOENIG I think it's no coincidence that all the internationally known musicians from that Berlin scene – Ash Ra Tempel, Tangerine Dream, Klaus Schulze, Agitation Free – practised in the Electronic Beat Studio. We all profited a great deal from Thomas Kessler, in my view, both from the contemporary techniques he showed us as comparisons and from his wonderful enthusiasm. In retrospect, it was probably the most successful German rock academy that ever existed, if you ignore the fact that it wasn't an academy and the head was Swiss.

THOMAS KESSLER They only ever smoked joints in the studio; it was like having a beer. There was no excessive behaviour. No one was ever babbling on the floor, with glazed eyes fixed on seventh heaven, at four in the morning. I presume the joints were actually a distraction from alcohol. We certainly never drank in the studio; I'd have been annoyed if there'd been empty bottles down there. But nothing was banned – it didn't have to be, everyone was astoundingly sensible.

MICHAEL HOENIG There was an insane amount of discussion in Agitation Free. As I said, it arose naturally from the way we permanently recorded everything. We were constantly discussing both the music and the group dynamics. In retrospect, it's pretty amusing how much time we spent verbalising everything. There's a wonderful radio play by Alfred Bergmann, by the way, a writer and an Agitation Free fan who did radio plays for the SFB. He invited us to his house on the Lüneburg Heath in 1972, and he recorded all our conversations from morning to midnight, and of course also the music we played in his barn. The result was a wonderful document of our group dynamics. I don't know if it was down to our egos, the group or the questions the writer asked, but we seem to have spent the whole time arguing. The wonderful thing about it was that the verbal aspect was always immediately expressed in the music we played the same day. The band thrived on that dynamic.

THOMAS KESSLER There were always different numbers of people coming together in the studio. One night there might be only three of us, and the night after that the place would be full, maybe thirty or forty people. There were no rules. I didn't really analyse what we got up to. At least not in the way German music critics would have done at the time. I was on an equal footing with the musicians.

LÜÜL Once, Thomas took us aside and gave us written notes for various instruments. We thought it was something he'd composed. We played fragments of it, he recorded it, and afterwards he said: 'Right, now listen to the original.' It was excerpts from *Church of Anthrax* by Terry Riley and John Cale. When I told Cale about it later, he really wanted to hear it, but the recording doesn't exist any more. Cale was very disappointed.

MICHAEL HOENIG We were very surprised by *Church of Anthrax*, because we'd had no idea before that there were minimalists in New York as well.

LÜÜL People like Terry Riley and Steve Reich became important for us then; you can't tell with Agitation Free, but later with Ash Ra you can clearly hear that influence. Manuel Göttsching's solo album *Inventions for Electric Guitar* has echo effects that sound a lot like minimal music. And one of the greatest live shows I ever saw was Steve Reich's *Drumming*.

THOMAS KESSLER The actual electronic revolution was the EMS Synthi-A from London, though. The Brits were a leading force in synthesizers at the time. I'd heard it in 1971, when Stockhausen's *Sternklang* premiered at the East Berlin zoo. And Hugh Davies from London was sitting up a tree with his little improvisation group. They had with them little black cases with the first portable synthesizers that made electronic music, the first portable analogue synthesizers with voltage control. I started saving up straight away – I was still a student at the time. Once I'd got enough money together I went to London and got myself a little case of my own at Electronic Music Systems. It cost me DM6,000, a whole lot of money at the time, but the machine was a sensation in Berlin. When I got back with it I was invited to every party in town, but I always had to promise to bring my case along, and then we'd all play around on the synth. There were no instructions, no one had worked out any lessons for it. You had to work everything out for yourself, and that was a good thing.

MICHAEL HOENIG On the radio – it was RIAS, where Walter Bachauer made excellent contemporary music programmes – I'd heard a piece with a piano and a ring modulator, a surreal, fantastic sound. Once I'd found out what the electronic component was, I immediately built myself one, with a mic input and a sine wave generator. I wish my first experiments still existed, especially the stuff with my zither.

THOMAS KESSLER Hugh Davies had given me a little plan for how to build my own ring modulator; it was very easy. You could get the parts in a shop; all you had to do was solder them together, and it worked. You could produce amazingly strange sounds with it, with voltage control and functions like that. In combination with the Synthi-A, it was a wonderful tool for musical experimentation.

LÜÜL We had a tape recorder on for almost everything, but we usually just taped right over it again. We just couldn't afford to keep it all.

THOMAS KESSLER I've only got very few tapes left from those days. It's sad, but we didn't know what we were doing. I was just a student from the conservatory, and there were a lot more important and more talented people there than me. And the musicians from the Electronic Beat Studio were straight off the street, if you like. We were like a refugee camp for homeless musicians. Sometimes famous people did put in an appearance – one of the Stones came by, but I can't remember who it was. But we always stayed in our niche. And my niche was even smaller than Agitation Free's or the others' because I never changed camp, my music was always very different. As soon as the bands from my studio made a bit of money, they'd buy their own electronic equipment and bring it along to the studio. Even the first big Moogs, after a while. We tested a lot of machines there. It went on that way until I was called back from Berlin to Switzerland, for a position in Basel. Once, much later, I was in a WDR studio, and the editor told me Stockhausen had worked at the mixing desk and no one knew how much of him was still inside it. That might be true of my little black case with the EMS Synthi-A inside it too – I've still got it. It's a bit scruffy but it still works just as well, squeaks and buzzes and hums and does what it wants. It's the first of its kind that ever came to mainland Europe. Or that's what they told me in London when I bought it. That machine made a big difference, more than I did. That's how it is in electronic music – humans aren't that important. At any rate, that little case set a lot of balls rolling in Berlin.

TANGERINE DREAM

'We were stoned. The crowd was stoned.'
KLAUS SCHULZE

JEAN-MICHEL JARRE I once had a debate with Edgar Froese about which of us had started making electronic music first. I was certain Tangerine Dream came before me, but Edgar said it was me, and Tangerine Dream had still been playing prog rock at the time when I was already working electronically. It was a funny argument – neither of us wanted to have come first.

IRMIN SCHMIDT I went out with a schoolfriend in Berlin one time, the painter Peter Sorge. One night he dragged me along to the Zodiak, said there was a great group there, the musicians all completely barmy, and the guitarist in particular was amazing. So we head over, sit around there for ages, and nothing happens. Someone kept coming and saying they'd be starting any minute now. But then it was a good hour before Edgar Froese came on stage on his own with a guitar and made this grumpy announcement: 'My band's left me. I'm gonna play on my ownsome!' And then he played guitar all alone for two hours, the wildest free rock, he was up to his eyeballs, letting off steam and really getting his anger out. I was incredibly impressed. Afterwards we had a bit of a chat, but he was still far too angry for a long conversation. Still, I thought he was really amazing. That was at the end of 1967, and then we lost track of each other for a while. Then when I had the idea to start Can and was thinking about guitarists, the first one that came to mind was Edgar. But before I could make contact, Holger suggested Michael Karoli as a guitarist. I met Michael and was really into him right from the first second. But it would have been exciting with Edgar Froese as well. Then there wouldn't have been any Tangerine Dream, and Can would have turned into a very different band.

KLAUS SCHULZE Schnitzler and I used to have day jobs with the post office, delivering telegrams to pay the rent. Edgar was still painting buses at the time, painting ads on them; he'd studied graphic design. Everyone in Tangerine Dream had day jobs. You'd get DM50 a night for playing in small clubs like the Magic Cave or the Silver Apple, and you couldn't live on that, even in Berlin. We never even thought of being commercial, because then we'd have had to adapt our music and there was no way we wanted to do that. All we were interested in was making our own new sounds – we didn't really care whether they sold or not. That's why we did so much experimenting. What you can hear on the first Tangerine Dream record, *Electronic Meditation*, was our musical act of liberation. Compared to later, it's not particularly electronic or particularly meditative, more like *tabula rasa*; it's punk, actually. The real electronic music came later, but we didn't know that at the time.

MANFRED GILLIG I first saw Tangerine Dream in one of their earliest line-ups in February 1969, when they were mainly doing free jazz, at the student bar Litfass in Berlin-Charlottenburg, where Reinhard Mey used to sing as well. Froese was already playing around a bit with electronic stuff, but the saxophone was still basically dominant. There were five or six people on a small stage, right up close to the tables where people were sitting, and it was clear that Froese was the man keeping it all together. Like a conductor, he made the music louder and quieter with his gestures and he seemed to be controlling everything, but he also allowed long solos. There were two or three long pieces with a lot of improvisation which felt like they'd never stop. They didn't use classic song structures. But what later made up a whole album on *Phaedra* was divided up into chunks, all very free and intuitive, and of course also wild and loud and noisy. They might have already had a Mini-Moog and played around on it a bit. It was over after a good two hours. The audience, about fifty people, were fascinated and excited. I was amazed too by what happened there. But the electronic side wasn't that important, although the first real electro records came from the US in 1968, Wendy Carlos's *Switched-on Bach* and the first Silver Apples album. Still, I came out of that Tangerine Dream gig and thought: 'This is going to be good.'

STEVE SCHROYDER My first encounter with Tangerine Dream was at the Essener Songtage. I didn't know the band that well yet, but their gig was really impressive. The 'politicos', the political students, cut their power cables while they were playing. There was a permanent fight raging between the people who wanted to listen to music and the ones who wanted to debate politics, or about whether music was essentially crap if it wasn't a protest song. So the sounds from Tangerine Dream turned into a kind of contribution to the discussion.

WINFRID TRENKLER I was at the Essener Songtage to write up the festival for *Sounds*. I had my first personal encounter with Edgar Froese in the lobby of the Grugahalle, and he said to me in his broad Berlin accent: 'Whenever a journalist or someone comes to me and says he can do us a favour, I just wanna punch him straight in the gob.' He'd had enough of media people.

STEVE SCHROYDER Politics students cut through the cables during Tangerine Dream's performance in the Grugahalle. Hardly anyone noticed in the auditorium, word just had it that there'd been a power cut. When they couldn't play any more, Tangerine Dream went to the front of the stage and just sang. I was bloody impressed. And their act up till then had already got me all fired up. At the beginning, when they still had power, Edgar stood there and just played guitar. I heard things I'd never heard before, which really fascinated me, like singing choirs of angels! In the end, though, the political students yelled down Tangerine Dream.

KLAUS SCHULZE Tangerine Dream shows were like rehearsing again – just after the rehearsal and with an audience. The Brits call it an open rehearsal, we called it a gig. We never composed anything in Tangerine Dream, only ever improvised. Our gigs were usually just two long pieces with a break in between. That's why they couldn't compare us to Jimi Hendrix or the Grateful Dead. It was just really our music and nothing where anyone could say: 'That sounds like . . .' It's not a compliment to be compared with something that already exists. If you listen to *Electronic Meditation*, you have to say there wasn't any music like that before. Even Pink Floyd had only one long and really crazy track on *A Saucerful of Secrets*.

STEVE SCHROYDER I had a life-changing LSD experience in Finland in 1969 and came back that summer a different person. But since the rest of society hadn't changed as much as I thought, I ended up a year later in a mental hospital in Berlin. I'd been picked up in a department store because I wanted to stroll out with Deep Purple's *In Rock* LP without paying, and made no attempt to hide it. I told the staff the record had been made just for me so I didn't need money to pay for it, and anyway money would soon be obsolete in the modern world, since everybody knew it would soon be abolished. So I was promptly arrested and handed over to the police, where a psychologist diagnosed me with depression, and I was taken to Bonnie's Ranch – the infamous Karl Bonhoeffer mental institution where terrible things were done in the Third Reich and all Berlin's drug cases were admitted in the early seventies. But I climbed out the window with another guy the next day and split. Since my Finland trip I'd been hearing voices from outer space, my own cosmic advisers whispering things in my head. I never talked about it publicly but it was a new truth for me. At some point I heard the first Tangerine Dream record, *Electronic Meditation*, and an inner voice told me Tangerine Dream could help me. Someone in a record shop gave me Edgar Froese's address because I wanted to talk to him right then and there. But the address wasn't for Edgar, it was Klaus

Schulze's. I went to visit him in Steglitz – I think he was still a postman at the time – but Klaus told me he'd just left Tangerine Dream, and gave me Edgar's address: 7b Schwäbische Strasse. I went right round there and rang the doorbell in the middle of the night. Someone looked out of one of the top windows and said: 'Hello?' And I answered: 'I'm your new organist, appointed by the cosmos!' 'Fantastic! I'll be right down!' Edgar yelled, and he came down and opened the front door and invited me up to his flat. Then me and my girlfriend went up – I'd taken her along with me – and we spent all night talking to him and his girlfriend Monique. The most interesting thing about my time in TD was the conversations I had with Edgar. We'd talk at great length about metaphysical subjects, out-there things, everything that wasn't real. We talked a lot about time and space, especially. All things that were later formulated in music too. After that night, I was in the band. Edgar was in a tight spot at the time, though: Schulze had just left, Schnitzler was gone too, so the band was just him. That's why he'd just got in touch with Christopher Franke as well, who then joined as our drummer. Anyway, he invited me along to a meeting with Christopher the next day. The two of them came over to my place and I played them my organ improvisations, and they liked them.

KLAUS SCHULZE Everything came about by coincidence, really. We never theorised about our music. We actually hated discussing music. We'd talk more about art – Andy Warhol, David Hockney and that kind of thing. But Stockhausen's avant-garde music wasn't for us; it seemed to be all about avoidance and breaking things, ultimately doing things that aren't nice. Pierre Henry was halfway all right, but even that became less and less appealing – we wanted to have something harmonic in our stuff. Not along the normal scheme, though: chorus, middle eight and then back to the chorus. But just not as structuralist as the new sound people. We wanted neither chart pop nor avant-garde art. We wanted a third way: underground music.

STEVE SCHROYDER That love of improvising and experimenting is what marked out Tangerine Dream from the beginning, that always starting over at zero. I still remember our very first session, very clearly. Tangerine Dream had a studio on Ku'damm where we rehearsed. Before we kicked off we turned the lights out. The point was to achieve absolute silence as inspiration. It was pitch black, only the LEDs lit up on the amps. Edgar kept going 'Shhh, shhh'. So we sat there motionless in the dark for a few minutes and listened to the silence. After a while someone started making sounds out of that atmosphere, and then the others joined in. That was how we made our tracks back then. Tangerine Dream were much more at home in the art scene than the rock world. And the gigs were a meeting place for the LSD faction.

KLAUS SCHULZE We were stoned, the crowd was stoned, people did moderate dancing or just lay on the floor. It was all about listening. But it was a peaceful scene. It was music that made a lot of people think – they had to decide for themselves about what. But there could always be surprises at Tangerine Dream gigs, anything could happen at any moment.

STEVE SCHROYDER When people asked me about *Alpha Centauri* they'd often say it was a 'crazy trip', because they needed that kind of music for their quiet sessions. No one ever said it was a 'groovy record' or anything, it was always about the trip.

KLAUS SCHULZE Our music was improvised from beginning to end. That's why it was hardly possible to repeat certain songs, which made it tricky for the recording studios. It was a 'take it or leave it' situation; they couldn't say their usual stuff like, 'OK, let's do that again, but make it cleaner this time.'

STEVE SCHROYDER The first TD gig I played was in September 1970, for Austrian TV, a performance with pinball machines. We played in the Austrian studio on a staircase, me on my Farfisa organ and a real Marshall amps stack, Edgar had his Gibson guitar and Christopher Franke his drum kit. And there were four pinball machines as well, hooked up to speakers and operating randomly; the balls got sent up automatically. The sound of the balls in the pinball machines, the rattle of the gaming machines was integrated into our improvised music by contact microphones. I was looking at the potential of spiritual energies at the time and I thought a lot of improbable things were possible. I even had a telepathic experience with Conny Schnitzler, when we were working in adjacent studios. We were both playing at the same time in our practice rooms without knowing about each other, and after a while I got the feeling someone else was playing along, so I left the room, and at the same moment Conny Schnitzler left his room as well; he'd felt the same thing as me. It was pretty phenomenal. And because I was convinced of my telepathic powers, I'd come up with something special for our Austrian performance: I wanted to send energy to America through my music, to give President Nixon a heart attack. All right, that was intent to kill, it horrifies me to think about it now, but at the time it seemed worth a try. So when we started playing I concentrated really hard to send my deadly beam from the TV studio to Richard Nixon, when suddenly there was a BOOM! What happened? My Marshall amp had burned out. We had to break off the performance and start over. But for me, it was all over from that point because it had really taken it out of me. I'd used up all my energy and shot it off in one moment. Obviously, I was glad the universe had intervened to rescue Nixon from me, because I wouldn't really have wanted an American president on my conscience.

KLAUS SCHULZE At the time Tangerine Dream and Ash Ra Tempel weren't rock bands playing in entertainment venues; they were more like gallery bands who often performed at exhibition openings. It wasn't thought of as a show, more like a musical backdrop to various art happenings. We were regarded as avant-garde, so they called us when people like David Hockney had an exhibition on. It only came about little by little that we played gigs as a band and weren't just an accompanying cultural event.

STEVE SCHROYDER When we recorded *Alpha Centauri*, what we wanted was to reach other worlds with our music and embrace phenomena like telekinesis and telepathy. We consciously used the term 'cosmic music' for it. We didn't want to just give an impressionistic picture of cosmic spheres; for me, at least, it was also about creating an energy ray with music that would carry us through space. That was my declared intention. Christopher played the drums, I played the organ with an effects device, and Edgar played guitar. Our sessions were a constant seeking, never defined playing. We didn't know exactly what we were doing. No one ever said what to play and when to stop. *Alpha Centauri* came about in the moment. A spontaneous thing from beginning to end. We just had a kind of feeling for when something worked. On 'Sunrise in the Third System' I play this organ part at the beginning, and I'd just found it at the moment we started recording. A Gothic theme, but I couldn't remember how I'd got there and I didn't want to either. I thought my organ was from the cosmos as well and had all music stored inside it, just waiting for me to call it up. I never saw myself as a creative person, always just as a medium to transfer cosmic sounds that already exist somewhere. The whole record is improvised, in that sense; the only thing Edgar had before was the organ theme at the end of 'Fly and Collision of Comas Sola'. I thought it was too close to Pink Floyd, though, so I only went along with it against my better judgement. I didn't have a clue about chords, either, but I did know what the notes are called, and I arranged them so that they went together nicely, to my taste. Then I brought along Udo Dennebourg, who plays the flute on *Alpha Centauri* and was a great theorist – a philosopher and professor of psychedelic society, if you like. Unfortunately his behaviour was so counterproductive that no one wanted to work with him again. I still regret bringing him along, because in the end the flute on the B-side of the record is totally out of place. Then a synthesizer was flown in as well, this little Japanese guy came to the studio in Stommeln with an EMS synthesizer from London. We played around with it and produced all kinds of noises and strange sounds. We all had a bit of a go on it, but it was the technician Roland Paulyck who took real care of it, which is why he got the credit for it. I wasn't that impressed by the EMS so I didn't pay it much more attention. Then we went to Stockhausen's studio in Köln and watched one of his concerts. The choir at the end is based on the Essener Songtage. The critics panned *Alpha Centauri* at the time – it only got appreciation much later.

KLAUS SCHULZE We all developed pretty quickly, but not always in parallel. I was more or less thrown out of Tangerine Dream in those early days; Edgar insisted on me only playing the drums and he wanted to be the guitarist. Thank God, then Schnitzler joined, a student of Joseph Beuys with lots of avant-garde ideas. That made two of us who had different plans to Edgar. But I was increasingly busy making sounds on the electric guitar myself and altering sounds. Edgar stuck to his position, though: 'You either stick to drums or you leave.' At some point I really did leave, and set up Ash Ra Tempel with Manuel Göttsching and Hartmut Enke. That only went well for a certain time, again. At the start we were all on the same page, and we recorded our first LP together in 1971, something genuinely new: a thirty-minute track on vinyl, using the whole record up to the run-out groove, pure improvisation, recording in the studio but without a concept, the way we played on stage. No one had ever done that before, not even the Grateful Dead or Pink Floyd. But then Manuel and Hartmut, who'd done blues before, wanted to make more hands-on music rather than experimenting with electronics like before. After that I'd had enough of bands and I worked solo – that way, no one could stick their oar in any more.

163

THOMAS KESSLER Tangerine Dream only became an electronic group through Christopher Franke. He was a drummer originally, like Klaus Schulze was, but then he took care of the synthesizers in Tangerine Dream. I played a part in their music a couple of times with tape feeds I'd spliced together, but only at studio sessions, never live on stage. But ultimately it wasn't my music and I didn't want to intervene, although I thought their concerts were amazing. I knew they'd be successful, but their way was different to mine. I was all the more impressed by how they produced music without having attended conservatories, music that reached so many people – which I could never do, even though I'd studied so much.

STEVE SCHROYDER When we finished mixing the record on the last day, I didn't feel good about it. None of it was my thing any more, somehow. And then there were a few little misunderstandings between us. Working on *Alpha Centauri* had really exhausted me, partly because of the voices in my head with their constant cosmic inspirations. Driven by them, I went to Köln Cathedral one day to get hold of a choir and an organ for a Tangerine Dream session. I told the people in the cathedral the session would be 'the shit!' Of course, I got neither an organ nor a choir, a huge disappointment for me, one of many . . . On the last night of the record production I decided it was all getting too much for me and I had to get out of there and do something different. I didn't say goodbye, just packed my things, including the organ, chucked it all in the car and headed for Paris to visit Pierre Henry, which didn't work out either, naturally. Instead, I ended up in jail in France because I'd 'borrowed' a car. I mean, the apartment door had been open and the key was on the table, and anyway I'd left the owner a tarot card in exchange. But since I'd read the guy's tarot cards in a bar beforehand, they picked up on me pretty quick. After forty-five days in jail, I hung out in France for a bit, where a pal of mine stole my organ. So making music just faded into the background.

PETER BAUMANN One day I was at an Emerson, Lake and Palmer gig and they were running late, and I turned around to see who'd come along and find someone to talk to. Sitting behind me was Christopher Franke, and we ended up in conversation: 'What do you do?' he asked me. 'I make music. But what I'm most interested in is experimental stuff.' He said: 'That's interesting, where do you live?' Then later I found a note in my letterbox: 'Hello from Christopher, we're looking for a new keyboard player.'

STEVE SCHROYDER No one in Berlin knew where I'd gone. People asked my relatives, but they had no idea either; I had no contact with my family at the time. 1971 was a terrible year for me. I didn't feel the need to get in touch with Tangerine Dream for a long time, but I did go and see them in the summer. They gave me a euphoric welcome because *Alpha Centauri* was doing great, but that spark between us was gone.

PETER BAUMANN Steve Schroyder didn't fit in with the band any more; he was having personal problems.

STEVE SCHROYDER My conversations with Edgar were still good but everything else had changed, somehow. And I was in a really bad way that year, a deep psychic disaster.

PETER BAUMANN When I found the note, I thought: 'Great, where do we meet?' I picked up my organ and met up with Edgar and Christopher, and then we started making music in a basement room with blue light. I brought along a Farfisa organ I'd had for four years. I loved its great reverb and vibrato. Edgar played guitar, Christopher was on drums, and I set up my organ. Edgar made pretty weird sounds on the guitar, Christopher played something similar on the cymbal, and I joined in with a couple of odd notes and started shaking the spring reverb. We stopped after about an hour, and Edgar said: 'Pretty good stuff, so here's our next gig. Then we'll see how it goes.'

STEVE SCHROYDER Peter Baumann had replaced me, but I didn't feel the slightest inclination to get into it with him. And I didn't even have my organ any more either. That was the end of it for me. I was asked to work with them on the next record, *Zeit*, and I did make a minor contribution, but you can't compare it to my part in *Alpha Centauri*.

STEVEN WILSON The first German band I became aware of was Tangerine Dream. A friend a few years older than me had a couple of their records, like *Phaedra*, *Logos Live* and *Zeit*. And that was the exact order I listened to them in. The first time I put on *Phaedra* I was blown away, and *Logos* was the same. But when I listened to *Zeit* I just thought: 'What on earth is this? There's nothing happening.' Over time, though, *Zeit* became my absolute favourite album. It wasn't music any more, it was more than music. Some of the very best records don't work on your first listen. You just get a sense that something about them is special. *Zeit* is one of those records. And I listen to it at least once a month. I've got various editions, on CD and vinyl. I love *Zeit*, it's where everything started!

PETER BAUMANN The first album I worked on was *Zeit*, which came out on Rolf-Ulrich Kaiser's Ohr label. I got to do what I liked during the sessions, and everything just slotted together. The chemistry worked between the three of us. Edgar only had a guitar at first, then he got a noise generator and Christopher got a couple of oscillators. It was really primitive at the beginning but then we got more and more devices. Each of us developed our own sounds.

STEVEN WILSON *Zeit* sounds like so many feelings: wonderfully organic on the one hand, and on the other uncanny, disconcerting and actually weird, which I love. I don't even want to know what the record's about; then it would lose its magic for me. A lot of people have since done similar things to what you hear on *Zeit*, but there's still something on the album that I haven't worked out to this day. And that's all the more amazing when you think how long it was before computer technology was introduced in studios, which is used to perfect everything now. On *Zeit*, you're listening to imperfection, in the very best sense. These days you'd probably call the sound 'lo-fi'. Even the genius beginning, with seven minutes of cello players who keep sounding out of tune: breath-taking. On my first listen I asked myself: 'Where's the tune? Where's the structure?' There were just these big sound clouds, just textures and atmosphere. I'd never heard of ambient music at that point.

SIMON DRAPER Tangerine Dream records were in huge demand via our mail order and in the shop. And when we decided to start Virgin Records in 1972 and I was on the lookout for artists that suited us, I soon thought of Tangerine Dream. I wasn't all that surprised when they were such a success for us. What made it much easier for them as a German band in the UK was that they didn't have vocals. Back then it was still a massive problem selling anything on the English market with non-native speakers singing on it, either in their own language or in broken English. So rock music from France, Holland and Germany made modest sales. That's all in the past now, thankfully. But krautrock was mainly instrumental and often electronic as well, so there was no resistance.

STEVEN WILSON Once you've discovered one krautrock band, it automatically leads to the next. After Tangerine Dream I found this guy called Klaus Schulze, who used to play the drums with Tangerine Dream. He led me to Manuel Göttsching and Ash Ra Tempel. Then came Conrad Schnitzler and many more, just the way you always discover music.

PETER BAUMANN The first synthesizer came from England and was called EMS, which stands for Electronic Music Studios. Our version was an AKS1. It was a case with a little synthesizer in it. After that things really kicked off for Tangerine Dream, because we suddenly had a way to shape our very own sound. Christopher Franke was the first one to have a synth; it must have cost about $1,500 at the time, a lot of money for us. Christopher made these brilliant sounds on it, and he lent it to me one weekend. After that I decided: 'I'm getting one too!' It all went pretty fast. Another helpful thing was a visit to the Farfisa company. We went by after a gig, and they gave us all this equipment as a promo opportunity. That must have been 1972, so early on. They were already confident we'd make it big.

SIMON DRAPER Christopher Franke was a bit taciturn to begin with, while Peter Baumann was very chatty. But it was always clearly Edgar in charge. He was the one who made the decisions and dictated what they did.

MANFRED GILLIG I saw Tangerine Dream in the Royal Albert Hall in 1974. That was my first big trip for *Sounds*; I was invited by Virgin Records. I'd missed my flight because I'd been partying too long the night before and got there late, so they let me go in the last car from the Virgin office to the Royal Albert Hall. There was this young beardy guy in the car as well, and we talked all the way there. He wanted to know what *Sounds* was and asked me about the German music scene. At some point I asked him who he was, and he introduced himself as Richard Branson and told me what he'd done so far. Tangerine Dream were the first big thing for Virgin after Mike Oldfield.

PETER BAUMANN We weren't a rock band in the usual sense. We didn't talk to the audience. When we came on stage the lights went off, just a few blue lamps were on, and we'd sit down and make music, there'd be applause two or three times in between, and then two hours would be up, we'd wave goodbye, and that was it.

MANFRED GILLIG We got to the hall just as Tangerine Dream were starting to tune their gigantic Moog rack, all three of them getting all the settings right. Then they kicked in, playing *Phaedra*. After fifteen minutes I nodded off for a bit; the journey to London had been exhausting but it was also partly the music, which had something relaxingly meditative about it. Plus the solemn, sacred atmosphere. The three of them were wearing long robes and the hall was barely lit up, everything was pretty dark. There were just all the synthesizer lamps flashing away. Once it was over they got a lot of applause from the Brits, who didn't seem to know that kind of music very well, and I left the hall in a buoyant, relaxed mood. It certainly wasn't the normal Royal Albert Hall crowd. But unlike Faust, Tangerine Dream's music was on a popular level. So there were some pretty big freaks there, but also a pretty big crowd of them.

SIMON DRAPER Tangerine Dream had a big fan community in the UK in the seventies. There was a lot of interest in Edgar Froese and the others. They acted anonymous on stage; they weren't rock stars, they hid behind lighting effects and dry ice, but then so did Pink Floyd. The British music press, like *Melody Maker*, which had huge influence and power at the time, wrote a lot about Tangerine Dream.

MANFRED GILLIG After the gig Branson invited me to a party in the basement of his house on Portobello Road, that red-painted Virgin house. Tangerine Dream came along too. Froese wasn't very communicative, rather withdrawn. I spent all night with Christopher Franke, who talked mostly about the future of computers and the digital explosion. It was early 1975 – he was way ahead of his time.

PETER BAUMANN People were much more open to us in the UK than in Germany. John Peel played our music intensively on his show, especially *Phaedra*, and that had a great effect.

SIMON DRAPER John Peel was important for the music. We knew him well and he supported Virgin from the outset. He loved Mike Oldfield's *Tubular Bells* and played it in full, which was a big help, of course. A band like Tangerine Dream would never have got as big in the UK without Peel's help. How else would people have heard music like that on the radio? Tangerine Dream didn't even release singles. But whenever he played something from one of their albums, sales shot right up.

PETER BAUMANN We played a lot of gigs in the UK, and after that things really took off there. Richard Branson was a fun, crazy guy who put a cheque down on the table for us and said: 'Here's a studio for you to record in.' That was the only thing that interested us. He let us do what we liked, partly because he didn't really know much about music. He had Simon Draper for that, who ran the label. Draper came to the studio once and asked us to play him something. So we played him the first side of *Phaedra*, and he didn't know what on earth to say. 'A very unusual piece of music.' He must have liked it, he was just confused because there wasn't a pigeonhole to put it in yet.

SIMON DRAPER Tangerine Dream were pleasant to deal with. By the time they came to us in the UK, they were already selling well and they knew we could use their records.

PETER BAUMANN Virgin took a big financial risk on us, but they had a good instinct and they saw there were interesting things going on in Germany. I suppose they found Tangerine Dream most exciting, so they took us on.

SIMON DRAPER Tangerine Dream recorded their albums in our studio – the Manor – and they'd always stay for about three weeks. They brought their own synthesizers, but they also used our equipment. The Manor wasn't up to the latest technical standards, but we made our artists use our studio for financial reasons; that was part of the contract.

Only a few refused, like Faust, for example; they didn't want to go back there after the first record.

PETER BAUMANN We'd recorded *Phaedra*, our first record for Virgin, in Oxford. I was in Italy with my girlfriend when it came out, and I got a telegram from Richard Branson telling me to come straight to England to do interviews because our record was in the top ten. And I just thought: 'What top ten?' We'd never really imagined we'd ever have more than a couple of hundred listeners. I called Richard Branson, and he said: 'It's unbelievable, the record is selling very well – you have to come to London.' So we all flew to London and did dozens of interviews.

SIMON DRAPER It wasn't that easy to promote Tangerine Dream because it was clear from the beginning that they wouldn't get airplay on normal daytime radio. John Peel played them at night, but that was it. That's why magazines like *Melody Maker* were so important for us. We could grab people's attention there with sensational ads. I came up with the slogan 'Music that melts'. I'd been thinking of Salvador Dalí's painting with the melting clocks. So we melted black vinyl records, hung them in record-shop windows and printed the slogan 'Music that melts' on posters. It was a bit of a stunner. Later we hired a famous cartoonist to draw us a big 'Edgar rules' picture of Edgar Froese breaking through a wall. We did some fun ads with Klaus Schulze as well. The audience was pretty into it.

MANFRED GILLIG *Phaedra* went into the British charts quite high and sold well for a long time, as did their next albums. And that triggered UK interest in other German musicians. Magazines like *Melody Maker* and *New Musical Express* had huge print runs back then. And Virgin also imported records or licensed them, like with Klaus Schulze and Can.

SIMON DRAPER Our technicians didn't like working with Tangerine Dream because they did everything themselves. When we sent the recordings for their *Phaedra* album to the pressing plant, one of our technicians, Phil Becque, went along to keep an eye on things. Anyway, then the record accidentally got cut backwards and none of the tech guys noticed. It all sounded the same to them! When we finally realised, I said to Edgar: 'It's great, now we can bring your records out again backwards. We've got a real treasure trove here.' He laughed at that. If you play most albums backwards, they just sound like weird noises, but Tangerine Dream backwards sounds just as electronic as their usual music.

GABI DELGADO-LÓPEZ *Phaedra* really impressed me – the music on it sounded like freedom. I thought the sequential, serial aspect to it was amazing. I'd never heard anything like it before.

JEAN-MICHEL JARRE I went to the legendary 1974 Tangerine Dream concert in Reims Cathedral. I just happened to be there by chance, working on an installation with tape machines and electronics. I heard a German band would be playing in the cathedral with synthesizers, which obviously interested me. And then it was absolutely grandiose. I'm very happy I was able to talk to Edgar about it before he died.

HARALD GROSSKOPF When Tangerine Dream played in the cathedral in France, people took a crap in the corners. It was a huge scandal that really pushed their sales. Scandals are a good thing. Ash Ra also often performed in special places, like planetariums and churches. The audience looked as unusual as we did, long-haired hippies in sacred spaces.

SIMON DRAPER Tangerine Dream gigs were exciting because there was a great light show and it was very loud, but they still bored me a bit because I often couldn't make out any structure to their live music. It was all improvised, of course, but that doesn't automatically make it particularly inspired. They did get more rhythmic over the years, which gave the shows a bit more pep. And at some point Edgar started playing guitar again as well. That made their sound more commercial and accessible, but also a bit more normal with fewer surprises; their pure electronic music was more special. Tangerine Dream sold a lot of records everywhere, not just in the UK but all over Europe, even in the States. I wasn't surprised when they got booked for Hollywood soundtracks – it was the perfect fit.

PETER BAUMANN Money wasn't important, but then our album *Phaedra* was very successful, and *Rubycon* as well, the next record, and that does influence you in some way, naturally, because you wonder what you did to prompt such a big reaction. But for a long time we didn't talk about it, just went on making music. We could afford to because *Phaedra* sold a million copies and we could live off the money very well. Later on, after me and Franke had left, money did become an issue for Edgar. I earned almost a million marks at the age of twenty. I bought new instruments with the money. Everything was great and I never thought about saving it for my old age.

STEVE SCHROYDER Tangerine Dream was never into following existing models, only into seeing what didn't yet exist: what are notes? What are frequencies? What is silence? Those were the things we thought about. It was an attempt to get different sounds out of the usual instruments. Later, they switched entirely to synthesizers, unlike the many other bands where synthesizers only played a supporting role. When I was in the band with my organ, I said to myself: 'Standard harmonies don't exist any more, I have to find my way around this system of keys differently.'

SIMON DRAPER Tangerine Dream was essentially easy listening, if you like. And Klaus Schulze as well, of course.

STEVEN WILSON I love listening to *Zeit* late at night when I'm reading. *Zeit* is one of those records that can utterly change the atmosphere and feel of a room; it has almost the same effect as a scent. It works like ambient music, in the sense that you're not supposed to listen closely. *Zeit* alters how you feel. Ultimately, we don't have the appropriate words to describe the music's effect. I never met Edgar Froese but I think even he couldn't have explained the secret of his early music. Later on, Froese, God rest his soul, kept trying to improve old songs through new recordings, and that always made them worse, which is what makes me think he didn't understand the magic of his early records, because otherwise he'd have left them as they were. He even re-recorded his solo album, *Epsilon in Malaysian Pale*, another big favourite of mine. When I listened to it I almost lost my temper, which doesn't happen often. I once met his son, Jerome Froese, and I begged him to stop his father from messing with *Zeit*. He laughed a lot. But it's similar with a lot of artists from that era. I've worked with many of them and I've noticed that very few of them realise what makes the magic of their music. If they knew that, they'd keep on doing it. Froese would presumably have dismissed *Zeit* as a primitive early work. Inevitably, Tangerine Dream got 'better' after it, if you like; *Phaedra* is much more sophisticated, of course, a better recording, and it has its own magic. I love it too, but for me *Phaedra* can't match that feeling of withdrawing from the world that I always get from *Zeit*.

SIMON DRAPER It's surprising, all the places where people are into Tangerine Dream. I once went to New Orleans to make an album with the reggae band the Mighty Diamonds. What I wanted most, though, was to work with Allen Toussaint. I asked him what he thought of our band, and he said: 'Well, it's reggae, isn't it?' He didn't have any more to say about them. Then I wanted to chat with one of Toussaint's technicians, but all she wanted to talk to me about was Tangerine Dream. It was really bizarre. We were in the deep south, Black musicians playing the Blackest music, but somehow everyone only wanted to talk about Tangerine Dream.

COMMERCIALISM

'Future? So what?'
JEAN-HERVÉ PERON

BERND WITTHÜSER Commercialism was never my thing. I mean, it was great to get occasional royalty cheques but it was never important to me. I got a cheque for Witthüser & Westrupp yesterday: sixty-seven euros. Great – that'll top up my pension.

GERD KRAUS Obviously, we wanted people to listen to Limbus's records. If you write a book, you want it to be read.

HELLMUT HATTLER Seymour Stein, who later discovered Madonna, liked Kraan and gave us a contract. So some of our records also came out in the States. But we didn't want to tour there, so not much happened. We claimed it was for political reasons, Vietnam and all that, but that was rubbish, it was just too stressful for us. We even played at a couple of US festivals, but we didn't want to put more energy into it. The band just wasn't ambitious enough for that.

SIGGI LOCH Like every label-maker, I tried to make Can and Amon Düül into commercial successes. And it worked, to a certain extent.

HARALD GROSSKOPF Success is important. It's not just about money, it's also about recognition. They're closely related. And I wouldn't have minded a better living standard.

HANS-JOACHIM ROEDELIUS As Cluster, we didn't care about money, we just wanted to do what we liked, which we did very thoroughly, in all our phases. Once we played in Kiel, and they didn't even want to pay us a tiny fee afterwards. I cursed the organiser, which I felt sorry about because he died the next day. He was a disco-owner who'd got into trouble and been wiped out by his gang.

HARALD GROSSKOPF Ash Ra wanted success as well. But we were never as successful as Tangerine Dream or Kraftwerk, never mind the Scorpions.

PETER BRÖTZMANN Commercial success was never important to me. Of course, it's nice to earn money, especially if you haven't got any. For a long time, radio stations were really helpful for our work, unlike these days. But it also helped that we sat down with other musicians from Britain, Holland and France and organised and did things together.

JEAN-HERVÉ PERON Zappi and I never talked about money. All that talking annoyed us anyway; we preferred to spend time with our dogs.

MICHAEL HOENIG No one ever thought about a 'product', we just wanted to do whatever we were into at the time. There were a few forerunners here in Germany who started talking about commercial rights for the first time. But all we were interested in was expressing ourselves. At best, we planned from one week to the next: 'Who's playing with who?' And one very important thing: there was no such thing as branding. None of us ever thought of making a buck out of it. We all had random jobs to pay for the equipment we needed. When I started playing with Agitation Free in 1970 I was studying theatre studies, journalism and sociology and had little jobs on the side, like all of us. It was all really easy – first uni, then your job, and once you'd knocked off for the afternoon a new reality began.

HANS-JOACHIM ROEDELIUS A while ago I got an offer to make a record with Lloyd Cole. He was also very much on board because he felt like making music that he really likes for a change, but can never do because he has to feed his family, pay the mortgage and get the roof fixed. But it's clear we can't go on this way forever. I was different, I always did more or less what I wanted, and felt good about it.

ASMUS TIETCHENS It was never about money for me; my music was never going to make me a millionaire.

JAKI LIEBEZEIT We never cared whether our records did well, never even made an effort to appeal to audiences. We were never as conformist as a lot of bands these days. The first Can record came out on a tiny München label. All we wanted to do was make our ideas happen. If we happened to sell a few records as well, that was a stroke of luck. It was particularly difficult at the beginning. We always threw our money in together and each of us got a monthly wage, the same for everyone. We had to get by on that. We invested the rest in our equipment – tape recorders, speakers, a PA – for tax reasons alone. Irmin's wife Hildegard took care of it all; she used to be a personal assistant and she had a good head for business – the rest of us were bad businessmen, we only ever thought about music. Thanks to Hildegard, we never had financial problems. In the end we even had our own professional studio and a truck for touring. It's different for me now. When I'm on the road I've just got a little case with my drumsticks, and a snare drum with little cymbals. I borrow the rest from the organisers. And it always works out.

IRMIN SCHMIDT Commercial success was very welcome, but not important. We never did anything with the idea at the back of our minds that it had to be a hit. And I'd always take the mickey out of people who thought they knew what was commercial. I'd say to them: 'If you know so well what's commercial, how come you're not a millionaire?' I'd always have that discussion in München with the guys from Amon Düül. They were always going on about commercialism. But for people like the Beatles, that just happened. They didn't consciously make commercial music, they were catalysts of a zeitgeist that struck and suddenly made them the Beatles.

RENÉ TINNER Can didn't care about the commercial aspect. All right, there were a couple of songs that were meant to be successful, like 'I Want More'. It was recorded according to a certain plan, with a particular tempo.

LÜÜL We just made music without thinking about money. These days I wonder what we even lived on. We once went on tour in France and we had a budget of twenty francs a day, per head. Even a croque-monsieur cost four francs. But it always worked out somehow. You just slept on a sofa somewhere. We only had to make enough money to cover our van, for example, and things like that. But none of us made big bucks. The subject was way down our agenda. We lived from hand to mouth.

MOOG

'Violins don't grow on trees.'
KLAUS SCHULZE

HARALD GROSSKOPF We had a connection to Popol Vuh in München, who I was also supposed to play with. Florian Fricke called me up and said he'd heard I was free and did I fancy coming to München? Because Daniel Fichelscher, who played guitar and drums with them, couldn't always do both. I was interested and I liked their music, so I packed my stuff in my VW and chugged off down to München. Fricke had just sold all his electronic equipment he didn't want any more to Klaus Schulze, most notably his altarpiece, the 'big Moog'. Florian came from a wealthy family – his mother was an opera diva, his father was a famous jazz musician – and he had classical training; he was supposed to have a career as a pianist. But he didn't want to, and he was looking for new forms of expression on the Moog. Just as I got there, though, he went back to classical piano and acoustic instruments. They were playing this gentle melodic stuff at low volume. I couldn't deal with it at all – I was used to loud rock music. I left town again a few days later, and I was pretty sad about it.

KLAUS SCHULZE I started off only playing normal instruments, but as time went by it bothered me more and more that the sound was always the same, and all kinds of music were supposed to have fixed boundaries and rules. When the first ARP and Moog synthesizers came on the market, they meant I could not only compose my own music – I suddenly also had the freedom to choose and create my own sounds. An organ always sounds the same, but the early synths never did! The sound became more and more important to me, almost more

179

important than the music I could compose out of it. Electronic music opened up paths that I absolutely wanted to take. Buying the big Moog from Florian Fricke was the logical consequence.

HARALD GROSSKOPF For a lot of people at the time, synths were a nightmare. When I got friends to listen to the first Kosmische Kuriere sessions, they thought they were terrible [Rolf-Ulrich Kaiser's Kosmische Kuriere label ran a series of very stoned sessions involving a shifting group of musicians collectively termed the Cosmic Jokers; see below]. It was incomprehensible to me that they didn't like them. No one had ever heard of sequencers, so they were confused and rejected the music. I was one of the first people in the world to drum to sequencers. But you had to explain it to people first: they're machines where you can set the pitch level and pauses and patterns. 'Anyone can do it!' they'd say. 'It's artificial music!' Klaus Schulze used to say: 'Violins don't grow on trees, you know.'

JÜRGEN DOLLASE Klaus Schulze was an absolute zero on keyboards, in my view. It was incredible how bad he was. Making music with Schulze was always a problem for me. His tootling around had to be processed and concretised for the records – you couldn't have sold them otherwise.

HARALD GROSSKOPF Trenkler had played Schulze on his WDR show, and I just thought: 'Wow!' I didn't know how he did it but I was so enthusiastic that I went right ahead and wrote to him. He wrote back – we still wrote letters in those days – and told me to come by. In his basement, he showed me his big Moog, the exact same one he'd got from Fricke, which I'd just missed with Popol Vuh. I'd seen something like it before but never really experienced it in action. In any case, Schulze switched it on and I got goosebumps. The sequences grabbed me so hard I picked up a bucket and started drumming along spontaneously. And that got Schulze so fired up that he said we should definitely do something together.

KLAUS SCHULZE At the end of the day, that joy in experimenting with sounds was the dynamo that gave me my drive. There were no pre-set synthesizers in the seventies; they didn't come along until the mid-eighties. So it was actually impossible to find sounds again – for instance, the great sound from the previous night's gig. You just couldn't do it. You turned a knob a fraction of an inch and everything sounded different. So we twiddled the knobs from scratch every time until we liked what came out, and that had to do. Until that setting got lost again. I liked it, to be honest, because every night had its own special feeling, it sounded different every time, so you played differently as well. For me, that was the most interesting way to make music, because I was constantly surprising myself.

HARALD GROSSKOPF Electronic music put me on a huge high. The absolutely free and new side to it. I had to make that music and I knew it would be a success. I could only be a success, because it had so much energy.

KLAUS SCHULZE The audience noticed as well that it wasn't just someone playing by rote. But they didn't like it everywhere. We'd fill venues in France, but often in Germany only twenty people might turn up, and ten of them would leave pretty quickly. That didn't bother me much, though.

GERHARD AUGUSTIN Before I produced *Affenstunde* in 1970, the first Popol Vuh LP focused around the big Moog, I'd already made a soundtrack for a porn movie in San Francisco with Dave Brown from Santana, who had a small Moog. That meant I had an idea of all the possibilities a Moog synthesizer offered. In Germany at that time, only Eberhard Schoener and Florian Fricke had Moogs. Schoener had this synthesizer that Florian had seen at his place, and after that he wanted one of his own. But Schoener, who also ran the München Youth Orchestra, wasn't interested in what Florian was doing, even though they were nearby in Miesbach.

FRANK FIEDLER I met Florian through my work as a cameraman, through friends we had in common. We got on well and spent whole nights talking about politics and society. One of our many inexhaustible conversation topics was the sacred book *Popol Vuh*, which we'd both read. One aspect I was very interested in was that the K'iche' people had no terms in their language for 'future' or 'past'. Instead, they'd expanded their concept of the present so far that it included everything. That opening-up into the universal impressed us both. So at some point we got stuck on the name Popol Vuh. The debut LP *Affenstunde* was also inspired directly by the book; the title comes from a chapter near the beginning, part of the creation narrative about the initiation of the next generation, the 'Hour of the Monkey'. It fitted well with the openness inherent to working with a machine like the Moog.

GERHARD AUGUSTIN The big Moog cost DM65,000 at the time. Fricke had got it as a wedding present from his wife, who'd inherited a lot of money. I'd heard about it and asked friends to introduce us. Soon after that, Florian came over to my office. We gradually became friends and he ended up coming by often. For the people at the record label, though, he was a real alien with his long hair and weird look.

FRANK FIEDLER Sometimes he had a tendency to let himself go hygiene-wise, but that's what it's like in work phases – you can't always be a blow-dried beauty. Gerd was a department manager at United Artists. He took Popol Vuh under his wing and we were snapped up by Liberty. But we knew a few people at the company wouldn't be into us. It didn't bother us, though; all we wanted was one person to stand by us so the records got pressed.

GERHARD AUGUSTIN Florian was an earnest and introverted person. But he also had a big ego; he never saw anyone other than himself as part of Popol Vuh. For him, it was a solo project and all the others were guest musicians. That showed in the interviews he did as well. But he still always had good people, who certainly contributed something.

FRANK FIEDLER Popol Vuh wasn't a band in the usual sense; it rarely played in public. Popol Vuh was actually more of a studio project of Florian's. Even though various people were always part of it, some of them for a while longer, the impulse for the music always came from Florian.

GERHARD AUGUSTIN Florian wasn't one to put himself out there. He was still living in Harlaching, in a nice house on Ulmenstrasse. He had his synthesizer in the basement. It was basically four different-sized boxes with lots of cables to plug in between them. You had to know which frequencies you could modulate with which other frequencies, in which conjunctions. Florian tried to process human voices on the Moog. He played me how he imagined it, in his basement. Then I arranged for a spot on the TV show *Beat-Club*, where Popol Vuh performed the song 'Bettina', which helped a lot.

FRANK FIEDLER We could use the Moog to invent fantasy sounds. What we were doing was absolutely new at the time. We imagined what a drip falling in a limestone cave sounded like. We partly managed to make fantasies like that happen on the Moog; you just had to connect everything up the right way. But the Moog was also relatively unstable, and the voltage was always varying where we were working, in the countryside. When the voltage went down the lights in the house went darker and the Moog went down a quarter tone. So we preferred working in the daytime to the night. We'd go hiking between sessions to keep fit.

LIMPE FUCHS Fricke was practically in the same building, but we were very different, musically. We did our Anima thing in the separate servants' quarters – and they did their Popol Vuh thing in the big parsonage. The parsonage in Peterskirchen was actually meant for the bishops in Passau. When the bishops went to Rome they'd stop off in parsonages like that one, which were built especially for them 800 years ago so they'd be well looked-after on their journey. We had a stove and water from the well. People came and went, like [composer] Helmut Lachenmann or [photographer] Gunter Sachs. And the model Vera, who called herself Veruschka later, she lived there with [artist] Holger Trülzsch, but it wasn't a commune.

GERHARD AUGUSTIN We played *Affenstunde* to the production committee at Liberty. There were six of them and they thought it was terrible because they didn't understand it, not even the instrument, the Moog. They were completely out of touch with the culture. I was head of production at Liberty at the time and I came up against all sorts of resistance. And they just didn't want to release Popol Vuh, let alone spend any money on promotion. I said: 'This is the sound of the future!' And the others said: 'No!' Then we got into my VW bus – Florian, Frank Fiedler, Holger Trülzsch and me – and drove off overnight to find another record label. But while the negotiations were happening with others, the Liberty management changed and they did let me bring out *Affenstunde*, which I'd even co-financed. Florian and I were friends by then. There'd never been music like that in Germany. Sadly, we only sold 2,000 or so copies, partly because the record company wasn't on our side. They practically wanted to prove it couldn't be a success, they threw stones in our path whenever they could. It was sad. For Florian, it wasn't as bad as expected because he wasn't that crazy about commercial success; he already had money.

FRANK FIEDLER Then he had his Moog 3 in the house at Stadlberg, outside Miesbach where the mountains start. The rooms were huge, the Moog was set up in this enormous attic room. It was a 400-year-old farmhouse at the top of a hill, with a view of the Alps and the highlands. You could look down at the valleys as you played the Moog, with the

Alps looming behind them, which was obviously very inspiring. Even just the crazy play of light when the sun went up in the morning. That's where we started Popol Vuh and came up with the music. Technology doesn't really impress me, I don't worship at its altar, but that Moog was something special. I'd trained at Siemens and I was impressed by the machine's system. I worked out the technology pretty quickly – the modules were connected with jacks and it was easy for me to work out what corresponded with what. All right, all the different filter banks and interconnecting the individual oscillators was pretty complex. But we always had our own guidelines for the things we wanted to play, and also for Holger Trülzsch, our percussionist. We didn't have much studio equipment, just two Revox machines. Sometimes we did struggle with the Moog, of course; when we'd taken it into inaudible spheres it was hard to get it back to the original positions. So it stayed that way. And then we just unplugged it, let it cool down and plugged it back in. Then it was like new again. All in all, it was a joy to play around with it.

GERHARD AUGUSTIN Florian didn't care that Liberty didn't want to use its option for the next Popol Vuh album, *In den Gärten Pharaos*. He said he felt liberated. And he already had an offer from Rolf-Ulrich Kaiser to release it on Pilz.

FRANK FIEDLER At that time, we were thinking a lot about Buddhism. The cover of *In den Gärten Pharaos* comes from Indian Buddhism. The motif touched us, somehow. There was always a lot of discussion, and we'd drink a sip or two of wine. Florian and I could easily get stuck on one subject for two or three hours; it could get pretty deep. Florian was a bit lonely, too, despite his wife and children. He had to make all the decisions himself, for his art.

GERHARD AUGUSTIN Florian was very critical of himself and hesitated for a long time before he released anything. Feedback from the people around him was important to him as well. And he often changed the style of his music, from *Affenstunde* all the way to *Messa Di Orfeo*, which I call his 'bee record'.

FRANK FIEDLER Florian decided what went on the albums. He was a master composer and a very good pianist. The record company wasn't involved at all. We made the music entirely freely; we were really into what we did.

GERHARD AUGUSTIN Florian knew the film-maker Werner Herzog from the München scene. Actually it was Bettina, Florian's wife, who was friends with Herzog. Then when Herzog found out what kind of music Florian made, he went out to see him on Ulmenstrasse and listened to his stuff more closely. And if he liked something, he'd raise his finger and say: 'We'll take this one.' Later on, Florian played live to video recordings of Herzog's film scenes, improvising. For example, with *Aguirre*. What happened with *Nosferatu* was, Werner Herzog was working on the film in Rome but he didn't have any music for it yet. What he had wasn't working, so he flew Florian out to Rome and told him: 'I'd like music that scares people! Have a look at what you can find in your box of demos.' Florian always had a big box of unreleased music. Herzog listened until he said: 'That's it!'

FRANK FIEDLER Herzog and Florian had known each other since they were sixteen; they'd even once tried to make a film together. But it never got edited and it's probably lost now. Anyway, the two of them were friends. When Herzog needed new film music they'd talk for hours and hours. Then Florian would sit down at the piano and play something for Herzog. He was very familiar with Florian's music because they'd known each other so long, and he knew exactly what he wanted. When we made *Affenstunde*, *In den Gärten Pharaos* and *Hosianna Mantra*, they just sparked with Herzog. That's when he must have realised the music went well with his film work.

GERHARD AUGUSTIN I often put on Popol Vuh records to go to sleep at night. Florian found out and he told me once that it bothered him a bit. But listening to *Affenstunde* just makes me fall asleep, I'm afraid. Once I asked Florian why he always uses the same melodies in his music. He answered: 'Ask Mozart!'

ULRICH RÜTZEL People didn't yet understand things like Popol Vuh at the time, especially in the media. It was a bit of a coup, of course, that the music was part of a few of Werner Herzog's films. But people only started taking notice of Popol Vuh in Germany when interest came up in America and the UK, and people like Brian Eno talked about them. That hasn't changed, even now.

AMON DÜÜL

'We just wanted to make some noise!'
RENATE KNAUP

CHRISTIAN BURCHARD I've been friends with the Amon Düül drummer Dieter Serfas since I was ten. We did our A-levels together. Most of Amon Düül are from the Allgäu region, but Embryo is a Franconian band [Franconia and Allgäu are both in Bavaria]. There was a piano in some school camp or other that you were allowed to play. I tinkled away at it, Dieter drummed along on saucepans, and we were surprised to find the other kids liked it. It was so much fun we dived more and more into music. Then we discovered jazz, and things like flamenco and bossa nova as well.

DIETER SERFAS Jazz was the starting point for Amon Düül. Ornette Coleman and Don Cherry were our role models. All the krautrock apostles were actually jazz fans who went a step further. When the other kids in our generation started listening to the Beatles and the Rolling Stones, we stayed true to jazz. That's why our rock was so different, later on.

CHRISTIAN BURCHARD Dieter and I got in touch with Black musicians stationed as soldiers in Germany, when we were still quite young. There was a big US Army barracks in Hof, with loads of musicians running around. We met a bassist from Little Richard's backing band there. He was ten years older than us but he thought it was great we were so interested in Black music. And then we started a combo with all these Black guys. All the other kids our age ever listened to was Elvis. And they wanted to be Elvis themselves – you got the feeling there were

188

thousands of Elvis copies out there in Germany. They looked exactly like him, had the same guitar and played the same songs. And then when the real-life Elvis came to Germany as a soldier it took off even more. The Black soldiers weren't into Elvis, though – they listened to music I hadn't known before, the whole rhythm 'n' blues culture with gospel and jazz. When Dieter and I played music with them we got to know that repertoire, covered Chuck Jackson or copied James Brown, who was brand new on the scene back then. Anyway, the soldiers let us join their jazz band, which was already playing in München at that time. I first went on stage with them there in 1963.

CHRIS KARRER In the Allgäu, jazz was the most progressive thing you could imagine. We played in various Kempten Dixieland bands, and later modern jazz and free jazz. It was a kind of liberation. Other than that, there were the beginnings of rock 'n' roll with Elvis and so on. I was into that for a little while but then I switched to jazz and stuck to it until I was eighteen. There was a shop in Kempten that always had jazz records. What they didn't have, I'd get hold of in München. Later on, I met Falk Rogner and the Leopold brothers at boarding school. We had a free-jazz combo, must have been around 1963.

DIETER SERFAS Chris Karrer, Peter Leopold and Rainer Bauer were a boarding-school clique from Marktoberdorf. After they left school they all went to London and discovered first Hendrix and Pink Floyd, and then communal living. That was the groundwork for Amon Düül.

CHRISTIAN BURCHARD Once we'd done our A-levels in Hof, we got straight out of town. Dieter went to the art academy in München, where he met Chris Karrer.

RENATE KNAUP I was born in the Allgäu, in Sonthofen. My boyfriend at the time, a guy I went to vocational college with, was a friend of Chris Karrer and Peter Leopold, and that was how I met them.

Chris played flamenco guitar back then, and my boyfriend did too. And we all listened to jazz: John Coltrane, Don Cherry, Albert Ayler, the really wild stuff. We'd get the records in München. The crucial factor might have been that Peter and Chris went to school together in Marktoberdorf, about twenty kilometres from Sonthofen, and they had a gay art teacher there, Gerlach Bommersheim, who introduced them to art, music and technique. He was a wonderful man, made a name for himself later in the München scene.

CHRIS KARRER Bommersheim was a jazz musician as well, played vibraphone and piano. He encouraged us to start a jazz combo, but he had problems at the time, sadly, because he was gay and always had to hide it. When it got out at some point, he got thrown out of his teaching job.

CHRISTIAN BURCHARD I already knew the Amon Düül people back then. First Renate, Falk, Chris Karrer and Peter Leopold. John Weinzierl only joined later. Anyway, we played together even then, mostly free jazz because normal jazz was for squares.

DIETER SERFAS My drum kit was really loud, so we often went underneath the bridges across the River Isar to play. Chris Karrer would come along, and sometimes Christian Burchard. That was in 1966, before Embryo and Amon Düül started up.

RENATE KNAUP My father was very combative towards me. When I put a picture of John Coltrane up on the wall he flipped out; he was a bit of a racist. He tore the picture down, and I said: 'Dad, you can tear the pictures down as much as you like, it won't change anything. They're in my heart.' Other than that, I listened to Radio Luxembourg until it came out of my ears – Beatles, Animals, Stones and soul. I was sixteen and I had a slightly older boyfriend with a royal-blue Citroën 2CV. Back then Peter Leopold, Chris Karrer, Al Gromer and I would meet up down at the railway station, this desolate brain-dead spot in the Allgäu. There was a cake shop there, where we'd buy apple cake with ice cream and whipped cream. We had a battery-powered record player and we put it on the car's roof to listen to really loud jazz. Our mood was hanging out, zen, edelweiss, Jack Kerouac! And our message to the world: 'Hey, what do you stupid idiots want from us?'

CHRIS KARRER It all started for me with a Jimi Hendrix gig, 1967 in München. I went along by chance because I'd only ever listened to and played jazz before; I thought rock music was dull, and I said to myself: 'This Hendrix guy's a blues musician, I'll go and take a look.' I was a bit surprised by how many girls turned up in miniskirts. I didn't know them from the jazz clubs – the drab stinky-socks look was all the rage there. Anyway, at the Hendrix gig they'd set up amps all the way up the wall. And then this sound came out of them like I'd never heard before, at a volume I'd never experienced. After that performance I was a convert. In a matter of hours, I'd gone from a jazz musician playing soprano saxophone to a rock musician. A week later, I had an electric guitar and I'd given away all my jazz records. Then I went to London to take a closer look at the scene there.

ALEXANDER VON SCHLIPPENBACH Amon Düül played a kind of rock that people do when they've only just discovered it. They definitely learned it from Hendrix, but they made something of their own out of it.

CHRISTIAN BURCHARD Embryo played at Jimi Hendrix's very last gig, by the way, on the [Baltic] island of Fehmarn in September 1970, right after him. The festival was mainly sponsored by the sex-shop impresario Beate Uhse, although her sales stalls got smashed to a pulp at the end, like everything else there. It was a bit of an inferno, financially and in every other sense. But Hendrix's performance was great; there was no way of knowing he'd die so soon afterwards.

RENATE KNAUP I went to London as an au pair girl, at seventeen. My boyfriend was a draft-dodger who would have been called up in Germany. He went to England to get out of it, and I wanted to join him there. But I was only seventeen so I had to fight with my parents to go; I was constantly begging them to let me go to London. The sign of their permission was when I got a suitcase and a travel bag for Christmas. Then in February I took the ferry from Ostend to Dover. There was a real storm blowing, gale force eight, good grief! I stayed in London for a year and a half. My parents didn't have a phone in those days, so I just wrote occasional letters home. Germans got a bit of a cold shoulder in England, but I mainly hung out with young people in London, which was pretty easygoing. I worked in a Jewish club in the middle of Soho, right opposite the Marquee Club. That's where I saw the Kinks. My boyfriend was more interested in Indian stuff. He'd learned to play the sitar, and I once had the great honour of seeing Ravi Shankar in a living room, in front of ten people. He played after breakfast for a few friends. I've always been open for all music. When I was little in Sonthofen, we had a great pastor who went to a lot of effort to introduce us to music and dances from all over the world, and that was wonderful for me because I liked dancing. After I split up with my boyfriend I went back to Germany, and the first thing I did was see where the others had got to, Chris Karrer and so on. All I knew was that they were somewhere in München. In the end I found out they were living in this fancy five-bedroom apartment on Prinzregentenplatz. I went to see them, but they acted ultra-cool and said: 'What are you doing here?' I thought: 'You idiots,' and I left. But then they called me straight up and said: 'Why did you leave? Come on over.' I moved in there a couple of days later.

CHRIS KARRER We'd rented this huge flat in München in a fancy area and we were operating from there into the whole wide world. We got our parents to pay for it. A lot of us had parents with their own businesses, and my mother was very generous as well. Later on, it was her that enabled me to get the house in Herrsching. Someone once wrote that we were 'the juniors of the Mercedes generation' – that's not wrong; none of us earned any money at the time and we couldn't have afforded the flat ourselves. But at the same time there were lots of restaurants that wouldn't serve us because we looked too freaky. The old Nazi elite was still running around, especially in München. You'd get yelled at that you ought to be gassed. The more harmless of them just told us to get a haircut. But there were still plenty of that kind around in München. Our arch-enemy was the Bavarian conservative Franz Josef Strauss. He'd go into schools and give teachers a dressing-down. I once saw for myself how he laid into our Latin teacher. I was about twelve at the time and I didn't know left from right yet, politically. But after that I knew who Strauss was.

RENATE KNAUP I was part of the riots in München as well. But mostly I just watched, with Falk. I wasn't one to tip a car over, although I thought it was good that something was happening. Everything in Germany was so incredibly dull back then, like Dieter Thomas Heck with his horrific TV hit parade – that was new at the time.

CHRIS KARRER We soon got a rehearsal room for our sessions, because we were too loud for the flat. It was only two hundred metres away but walking there was like running the gauntlet, getting spat at and insulted. Once we had our own house later, things got better. We set up a practice room downstairs.

RENATE KNAUP München's just a shitty city because they've always killed off all subculture there. As soon as something manages to get bigger, the Bavarian state government immediately clubs it to death.

CHRIS KARRER At the very beginning, our music was pure hippy fantasy. We just wanted to get started somehow. Our role model was the Incredible String Band, alternative folk from England, and the bands Hapshash and the Coloured Coat and Art, with their album *Supernatural Fairy Tales*. We were still playing entirely acoustic, with Rainer Bauer on vocals, partly in German, plus the two Leopold brothers on bass and drums, and me. And out of that came Amon Düül – let's call it 'Amon Düül zero'.

RENATE KNAUP To begin with, Amon Düül was just a little gang of musicians. We were always playing and jamming, and we just realised along the way how much you can express and change with music.

DIETER SERFAS There was a great sense of life that washed over München – like over Hamburg and Berlin. You could see it in parallel in the film world; the Hof film festival started in 1967, and people like Fassbinder and Herzog were experimenting as directors. There was a sense of new beginnings in all the arts.

RENATE KNAUP One day, all fourteen of us in the commune did a trip together. Gerlach Bommersheim took care of us, he was our travel guide. He sat in the middle and we sat around him in a circle, and then we all took the trip at the same time. Beforehand, we'd been to a record shop on Leopoldstrasse and picked two records we didn't yet know. And we had this reverb machine that was in fashion at the time, which made a spherical, broader sound. We played the records through it and the sound was insane. One of the records was *Tanyet*, by a Californian band, the Ceyleib People. Their music had this Indian touch to it but it was also experimental, with vocals in between. Anyway, they had one track called 'Dyl', and that was what inspired our name. The men always said it had something to do with a god, but that's nonsense. It's about time we took the mystery out of it. Only 'Amon' was derived from the Egyptian god, and that fits because Chris was a pretty mystical and esoteric guy. He had a passion for Arab music and spent a while in Morocco; he was really into Egypt.

CHRIS KARRER I was the first one to give up LSD. I'd had some experience with it earlier, around the mid-sixties. I did about twenty trips and that was enough for me, for life.

RENATE KNAUP I hadn't taken any trips in London, we just smoked joints and ate hash cakes there; acid only came along in München. It was uplifting to sit in a circle because you felt this force, this sense of togetherness. It lasted about twelve hours. Falk Rogner sat next to me, who did all the Amon Düül cover art. After that trip I was with him for eight years; we didn't let each other go for a very long time. There were ups and downs, of course, pulling faces in the mirror, and then music again. Sometimes we just felt normal. That's what makes tripping so crazy: you zoom off and then you're back in the here-and-now for a moment. But I never took that many trips, it got too predictable for me. If I sit down with a flowerpot on acid, the flowers change and it does something to me, sure. A construct grows out of it, and perhaps you really do have an added experience compared to people who've never had that kind of insight. But I never saw anyone achieve anything creative on a trip, nothing that lasted.

CHRIS KARRER It just spooked me, people flipped out completely. We had to walk Peter around holding hands for a while because he wasn't capable of going anywhere on his own. There were a lot of LSD casualties. I only smoked hash then, never made music on acid; it's not possible to compose or write anything meaningful. The experience of tripping only flows into music indirectly, if at all. We were never LSD advocates, in any case, not a head band like the Grateful Dead.

RENATE KNAUP I wanted to be a singer and I had really beautiful songs in my head – but 'beautiful' in the normal sense, not the freaky stuff we produced at the beginning. We mainly improvised, or more like: everyone played whatever they wanted. If they even knew how to play their instruments properly! Anyway, all that was left for me was vocals, and I improvised those too. I used to sing in the church choir, and the choirmaster had always told me I was talented, so I had enough confidence to use my voice as an instrument and integrate myself into the band's sound.

DIETER SERFAS I first saw Amon Düül in the atrium at München Uni. They were a crazy bunch of noise-makers, unbelievable. It was still the original quartet at the core, ur-Düül, if you like, with the two Leopold brothers, Chris Karrer and Rainer Bauer. But the communards had gathered around them, women shaking their bodies, Uschi Obermaier banging the tambourine, loads of people tootling around. Watching them was pretty impressive because it was so free and had nothing in common with the usual rock beat.

RENATE KNAUP Then came the split between Amon Düül and Amon Düül II. And absurdly enough, it was the un-professionals, exactly the ones we thought were esoteric losers, who suddenly said: '*Auf Wiedersehen!* We're off to make music professionally!' That was what we actually wanted too, just not that fuzzy feel-good sound for the wellness oasis with birdsong and whatever – we wanted to make some noise! The final separation happened at the Essener Songtage.

CHRIS KARRER The whole commune gang always wanted to let all the women and children sing along – but I was dead set against it. It was unbearable in the long run, girls who'd never played parping around on the saxophone or jangling tambourines. And the men who absolutely couldn't play were just as annoying. It really rubbed me up the wrong way – it was so bad they chucked me out of the commune.

DIETER SERFAS He didn't get chucked out, he just left. Chris had always had his own flat anyway, he was never purely a commune guy. When I packed sandwiches for everyone on the road for our gigs, he'd say the whole boy-scouts feeling got on his nerves. Chris was always a loner, but it was him who brought the dramatic structure into Amon Düül II's music. When he learned guitar he wrote a song for every new chord he mastered. Chris Karrer shaped ninety per cent of the band's output.

CHRIS KARRER I was in bed at my mum's place for a few days; nervous breakdown. And that was where I had the idea for *Phallus Dei*. I composed the songs in bed and then gathered my own team around me: Renate, one of the Leopold brothers and a couple more. That's how Amon Düül II came to be. Then we rented a house in Herrsching on Lake Ammer and bought a van and equipment.

DIETER SERFAS At that time, I was sharing a rehearsal room with Chris in München. He was playing with the original Düül quartet, and I was with Christian Burchard and Mal Waldron. We all jammed together there now and then. I was playing jazz but I also liked modern stuff like Hendrix. Even before the Essener Songtage, he told me once Amon Düül was getting too much for him, he couldn't stand the women's jingle-jangling any more and he wanted to make proper music. Soon after that, he came to me and said we'd had some good jam sessions and I was his man. He wanted to start his own band, he said, and now he knew how to. We got on well, and apart from that I was impressed that he knew his way around the music of Ravi Shankar and Nusrat Ali Khan so well, so I said yes. Then he left Amon Düül and grouped his own people around him: John Weinzierl, Falk Rogner, Peter Leopold and me. That was the primeval soup of Amon Düül II. We all moved to Herrsching on Lake Ammer and spent ages looking for a new name. We almost called ourselves 'Sportsfreunde Herrsching', like an amateur football team, but then we stuck to Amon Düül, just 'mark II'.

GERHARD AUGUSTIN There were probably more than 120 musicians who called themselves Amon Düül over the years, because there was always a lot of rotation. But the hard core of Amon Düül is just Chris Karrer and Renate Knaup.

RENATE KNAUP We played at the PN-Hithouse on Leopoldstrasse every Monday. Peter Naumann was this great guy who had a basement bar there with a little stage, with a capacity of 250 at most. He booked people like Jimi Hendrix and Arthur Brown. He gave us a chance on Monday nights; he said: 'Monday's your night, you can play every week.' We all squeezed onto the miniature stage like sardines, five or six of us, but it didn't matter – the place was packed every Monday. And soon people would say: 'Amon Düül play there!' It was one of those places you just had to go to.

CHRIS KARRER All the British bands played on the weekends. We were the contrast act on Mondays. Word got around quickly, and by the end up to 400 people would turn up. We made it our principle to play something new every Monday, and we invited guests as well. Once we had a guy with a graveyard bell on stage; he had a naked woman with him, stuck a finger up her bum and dinged the bell. And we had our own light show. There were at least six of us, sometimes as many as ten people on that tiny stage: apart from me there were usually two drummers, Renate on vocals, Falk on the keyboard and a bassist.

GERHARD AUGUSTIN Wim Wenders filmed one of their gigs back then.

WIM WENDERS I often saw Amon Düül in their early days, and I went to their legendary concerts, like at the München art academy. I visited the band several times out at their commune as well, and then John Weinzierl appeared in two of my films, *Alabama* and *Summer in the City*.

CHRIS KARRER We never had a band leader, we were a kind of communist party where everyone had the same rights and we earned the same money. A lot of American and British musicians didn't understand how it could possibly work. But we never had problems over authority. Weinzierl and I wrote the songs, like in the Beatles. To this day, each of us gets the same amount.

RENATE KNAUP We absolutely did not have equal rights. I had to fight so hard, it was really brutal. Peter Leopold was my special favourite, he could say things like: 'You don't have a say, you don't even have A-levels.' Thankfully, the other men would stand up for me, but it was still sometimes really, really terrible and disgusting for me. When *Yeti* came out, with my breakthrough track 'Archangels Thunderbird', I really had to fight for my rights. And in other cases, too, the melodies often came from me. They'd give me the half-finished piece, and I'd improvise to it until I had a hook-line. And on the very complex 'Thunderbird' it was my melody as well. But John Weinzierl claims he wrote it. I've never seen a penny in royalties for it.

CHRIS KARRER Once we got arrested by the police in France, because we'd taken a ride in a dealer's car. When the gendarmes realised we had nothing to do with the deals they let us go, but before that they shaved our heads. So we got back to München without our long hair, it was all gone. It was a freezing-cold New Year's Eve and we bought wigs so our heads wouldn't get too cold. So the next Monday at the PN club we had these wigs on, and a week later our fans all turned up in wigs as well; they thought it was the next big thing.

RENATE KNAUP A couple of metres on from the PN club there was a great record-store woman, Irmgard Weigelt, really bright and interested. People kept turning up there and asking if she had any Amon Düül II records. But there weren't any, of course. So she collected signatures of people who'd buy an Amon Düül II record if there was one.

Once she'd got more than a thousand signatures Olaf Kübler got wind of it, and he smelled blood. He suddenly turned up in Herrsching and acted like a manager, and he had the contact with Siggi Loch. From then on there were always seven of us at appointments for contracts and that kind of thing. Imagine it: seven crazy cats at the negotiating table with the suits. They'd never seen anything like it. They almost went mad.

STEFAN MICHEL Gerd Augustin was one of the few people to recognise that an autonomous rock scene was forming in Germany. And he wanted to be part of it.

GERHARD AUGUSTIN The Americans helped finance Amon Düül II. The anglophone media had got wind that German underground bands were doing exciting things. In the end, we handed the group DM250,000. And rented the house in Kronwinkl for them, which cost another DM4,000 a month. It was a huge mansion but it soon stank of cat shit, unfortunately, because John Weinzierl was so into cats that he kept a few too many of them in his room. The others got pissed off about the stench, obviously.

DIETER SERFAS We recorded *Phallus Dei* live in two days. We'd already played the tracks on stage, so we knew them well enough. We just played them all the way through once, and then we did a second take. It's a live record in the end, recorded in two takes over two days. On the day after that we did overdubs. Christian Burchard came along with his vibraphone and Chris did a bit of tambourine-jangling on top, all without multitrack technology.

GERHARD AUGUSTIN *Phallus Dei* was made in two days in the Trixi Studio in München. And it's those early, musically chaotic albums that are the classics these days.

SIGGI LOCH I was twenty-six in 1968 and I'd just started my job as founding managing director at the Liberty label in München. One of my main tasks was to find pop artists for the German market. I somehow came across Amon Düül II, probably via their producer Olaf Kübler. I came more from the jazz and rhythm 'n' blues direction, but I was impressed by Can and Amon Düül II and I decided to make them the promotion and distribution focus for new rock music at the young Liberty Records. We took on *Phallus Dei* as a finished LP; it had been rejected somewhere else before us.

GERHARD AUGUSTIN It was utter chaos, nothing was organised. There were various different people claiming to be the band's manager. Olaf Kübler ended up taking care of the chaotic kids and representing them. We were interested as a record company, because we saw the whole German press getting into the band, this 'new thing' out of München. When I was still living in Los Angeles in 1969, Lee Mandel, the international president of United Artists, showed me a copy of *Phallus Dei* and asked me: 'Gerhard, what do you know about this band?' And all I could say was: 'Nothing.' At United Artists, they put their money on Amon Düül more than Can, probably partly because their manager at the time, Olaf Kübler, had everything tied up. Siggi Loch didn't even know at the beginning that there was Amon Düül and Amon Düül II. Amon Düül was the political faction, they'd moved to Berlin and couldn't actually play. Amon Düül II were the musicians, though, and the hard core knew each other from their boarding-school days in Kempten. No one at Liberty even knew they'd split up. One day Siggi Loch called Kübler and said: 'Hey, Olaf, did you know there's another band calling themselves Amon Düül in Berlin?' That's how our group became Amon Düül II. But it was a stupid situation – all of a sudden there were two underground bands with the same name, and of course the media got confused.

RENATE KNAUP The contract gave us a whole different push, but it also raised our expectations of ourselves. Now it wasn't just ourselves we had to prove it to; it was the whole world! It was a new kind of pressure.

GERHARD AUGUSTIN The record company financed the group's entire life.

RENATE KNAUP It might have been wiser to sign with a smaller label or set up our own company from the start. But maybe we just didn't have the courage. Getting signed by a major label is a pretty good pat on the back. The press guy there at the time was Gerhard Augustin, who later became our manager. I never read contracts; I can't do it, even now. And I don't care anyway. But a lot of things went wrong for us because of contracts. All in all, we must have been tricked out of a quarter to half a million.

SIGGI LOCH For the next album, *Yeti*, I went along to the studio because I thought the music was so interesting, and I helped a bit with the production. The recording situation was extremely exotic. I was familiar with excessive drug consumption from jazz, but I'd never seen it done so openly. It was interesting to see how long it took them, how many 'pipes' they had to smoke before they were all on the same level above the Earth. It took hours. Peter Leopold sometimes wasn't even capable of playing for long periods. But once they got there, they played divinely. It was a new and unusual experience for me. I didn't join in the drug sessions, though; back then I was still a big fan of alcohol. I only had the occasional toke on a joint, which sometimes made me feel rather isolated at the sessions. But I really wanted to be there while the music was made so I could intervene and say what we'd take and what not; it was purely about the music for me. And I still consider *Yeti* the best Amon Düül album.

CHRIS KARRER Siggi Loch was a nice art appreciator who didn't intervene much. Good recordings were important to us. Even for *Phallus Dei*, we had one of the best studios in München, like we did later – always the best studios with the best engineers. It did cost us a whole lot of money, though.

SIGGI LOCH They had a clear vision of what they wanted and what they didn't want. But I still sometimes tried to exert a gentle influence, without imposing my wishes on them. We recorded huge amounts of material and then cut it together later. I don't think any of the tracks came out on the record the way it was recorded; *Yeti* is ultimately a collage, but with an incredible number of amazing moments.

RENATE KNAUP When I played *Phallus Dei* to my father he lost his rag: 'That's not music!' But then when word got back to the Allgäu about our success, he'd show off to his drinking buddies: 'See, I always knew it, that's my lass . . .'

SIGGI LOCH When I started as head of WEA in 1971, the then-manager of Amon Düül came to see me and asked if I could help the band make it big in the US, and then they'd switch to Warner. I was in New York soon afterwards and I played them to Jerry Greenberg, the president of Atlantic Records. He just looked at me, dumbfounded, and said: 'Are you crazy or something?' So I went back and told the band I was terribly sorry but I couldn't do anything for them in the US for the time being. But I would guarantee full European distribution for them. That wasn't enough for them, so we didn't make a contract. Six months later, the same Amon Düül manager flies to New York and meets the same Jerry Greenberg and sells the same album for a $50,000 advance. Greenberg didn't want it from me; he wanted to sign them himself, play the big discoverer! That same man also turned down the Scorpions from me, by the way.

CHRIS KARRER It was important to us that the records were a commercial success. If you're entirely idealistic, music's just a hobby. That's nice if you can afford it, but we had to live off our music. At some point our parents were dead or no longer prepared to support their children. When we got our first GEMA fees for performance rights, we treated ourselves to proper guitars and a van, and went shopping for equipment in London. It's all so expensive. The way things developed financially was a good thing for us, with the international tours and contracts.

STEFAN MICHEL In Paris, we had a fabulous line-up: first the Groundhogs, then Amon Düül and then Hawkwind last of all. But the people from Olympia didn't really want the bands inside the hallowed four walls of their venue, you could tell straight away. They thought they weren't worthy, so they closed two of the bars at the back of the hall, which meant everyone crowded around the bar at the front. And they started pushing and shoving because it took ages to get a drink. Because everyone was so crowded together, it was hard for people to get into the hall, and the moment the Groundhogs went on stage the riot kicked off. A few people started ripping up the seats, the nice padded rows of seats were just ripped out and all hell broke loose. The Düüls were supposed to go on second but they were all scared and didn't want to go out there. All sorts of stuff was getting thrown on stage. At some point Lothar Meid just said: 'Fuck it!' and went out and played a bass line that really hit home, and the first time a chair came flying at him, he chucked it right back. That was exactly what the people wanted, and it turned into a really good gig – the whole hall was floating on air! And after that they got Hawkwind – you couldn't get better than that. Then again, the Olympia manager had called in the Garde Nationale and they soon surrounded the whole place, itching to arrest everyone and beat them up. The Olympia staff wanted to get us out of there quick, but we refused because we knew it would be a bad move, health-wise. We waited until things had calmed down. In the end it was great PR for us. The press was really into it and ran lots of big stories.

A.R. & MACHINES

'Suddenly it went: dabadada dabadada dabada!'
ACHIM REICHEL

FRANK DOSTAL At the beginning of the seventies, Reichel and I were broke. We'd spent all our money on the Star-Club, we were completely skint and we were several hundred thousand marks in debt. But we just wanted to make music, even though that wasn't the sensible thing to do. At some point we worked out that our stuff was best when we liked it ourselves. I've never been able to imagine what other people like. And I think Achim was similar. Usually, I'd write lyrics for other people, and I'd always wonder what it would sound like if such-and-such a person sang it, how my words fit to their voice and what their face looked like singing them. But I never spent much time thinking about whether something might be successful. I've never understood what makes a hit, not in all my life. The only thing clear to me was that the music we'd been making up to then, with the Rattles and Wonderland, had burned out for us by that point.

HANS LAMPE There was a scene in Hamburg where a lot of people went along to little places at night to jam, especially on Grosse Freiheit and Pferdemarkt. Achim Reichel often came along. Ritchie Blackmore even came once, at Christmas 1968; he was living in Hamburg and he just joined in. There was this general mood of wanting to make music differently. Once Achim Reichel and Frank Dostal had taken over the Star-Club I often used to head over there. Bands like Taste and Black Sabbath played there, three or four nights in a row, a few sets a night. I worked behind the bar, and that was how I met Achim and Frank. One day, Achim took me along to the studio when they were recording

A.R. & Machines' *Die grüne Reise*, with Conny Plank on the mixing desk, and that's where I met him.

NIKEL PALLAT Achim came from beat music but he was always looking out for contemporary forms of expression. He's not an intellectual who reflects endlessly on himself; he just gets down to it.

ACHIM REICHEL At that time I also started listening to different music, like Ravi Shankar – wow! I saw him play at the Musikhalle and I almost sank into the ground in awe. That massive clunky instrument, the sitar, and then he starts playing at a tempo that makes you think: 'That's not possible!' There were three of them and not a note out of place. Incredible. That's where we learned that music can be more than a three-minute single. Space! Room to breathe! A revelation! It was a liberation from the whole copying thing as well. With A.R. & Machines, we noticed we were offering people something they'd never heard before.

FRANK DOSTAL Achim discovered a really unique echo effect on a tape machine and soon noticed he could play together with the machine; these repeats offered entirely new possibilities. For example, he could jazz his solo voice up into a whole choir. Nowadays anyone can use sampling technology to do that, but he was the first one to really make music using that effect. It quickly took on a life of its own, and especially after consuming certain substances, completely new dimensions opened up, entire universes where you'd race through at warp speed and experience things that truly impressed you. It's a miracle that Achim was still capable of playing his guitar with the machine, under the circumstances, but he's one of the best rhythm guys I know.

ACHIM REICHEL Before '68, we thought just writing our own songs was something special, even if they came across stylistically like Beatles tracks, like in the Rattles. I was looking for something of my own and

I came across echo. Completely by chance – I'd just pressed the wrong button when I wanted to record something else entirely. But suddenly it went: dabadada dabadada dabada. It sounded fun and I thought: 'Hey! What's that? Wow!' I added a second vocal, then a second guitar, all in the rhythm of the echoes, and I thought it was amazing! It just tended to be annoying for drummers, because it wasn't them setting the rhythm any more, it was the machine echo. But that experience of playing a guitar that sounds like ten guitars – it was irresistible. We immediately started playing sessions with the new sound.

HANS LAMPE What Achim did there was an expression of a shared perception, far removed from all traditional song structures. He jettisoned the usual scheme – intro–verse–bridge–chorus–verse–bridge–chorus–fadeout – and instead he let the music flow freely, and that was great. It was just a case of playing and listening to what happened, and that would take you to completely different results. At most, you'd ask: 'Are we playing in D or E?' That was the beginning of experimental music in Hamburg. It's just that no one understood that at the time; it was too soon. The people at Polydor must have been expecting something else; Achim Reichel was well known, just with a different kind of music, and at that time he didn't want any more to do with the Rattles and Wonderland.

ACHIM REICHEL Because it was so new, we took it pretty slowly, only met up occasionally at the studio, had a joint or two and let the mood take us, saw what happened. There wasn't yet a plan to make records out of it. But it was the time of so-called progressive music, after all, and hair and solos were getting longer. Then I happened to mention the sessions to someone at Polydor and he asked me if there was anything he could listen to. So I played him a few echo things, and he liked them. Polydor had just set up a new branch for progressive music. They didn't actually know what 'progressive' was supposed to mean – as long as it was unusual in some way. So the Polydor man says:

'Achim, it sounds interesting. How long would you need for an album of this music?' They always had the studio costs in mind. I said: 'It'd definitely take me three days.' And he asked if I hadn't meant thirty days. No, only three. So he said: 'OK, I'll pay for it!'

FRANK DOSTAL The first idea was: let's just record something. But at some point, we worked out that something was missing, because it was purely instrumental. No one can stand pure machine music, we thought. That led to me suddenly sitting there and having to think what kind of lyrics would even fit. There were no verses and choruses any more, so I let go of that structure and concentrated entirely on the words' sounds and associations. Having sung myself was an advantage, since it meant I knew what's singable and what's less so, but also that it's good for something to sound a bit 'wonky' now and then. I remember the line 'Thin is the skin of ecstasy' – the sound's the thing! You don't ask yourself what it might mean until later, if at all. It's certainly not a treatise on ecstasy; it's all far from any logic, purely about the word sound. All right, here and there I did say the odd thing I wanted to get off my chest. But I didn't intend to write a political thesis. And least of all with A.R. & Machines. Most people aren't interested in the meaning anyway, especially in Germany – they're into the sound of the words, at most.

ACHIM REICHEL On *Die grüne Reise* I thought: 'Symphonies can go on for whole records, so why shouldn't I do it too?' There were already a couple of international rock bands doing tracks that took up all of one side. These days, though, I wonder where we got the courage to do it. We were already in a good place, we'd made good money with the Rattles. Thankfully, I didn't realise I was on dangerous territory, risking my reputation because it didn't fit my image. It was just too exciting. The marketing crap, all the 'Where's the target group? How big is it? How do we reach them?' – none of it mattered! The music is good. Full stop. If you get it, you're welcome, and if you don't . . . you need a bit more time.

HANS LAMPE For *Die grüne Reise* I made howling wind noises in the studio with a hosepipe.

ACHIM REICHEL *Die grüne Reise* was actually a success with critics, as it turned out.

FRANK DOSTAL They released two tracks as singles even, and they did quite well on the radio, to our great surprise, even though they were completely unsuitable, structure-wise.

ACHIM REICHEL Polydor wanted a second record quickly at least. So we did two for them in one, a double album, and then came a legendary listening meeting: the Polydor people sat there, listened to our over-hour-long opus *Echo* – and were speechless. They didn't even know where they were at the end. At some point the Polydor man Karl Faust piped up: 'Well, Herr Reichel, it's all very interesting, but does it really have to be in the same key all the way through? It's not one song, is it?' They genuinely thought I was taking the mickey. Apart from that they went on about how I'd been such a teen-pleaser just recently. 'And now you want to be taken seriously all of a sudden?' George Harrison once put it like this: 'Of course we wanted to make money, a lot of money, fast. But once that had worked out, we asked ourselves why we actually wanted to make music.' It was like that for us. We didn't earn as much money as them, obviously, but once it started working, you did ask yourself how you wanted to go on. The worst thing that can happen to you in this business is cynicism, when you tell yourself: 'OK, the masses are dumb, they just want to sing along to a nice groove.'

FRANK DOSTAL Despite not understanding us, the record-company people we dealt with did show great respect for our work, ultimately. *Echo* came out on Polydor, a gatefold double album. After all, they were used to new things happening all the time in so-called pop music, things they didn't understand to start with. But sometimes they understood them pretty quickly, sometimes even while something was being made. It could be pretty inspiring. Back then, people still talked about music, not just about marketing plans, full-page ads and that kind of crap.

ACHIM REICHEL We were at this party once, we'd all taken something or other, and all of a sudden there was this ancient old man sitting around, in a turban with a brooch on the front of it. It seemed a bit strange to me. Anyway, then the guy puts on my *Die grüne Reise*, leaps up with his turban and starts doing these crazy pirouettes. After a while he sat down next to me, out of breath, and said it was outstanding music, he'd listened to it back in the 1920s. He was an old dancer from the state opera. Those were pretty crazy times.

FRANK DOSTAL All in all, the *Echo* stuff wasn't that unsuccessful, even though we'd been used to different reactions up until then.

ACHIM REICHEL We played with Rory Gallagher and Taste at the Musikhalle. And in the Hamburg municipal park we hung speakers for the echo effects in the hedges. They thought I'd lost my marbles.

HANS LAMPE It was very varied; sometimes we'd play in front of three people in a hall in Lower Saxony, and shortly after that at a festival in the Ernst-Merck-Halle for a crowd of 6,000. We always played the whole thing whatever happened, that was the concept. A piece lasted forty minutes, never mind how people reacted. But the 6,000 were completely blown away, cheering and clapping so hard it surprised even us. It was incredible. We even played an encore, which wasn't usually done at festivals at the time. People were amazingly open for that kind of thing. It was just the records that didn't do as well, sadly.

ACHIM REICHEL I stayed true to it until 1975 and made a total of six records; the last one was called *Erholung*. But at some point, I thought

I'd probably end up alone with the music. The people I'd have liked to get recognition from all ducked and dived, and that sadly spelled the end of it for me. A.R. & Machines was a great phase, I got really into it and gave my statements, but I had to go on with my life. Especially with my music, if possible. So I took another radical step with my shanties album. And then I produced a lot of stuff in that direction, [the bands] Ougenweide [and] Novalis and that kind of thing, and [the singer] Kiev Stingl as well. These days, people see Ougenweide as prophets of medieval rock. Back when I met them they were still covering Fairport Convention. I said to them: 'Play [the *Minnesänger*] Walther von der Vogelweide instead' – a nice bit of medieval German poetry.

FRANK DOSTAL A few years later, a journalist from Australia sent me a review out of the blue, going into my lyrics on *Die grüne Reise* in immense depth. There were always particular appreciators of the music, especially in the UK, France, Italy, America and Japan, but there've been more and more of them in the past few years.

NEW PATHS

'I wanted total liberation.'
SUZANNE DOUCET

ASMUS TIETCHENS I discovered Neue Musik on the radio. First on WDR, then from the mid-fifties on NDR. The two stations were keen to report on what was happening in Köln, in the Köln Studio for Electronic Music – once a month, which was a great deal, compared to the fact that only Deutschlandradio reports on that kind of music these days.

LIMPE FUCHS As a sixth-former, I visited Josef Anton Riedl's new Siemens studio in München in 1960. That was my first impression of electronic music, of the possibilities electronics offer for generating and varying sounds.

SUZANNE DOUCET For me, the cassette recorder was like an instrument I could use to do anything I liked. My sister inspired me; she and I just started recording things: I played guitar and recorded that, went to the funfair and recorded it, went to Prague and recorded the sounds there.

WOLF SEESSELBERG In the mid-sixties my younger brother Eckart was living in Hamburg and I was in Düsseldorf. Whenever I visited, we'd sit down and experiment with the electronic devices he was developing. Eckart was constantly working on his synthesizers, so they were never really finished, but that produced more and more new possibilities for experimenting.

212

ASMUS TIETCHENS Those night-time electronic music programmes and similarly ambitious radio shows interested me – I was about eleven – for a very simple reason: I'd just started at grammar school and I thought to myself: 'It's a higher school, so I have to take an interest in higher things.' At twelve, I walked around toting a paperback of Camus' *The Myth of Sisyphus*; I didn't have the slightest idea what it was about. All I knew was that it was important somehow. It was exactly the same with the outrageous music broadcast on the radio at night: I pretended to understand it. Karlheinz Stockhausen's *Gesang der Jünglinge* left a lasting impression on me, as did Gottfried Michael Koenig's *Funktion Grün*. I've forgotten many of the artists' names whose music I heard there, sadly, but I have a lot of it still in my head. Of course, I didn't understand a thing. But I was all the better at showing off with names and words I'd picked up, because the people around me understood even less. It might not have impressed the girls, but a few of the other boys at my school were a bit in awe of me. At any rate, that was the original reason why I took an interest – a pretty base motive, but never mind. I didn't actually like the sounds at all, to begin with – I was really into other things. I only paid serious attention to Neue Musik after I turned eighteen.

LIMPE FUCHS I owe my helpful knowledge of music development to the conservatory, from Schönberg to the equality of sounds. Thanks to that knowledge, I was far better able to integrate Paul Fuchs into my work, the sculptor who was so interested in making music with me. But he wasn't traditionally familiar with an instrument, so we tried out material together. Sounds have always been particularly interesting for me. Even as a child, I'd nag my father to turn the radio dial so I could listen to the shortwaves.

SUZANNE DOUCET I produced a feature for Bavarian radio in 1966. They gave me a NAGRA, a portable audio recorder. I went out with it and interviewed children for a project about children's songs. That mobile recorder was such a liberation; it meant I could record independently of a studio, by myself. And then my recordings could have effects added, in the studio. You were always your own producer. At my first TV shows as a singer, the cameras interested me more than my own performance. I was soon editing films and learning sound engineering in a studio. I was very interested in the technical side. That's when I had my first 8mm camera as well. So I recorded things for three months, at home, outside, wherever, whatever came along. Then we somehow spliced it all together. Some of it was reel-to-reel tape, some of it was cassette recordings, and TV clips as well. At home, I added other things with the tape machine. The process took several months. After that I put the best parts together and edited a collage out of the entire material. It was such a lot of work back then! But it was an adventure.

WOLF SEESSELBERG My brother and I were born in Hamburg. Eckart was twelve years younger. Our father was the orchestra leader at the Hamburg State Opera and Philharmonic, which gave me early access to the opera rehearsals. At eighteen, in 1959, I started studying under Teo Otto, the professor of stage design at the state art academy in Düsseldorf. The stage design class only had five students to begin with. After six months, we were travelling to major theatres as assistants to our famous professor; Otto had up to eight premieres a month at that time. In the early sixties I was his assistant at the Hamburg State Opera, when the composer Rolf Liebermann was artistic director there and working on his *Les Echanges* symphony for sixteen typewriters and other office machinery. Otto had designed the sets for the world premiere of the first space opera, *Aniara* [based on a book-length 1950s Swedish poem by Harry Martinson]. The Swedish composer Karl-Birger Blomdahl had composed it for an orchestra, but he also provided various tapes with celestial sounds and recordings of ultra-shortwave noises from the radio, which I found extremely inspiring. Almost at the same time, I was experimenting at the Düsseldorf academy with blank film, painting directly onto the film material, sticking sugar on it or piercing it with a sewing machine. The result was abstract films without a camera; I'd have liked to have given them an equally abstract soundtrack but I couldn't see any way to do so, for the moment. As it happened, my brother [Eckart] was looking at constructing walkie--talkies, which was still banned at the time [by the Allies until 1949 in West Germany; until 1953 in the GDR]. He secretly presented his latest creations in our parents' attic in Hamburg, but he saw the ambient noise they produced, the crackling, rattling and whistling, as a defect that had to be fixed. Those sounds reminded me of *Aniara*, though, so I asked my brother whether he could isolate the 'defects' for me. And he could. That was the start of our excursion into the electronic sound cosmos.

ASMUS TIETCHENS At the age of ten, I'd already heard you could make music without instruments and only needed a tape machine and a microphone, plus scissors and glue. At fifteen I had that equipment, so I cut up a strip of tape, put the snippets in a box, shook it and then stuck them all back together randomly. The upshot sounded very interesting! My first planned work with tape, carried out deliberately based on an idea, is from 1965. The piece still exists. My plan was very simple: I had a tape machine with three tape speeds and the possibility to record over an already used track without deleting it. That's what I did; first I clanged around on tin cans and saucepans and then I played it back at half speed. It sounded completely different. Then I recorded something else over the top, at normal speed! I played the whole thing back at triple speed. I spent a whole afternoon on it, and the result was seven minutes long. And I realised I could use a tape recorder and microphone as tools to do anything I wanted.

LIMPE FUCHS My father didn't want me to study free piano as my major, so I was forced to study violin and harmony theory and com-position and conducting, and so on. That's how I came to appreciate the diversity of Béla Bartók's rhythms. My maternal grandmother was

Slovenian, so free rhythm structures come naturally to me. The most important thing for me, though, was that I bought a snare drum at the conservatory after I saw it advertised on a noticeboard in 1963, and after that I played in a girl band. After that brief excursion I got myself a drum kit, with bass drum and hi-hat and so on. It was a beat band, covering the Beatles and that kind of thing. Paul [Fuchs] played his new-built horn on 'Yellow Submarine' and blew everything away. That was when I gave myself the name Limpe, my own invention. But after a show, a linguistics scholar came up to me and said he knew where my first name came from, said it was of Celtic origin: a Celtic water goddess. And there's a place called Limpach near where my son lives.

SUZANNE DOUCET I'd gone out into the world with my tape recorder. And I already knew the music business through my schlager records. My third LP, *International*, was produced by Siggi Loch for Liberty in 1969, when he was already working with Can and Amon Düül. But the actual origin of Zweistein's music was neither the tape recorders nor my previous pop career – it was down to my first experiences with drugs and my first LSD trips. After those experiences on acid, I wanted to do something completely removed from what I'd recorded as a schlager singer. I wanted total liberation.

WOLF SEESSELBERG At first my brother built various small modules in soap tins with switches or knobs that made different noises and sounds but couldn't be combined. He'd worked out very quickly what I was looking for, and then he caught the bug as well. He pulled all the modules apart and put them together on one circuit board, and over the next two years that grew into his first synthesizer, which we used to make sound for my films in the mid-sixties. Once they'd been shown in 1965, there were a lot of enquiries, including about the sound. By that point I was a lecturer for the Düsseldorf academy's stage-design class, and later I led the class on theatre and film. Our first synthesizer had about a hundred switches and knobs, which could be combined with

At the Internationale
Essener Songtage in 1968:
Johannes 'Buschi'
Niebergall, Peter
Brötzmann, Willem Breuker
(photo by Krista
Brötzmann)

Asmus Tietchens, 1981
(photo by Kim Suprare;
© Bureau B/SKY)

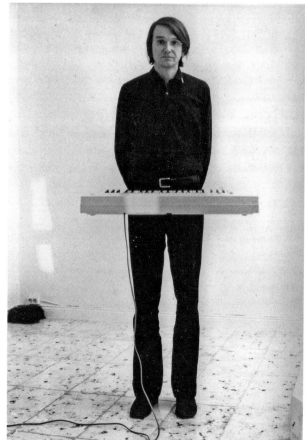

Tangerine Dream, 1970: Klaus Schulze on drums, Conrad Schnitzler on synthesiser and Edgar Froese on guitar (photo by Wilfried Bauer)

Michael Hoenig, Berlin, 1972 (photo by Hans-Georg 'Putti' Losse; from Michael Hoenig's personal archive)

Cluster: Hans-Joachim
Roedelius and Dieter
Moebius, 1971/72
(photographer
unknown; © Bureau B)

Thomas Kessler, 1974
(photographer
unknown; from
Thomas Kessler's
personal archive)

Tangerine Dream, Peter Baumann, 1972 (photographer unknown; from Peter Baumann's personal archive)

Frank Fiedler and Florian Fricke with their Moog-3 synthesiser, Peterskirchen, 1970 (photo by Bettina Fricke)

A.R. & Machines, Achim Reichel, British-German Pop Meeting in the
Ernst-Merck-Halle, Hamburg, 18 September 1971 (photo by Hans-Jürgen Dibbert)

Wolf and Eckart Seesselberg with two home-made synthesisers, 1972/73 (photographer
unknown; from Wolf Seesselberg's personal archive)

Limbus 4 at the German Jazz Festival in Frankfurt am Main, March 1970 (photo by Wilfried Bauer)

Christian Burchard of Embryo, early seventies (photographer unknown; from Marja Burchard's personal archive)

Faust singing in Wümme, 1970/71 (photographer unknown; from Hans-Joachim Irmler's personal archive)

Jean-Hervé Peron of Faust, Wümme, 1971 (photo by Gunther Zint)

Faust gig at Musikhalle
Hamburg, November 1971
(photo by Heinrich Klaffs)

Irmin Schmidt (photographer
unknown; from the Spoon
Records archive)

Poster from the second Guru Guru tour, with Xhol Caravan and Tangerine Dream, August 1969 (photo by Mani Neumeier)

Holger Czukay and Damo Suzuki in the studio in Schloss Nörvenich, early seventies (photographer unknown; from the Spoon Records archive)

Holger Czukay, Jaki Liebezeit, Michael Karoli, Irmin Schmidt (photo by Mick Rock; from the Spoon Records archive)

Michael Rother and Klaus
Dinger (photo
© Thomas Dinger)

Ulrich Rützel (photographer
unknown; from
Ulrich Rützel's personal
archive)

A session with the Kosmische Kuriere, early seventies (photographer unknown; from Jürgen Dollase's personal archive)

each other. That made the device comparatively easy to use at concerts, without endless cable connections and plugs. Our first performances were mostly improvisations on various sound sequences in 1967, at places like the Düsseldorf art academy, the Fabrik in Hamburg, in various Köln galleries and in London's Gallery House. In Düsseldorf we'd sometimes meet up with Conrad Schnitzler and play together – across three rooms – with our very different set-ups. And Joseph Beuys always liked coming over. He's an artist I really admire who was omnipresent in those years; he didn't have any influence on our work, though.

ASMUS TIETCHENS My friend Okko Bekker went to India at the end of the sixties like so many people, got jaundice there like so many people, and ended up spending four months in hospital, where he learned how to play basic sitar. He had enough cash with him to hire a teacher who showed him how to play. When Okko got back to Hamburg a year later, he had his sitar with him. Then he got the opportunity to take part in a professional record production with his sitar, which was very much in demand as an instrument at the time. He didn't get paid in money; he got a synthesizer. That was in 1971, when electronic instruments were out of our league, financially. The first synthesizer you could seriously save up for was the Minimoog, and that cost around DM3,000–4,000. And that's what Okko got as his payment. So I suddenly had access to a synth. Working with him was always fun anyway, and very productive. And now we had a synthesizer as well!

LIMPE FUCHS I met Paul after a school trip, when I'd just turned eighteen. He'd just finished training as a blacksmith and was studying sculpture at the academy. He came from that background of working with his hands, learning a trade – and realising that you can build something yourself, put something together, was a wonderful experience for me. It was a liberating kind of self-determination, whether you're building a house or making music that way. And the idea of moving to the country together, the possibility of creating a house as poor students, people with no money, was so convincing that I got together with him. But we were lucky that Countess Lehndorff gave us a guarantee at the bank, which meant we could get into the project. It was a group project that was partly religiously motivated. The group had moved away from Catholicism but still used to worship together. We started off in Peterskirchen. And that's where I still am now. Between then and now, though, we moved to Tuscany, near Massa Marittima, to get even more isolated. But not where the expensive property is; we were in the middle of the forest. It was really remote. I've always liked being in the wilderness. There was no road to the house, neither electric light nor running water. We could only get there in off-road vehicles, and only in the daytime; we wouldn't have found it in the dark. Because we were travelling so much, I didn't put our two sons into school. Home schooling is allowed in Italy, unlike in Germany, so I taught them myself. Our children knew we had to get by on very little, but they had the kind of freedom that children who go to school in a town don't have.

SUZANNE DOUCET My good friend Peter Kramper, who was later the sound engineer for Amon Düül and Popol Vuh, listened to my recordings and suggested going to the studio together to add electronic effects. I said: 'Do whatever you like! We recorded it in complete freedom, and now it's your turn.' Once we got it all done, we had an hour and a half of music – so much material that it became a triple album. But the three parts went together with the concept. For me and many of my generation, the first drug experiences were totally mind-expanding and liberating from the conventional hurdles of everyday life. All of a sudden you saw how things really are, and not how you thought they were. That expansion is what the first of the three records is about, which is why it's called *Trip*. A lot of people took drugs and lost themselves. That experience was embodied on the second record, *Flip Out*. And the third one was about coming to a higher synthesis from those positive and negative poles, to *Meditation* and introspection, where everything comes together to achieve a deeper meaning. Then we played the result to friends, and they all loved it. They lay on the floor for an hour and a half, listened to our tapes, and afterwards they said: 'Make a copy for me, please!' Once I had more than thirty requests for copies, I thought to myself: 'Let's make it into a record.' So I called up the Philips label and said I'd made a great production in München with an avant-garde group that I'd like to play them. Then I flew to Hamburg with my sister Diane and played it to the record company. Mind you, I claimed I was just the producer, so they had no idea my sister and I had recorded it ourselves. I remember it to this day – it was a Monday morning, eleven o'clock, the whole marketing team had come together. My sister made tea, filled a pipe and closed the curtains. Then all the record-company people sat in the dark, smoking and listening; after an hour and a half we knew they thought it was great and wanted to do it. Anyway, we had the signed contract in the bag by three in the afternoon. All we did then was go to the graphic designers, although the liner notes and the cover concept with the mirrored cover were already finished. I'd already got everything ready, and it was done that same day. The record company were really keen; they signed Kraftwerk at the same time. They wanted something entirely new at that moment. I played it for the producer Christian Bruhn, who was also really into it and wanted to make a single right away. So while the three-LP set was at the presses, we went back to the studio and recorded a single, produced by Bruhn. It didn't bother the Philips managers that one of the records was about a trip – it was 1970. *Trip – Flip Out – Meditation* was a radical statement. And for me, it was a total liberation from German clichés.

WOLF SEESSELBERG Eckart was still living in Hamburg, and even just that distance often made it difficult for us to get together for shows with all the equipment. I often had to take care of the assemblies and arrangements alone. In 1970 we decided to make a record out of live recordings and the film music: *Synthetik 1*, which we finally finished in 1972. That same year, Eckart finished his second synthesizer, with much wider new possibilities. But it turned out that Eckart was mainly interested in developing his devices and was hard to persuade to play live. We couldn't make money out of our music back then, and the record initially sold very slowly. In that respect, Kraftwerk were way ahead of us, with their very different concept. From 1970 we'd run into each other occasionally in the old part of Düsseldorf. Dressed all in black leather down to their gloves, with white trainers, they could hardly be overlooked. I liked their work, but we never came together.

ASMUS TIETCHENS Tangerine Dream, Klaus Schulze, Ash Ra Tempel – all those mumbling bumblers from the so-called Berlin School went completely over my head. It was probably because I didn't take drugs, because their music's actually dull as dishwater. Those tracks that took up a whole side of an LP were so musically empty that you had to take drugs to like them – while I had the misfortune of having to listen to what they'd actually recorded. I was more encouraged by the first Cluster and Conrad Schnitzler records, which I heard early on. Cluster didn't have synthesizers yet; they had a sine-wave generator and an electric organ. The first Kraftwerk records, the ones with the cone on them, sounded very different to what came later as well. They made us feel we weren't the only people in the country fiddling around with this stuff, that there were like-minded people in Berlin and Düsseldorf who were even making records. The idea of doing something together came from Moebius, after Roedelius had made his first solo record. Konrad [Conny] Plank was still alive at the time, and when he got suggestions like that he'd look in his diary and then say: 'I've got six days then and then, but really only six days.' We managed to record *Liliental* in 1976, but it didn't come out until 1978.

LIMPE FUCHS We started by banging rocks together. We were a group of ten people and each of us had two stones – it was all about the rhythm of the community, whose turn is when, when to get heavier, when lighter. Essentially, it was a stone meditation, and that was the start. Then we added percussion instruments, and then we built a harp and a horn. Essentially, it was music that we developed just for ourselves, house concerts in our home and studio. It was far removed from any performances or audiences. Music has to have a name, and because we were great admirers of the work of C. G. Jung at the time, we called ourselves Anima, because I was Paul's *anima*. And then we made a short film where I'm naked and painted black, and he's naked and white, to start with. And then he turns black and naked, and I turn white and naked. We showed the film in a München cinema. But the decision to perform live like that was essentially a male decision. I didn't really mind, but I was always perceived as being behind Paul at the time. People always said: 'Paul and Limpe Fuchs.' I was the family, I was the orchestra in the background. And Paul was up front with his horn. I was only naked at five festival performances, though. The main shocking thing was the poster. I wasn't a pin-up girl at all, I was quasi a philosophy: Jung's philosophy. That's what I wanted to illustrate by being naked. But, of course, that point never got across. One time, a journalist asked me if I could only play naked and black, and that's when I decided never to play like that again. We did come very much from the visual side, though, and there was nothing pornographic about our intentions – it's just that not everyone understood that. But I never saw myself as a frontwoman, I always did the background: in the family, in our music. I'm more the clownish type, and Paul is all about pathos.

SUZANNE DOUCET People in München kept raving to me about the Zweistein LP, but most of them had no idea I was involved in it; I was only mentioned in the small print, as producer. It was great because it meant I got to hear honest opinions. I never owned up to it, either, all I ever said was: 'Sounds great, I'll have to buy myself a copy.'

WOLF SEESSELBERG When my brother started at university and I went back to my very time-consuming job as a film architect, we couldn't find time to work together, and we decided to give up playing live. Forty years later, young producers started getting interested in our old *Synthetik 1* LP. Record companies from Spain and Italy re-released it. And this time sales were pretty brisk. We even got enquiries about re-releases of *Synthetik 2*, which never existed – although we did have a lot of unused recordings and tapes. The big electro-boom associated with techno only happened long after we'd stopped making music. My brother has since passed away.

ASMUS TIETCHENS My music was just a hobby for a long time; I never even thought about putting out records under my own name. When Cluster recorded their album *Grosses Wasser* with Peter Baumann, Achim Roedelius happened to have a cassette of my music with him, which Baumann then happened to hear, and he asked who I was. I'd heard of Baumann, of course; he'd just left Tangerine Dream and opened up the Paragon Studio in Berlin. One day he called and invited me to bring a few tapes to Berlin. And then we made an album out of them. The French record label Barclay had hired Baumann to produce three albums of German electronic music. They were obviously hoping to discover the next Kraftwerk or Tangerine Dream, but instead, Baumann picked the poorest of the poor – Conrad Schnitzler, Achim Roedelius and me – and made one LP with each of us. Mine stuck to the shelves like glue; they only sold 800 out of 2,000 copies and they melted down the rest. The other two more or less broke even. Barclay didn't extend the project after that. But at least that was how I got my first record out in 1980.

LIMPE FUCHS The Tractor Tour was in 1971. Rolf-Ulrich Kaiser had recommended us to this festival in Ossiach in Austria, and Friedrich Gulda invited us. He'd listened to our first LP, *Stürmischer Himmel*, and liked it. We started out in a VW bus, but it broke down in

Schorndorf. After the gig, people gave us a lift back to Peterskirchen, but we didn't have a car any more. That's when Paul had the idea of using the tractor, a tractor with a wooden house we'd built on top of it. So in 1971 we went on our Tractor Tour, from Peterskirchen to Düsseldorf, and Aachen to Rotterdam. And back again. With small children, no running water or toilet – it wasn't easy, obviously. But we were lucky enough to meet nice people everywhere who helped us. The audience reaction was very mixed, but there was always a lot of spontaneity. You don't get that any more. Sometimes we'd get loud protests at concerts, usually from the classical listeners who'd come for Friedrich Gulda. And sometimes the audience started arguing amongst themselves – it was unbelievable at times. But Paul had great ideas as well: in the Berlin Philharmonic he sawed up a big tree trunk, after attaching a contact microphone to the hand saw and putting on ear protectors. The sawing sounds were amplified to the extreme, and the people in the auditorium yelled along: 'Hooo! Hooo! Hooo!' There was thunderous applause when a piece of wood fell down. Some just enjoyed the provocation in the classical music space. Others walked out, slamming the doors, or threw paper planes. The best thing was when the grumpy cleaning women swept up the sawdust, as if it was an insult to their nice parquet floor.

SUZANNE DOUCET After the end of the Zweistein recordings, we took the tape and flew to London, in search of George Harrison. It's a bit of a strange story: we set off intuitively on the Tube, changed a couple of times and eventually arrived in Henley-on-Thames. It was midnight, and we just walked out of the station and ended up at George Harrison's place. There was a huge park where we climbed a hill – 'Fool on the Hill', obviously. It sounds crazy but that's how it was. Anyway, we got to a big gate that was open. We went inside, past this little house, and someone came out, so we said we'd come to see George, and he said: 'Yeah, yeah, George is in.' So we walked on until we reached this mansion, and we were standing outside the door when someone said: 'Why don't you open the door? The door is always open.' We went in and we stayed for twenty-four hours. There were seven or eight people there, and we listened to music with them the whole time. We listened to Zweistein as well. George and his friends really liked it. It was a great experience.

ASMUS TIETCHENS My first foreign tour was organised by the Goethe-Institut [the German equivalent to the British Council] in 1986. My first big trip abroad was to Brazil, where there were always about 150 people in the big cities who wanted to hear my music. People often said you could tell a lot of effort went into it in the studio. Which is true, because my friend Okko Bekker decided to work commercially early on in the seventies and set up a perfect studio – which you could hear in my music, in that it was at least perfectly recorded. Lots of Brazilians couldn't imagine how I could possibly record unsellable records released in batches of 500 in a studio that cost DM1,200 an hour. It was a contradiction, for them. For me, it was an interesting idea as a confrontation.

LIMPE FUCHS When we were making our album *Anima* in 1972, I spent a lot of time knitting jumpers in the studio. We had sheep, and all that happened in the studio was editing the live material from the concerts with Gulda. I've always been interested in everyday sounds being added to music: sheep bleating, the dustcart, the fishmonger or just something being torn in two. Soundscapes like that were just my thing. Later I also made audio plays for Bavarian radio. We had nothing to do with the other bands in München. We only picked up on them if they were in Peterskirchen.

SUZANNE DOUCET Zweistein was always planned as a one-off, and then I lost touch with my sister when she moved to America. It was clear we couldn't do anything else like it, and there was never an idea for a second record. The experience with Zweistein was a transition that eventually led me to New Age. I'm still into it. After Zweistein I went to India for a year, and when I got back I did the musical *Godspell* with Donna Summer. After that I only did producing for a while, more or less. The Zweistein thing was gradually forgotten. I'd only made a licensing agreement with Philips, so the rights reverted to me after ten years. Philips had stopped selling the record after a couple of years. At some point no one was interested in it. I've been living in the States for years now. One day I looked on the internet to see if I could find anything about Zweistein. And I saw that it's a cult album and read these amazing stories. Anyway, then I contacted one of the blogs and said: 'No, it was all completely different.' That was the first time I came clean and told the world how it all happened.

ASMUS TIETCHENS I've been convinced for decades that I'm incapable of making commercially viable music. It was never important to me, either. I just can't do it. Any attempts to inch towards pop came out so embarrassing that I can't even think of them without blushing. I had to try it out, to show myself it wasn't possible.

GLOBETROTTING

'They wouldn't let Embryo into Morocco
because our hair was too long.'
CHRISTIAN BURCHARD

MANI NEUMEIER We put everything that came into our heads in our music: Stockhausen, Coltrane, industrial noise or nature sounds, even sounds from Africa. Our ears were wide open, and maybe the drugs helped a bit as well. The three of us created a sound that other bands needed ten people for.

GERD KRAUS We were influenced by Mani Neumeier and Guru Guru. Seeing them live changed us, it was a milestone. We wanted to make music that way too. Our band was called Limbus 3 because there were three of us. As simple as that. That was the Limbus principle. Mani had spent a long time in India and learned to play the tabla there. And when he got back we played gigs together in a commune in Heidelberg. Absolute highlights. He played the tabla and I played the sitar, in front of people in Afghan coats. You can't imagine these days how fluid life was back then. And the music was just as fluid and free. At gigs, we basically only played one piece that went on for two to three hours. It wasn't jazz, it was something new, evolved out of various different impulses. We recorded everything and then listened to it for usable ideas and themes. And we listened to records from all over the world – Indonesia, Africa, and so on. We had this Asian-inspired spirituality, so the titles of our pieces had names inspired by Hinduism.

LÜÜL Indian ragas were very influential for us at the time. We all discovered that kind of thing and the sitar through the Beatles, but it wasn't just about the exotic sound, it was about expanding our horizons. To this day, I think that people who are too used to the rules don't know how to just dynamite whatever you've learned. The parameters of classic European music often prevent you from finding your own way. The ragas showed us that music can be completely different.

MANI NEUMEIER The traditional structures had to be broken down, classical and jazz and pop structures. We didn't just have a different sound, we also played differently to the Brits and Americans, very consciously. The pieces would last half an hour or a whole hour, or two. We just felt the need to play for longer. Why stop when it's going well? Of course, we didn't invent that, we took it on from Indian music and people like John Coltrane. But that basic attitude that you can let things go on, and then really letting them go on – all the interesting musicians back then had that in common. Even Kraftwerk, whose stage outfits looked like they'd just gone to the bank to open a savings account, had that basic attitude, and that took them to new things, which was why they were interesting.

GERD KRAUS At our Limbus gigs, we'd have about thirty instruments on stage. As we saw it, anyone could play anything, although obviously everyone preferred particular instruments, like me with cello and electrified viola, plus flute and all sorts of whistles, recorders and so on. We bought some of the instruments but we built some of them ourselves, for instance the totalophone, which was a grand-piano frame resting horizontally on a board, just the frame with the strings, not the wooden case. The concept was to detune the strings and improvise. Or the soundstring guitar – I sawed the neck off a guitar and put a hinge on it so the pitch could be raised smoothly by angling the guitar neck differently to the body. We often used our handmade instruments. There must be piles of them, and similar relics, in old communes' barns and cellars.

LÜÜL Agitation Free have been called pioneers of world music for a while now, which we were never aware of at the time. Through Thomas Kessler and the Beat Studio, we'd picked up a passion for working with tape recordings. Luckily, we had an Uher reel-to-reel recorder with us when we set off for the Middle East, and we pressed 'record' whenever something sounded interesting. We got lots of original sound footage, from belly dancers to street noise. Our album *Malesch* starts with us boarding a plane from Cyprus to Beirut, and the pilot saying: 'You play for us, and I fly the airplane.' That was the kind of material we worked with. We spent a week in Egypt, which was a culture shock for us eighteen-year-olds. There's a video of us meeting Bedouins at the pyramids. I had a guitar organ with twenty-four buttons, super-avant-garde stuff, and people there were hunting fish with spears. Those experiences were incredibly intense for us, like a high. We got back and went straight to the studio, which was very exciting. There were a few hotels in Cairo where bands played, but more for the tourists. We got taken along to a tent by the Giza pyramids, where a grassroots orchestra was playing music for belly dancing. We recorded stuff there too that made it onto our record. They were sounds we'd never heard before.

CHRISTIAN BURCHARD Embryo's trips to the Middle East drastically changed our music. That was my initiation, because I realised I couldn't actually do anything. That's why I started looking into the theory of Middle Eastern music. I looked for information everywhere: what kind of scales do they have? What kind of tonal systems? Arabic music has 600 different keys. Completely different to our chord systems, and no well-tempered tuning either. Anyway, we had to find out about it first, which took years. I was travelling a lot at that time – I went to India for a year, cross-country through Iran, Afghanistan, Pakistan, and I learned a huge amount. We went to Japan as well.

MICHAEL HOENIG We went to the Middle East early on. The Goethe-Institut still had money back in 1971. Hartmut Geerken, a wonderful man who worked in the cultural department in Cairo and brought the Sun Ra Arkestra out there as well, had heard us in Berlin and set up a Middle Eastern tour with concerts and workshops. So we went to Egypt at the age of twenty. The tour started in Cairo, and it was divinely surreal. Agitation Free was the first rock band ever to play there with guitars and drums and electric amplification. In Cairo, maybe 1,500 people came to our performance. They were really enthusiastic, but the most surprising thing was the detailed audience questions afterwards. They paid incredible attention to the details of our music, things we weren't necessarily aware of ourselves, which we'd just improvised in the heat of the moment. And the seminars at the Goethe-Institut only increased our impression of the local audiences' enormous thirst for knowledge. In Europe, we could only have dreamed of the precise intensity of that listening experience. I'd never have thought our music could make such a deep impression on a completely different culture. It influenced us so strongly that we put the impressions from that trip into our first record. The problem was that I found it very difficult at the time to adopt my musical discoveries from there directly into our music, to use details from another musical culture in our own music. I thought it was disrespectful and exploitative, little more than plagiarism, so you couldn't do it under any circumstances. I resisted it for a long time, which was probably a mistake, in retrospect. When Peter Gabriel did it later on a grand scale, people seemed to have no problem accepting it.

CHRISTIAN BURCHARD They wouldn't let Embryo into Morocco because our hair was too long. They only wanted posh tourists, or at least package holidaymakers who brought hard currency, not guys like us. Hippies were too poor for them. So they passed a ban: no long-haired men allowed into Morocco! When we got to the border there was this huge pile of hair, because a lot of freaks had just said goodbye to their locks to get in; I mean, it would grow back anyway, right? But I refused to part with my long hair, and I said: 'I've come to make art in your country, we're not tourists – why should I cut my hair off to get in?' In the end someone from the German embassy had to come and negotiate, and there was a lady from the Goethe-Institut as well, who said: 'Come now, Herr Burchard, can't you just cut your hair? It's not that bad.' But I stuck to my guns and threatened to go back home if my hair had to come off. In the end they did let us in with long hair. Our gigs were a huge success – the Moroccans cheered us like pop stars.

LÜÜL The first time I felt like a German was when we performed abroad for the first few times and the subject of guilt came up. It was on our Middle Eastern tour in 1972. We were told the Arabs thought Hitler was great, and the state of Israel had paper stuck over it in Egyptian school atlases. We were confronted out of the blue with Hitler and Nazi Germany, and we had to find some way to respond. We were pretty perplexed in the band, to begin with, because we couldn't understand what they wanted from us. The sympathies for Hitler in the Arab world were a real shock to us.

CHRISTIAN BURCHARD Algeria was very odd, compared to Morocco. We had two gigs in a hall in Algiers. So we went ahead and played, the people totally rocked out, all great. Then we take a break, and this guy from the Goethe-Institut comes up to me and starts in: 'For God's sake, can't you play something quiet? The crowd's too boisterous and someone from the communist government's already complained that young people are too into Western music.' So in the second set we started off with just quiet stuff, space music kind of thing. But at some point, Dave King kicks off with a fat bass groove and I join in, and the whole hall starts rocking out again: 'WOOOAAAAHHH!' They were totally flipping out. Then the government just went and banned our next show. Young people complained to us that it was a really bad dictatorship. It was a bit better in Tunisia, but still strange. We played in Tunis in a big cinema, and if anyone in the audience flipped out too much, got too enthusiastic, the security people guarding the thing came along, grabbed them and threw them out. I've been back to Morocco many times since then, but I prefer not to go to the other countries. They were too stressful.

MANI NEUMEIER People who came to see bands like us abroad were pretty open and presumably not German-haters. We were always welcomed as musicians, not as Germans.

CHRISTIAN BURCHARD I was always treated well on my travels. But I was often ashamed to be German. You hear a lot of nonsense about Germany abroad. One time, we were invited to the home of this really old singer in Japan. His family entertained us beautifully and he gave a concert just for us of old Japanese music, it was all wonderful, but after that he came out with all this stuff about knowing Germany well, especially the Hitler Youth. Stories like that are always strange, every time. Or in the Arab world, when people hear that you're German they'll say that it was good that the Germans killed so many Jews. They'll just say it openly, when you're buying fruit from them or something. Obviously, you answer that it's rubbish. But it's no use, a lot of people refuse to listen.

LÜÜL In France, where I lived for a while, I sometimes still sensed an aversion to Germans. But that was isolated cases, and always old people. I've never had problems abroad with people our age. All right, I was in a bar in Paris once in 1974, and a woman looked me up and down, liked what she saw, but then said: 'Yes, you've got blue eyes and blond hair, like my son. But I hate the Germans.' Her son had been killed by German soldiers, and of course meeting someone like that does something to you. In moments like that, you really realise that you have to live with that guilt, as a German. But as musicians, we had it good abroad, we usually got a friendly reception.

FAUST

'The stage looked like the aftermath of war after every gig.'
WERNER 'ZAPPI' DIERMAIER

JEAN-HERVÉ PERON Hamburg was great: demos every day. It was like going to the cinema. 'What shall we do today? Hmm, let's see what demos are on.' And there was a lot going on musically in Hamburg as well. There were various scenes, especially around Grossneumarkt. And of course the Onkel Pö. We were the radicals, at any rate; we'd hang out at the Toulouse Lautrec Institut, a bar on Grossneumarkt. The film-maker Andy Hertel ran the most exciting bars and places, and I ran the Toulouse Lautrec Institut for him for a while; he made me managing director. I lived upstairs in the same building, in a flat where loads of people would come by. I started my first band there with Rudolf Sosna and Gunther Wüsthoff. We didn't have a name at the time, but now we call it Nukleus.

WERNER 'ZAPPI' DIERMAIER I was the drummer for the band Campylognatus Citelli, named after a [perhaps fictional] Swabian ptero-saurus, and Hans-Joachim Irmler was in the band already. Arnulf Meifert joined us as a second drummer. We rehearsed in a bunker at Hamburg's Sternschanze station, a long, narrow room. I was living in a shared flat at the time, and one day one of my flatmates brought Jean-Hervé back for the night, from uni. We got talking, and he said he had a band as well: Nukleus or something. I invited him to our rehearsal the next day. He liked it a lot and we decided to put the two bands together. But not everyone, because there would have been too many of us. I brought along Hans-Joachim Irmler, who made great sounds, and Arnulf Meifert. Jean-Hervé took Rudolf Sosna and Gunther Wüsthoff with him.

232

HANS-JOACHIM IRMLER The Campylognatus Citelli gang had a few psychedelic dents in it. We weren't capable of writing songs, but we'd have liked one or two. Then our drummer Zappi met a woman who was Peron's girlfriend. His band was called Nukleus. And then we fused with them: they came up with the songs, and we took care of the sound. Our joint rehearsals went well. And when we wanted to make more out of it, someone suggested Uwe Nettelbeck as a contact to the industry. He was a great guy, had a lot of nous and guts. He wasn't afraid of anything. He actually came and listened patiently to our ideas and conditions and expectations. We had all sorts of fluffy ideas in our heads and we were good at making demands. We even asked for our own studio.

JEAN-HERVÉ PERON Uwe Nettelbeck was a very dedicated journalist with contacts in the extreme left. He was an early follower of US underground music and he wondered why all the schlager musicians here could do whatever they liked, while the experimental musicians had to live from hand to mouth. Uwe's plan was to give the established music industry the runaround by obtaining mainstream means for a nonconformist group, no matter if they were well known before or not. And we were that kind of uncompromising band. But, for us, being political didn't mean writing agitational leaflets. Our politics were non-verbal, our politics was the music itself. Avant-gardists have always been a danger for the establishment, no matter whether they paint, write poems or make music. We stimulated aspects in the population that the powers-that-be didn't want to be stimulated: thinking, doubting and asking questions. I think we shook people's feelings of security. If you push people out of what they're familiar with, in the best case they start asking questions. Even those who came out of our gigs unhappy might have been changed slightly. And exactly that is political.

SIMON DRAPER Uwe Nettelbeck was an intellectual and a thinker who was especially fascinated by the idea of Faust. He talked Deutsche

Grammophon into signing them as an important avant-garde band. Genius. But he produced other strange music as well, like Slapp Happy and Tony Conrad. It was Nettelbeck's idea to use a Bridget Riley picture on the cover of *The Faust Tapes*. I have to admit I had no idea who she was. But then we had to meet up with her to get her permission for the record cover. So once we'd been to her gallery and agreed on a motif, we told her what we were planning to use her picture for, what kind of band Faust were and what it was all about. I started collecting art in the nineties and tried to buy the original painting from *The Faust Tapes*, but I couldn't because it's in a museum. Instead, I bought two of her other black-and-white pictures for £20,000 each, also painted in 1964. One of them's called *Shiver*. It's valued at about £4 million these days. Anyway, I'm annoyed that I didn't buy the Faust painting back in the day – we'd have made a lot more money out of it than Faust ever brought in.

HANS-JOACHIM IRMLER Uwe Nettelbeck was pretty well known as a journalist at the time. Long hair, not all that tall. You could spot him by the way he always had a carton of really strong Roth-Händle cigarettes wedged under his arm. We made the whole thing sound palatable to Uwe, with lots of laughs and jokes. After a while we suggested we could act like we were the German Beatles. That's how we signed with Polydor, who had cheesy stuff like Bert Kaempfert and Freddy Quinn on their label, plus a couple of licences for the Who and Hendrix, but mainly that light-entertainment stuff. It was hilarious for us to get a contract with them, of all people. Uwe was a very eloquent person; it would never have worked without him.

WERNER 'ZAPPI' DIERMAIER Uwe wanted to be a music producer. He took our demo tape to Polydor, and they liked it. Uwe told them we were doing something completely new, we were 'the new Beatles'. And of course Polydor didn't want to risk letting the new Beatles slip through their fingers, what with not signing the old ones in the first place. At our next meeting, Uwe brought us a briefcase full of cash. We were so poor we hardly had anything to eat, and we signed the contracts straight away. That's how it started. Then we spent a long time thinking about what to call ourselves.

JEAN-HERVÉ PERON There are two theories about how we got our name. Theory A: revolution. Theory B: taking the mickey out of Polydor. They're both right. It was actually the way it often goes with bands – the musicians sign a record contract and think: 'What the hell is our name?' We didn't have a name at all for ages, neither Nukleus nor any of the many previous names. Then Uwe Nettelbeck came along and said: 'OK, we need a name for you now.' So we met up for a big, long meal. We smoked lots of joints and thought about the name.

WERNER 'ZAPPI' DIERMAIER Nettelbeck suggested Götterdämmerung, but we all thought that was really dumb.

JEAN-HERVÉ PERON Götterdämmerung? Blah blah!

HANS-JOACHIM IRMLER We thought briefly about Götterdämmerung, because we thought it would be funny to hear Americans trying to pronounce it.

JEAN-HERVÉ PERON The first thing we agreed on was that the name had to be short; there's nothing more annoying than long band names. And short so that it was easier to write; and also international, so people could understand it in different languages. Plus, it had to have a deeper meaning.

WERNER 'ZAPPI' DIERMAIER Then I had to go to hospital for three weeks, and while I was away the rest of the band decided we'd be called Faust. A short name that English-speakers could pronounce.

JEAN-HERVÉ PERON Faust? Faust! The clenched fist of the revolution and also the pact with the devil. Faust fitted perfectly.

WERNER 'ZAPPI' DIERMAIER Aside from that, you can associate all sorts of things with it, from Goethe to a clenched fist.

HANS-JOACHIM IRMLER But we wanted a name that had more than one meaning. So Faust was ideal for us, uniting physical and intellectual struggle.

WERNER 'ZAPPI' DIERMAIER There's no more specific explanation, though, and that's deliberate. Rudolf Sosna came to visit me in hospital and said: 'We're called Faust. All right?' Uwe Nettelbeck insisted on Götterdämmerung for a while longer, but one day Rudolf Sosna went to his house and stuck a note saying 'Faust' to his front door with a knife. That was that sorted.

HANS-JOACHIM IRMLER In general, a lot of things got talked to death back then; we had endless discussions about absolutely everything. You had to avoid certain bars if you didn't want to get trapped in discussions for days on end. If you went in on a Monday, you could think yourself lucky if you got out again on a Wednesday. They were great times, really.

JEAN-HERVÉ PERON Uwe never tried to influence us, he just diverted our wild energy in clever ways. His wife Petra always supported us as well. I'm certain Faust would never have existed without Uwe Nettelbeck and his wife. We certainly made some bold demands of the record company, Polydor: first of all that we didn't want to deliver anything for a year, but we wanted a fully equipped studio available day and night, including a sound engineer. Plus a PA for playing live, and bread on the table. And Polydor said yes. That was down to Uwe; he could be very convincing. That's when we moved to Wümme.

HANS-JOACHIM IRMLER Part of the agreement with Polydor was that we'd leave Hamburg to work on our music. We were aiming for conscious isolation. We wanted to get out of Hamburg as fast as possible, because we had musicians clinging on to us like vultures. Or that's what we felt like, at least. I must have had three different address books where Udo Lindenberg kept writing his number down.

WERNER 'ZAPPI' DIERMAIER The other Hamburg bands didn't want anything to do with us. They said we couldn't play properly, we just messed around with effects and got loads of money for it. They were all just jealous. Carlo Karges, who was in [the rock band] Tomorrow's Gift at the time and played with Nena later, once told me it took him a while to appreciate Faust for our experiments.

JEAN-HERVÉ PERON First we moved to Schwindebeck. Petra Krause, Uwe Nettelbeck's wife, had a family house there that we got to use. It was a big mansion on a tank range in the Lüneburg Heath. But we only spent a few months there until the former school was done up that Polydor bought for us in Wümme, where they had a studio installed especially for us, and beds. We had a very nice life there, with the Polydor record company paying for everything. Apparently, we still owe them 50,000 euros, or so they say. At the time it was several hundred thousand. A lot of musicians think we were a boy band with endless money, designer labels, drugs and whatever else. Faust didn't have a good image. In fact, there were times when we had so little money that we only ate porridge with syrup and tripe dog food. But we still savoured the *dolce vita* while the tanks manoeuvred around us.

HANS-JOACHIM IRMLER First we moved into Petra Nettelbeck's father's hunting lodge on the heath; he'd made a fortune in shipping. We stayed there until they found us a suitable studio. It turned out to be a former village school in this hamlet called Wümme, near Hamburg. We did have a good budget, though. For one thing, they put in such effective heating that you had to walk around naked – even if it was set only on one, even in winter – it got so hot there. Of course, we liked walking around naked. It'd be inconceivable these days, but it was no big deal then. We were very isolated there, though – we didn't have any visitors at all. That was part of the communication ban we'd imposed on ourselves. We wouldn't let friends, relatives or girlfriends come. There was no radio, record player or TV either. It was a six-month quarantine. The objective was to concentrate entirely on ourselves! We wanted to get what was inside us worked out, unfiltered. Excursions into unfamiliar worlds would only hold us back. Despite our isolation, the neighbours soon thought we were the devil incarnate.

KURT GRAUPNER I was working for the Special Projects department at Deutsche Grammophon Gesellschaft. There were two of us in charge of expanding recording technology and the calibration of control rooms and release rooms for records, and we developed a procedure for stereophoning the old classical mono recordings. Deutsche Grammophon sold them on the Heliodor label. I was mainly responsible for the technical development and processing of the recordings. Then I left DGG to work freelance, mainly so I'd be independent of office hours, but soon afterwards I was asked – again by DGG, this time their pop label Polydor – if I'd be interested in setting up a studio for a fee and doing recordings with a group. DGG would take care of technical support, including an experimental workshop. The idea was very tempting and I immediately accepted, so they put me in touch with Polydor and Uwe Nettelbeck.

JEAN-HERVÉ PERON Wümme was a microcosm. It's a village on the B75 highway, with no one around for thirty kilometres either way. Absolutely no one for miles. And we had no TV, radio or newspapers – nothing! The end of the world. No outside influences, just us and the loneliness. But we loved that loneliness. We rarely had visitors, and if we did get visitors, we'd end up having great big orgies. But that was normal, especially if you get young men living cut off from the world for months and then young women come by in hot pants – your hormones go off the scale. That seclusion distinguished us from other communes, though. They'd normally get plenty of visitors. In Wümme, we were usually alone, just the six of us and the music.

KURT GRAUPNER I brought along various equipment and my experimental mixing desk from Deutsche Grammophon. I'd had the desk built especially for processing the old classical tapes. Once I'd left Grammophon they stopped using the equipment, so I could do what I liked with it. That meant we could do lots of things that wouldn't work with a normal mixing desk. The musicians had their own instruments and effect devices, but they weren't usable for studio recordings because they produced crackling and buzzing. So it was clear they needed high-quality effect devices, and I developed black boxes that integrated all the effects: delay, reverb, ring modulator and other effects. Then I developed light-activated multifunctional foot pedals that worked cleanly and didn't cause any noise interference. You could use the black boxes to preset various sounds on three signal pathways, and cross-fade between them. All that meant we were pretty perfectly equipped in Wümme. Unfortunately, they put increasing time pressure on us to deliver the recordings. It takes time to develop and build equipment like that, but it was still a lot of fun.

HANS-JOACHIM IRMLER We didn't have much contact with the outside world, but we still had to go shopping now and then. There was also a pub nearby where we were welcome, because the landlord and our drummer Zappi were both Austrian. We'd always go down there, but if other people came in, we had to go in the back room. The landlady worried we'd scare off the locals. We did look a bit wild, especially Zappi. He's two metres tall, and he had shaggy hair and a dog, to make matters worse. Running into them on a foggy night on the moor would have been really creepy.

WERNER 'ZAPPI' DIERMAIER Jean-Hervé and I had dogs, but the others didn't like them. So we built a kennel in the garden and slept there on straw, with the dogs. It was nice. I once dug a huge great hole outside the front door, just for laughs. The authorities came round and ordered us: 'Fill it back up! Someone might fall in!' Then I dug another hole, and they came back again, and it went back and forth like that. The locals soon started calling us 'the commune', although we never called ourselves that. On the odd occasion when we did the washing, we'd hang it out to dry outside. And if someone needed socks, he'd just pluck a pair off the washing line and put them on. There were no real belongings and no fixed rules. We did try and make a cooking and washing-up rota, but we quickly abandoned it. It just didn't work that way. I often did the cooking, but most of the others didn't like what I made. One day I said: 'I'm never cooking again!' And Arnulf just said: 'Thank you!' Breakfast was our most important meal. We did a lot of shopping: fish, meat, cake and veggies. Everything you can think of for breakfast. We were night owls, so we didn't have breakfast until around two in the afternoon, and then we'd be full up for the rest of the day. Music was mostly made in the evenings. One time I was asleep, when Rudolf Sosna came in my room and woke me up: 'You've got to come right now!' I went into the studio, still half asleep, and he said: 'Knock: DUM DUM DUM,' and he sang along: 'Rainy day! Rainy day!' The next day, the others joined in as well. And 'Rainy Day' became a kind of hit for us. People still want to hear it these days. But I don't really want to play it any more.

JEAN-HERVÉ PERON One morning, we woke up to find machine guns trained on us. That was in the terrorism days. We only found out later that Uwe Nettelbeck had contacts with left-wing extremists, the Red Army Faction and so on. And we looked kind of similar, so we aroused suspicion. I can well imagine what people in the village pubs around there thought about us: 'Oh, those long-haired hippies in Wümme, those weirdos!' Anyway, the state came at dawn with dogs one day, a great big kerfuffle.

HANS-JOACHIM IRMLER They weren't normal policemen, it was Federal Border Guard officers who'd surrounded our house. It was probably down to the attendant at a petrol station not liking the look of Zappi. He suspected terrorism and called the police.

JEAN-HERVÉ PERON There were loads of policemen, probably a hundred. They got in no problem because we never locked the doors anyway. We were all naked. I just thought it was funny and I laughed and laughed – you could tell the police didn't really know what they were doing there either. It was just too surreal to be scared. For me, it was nothing but a stage play, they couldn't be serious.

HANS-JOACHIM IRMLER Luckily, I wasn't there that day, I was visiting the Nettelbecks. Anyway, we got a call from Wümme: 'Come quick! We're surrounded!' More than ten officers had turned up, all armed with machine guns, and stormed the rooms. It's amazing that nothing happened, actually. It wouldn't have been that unusual to fight back. We hadn't done anything wrong. Anyway, it went on from six in the morning to three in the afternoon. They turned everything upside down, and presumably at some point they started wondering what they were doing there. It only happened once, luckily, but once is enough for a lifetime.

JEAN-HERVÉ PERON Our decision-making processes were always chaotic. Arnulf Meifert was the most political of us, for example. He always had explicit opinions on everything and wanted to discuss everything. Irmler was shy, often shut himself in his room and listened to the Beach Boys. Zappi and I were always making music and jamming. Rudolf would always be playing as well, guitar or piano. We'd even installed microphones in bed so we could record everything – I recorded a few things on the guitar in bed. Sometimes I'd lie there and yell: 'Kurt! Press "record"!' Kurt Graupner was our sound engineer, booked by Polydor. But he wasn't always there because no one would have put up with us permanently.

HANS-JOACHIM IRMLER Kurt Graupner wasn't some jaded engineer; he'd just finished his training and he brought along a lot of great ideas. But it must have taken us three months to persuade him to let the levels go over into red now and then. Graupner became a member of the family and we set up another room for him in the attic.

JEAN-HERVÉ PERON He'd come for two or three weeks and then head off again. But when he was there, we'd always go: 'Kurt! Press "record"!' And then we'd start jangling away. That was how the famous *Faust Tapes* came about. Polydor hoped to have found the German Beatles, but the label never understood how valuable our Faust record really was because they'd expected something completely different. If they hadn't been such imbeciles, they'd have advertised us with much more euphoria and intelligence: '*Achtung*: here come the next Beatles!' But they were scaredy-cats. They were fairly relaxed in reaction to our album and even wanted a second one ASAP, but they wanted 'hits' on it. Uwe Nettelbeck was always on our side and gave Polydor the runaround. If it hadn't been for Uwe, we'd have been chucked straight out.

HANS-JOACHIM IRMLER All of us played the others' instruments, and all sorts of other stuff, so that we all understood how the others ticked. And we'd also agreed not to have a boss, all to have equal rights. That caused tension to begin with, because if everyone has to decide everything, there's a lot more potential for competition, obviously. We had constant discussions; every one of us was really done in by the group. I'd go as far as to call it brainwashing. It was a nightmare that you don't forget that quickly. But in the end, it worked.

JEAN-HERVÉ PERON We'd agreed with Polydor on a year in Wümme, but there wasn't a real deadline. Uwe didn't live with us, he lived with his wife and two daughters in Luhmühlen. But he came by regularly and stayed for a day, sometimes several days.

HANS-JOACHIM IRMLER Nettelbeck would come by regularly because he wanted to check if we were doing anything, of course. He'd want us to play music for him, he was very interested. We'd entice him by saying we'd let him play the drums.

JEAN-HERVÉ PERON But after a while the record company did put pressure on us, real pressure. Uwe came and said that Polydor wanted to see results and we had to deliver. In the end it was all stress, stress, stress!

HANS-JOACHIM IRMLER Polydor never said anything about our music. There were only two people in the whole company who could stand it. The boss was all right, but I think he had an accountant nagging him, always asking him what we were up to in Wümme. So that's why we had the idea of sending them a tape of music every week. Once we recorded 'The Blue Danube' especially for Polydor. We wanted to show them what a broad repertoire we had. But we swapped instruments to play it, which probably didn't do much for the harmony.

JEAN-HERVÉ PERON Our album concept was: one side of improvised live music from the studio, the other side properly composed songs. We'd recorded masses of music and there's still loads of it stored in boxes and crates; I've got some of them. But they're all just worthless sketches, like painters' drawings before they start a picture. All right, some of them might have some value, but most of it's just historically interesting. For us, what we were doing was perfectly normal, that was what music was supposed to be like. In my world, there was only music I was involved in personally. It was a world in which you snipped tape and happily recorded a cement mixer or wrote lyrics based on random choices. That was 'our' music. It's hard to say how many hours a day we spent making music, because we did things partly alone and partly in the group. The only rule was that we always played together for at least three hours, from six in the evening. But during the day everyone just popped into the studio at some point. We filled up tonnes of tape; that alone was incredibly expensive.

HANS-JOACHIM IRMLER There was this really cool steam hammer at Rödingsmarkt in Hamburg, which we recorded. And a big demo at Dammtor station. I remember a piece called 'Lieber Herr Deutschland' with all that in it. It got turned into a track advertising fully automatic washing machines.

JEAN-HERVÉ PERON These days you'd call it 'field recording'. We stuck the recorded sounds together into musical collages. On all the Faust tracks, we always composed and improvised together, even though we came from very different backgrounds. Gunther liked Stockhausen and Boulez, he had a mathematical approach to music; for example, he'd take a few notes and then mirror them geometrically, if you like. I'd call it 'conducted coincidence'. Irmler was the electronics man. And Zappi's a drummer who can link all those diverging elements together. He's got the groove.

HANS-JOACHIM IRMLER We once tried to translate a gathering storm into acoustic form. How do I represent crackling electricity in music? I can't really describe how it went, but it's definitely still on the tapes.

KURT GRAUPNER Polydor got more and more impatient, and in the end they insisted on a live show. Which then took place – and promptly flopped. Faust got famous anyway, though.

JEAN-HERVÉ PERON Our first gig was in the massive Hamburg Musikhalle. We wanted quadrophonic sound even before Pink Floyd, we were real pioneers. But unfortunately, we were too stupid to rehearse beforehand. At the Musikhalle, they just gave us a 500-metre roll of cable. We musicians had to wire up the hall ourselves right before playing.

HANS-JOACHIM IRMLER We'd been trying all year to do a kind of 3D installation. I'd say we invented the joystick along the way. It's just that none of it was ready when we had to play live, but there was no going back by then. And we liked the Musikhalle a lot, all that gilded pomp and splendour. We built a kind of watchtower in the middle of the velvet seats, with cables heading off in all directions. It looked a bit ghostly, to be honest. At five o'clock I drove off with Uwe Nettelbeck to get even more cable. The plan was to install surround sound, which was pretty complicated. Then we fetched about another 5,000 metres of cable. The gig was announced to start at eight, but it didn't quite kick off on time. Luckily, we'd also insisted on colour TVs, which were a new thing at the time. There was one for each of us on stage, so we could play the evening news for the audience in parallel from eight, while we were still laying the cable.

JEAN-HERVÉ PERON Rudolf Sosna was our genius; his mind was decades ahead. He already had this vision that David Bowie would play live in Tokyo, for instance, with musicians beamed in from New York. He actually anticipated the concept of what we now call a livestream, because even back then we didn't necessarily want to lug our stuff around the place; we'd rather have broadcast our gigs from one location. Irmler and Wüsthoff did a lot of thinking and were very good at imagining, but a lot of our plans were simply too far removed from the technical state of play and the realities at the time.

WERNER 'ZAPPI' DIERMAIER We wanted to play three-dimensionally. We'd practised it before, in a windmill in Hittfeld. We'd rented it for two weeks to try it out, with forty speakers that we installed at the top and bottom. And it worked there! An organ sound passed your ear from top to bottom, you could hear it clearly. Then there'd be a shot from the guitar straight across the space. Our sound man Kurt Graupner had two levers in the middle of the room, one for horizontal, one for vertical. He could move the sound from every track around the space – it was better than Pink Floyd's Azimuth Coordinator. It worked fine in rehearsal, but not at the gig in the Musikhalle. No one knows why.

JEAN-HERVÉ PERON What we really wanted didn't come across at the time. All the audience saw in the end was a band on stage who had no idea how to play live. True! Who were very bad at playing their instruments. True! Who made a song and dance about quadrophonic sound and then couldn't make it happen. True! But no one saw that we were daring to do something new, that we were a facet of a movement that would go on to make big changes.

HANS-JOACHIM IRMLER The Musikhalle gig was definitely one of the best we ever did. Opinions are pretty divided about it, of course, but you have to see it as a happening. The audience was more or less just invited guests, hand-picked by Polydor.

WERNER 'ZAPPI' DIERMAIER They'd invited fifty journalists from around the world. Nothing was working out, so we told them: 'You guys go to the disco next door. It'll all be fine by the time you get back in two hours' time.' They came back and it still wasn't working. We got a lot of negative press for it, but that wasn't a bad thing.

HANS-JOACHIM IRMLER When some of the guests had had enough of waiting, we recommended they go out to the Gängeviertel neighbourhood nearby, told them there were good bars there and they should come back around nine or ten. It was pure anarchy. Most of them really did come back. I'm probably the only one of us with positive memories of it. Nothing went to plan; either the vocals weren't working or the instruments. At some point we decided just to sing the whole thing. At one in the morning the janitor bustled on stage, bright red with rage, and screamed: 'Enough! Turn it off! My wife's just called to complain! What's going on here?' It was a phenomenal gig, really.

WERNER 'ZAPPI' DIERMAIER When we started playing live regularly, later on, we couldn't actually play our own tracks. Especially because we thought people would be better off listening to them on records. That's why we only ever improvised.

HANS-JOACHIM IRMLER We went on stage in normal everyday clothes.

WERNER 'ZAPPI' DIERMAIER On our first UK tour we didn't know what we'd do when we walked on stage, not the faintest idea. We'd just start somehow, knock over a glass or something. And then music came out of it, somehow.

HANS-JOACHIM IRMLER After the Musikhalle, that's when the rift started; it did strike a nerve. Things came to a head in the band, and with the record label as well. Arnulf kept saying: 'We've got to rehearse more!' And I'd say: 'Rehearse what?' Sadly, the way it developed was that Arnulf was thrown out of the band, I'm ashamed to say. He'd been very influential because he wasn't just the oldest, but also the most sensible. But perhaps a bit too sensible. If you're only ever sensible, you don't make progress. You can only create something new by overstepping boundaries.

WERNER 'ZAPPI' DIERMAIER After the second record, *So Far*, Polydor chucked us out for good.

JEAN-HERVÉ PERON One day we got a call from Herr Vogelsang, the big chief at Polydor at the time. He asked what it had cost to sign us. And how much had we sold? The first album hadn't sold that well. The second did better, but it still wasn't a big seller. After the third, Vogelsang stepped on the brakes and said: 'Stop!'

WERNER 'ZAPPI' DIERMAIER They'd realised we weren't the new Beatles after all. The sales figures proved it.

JEAN-HERVÉ PERON We just weren't worth it for them. So we all had to go, even everyone who'd worked with us, even Nettelbeck, we all had to go. We didn't care, though, we just wanted to make music. Whether it was released anywhere didn't matter to us at all. We didn't do a lot of thinking about it. Not out of stupidity – on principle. Money just had no bearing on us.

SIMON DRAPER Faust's debut album was easy to get hold of in the UK because the band was signed to Polydor.

WERNER 'ZAPPI' DIERMAIER Uwe Nettelbeck somehow came across Richard Branson in London, who'd just started Virgin.

HANS-JOACHIM IRMLER Then we all decided to go to England. Simon Draper had understood that our music was strange but had potential. He leaned on Branson to sign us up to Virgin.

SIMON DRAPER To get the contract done, Richard Branson and I went to Hamburg and stayed overnight with Uwe Nettelbeck and his lovely wife. Back then we negotiated mainly with Uwe, long before we were even in touch with the band. We only met them when they came to London to record their new album.

JEAN-HERVÉ PERON Branson wasn't yet one of the richest people in the world when we met him; he had a tiny office in London where we'd pop in every day, rain or shine. Branson never told us exactly what he expected from us. I think he saw us as the people from Polydor, like a racehorse you buy to see how it'll do. And the fastest horse in the Virgin stable was his favourite, of course: Mike Oldfield. Bingo.

SIMON DRAPER Faust were a good fit for Virgin. We stood for avant-garde music and strange sounds, Henry Cow and Kevin Coyne. That was the music that interested me personally. One music journalist who influenced us a lot at Virgin was Ian MacDonald, whose name was actually MacCormick; he was Bill MacCormick's brother. And Bill MacCormick was originally the bassist in the legendary Quiet Sun, and was playing at the time with Robert Wyatt's Soft Machine spin-off Matching Mole, and later for Brian Eno and Phil Manzanera. Anyway, that was the leading scene for me at the time, and Ian MacDonald was its most influential supporter at *New Musical Express*. Luckily, he seemed to love everything that came out on Virgin back then, which helped us a lot. But he was really fanatical about Faust, thought they were one of the most important bands of all time, even compared them to the Beatles. I was looking for music that had something autonomous and individual. I didn't care about the usual rock bands that just varied the same old stuff. So Faust were perfect for me as well. But they were tricky to deal with, they were pretty aggressive towards us. They were punks before punk was even invented.

HANS-JOACHIM IRMLER *The Faust Tapes* were our doorway to Virgin.

SIMON DRAPER Uwe Nettelbeck told us they had a whole lot of recordings they'd like to release. We responded that we'd prefer fresh recordings made in our own studio. So Nettelbeck suggested just giving us the old recordings, on condition that we didn't make any money out of them. We came up with the idea of making them into a record that we sold as cheaply as possible. We marketed *The Faust Tapes* as 'an album for the price of a single'. The price was forty-nine pence, if I remember rightly. And the record sold fantastically, although I doubt many people liked it – *The Faust Tapes* was a very challenging, difficult record that was presumably too much for most people. But I loved the idea of it helping Faust to break through.

HANS-JOACHIM IRMLER Branson agreed to us living in England under the same conditions as in Wümme. That was the Manor Studio, a nice old pile with a great studio and a good team.

WERNER 'ZAPPI' DIERMAIER Branson had a studio near Oxford, actually more of a castle, and that's where we recorded. Mike Oldfield used the studio in the daytime, and we went in at night. He'd made *Tubular Bells* there all on his own. It wasn't our bag, though – way too clean.

JEAN-HERVÉ PERON Mike Oldfield used to pop in and see us. He loved to sit under the table, barking like a dog. We'd give him a kick but only because he wanted us to; he was a bit mad. Or maybe he just wanted to take the mickey out of us Germans by pretending to be a German shepherd, I don't know. I didn't like him much.

WERNER 'ZAPPI' DIERMAIER Oldfield was barmy. We'd be sitting there, and Oldfield would get under the table and bite us on the ankles. Once I hit out under the table with a curtain holder and caught him right on the cheek.

SIMON DRAPER I kept out of the recordings Faust did there. Partly because I was so young, younger than most of the musicians I signed. I loved jazz and was generally into music, but I didn't have a particular concept that I wanted to suggest to our acts; I was more of a fan. As I got older I did give the artists advice, of course, suggested producers and that kind of thing. But in 1973 I didn't have the experience to do that, I just trusted that they'd make an effort in the studio. Mike Oldfield did what he liked there as well; he was living there at the time. He'd actually only had a week there to finish off *Tubular Bells* with our sound engineers, but he just stayed on. He had no fixed abode anyway, and no money. We didn't intervene, so he just hung out there for longer. The girls who worked there were nice to him.

JEAN-HERVÉ PERON We got to know Oldfield in the studio, when no one knew how big he'd end up, but we did pick up on his success building up. Branson was really into *Tubular Bells* from the beginning, partly because he knew it would sell and make him rich. Then he organised the famous concert at the Queen Elizabeth Hall, mid-1973, when Oldfield played *Tubular Bells* with this all-star prog orchestra, and he invited all the top acts along – we hung out backstage with Mick Jagger and guys like that. Back then Branson still thought we might wind up as successful racehorses as well.

WERNER 'ZAPPI' DIERMAIER Once Mike Oldfield finished *Tubular Bells* he invited a few musicians over. Keith Richards came in a sports car, and someone drove his Rolls-Royce along after him. We went to the pub later, but I stayed in the Rolls-Royce getting drunk, ended up pretty wasted. Then along came Keith Richards' bodyguard, dragged me out of the Roller and punched me in the face.

JEAN-HERVÉ PERON We weren't all happy with Virgin Records. The only people I had time for were the team at the Manor Studio and Simon Draper – they did a lot for us.

SIMON DRAPER We put them in the Manor Studio to record their new album – which I guess wasn't such a good decision. But it was part of the contract. Then they wrote me a list of everything they thought was '*Scheisse*'. They didn't even like the flat we'd put them in in London. I was twenty-two at the time, doing my best. I'd have given my right arm to live in a flat like that, but it wasn't good enough for Faust. They were very quick to pronounce all sorts of things '*Scheisse*' and they thought they were pretty big stars. At any rate, their demands always outweighed their sales figures.

HANS-JOACHIM IRMLER Then we started work on *Faust IV*. It had to be a pop album again. Although it did still sound pretty quirky. Simon Draper would come over and listen to the music. Uwe came too and commented on what we were doing. He had specific ideas as well.

SIMON DRAPER Despite all the difficulties, Faust were definitely one of a kind. The audience expected something unusual from them. And it got plenty!

STEPHEN MORRIS The Faust gig I went to when I was sixteen was really very, very odd. It must have been about 1973, in the Manchester Free Trade Hall. I remember they played in total darkness and only did two songs, but it lasted over an hour. The most exciting thing was that they seemed so mysterious, none of them appeared as individuals – the idea of the band as a unit eclipsed everything else.

HANS-JOACHIM IRMLER You concentrate much differently in the dark, as a band and in the audience.

SIMON DRAPER Around the time of *Faust IV* I saw a gig they played, which was one of the most incredible things I've ever experienced. They got this guy on stage with a pneumatic hammer, and he was part of a few of their appearances after that. The sound was fantastic, loud enough to drive you out of your mind.

WERNER 'ZAPPI' DIERMAIER The idea of the tools on stage was mine. I went for a walk round the block before a gig in Birmingham. There was a building site, and someone was breaking up rocks with a hammer drill. I asked him if he'd like to join in at a concert. He didn't know what to think at first, thought it was a joke, and then he asked his boss and said yes. That night we got them to heave a rock on stage and cover it with a blanket so no splinters came off. I'd asked the builder to come in his work outfit and arranged that I'd give him a sign when we wanted him to start, and another one to stop. And then, of course, he came in a bow tie and suit because it was a concert, and his mum and granny came along with him. The sign for starting went fine, but not the stop sign. I kept on signalling to him 'That's it! Enough!' but he didn't even look my way, and he went on hammering away until the end of the gig. The audience loved it. And it was certainly unusual.

JEAN-HERVÉ PERON Back then, at any rate, we started bringing industrial sounds on stage, almost ten years before the Neubauten. I was really into the idea of working with cement mixers, I was virtually in love with the cement-machine sound. As luck would have it, I met this French guy who composed contemporary music, at a party in the countryside somewhere. I told him what I did, and he listened closely. In the end I said: 'Couldn't you write a concerto for cement mixer and orchestra?' And he said: 'Absolutely, something like that needs to be written.' I was interested in sound symbioses, whether it was cement mixers, coffee machines or knitting needles.

SIMON DRAPER When they played the Rainbow in London they had TV sets on stage, and it worked like a dream. All the monitors showed an opera singer doing his thing. Henry Cow put on a big show before them – they'd decided to compete with Faust on the actionism front. They'd had ten brass players and dancers who ushered the audience into the hall to make sure everyone saw the support band. Some of the brass guys were pretty well-known British jazz musicians, and later on they parped away wildly at the back of the auditorium. Ray Smith, who'd done all the sock record covers for them, stood around on stage doing his ironing. Fantastic stuff.

WERNER 'ZAPPI' DIERMAIER We had welders, sculptors and knitters on stage. My girlfriend's kids did their homework on stage. They started off shy, looking down at the floor, but when people started clapping they had their fun as well. We wanted our shows to smell like hard work.

HANS-JOACHIM IRMLER Gunther, Rudolf and I were Dada fans. We did a play as well, called *Dr Schwitters*, pretty much pure blasphemy actually.

WERNER 'ZAPPI' DIERMAIER We started hiring power tools and using them ourselves, that was safer. We did overdo it a bit for a while. On a US tour the stage looked like the aftermath of war after every gig. Everything was destroyed. Sometimes we'd smash up a piano, sometimes there'd be a fire on stage and it'd be soaked in water afterwards. But at the end of the gigs people came up and took the wreckage home with them, sometimes even autographed. We often got banned for life in those places, but it made for good press: 'Day or Die Faust,' etc. We're still banned from the Great American Music Hall in San Francisco.

JEAN-HERVÉ PERON People never danced at our gigs. The audience was mostly older intellectual men with beards. Hardly any women.

HANS-JOACHIM IRMLER What I always wanted was for Faust to break down clichés. We wanted the shows to be as exciting as possible for us, which is selfish, of course. We wanted to be impressed by ourselves on stage. We played in a boxing ring once, in Liverpool.

JEAN-HERVÉ PERON Virgin had promised us a huge PA. That's nothing special these days, but at the time it was really cool for musicians. The PA was supposed to arrive on time for a show at the Rainbow Club in London, but no surprise it didn't. I decided to go on stage naked, in protest, and the club lowered the curtain instantly. 'What a scandal!' The English are a bit prudish. So I got dressed again and we went back on. The end with Virgin came because we had a different live philosophy to Richard Branson. I didn't pick up on much of it, though. Zappi and I were never into long discussions; either we'd be making music or we'd take the dogs for a walk. Anyway, they had a big palaver and something didn't work out. Branson apparently had a certain vision for Faust, and Irmler, Rudolf and Nettelbeck had different visions. The upshot was that Irmler and Rudolf hit the road. Gunther, Zappi and I stayed.

WERNER 'ZAPPI' DIERMAIER Everyone wants commercial success at some point, it just never worked out for us in the end. But Uwe always made sure we had money. Without a record contract, Faust probably wouldn't have lasted long.

HANS-JOACHIM IRMLER It was always a given for us that no one else was allowed a say in our music. At some point, though, Branson and Uwe tried it, which led to the break-up. I fell out with Uwe over it, and I refused to speak anything but Swabian to Branson. Then Faust split up for a while, to give us all a bit of a break.

WERNER 'ZAPPI' DIERMAIER Nettelbeck used to come on tour with us at the beginning as tour manager, but then he did other stuff.

JEAN-HERVÉ PERON There was a little tour lined up, five or six gigs, and we did them, partly with other musicians like Uli Trepte and Peter Blegvad. But after that tour we jetted back to Germany – and we all met up in München at the Arabella Hotel, where the Rolling Stones were staying as well to record in the Musicland Studio, down in the basement. Our roadie, a Dutchman called Ruud Bosma, booked us in there as well. He was a chameleon who could transform in one second from a roadie to a smart businessman. He went into the Arabella and announced: 'We're here with the band Faust from Virgin Records – *Tubular Bells*, you know. And we want the same studio as the Rolling Stones, for three weeks. Plus rooms for everyone – Virgin's picking up the tab!' They just said 'Sure!' and let us in.

WERNER 'ZAPPI' DIERMAIER After a while we'd had enough of staying at the Manor. We didn't like the food there any more. So we left and moved into a five-star hotel. We got them to send the bill to Richard Branson, and he even paid it, but then we left the UK and went to the Arabella in München. We spent two weeks recording there and sent the bill to Richard Branson again. He refused to pay that one, though, and the police turned up; two of our parents paid our bail. We paid it back later.

HANS-JOACHIM IRMLER I'd contacted Giorgio Moroder, who had this studio downstairs at the Arabella Hotel. I asked him what was going on there after 9 pm. Moroder said: 'Nothing, why?' 'Could we record there then?' 'Yeah, why not?' Moroder's an adventurer too. He had Donna Summer in there during the day, and Faust came in at night. We had a deal with Moroder that we'd pay something as soon as the songs we recorded there brought in some money. I tried to get Branson to cover the hotel costs, at least, but he refused. Still, we had a wonderful time in Moroder's studio.

JEAN-HERVÉ PERON So we recorded there, and after a while the bill got so expensive that the people at the hotel checked with Virgin if they'd really pay for everything. Virgin acted all surprised and said they'd chucked us out ages ago.

SIMON DRAPER They just had unrealistic expectations. We liked *Faust IV* as an album, but then they just buggered off and did more recording in München without consulting us. They ran up horrendous studio costs there and then they called us up and asked if we'd pay the bill. We said no, and I'm afraid we had to tell them: 'Guys, you're not selling many records and dealing with you's not much fun, so we don't want any more stuff from you.'

JEAN-HERVÉ PERON The hotel threatened to put us in jail, and one of us got in the car with the PA and all the tapes and crashed out through the underground car park barrier. The others hot-footed it as well and only three of us stayed: Irmler, Sosna and me. We let them arrest us – at least we'd saved our PA and the material.

SIMON DRAPER I can tell you with absolute certainty that we never made any money out of Faust's records. Whether we broke even on the tours I don't know, but I doubt it. Tours cost a lot and there's not usually much left over in the end. Virgin definitely sponsored Faust's tours – that's why Henry Cow played support, another one of our bands.

HANS-JOACHIM IRMLER Faust split up then, to let things settle for a while.

JEAN-HERVÉ PERON After that we officially went underground. Six days in prison, and then it was obvious we'd go our separate ways. We didn't fight, we just broke up.

WERNER 'ZAPPI' DIERMAIER After the Arabella, we didn't do anything with Faust for ten years.

JEAN-HERVÉ PERON I don't like talking about that time. Not because I've got anything to hide, but it's part of our legend. Let's just say that our musical life continued perfectly normally. We just went back to our roots, back to square one, back to Hamburg to the Toulouse Lautrec Institut. Zero hour.

WERNER 'ZAPPI' DIERMAIER A few years ago there was a huge long queue after a show in China, all the way out to the street. They had piles of Faust records with them to get them signed, and we spent two hours giving autographs.

HANS-JOACHIM IRMLER Faust always had a better reception abroad than in Germany. No one's interested in us here to this day, actually. We'll probably all have to die first before anyone in Germany takes an interest.

JEAN-HERVÉ PERON I don't see Faust purely as a music band – we're simply not good enough musically for that. But there are other things we're pretty good at. Not many people come out of a Faust show saying they had a dull time. Even if you say: 'That was a heap of shit.' Most people leave with stars in their eyes.

NETWORKS

'What does he want here?'
ACHIM REICHEL

HARALD GROSSKOPF You didn't pick up much on what the others were doing; you'd work autonomously.

MICHAEL ROTHER Of course I knew of other bands, but I wasn't interested in any kind of dialogue or exchange. I only paid attention to the few people I knew in Düsseldorf, that was enough for me. I wasn't interested in anything else and I was so busy – even with Kraftwerk I learned a lot, and then with Conny Plank, Roedelius and Moebi – I didn't need any more stimulus than that. I never went abroad in those days.

GERD KRAUS We'd meet up fairly often with bands we were friends with, because we were all permanently on tour: Xhol Caravan, Guru Guru or Amon Düül had an audience everywhere, but naturally it was more or less the same people wherever you went. With Limbus, for example, I was once invited to a festival in Kassel, and when we got there the first person we ran into was Ralf Hütter, who said: 'Hello, Gerd!' Similar people came to see Limbus and Kraftwerk at that time. So we'd chat away as we were rehearsing; for instance, Ralf would say: 'You know what, Gerd? I'm only playing quavers these days.' That was the kind of thing we'd discuss very seriously. I wish today's music scene had just ten per cent of that serious approach.

PETER BAUMANN There was very little contact between Berlin and other places. I'd meet Amon Düül now and then at festivals, but we never had any close exchanges. Agitation Free and Ash Ra Tempel I knew a bit better, of course, because they were from Berlin as well, but that's about it. Tangerine Dream really had very few connections outside the band. But I guess that's just the Germans for you.

GÜNTER SCHICKERT Our Berlin isolation was intensified by the fact that everyone always came here anyway. If I wanted to see Amon Düül, I didn't have to go all the way to München, I could just wait until they played the TU-Mensa [the canteen venue at the Technical University].

LÜÜL We West Berliners always just stuck together. Maybe Amon Düül were in Berlin fairly often, because Uschi Obermaier lived in Kommune 1. But we played most of our Agitation Free gigs with Ash Ra Tempel or Tangerine Dream. And you'd always run into people all the time anyway, at places like the TU-Mensa. That's how I ended up with Ash Ra later on, and Christopher Franke with Tangerine Dream. Or Axel Genrich joined us for a bit and then went to Guru Guru, who we were also in touch with. But the closest links were more between the Berlin bands. I guess there was a certain solidarity between all the Ohr bands, like Wallenstein or Witthüser & Westrupp, with Rolf-Ulrich Kaiser as the link between them all. We were more like outsiders in the scene, at any rate. There was only one time we hung out with Cluster: for two weeks, during the Olympics.

HELLMUT HATTLER To begin with, we didn't even realise there was a scene of sorts in Germany. You'd meet the other bands at festivals. The first time we met Kraftwerk was at a performance in Hamburg. There wasn't a lot of dialogue, though, we just said polite hellos and kept a curious eye on each other. We had closer contacts to some bands, like Guru Guru; we'd visit them and party together. They always wanted us to play on their records as well. Embryo came by once but they were too out there for my taste, too ideological, they had to have strict rules for everything – not my thing. I won't let anyone else dictate how I lead my life as an artist. I presume I had a reputation back then for being 'too straight'. But I can live with that, even now; at least I'm still around to tell the tale.

HANS-JOACHIM ROEDELIUS In the Zodiak days, we had no contact with other scenes. The Zodiak was its own scene. Once we left Berlin that changed, of course. We lived in Düsseldorf for a bit and a while in Frankfurt, München, Ingolstadt. But only ever partially. With Kraan for a while, and then I visited Florian Fricke in his studio outside München. I was in touch with the Embryo people too. And you'd know completely different scenes as well, via actors like Hanna Schygulla or via Fassbinder, whose house we stayed in for a while. It wasn't just about music, there was much more to it. I'd often meet Holger Czukay in Conny Plank's studio; I could chat to him for hours. And we were in contact with Brötzmann, the free-jazz man.

RENATE KNAUP Amon Düül didn't have many dealings with bands from other places. I don't know if that was down to us.

LÜÜL Perhaps the fact that Amon Düül and Can were a bit older than us in Agitation Free, on average, played a role. At that age, a couple of years make a big difference. We were a bit late with our first album release as well.

RENATE KNAUP We knew Edgar Froese, Can and Mani Neumeier. You'd run into each other at gigs, you know? We were always playing giant festivals with bands like Pink Floyd, but we barely had any contact with them. It never went beyond a quick 'Hello, how are you?' No idea whether it was to do with some kind of competition. That was more up to the men – I didn't have much of a say.

HOLGER CZUKAY We were in touch with Amon Düül now and then. It was almost a friendship, but their music was too driven by the Grateful Dead for us. Plus they were hippies, lifestyle-wise, they all lived together in a commune, and we didn't. In general, though, most bands worked pretty independently of each other, did their own thing.

MICHAEL ROTHER One thing that's hard to imagine these days is how little contact and exchange there was via the media. The only show on TV was *Beat-Club*, and that was almost all American or British acts; the music magazines tended to be similar.

JÜRGEN DOLLASE A while ago I was at an event in Köln with some TV stars or other. Someone came over to tell me: 'Irmin says hello.' 'What Irmin?' I said. 'You know, Irmin Schmidt. The one from Can.' I was surprised because I'd never had any contact with him.

KLAUS SCHULZE We had contacts to Frankfurt and München and to Amon Düül, who I drummed with very briefly at the Essener Songtage. But most of that was getting gigs for each other. Tangerine Dream brought Amon Düül to the TU-Mensa in Berlin, and we got to play in München in exchange.

ACHIM REICHEL There was very little contact and dialogue via the music itself in Germany. Everyone worked on their own little island. All the bands eyed each other with suspicion, more or less. And then when someone like me came along, I bet a lot of people thought: 'Hold on a minute, he doesn't belong here. What does he want here? Oh, he's calling it freedom? That sounds dodgy!' You'd run into the Kraftwerk boys here and there, or Can or Edgar Froese and Mani Neumeier. The interesting thing was that all of a sudden there were musicians on board who didn't fit the clichéd image of proletarian rock bands at all: Irmin Schmidt, with his classical music degree – 'Oh shit! Hope he doesn't start talking about diminished chords or something.' Or the Kraftwerk boys, from wealthy Düsseldorf families – 'Oho, goodness me, oho.' But in the end, all of us cast off together for new shores, no matter what different worlds we landed in.

CAN

'Rock was not the objective.'
IRMIN SCHMIDT

IRMIN SCHMIDT My favoured sound is silence. Even as a child. When I was five I had a den in a little patch of woods in Berlin-Charlottenburg, near where we lived. I'd sit perfectly still there for hours and I thought it was wonderful. Or I liked gazing at streams for hours and listening to the gurgling. I savoured all the sounds around me. The underground trains came out of the tunnel very close by. There were hardly any cars in those days. Sometimes my enjoyment of silence really annoyed my mother. It didn't bother me if she sent me to my room as a punishment. I'd sit there perfectly happy, sing quietly to myself and not feel punished at all. When we evacuated from Berlin to Austria, during the war, we ended up on an Alpine pasture, where I loved the quiet view of the valley. There have been experiences like that throughout my life. And I think you can find that yearning for silence in my music, no matter how loud it sometimes was. Silence played a major role in Can's work. Listening to the depths – there's a German word for listening: *lauschen* – such a great word! Sometimes we'd sit together for an hour, not saying a word. We'd smoke a joint or maybe not, and listen in to the space, like a sound installation that you can take certain sounds from. A tap dripping somewhere, a toilet flushing perhaps. And then at some point we'd get up and start to make something out of that quiet calm. A lot of Can's music came out of that feeling of listening to the space. Jaki could sit there for half an hour without saying a thing. He'd sit there as if frozen, but he was listening or thinking. He had that feeling for silence as well.

HOLGER CZUKAY It was always clear to me that there'd be no getting around music, in my life. But I soon realised that jazz wasn't my language. I even won prizes for jazz, but it still wasn't my language. Listening to Stockhausen on the radio in bed at night – that was it! I loved it, it was crazy! That's when I noticed he had something. I found that out when I was still at school. Stockhausen got a lot of joy out of shocking people, musically. Then after I'd met Stockhausen, I once saw someone call him out: 'Herr Stockhausen, all you want to do is shock your audience and make a lot of money out of it.' He replied: 'I can promise you I'm acting purely out of musical motivation. And when it comes to money, I don't need to worry because I married a rich woman.' That got all my bells ringing – it was right up my street! Exactly what I wanted to do too! When I had to make a living after university, it was a matter of finding a rich woman – so I moved to the homeland of rich women: Switzerland. And I picked a boarding school where the richest of the rich sent their children. I applied for a job as a music teacher there, and when the headmaster asked me about my training and my teaching qualifications, I proudly answered that I'd studied under Stockhausen. The headmaster had no idea who he was but he still gave me the job. But instead of a rich woman, in the first class I taught I met my student Michael Karoli. He was eighteen, in the upper sixth.

JAKI LIEBEZEIT In the sixties, other musicians told me everything traditional was old hat, and they pointed me to free jazz, where tonality and repetition were *verboten* – but that ultimately meant the end of rhythm, or was tantamount to unordered rhythmics, whichever you like. And yet I always felt I wanted melodic rhythm. The prohibitions in free jazz took away my conviction in it; what's free about it if I can't do what I like? You weren't supposed to play the blues either, although the odd blue note did slip out now and then. But free jazz and blues both came from America, or more precisely the men whose ideas generated free jazz, Ornette Coleman and Don Cherry. We free-jazz men wanted to do it too, but it was always a 'too'. And that 'too' was the mistake in itself. Can put an end to that 'doing it too'.

IRMIN SCHMIDT In the winter of 1966, the German Music Council sent me to New York for the Dimitri Mitropoulos conducting competition, and I ended up hopelessly immersed in the city's music venues. I spent three days lying on an air bed in some basement, for instance, listening to La Monte Young's drone put on by the Theatre of Eternal Music, where John Cale and others made that sound without pause, taking turns continuously, with Tony Conrad or Angus MacLise stepping up so the others could get some sleep. All they actually played was one chord, but at a hellish volume. Even after an hour you'd hear the angels singing, but it went on eternally, to eternity. I was utterly fascinated, and it was immediately much more important to me than my conductors' competition. I promptly forgot my score at the second orchestra rehearsal. I was supposed to conduct Mahler's fourth – I'd only got back to the hotel at five in the morning, the rehearsal started at ten and I left the score in my room on the way there. I'd learned it by heart, but that didn't help either. They must have noticed my mind wasn't really on the competition. I stopped turning up after that, but I met Steve Reich and Terry Riley instead. Terry had one of those basements in the Bowery, where we played minimal music for nights on end, him on saxophone and me on piano. That kind of music was actually a mystery to me, because it seemed so naïve and simple. Riley's *In C* with its short patterns – at the time it felt like a joke to me, going by the notes. It was only with Steve Reich, who'd just finished his first great loop piece *It's Gonna Rain*, that I worked out what was behind it. But I didn't get any more involved in the minimal-music scene than that. I preferred watching films like Warhol's *Chelsea Girls* in the cinema. I met the art historian Gert Schiff as well, who lived in the Chelsea Hotel, and he introduced me to the rest of the gang. The nights were long, with occasional LSD trips. There were beautiful pictures hung in the Chelsea Hotel, which suited my interest in new painting. One of the great Fluxus artists, Dick Higgins, lived around the corner from the hotel, and I visited him regularly and met John Cage there several times. So if there was something like a click effect for Can, then it was New York. And the main thing that clicked was that they made no distinction between 'great art' and 'entertainment' – unlike back home. It was so much freer than Germany, and liberating in that sense. I ended up extending my New York stay to two and a half months. They let me stay in my room even though I'd dropped out of the conducting competition. The competition was run by a rather quaint association, all lawyers and dentists' wives with blue-rinsed hair. The members were all about eighty, and they held these great gala evenings with their blue rinses. I stayed with a lawyer, and when I'd get home at six in the morning after skipping the concert the association had told me to attend, yet again, he'd be sitting at the kitchen table all on his own and he'd say: 'Oh boy, you're in trouble . . .' But he took it with a sense of humour. A wonderful man. I asked him why he got up so early in the morning. 'It's the only hour of the day when I get a bit of peace and quiet.' His wife ruled with an iron hand, you see. Wonderful people, but I still couldn't stand it and moved into a terrible hotel room. I preferred it to being mothered and getting told off all the time for missing some Haydn string quartet – that was really the last thing I was interested in there. I'd had my fill of that kind of thing for the past fifteen years, while New York was veritably exploding with new ideas; I had to get into that world. There's a side of me that tends to the excessive, and I could easily have lost myself there. Perhaps it was a good thing that I wasn't in direct contact with Warhol's Factory, although those what-ifs are always pointless. I've never regretted any of my decisions, at any rate, including giving up conducting. Sometimes I do get a spontaneous yearning, but that's over after a day or two. It's hard to say from today's standpoint how coincidentally or not it all happened back then. I very nearly went to San Francisco with the art history professor from the Chelsea Hotel; the only reason I didn't was money. What might have happened if I did?

JAKI LIEBEZEIT I already knew Schmidt. And the basic idea for the group came from him, I have to admit. The starting point was that all of us were unhappy with our various situations at the time, no one wanted to carry on doing what they were doing. Schmidt was working in classical music and theatre, that's how I knew him. There was a studio at the theatre where he was already making film music. And I was in the studio with him a few times even before the Can days. Two years later, he asked me if I knew a drummer, because he wanted to get a band together. I said: 'Yes, I do.' 'Who?' 'Me.' My answer to that standard question: 'D'you know a drummer?' is always: 'I only know one: me!' Who else can you say that about?

IRMIN SCHMIDT Before Can I was in Köln, at the conservatory with Stockhausen. I'd set up the Dortmund Ensemble für Neue Musik. I studied ethnomusicology under Marius Schneider, who'd been defamed by the Nazis and written the famous book *Singende Steine* [Singing Stones], and also a three-volume history of polyphony. I was still entirely in that other world but I wanted to go somewhere else. Unlike other conservatories, Köln was relatively calm in 1968, not like Frankfurt or Berlin. But Köln was still interesting, less the rebellion of 1968 than the cultural scene: Neue Musik, all the galleries, theatres and opera, the broadcaster WDR, there was a lot going on everywhere. That was more important to me than taking to the streets. I could never imagine what the students actually meant by 'the system' anyway. Radical changes were taking place in the art scene and in German theatre at the time as well. I was active in the art scene, ran around a lot of galleries, attended exhibition openings with young artists and curated a little myself. In the sixties, the Documenta festival had started changing everything in our minds. And then came the new American painting: Pollock, de Kooning and so on. The departure happened in art before music; there were only relative timid beginnings around Stockhausen, but they didn't have a broad influence. The new theatre people like Heiner Müller had a lot more resonance as well. Being able to make that sharp cut in my biography probably had a lot to do with what I'd experienced in art and theatre, that mood of change and radicalism – I was already familiar with it.

HOLGER CZUKAY I gave Michael Karoli guitar lessons. We got on immediately, played music together and jam sessions at night. People like Tony Ashton would come along now and then, but you could forget anything experimental with them. The only one I stuck with was Michael. He did his A-levels, and I got fired from the boarding school for being too rebellious, and then I took a teaching job in northern Germany, at a grammar school in Quakenbrück. I played things like 'Hey Joe' in a band with the students. One day I got a letter from Irmin Schmidt, suggesting we start a band. That was in 1968. I actually had other plans – I wanted to get a band going myself, with Michael.

IRMIN SCHMIDT I'd lost sight of Holger, so I wrote him a letter saying I'd like to get a group together. I said I had no idea how it would turn out but I wanted it to have everything in it, from jazz to the stuff we were doing. My instrument was classical piano, and Holger played bass. 'Do you fancy it?' And Holger wrote back: 'Yes, but I've got a young guitarist here, just doing his A-levels, and we were actually just thinking about starting a band. We'll come over and see you.' As I said, we all had a history, and that was important to me. The only one without any history was Michael, who was just an amazingly talented guitarist who could treat his guitar really rough, with the same radicalism that I found so fascinating in Jimi Hendrix. Michael and I got on at first sight, I liked him instantly, and it became one of my deepest friendships from that moment on. And that sealed Can's fate, really. The combination was what I wanted: a drummer with groove, a very young guitarist who lived in an electronic world, and me with my classical background. It was good luck that it all came together like that. The basic idea of Can was to combine various types of music, as I said, people who already had a path they were on, like me. Or like Jaki, who'd drummed his way through all of jazz history, from Dixieland to free jazz. When I met him, he was nearly thirty and he'd ended up playing with Manfred Schoof and Globe Unity – which didn't meet his needs, because he's the kind of person who has to make grooves. I came from the opposite end, from classical music. And Holger was somewhere in between, he'd done a bit of jazz, learned the guitar and pizzicato bass, but also studied classical music, proper classical orchestral school, and then composition with Stockhausen, longer than me, even. That's why he was more dedicated to serialism and other Stockhausen dogmas than I was.

HOLGER CZUKAY I learned from Stockhausen that music is something absolute. Before I started my degree, I went to Stockhausen and said: 'Herr Stockhausen, I can't play anything.' 'What do you want to be?' 'A composer!' He gave me a long, hard look. 'All right, I'll take you.' Schmidt only came to Stockhausen later. In the year when Schmidt came to us, Stockhausen took me aside once and said: 'Czukay, you think too much. You ask too many questions of music. You can barely compose because you're always asking questions. I've been at that point in my life too, asking myself so many questions that I couldn't compose. Only a few come up against that wall, but that's all the more reason for you to jump over it! No matter where you land afterwards.' It made me cry for a moment. He'd spoken to me man to man. A year later, he said: 'When a bird's ready to fly the nest, it spreads its wings: off you go!' And that's how I ended up in Can.

IRMIN SCHMIDT Stockhausen was a complex personality. On one side, he had his strict compositional technique, imposing forms on himself, no matter which. When I first went to his Darmstadt summer course in 1962, Stockhausen was still extremely dogmatic. Later he was more open and allowed a lot more. But it was always about form for him. And that's something that's essential to me too. A lot of Can's work came out of group improvisation, but it was always important for it to have a form – and that was also related to Stockhausen. Another side of him was the technical aspect, and that's where I owe him a great deal, for opening my ears to electronic music in the mid-sixties. There was very little electronic music back then that really sounded like music; most of it was more like device tests that no one would want to listen to these days. But Stockhausen works like *Gesang der Jünglinge* were real lessons for me, made it clear that you can make great music with electronics, that new paths were opening up! And that was key, because when I was studying composition in the sixties no one dared to compose anything – two months later a piece by Boulez, Nono, Stockhausen or Berio might come along and make you feel like you were lagging way behind. And that fear of somehow not being at the peak of your time, that was something Stockhausen imposed on you. I had a big row with him in Darmstadt in 1964. He spent weeks analysing his *Gruppen* for three orchestras and then wound up saying the last two days were reserved for questions from the students, but he'd only answer intelligent questions. And that was exactly what I objected to: 'You can't know in advance if a question is intelligent or dumb! Sometimes the simplest of questions are the most enlightening!' I told him he was intimidating everyone so much that the cleverest questions wouldn't get asked. Stockhausen did tend to polarise, but I still enjoyed my time with him. When I went on to study properly under him in Köln, he'd invite students home and hold all-night parties. He wasn't an unapproachable master; he had that Köln *joie de vivre* and sense of humour, he wasn't afraid to have fun.

HOLGER CZUKAY Can was the opposite of Stockhausen. Any approach to Stockhausen requires a lot of thinking – but that wasn't our intention with Can. We wanted to let the music happen of its own accord, purely intuitively. We didn't have much experience of that to begin with, but where there's a will there's a way: 'We'll record right away! We won't go to a studio! We'll do everything ourselves!' No one knew what would come out of it. I was still a dilettante, but I understood that a universal dilettante can overtake an expert, by all means. Experts are always afraid of making mistakes, instead of internalising the music. Only dilettantes can do that. Once I realised that, I was never scared again. There's no way I can be so bad that nothing works out at all.

JAKI LIEBEZEIT Musicians I worked with were always telling me: 'This is the music I grew up with, and that's what I'm sticking to.' I've never taken that standpoint. From the very beginning, I was curious and looking for change. In the sixties, most bands in Germany had bass, guitar, drums, vocals and maybe a keyboard on top. A few dance orchestras were made up of pretty good musicians; Kurt Edelhagen had good people. But apart from jazz, there was no interesting music in Germany, and not much else to build on either. So Can wasn't into the German thing. We didn't see ourselves as Germans, we thought of ourselves as citizens of the world. It was important to us not to concentrate on nations, not any more. Our music was based on a world-spanning idea.

IRMIN SCHMIDT Turning down a career as a composer was a drastic decision at the time, a very 1968 thing to do. My family thought I'd gone out of my mind. And a lot of my friends said: 'Are you crazy?' Or: 'Now he's really lost it.' I was known as a great proponent and interpreter of the newest of the new Neue Musik, I'd conducted the German premiere of John Cage's *Atlas Eclipticalis* with the Bochum Symphony Orchestra. Can already existed at that point, there was a bit of an overlap. I did Cage piano evenings as well, with *Winter Music* or his silence piece *4'33"*. That was pretty much the most radical thing you could do at the time. I found a letter recently from someone who remembered how dumbfounded the audience was that a highly concentrated pianist would do 'nothing' amid deathly silence; the unsettled atmosphere came about hesitantly. In other words: I was already known as a slightly crazy person. And that's why my veer to Can didn't come out of nowhere. My parents were sad about it, though, and I can understand that. We were badly off after the war. My father had difficulties getting work in his industry and making decent money. Despite our poverty, my parents gave me all the support they could for lessons and university – although my father thought my decision to become a musician was, well, questionable, because of the risk of not earning a living. He was a certified civil engineer and architect, he'd have liked to see me follow in his footsteps. Especially in the post-war years, architecture was an exciting career, always in demand. At the age of fifteen, at the height of my war with my father, I had lessons in architectural draughting and designing houses – and I'd sit with him in perfect harmony; that's how contradictory life is. But then he accepted me studying music without complaint. My mother had wanted to study music as well and would have liked to be an opera singer; she had an absolutely beautiful voice. She'd sing Puccini, and I'd accompany her on the piano. And she also had a much better ear than I ever had. When I was practising piano she'd pop up out of nowhere and point out my mistakes. I got a lot of support from my parents. And now I was just tossing it all overboard? They were really shocked when I started Can. Out of my friends, the only ones who really understood it were a few painters, who were just as radical at the time. They thought it was a good thing, naturally.

HOLGER CZUKAY For Irmin, Can was a typical 1968-style decision, a kind of radical leftist statement. For me, it wasn't. Irmin turned it in that direction, but I couldn't follow him. I was even embarrassed by his first TV interviews. I had nothing to do with what he said about politics and hegemony. For me, things only work as long as music and politics are kept separate.

IRMIN SCHMIDT I already had some distance from the 1968 move-ment, though. In 1968 I just wanted to get rid of all the dogmatism and do something concrete, not run from one pig-headed movement to the next.

JAKI LIEBEZEIT Can was a typical 1968 venture, pushing back against the past, a long-overdue radical change. And of course there were impulses from America too. Bands like the Velvet Underground had a major influence; not stylistically, more for the atmosphere.

IRMIN SCHMIDT A free collective with rock instruments and at rock volume, but not a rock band – that was the idea I started from. The rest we developed in the group; we all had equal rights. Malcolm Mooney turned up somehow, which became an initial thing between Malcolm and Jaki, who were suddenly a rhythm section. Malcolm is actually a vocal drummer. That's how the specific Can rhythm came about, and the whole thing took off from there. You could do something with Holger that I was also very much at home with: collaging – and we collaged until the cows came home. Holger had a lot of fun with it. Jaki never took part in that side, it bored him, he just wanted to play. But when the rest of us broke down a piece into its components and put it back together again in a new way, it was mainly Holger who developed enormous enthusiasm. He had the technical skills and he got very deeply into it. We didn't need a sound engineer; Holger did it all. He'd earned money as a teenager by repairing the neighbours' radios, something I was completely unsuited for. I only once mended a neighbour's television, and that was down to my daughter, who was four at the time. She was friends with the neighbours' daughter, and when their TV broke down my daughter said: 'Daddy can mend it.' 'How will he do it?' 'He'll just kick it and the picture will come back.' They really did call me over, and the neighbour said: 'Go on, give it a kick!' So I did, and suddenly the thing started working again. After that I was an absolute star for my daughter – I could mend televisions.

JAKI LIEBEZEIT We were prepared to sacrifice all prior knowledge, or at least question it. Schmidt turning up was a fortunate coincidence. We did have some influences. There was nothing we took from jazz in terms of style, but we did take on the idea of improvisation. That's why we never had musical notes in the Can days. The idea of the song-writer was alien to us – 'I wrote this song while I was on holiday,' what hogwash. Spontaneity was the name of the game when we were in the studio together. Someone had an idea, and then someone else had another idea that went well with it. It usually happened on the rhythm level: two people each throw in a chord, a third one comes up with a melody or a strange sound, etc. That's how a piece was born, sometimes. We almost always recorded, a tape was always running. We taped over most of it later because it was rubbish, but even the rubbish might have led us onto a productive path. Some things were tried and tried for so long until they took shape, and then we did the recording. For me it was key that it had to be rhythmic, for me never ever to lose the beat. And if something was just limping along: chuck it out! With free jazz, it was much harder to say if something was good or not.

IRMIN SCHMIDT We were never a commune, but Can did almost live together for a while, because we were making music together for twelve to sixteen hours a day, every day. There was one piece where we integrated chants from a 'manifestation' [demonstration] in Paris, and of course all sorts of politically active people came to the studio, but they were actually more of a hindrance. At some point I couldn't stand all that abstract claptrap about how everything ought to be; I'd had enough and I wanted to do something concrete. Not 'change soci-ety' but create something with this small cell that was Can, something that hadn't existed before: a group of people who didn't actually fit together, weren't even friends to begin with, but melded together to form a kind of common subject. That was more radical than a lot of what people were talking about back then.

HILDEGARD SCHMIDT The key thing was that everyone played an equal part in the music. There's not one who writes the lyrics and one who composes the music. Everyone was always involved in everything. Always! Always! Always!

IRMIN SCHMIDT Spontaneity was despised in the Neue Musik world I came from. Boulez said it openly: spontaneity is nonsense. But a unit like Can can only come about on the basis of spontaneous interaction, never as a construction or a plan.

JAKI LIEBEZEIT At some point in 1968, I went along to a demonstration in the Ruhr region with the actor and activist Wolfgang Neuss. The whole group was political, of course, which you'd see just in the way it worked, far from the principle of leader and led. As Can, we really overcame that old structure. We were anarchists, essentially. Or genuine communists, if you prefer. A British paper once wrote that 'C-A-N' was an acronym of 'communism', 'anarchism' and 'nihilism'. I liked that idea.

HOLGER CZUKAY Especially in contact with other musicians, we soon noticed we were on a completely different path. But despite that, we were very focused on American acts; Irmin was right about that, things like MC5 or the Velvet Underground. Their live recordings felt a lot like Can. What we heard on early bootlegs was often terrible sound quality but always very, very exciting. That was much more our thing than any ironed-out super-track. I heard that John Lydon felt similarly, that he wanted PiL to sound like us. He wanted to be our singer once as well.

IRMIN SCHMIDT Non-European music was a huge influence for Can. Holger had just made a record of Vietnamese music. And I studied ethnomusicology in Köln, apart from my studies under Stockhausen. The first time Michael Karoli came to my place to talk about Can, he took a look at the shelves and whooped with joy when he found two records of music from Bali, which I'd brought back from New York. Jaki not only played jazz with Chet Baker in Spain before Can, he also went to Morocco and played with North Africans. Every one of us was strongly influenced by non-European music. We always avoided the term 'world music', though, because it sounds so much like tourism. For our own excursions in that direction, we came up with the abbreviation 'E.F.S.: Ethnological Forgery Series', which works just as well in German: *Ethnologische Fälschungsserie*. It's all about the balance of closeness, distance and respect; so, immersing ourselves seriously, not just inserting it into our music like a souvenir, like you'd hang a sombrero on the wall, but at the same time not claiming to have an authentic grasp of the music or to be making a genuine contribution. Outside of that series, there were other influences of that kind as well – for example, *gagaku*, which you can hear in the music if you want to. That came about largely unconsciously, but it's probably down to my interest in medieval Japanese music. It has this incredible brutality that we arrogant Europeans will never understand. Humility towards the great cultures of Asia and Africa was immensely important to Can. In the knowledge that we knew nothing of it, we could use it as an influence.

JAKI LIEBEZEIT The first thing we had in common was that none of us wrote musical notes. The composer listed after every song was just 'Can'. Even the singer improvising his lyrics had no special rights to them. Everything was thrown in the pot, it was only ever about the group. I was naïve enough at the time to think all pop groups did it that way. 'The Beatles are friends! They share everything equally!' I didn't find out until later that Lennon and McCartney set the tone. Ringo will have earned enough out of it, sure, but still much less than Paul McCartney. That wouldn't have happened in Can. There wasn't one commander who had the say and wrote the songs and got the others to play them, and got rid of them if they couldn't or wouldn't go along with him. In the beginning there were five of us, so we could always make majority decisions, always at least three-to-two. That was a great advantage. There were certainly attempts to seize power over Can, but they were always blocked by the majority. We were absolutely democratic, almost socialist, as the liberal politician Guido Westerwelle would have said. That made Can pretty unique, as a group. There were some big egos involved, but they had no say in the matter.

IRMIN SCHMIDT Jaki always spoke of 'instant composing'. I think he got it from the Dutch free-jazz people: they called themselves the Instant Composers Pool. Around about 1968, though, Stockhausen also started referring to 'intuitive music', first just as an instruction in compositions, but then he moved more and more in that direction. Ultimately, it's about inventing the music on stage, highly concentrated, alert and in permanent reaction to what's happening around you, not as a solo trip. Part of that is a very humble attitude, not in the religious sense but out of respect for the other people making music with you. When the process works, it's one of the most wonderful things you can experience in life.

HOLGER CZUKAY What we did with Can was often perceived as improvising, but that's a misunderstanding – what we were doing was instant composition! The fact that no one understood it just brought us even closer together. That's probably why we stayed together so long, because it was soon clear to all of us that we were on a path no one had walked before us, one we could only walk together. Strangely enough, it was the Americans who understood it best, perhaps because there were parallels to us in their New Music. Steve Reich's *Drumming* is composed with notes, but it comes entirely out of playing as an ensemble, from listening to each other and interweaving to get an organic, dynamic ball rolling, like with Can.

IRMIN SCHMIDT Equal rights were difficult. We were five alpha males, each of us could have started his own group as a band leader. Especially me; I was trained as a conductor, after all. As a conductor, you have to stand there, and before you even raise your arm the orchestra has to trust you, you have to emit an energy that makes everyone think: 'We believe in him.' The audience has to believe in you too, the second you set foot on stage. That's the secret. And everyone in Can had that, which was why we accumulated such amazing energy. Naturally, this led to constant friction, but that friction itself also constantly led to new music. Arguments produce sparks and electricity, so even more energy, ultimately. None of us was gentle and pliant. But we had a shared objective.

JAKI LIEBEZEIT We chose our band name by secret ballot. We'd done a brainstorming session, everyone wrote five suggestions on pieces of paper and we put them in a tin can. I'd arranged with Malcolm Mooney to write 'CAN' as all ten of our suggestions. And that's what we ended up with.

IRMIN SCHMIDT We invented things together, and of course we talked as well. I'm sure we older guys all had a big influence on Michael, partly because he still saw himself as a kind of student at the beginning. But I learned just as much from him. It's hard to put my finger on what exactly, but I have a feeling I owe him a huge amount, in musical terms. Our way of making music was very intuitive. You'd just let the instrument do its thing, and Michael would correct that sound slightly, which sometimes came about of its own accord, sometimes with the bar on his guitar, sometimes with a fingernail, or by leaning his Fender against the speaker and stepping away. It was about the possibilities of not *mastering* an instrument, but really *playing* with it. Sometimes just by doing nothing at all. That way of making music, that modulating, letting things happen, none of us had that apart from Michael.

HOLGER CZUKAY Why should we have played blues? The Americans could do it a thousand times better. And others could do rock much better. Other people were superior to us in all other genres. From that perspective, we were an absolutely terrible band. We just had the good fortune of having our own studio where I could bring all sorts of ideas together. Our first record, *Monster Movie*, was effectively a collage.

IRMIN SCHMIDT The process was that we recorded everything we played and then listened to it together. Jaki always said: 'Throw it all away and start again.' If we'd have done what he said, we'd still be working on our first album now. So at some point we decided that there are three or four recordings that have great parts in them, albeit in different places. With Jaki's rhythmic precision, we could splice them together. And then Holger did that, an absolute virtuoso, with Michael and me looking on. The architecture of those collages was always a joint decision between Holger, Michael and me. Jaki found it boring; he was a pure jazz man in that respect until the end, he only ever wanted to make music in real time, in the act of playing itself, never outside of the primary playing time, which is unavoidable for editing and tape splicing – and was something Holger absolutely loved! So we always had to play the results of that cutting and pasting to Jaki afterwards, because he had to give his approval. With collages, I tended more towards radical, vicious breaks, in the style of Neue Musik. And we do have those in places, but as a rule the groove had to be strictly adhered to, no matter how many cuts we made. Jaki was our groove guardian, first during playing and then for final approval.

JAKI LIEBEZEIT We were ahead of our time on a few things that are normal these days. I remember getting in trouble with other jazz musicians because I played so strictly repetitively. 'Man, you only ever play the same!' Couldn't I come up with anything else? They were used to the avant-garde dogma of the time, that everything has to keep changing as much as possible. But that was exactly why I loved those minimal grooves after my free-jazz days, almost out of enjoyment of breaking taboos. On 'Halleluwah' there's one beat that runs through the track for almost twenty minutes, a constant underlying figure. All the other parameters can change – volume, timbre, etc. – but the groove stays the same. I designed a specific rhythm for every Can track, like the way a Viennese waltz has its own unmistakeable rhythm. The repetition I developed in Can is bang up-to-date now, but it's almost only ever machine-made, programmed. That's fine too. Back then, people weren't that into it yet.

IRMIN SCHMIDT You couldn't decide anything on your own, in Can. Holger would have liked to, of course, but even the montage of the LP tracks was always done collectively. A lot of crazy decisions got made. Michael might say: 'Why don't we do it backwards?' Or on 'Tago Mago' we copied snippets of older recordings into the mix, like phantoms from the past bubbling up and then disappearing again. That was my idea, for example, but Holger made it happen. The only discussions we had were about the music, whether the groove was right, whether the chords were OK, whether to add more, and if so, whether we could cut here, because otherwise the groove might get broken up. Or how to put it together differently.

RENÉ TINNER We really went to the studio every day, except when we were on tour. Either way, we were making music every day. The pleasant thing was that we were never under time pressure because it was our own studio. Sometimes we worked right through two days and nights, there was no time for sleep. And everything was always recorded. The Can philosophy was: the red light has to be on from the moment you walk into the studio, otherwise you might as well stay at home. You can't throw away what you haven't got. The usual process was to do only recording for four or five days. Then we set it aside. After a week or so we'd listen to it and see whether this or that section might be interesting. But it was all very free. And everyone almost always agreed on what was good and what wasn't.

HOLGER CZUKAY At the beginning I always wanted to play as many notes as possible. But Jaki said to me: 'Holger, just play a single note now and then.' So I tried it, and the result really was very interesting. That's how I realised I had to reduce things. It was actually the first elementary music lesson I ever got: the important thing is not to play as much as possible, but to let the others get a word in too. And even with just one bass note, you can make a big impression. Realisations like that were more important to me than any politics.

RENÉ TINNER Up to that point, I'd only known standard studios with a control room behind glass and the recording room. Everything that happened there went on in two separate worlds: one thing happened in the control room, something else in the recording space. That was different with Can because it all happened in the same room, and also it was a huge space, which other studios didn't have. There was no 'producer'. Holger played bass and also operated the recording equipment. The studio was completely different to anything I'd seen before. At first I didn't understand a thing, but I soon realised it was something special.

IRMIN SCHMIDT After we'd set up our studio and started playing pieces, Malcolm suddenly came along. He was very influential because he was really Can. His spontaneity and craziness and his understanding of music were very important for me. Malcolm had never sung before; he was a painter from Paris. I was actually supposed to introduce him to the Köln gallery scene, but instead I dragged him along to the studio, where he spontaneously started singing. A singer was born! Although the better word would be 'vocalist', because 'singer' is so closely linked to lyrics and Malcolm deployed his voice absolutely freely, like an instrument. I owe something key to everyone in Can: Malcolm the courage for shameless spontaneity, that high art of simply letting out a feeling, no matter with what instrument or how. If you're a classically trained pianist who goes on stage and gives an obedient rendering of Chopin, you can't do that. Malcolm taught me to trust myself and others, the others even more so. When Malcolm left, we carried on without a singer to start with, and it turned out fine. Then came Damo, who Holger discovered by chance in the street. But he was less a singer than a phenomenon.

HOLGER CZUKAY I saw Damo on Leopoldstrasse in München and I said straight away: 'Jaki, he's going to be our next singer!' That was typical of me. I like to decide things like that intuitively. Damo was just sitting on the street and worshipping the sun. Jaki was horrified: 'Holger! You don't even know the guy!' But I'd already got up and gone over to Damo. I said to him: 'Hello, I'm Holger. What are you doing tonight?' He said: 'Nothing.' 'Do you want to be a singer?' 'Yeah, why not? I've got nothing else to do right now. What do I have to rehearse?' 'Rehearse? Nope. You've got to dive right in.' 'OK, why not?' The place we were appearing that night was packed to the rafters. Damo started very gently, sort of Japanese. But then he got really aggressive all of a sudden, samurai-like, at the touch of a button. He screamed and yelled blue murder. And we reacted to it. The success was marked by a huge punch-up in the audience. I thought it was all incredibly funny. After a while the place was empty, but we just kept on playing. It wasn't a rock concert any more, it was a happening. The people running away was part of the performance – we saw it as a triumph.

IRMIN SCHMIDT Sometimes we were just plain provocative. At the performance in München where we'd just picked up Damo, we were at war with our manager Abi Ofarim, who was actually already our ex-manager. But he'd arranged the gig, in this dance club for people from the suburbs. And then Ofarim dragged along the actor David Niven, wanting to show him what a great band he had on his books. Holger had brought along a big cake and he was lying on the floor with the bass humming away on his belly while he ate the cake. Michael leaned his guitar against the speaker and set off terrible feedback, really awful. I'd brought along three concrete blocks from a building site around the corner, plonked them down on my organ keyboard and turned everything up to full volume. Then Michael and I helped Holger with his cake. Only Jaki was sitting at his drums, red in the face, and fighting like a lion against all the noise. And then there was our new guy, this Japanese whirlwind who suddenly turned samurai and started shouting and hurling insults. No one understood what he was saying, nobody spoke Japanese, if it was even Japanese in the first place. Damo screamed and danced like a whirling dervish, and after an hour of that the place was empty. Even before that the organiser came and wanted to throw us out, but we just kept going. He didn't have the guts to drag us off stage. Afterwards the only person left was David Niven, and he said to Holger: 'It was great, but I didn't know it was music.'

HOLGER CZUKAY Nico was supposed to be our singer once too. Or at least, a few people advised her to do it. We did play together once but nothing came of it. I was always in favour of singers; I discovered Damo Suzuki, after all.

IRMIN SCHMIDT Jaki always said: 'We don't need a singer, singers are just troublemakers.' And he wasn't wrong, in principle. Expressing yourself via your voice, purely via your own body, creates a certain sense of confidence, often a sense of mission. And we weren't interested in that kind of charismatic frontperson. Can couldn't be a mouthpiece, no matter for whom or for what. Our only 'message' was: we are an organism. People who worked with language, including journalists, noticed early on that it was pointless to search our lyrics for meaning. There was a special fan club that 'decoded' Damo's lyrics, but the only things that came out of it were bizarre. In Can, everything semantic was subordinate, there was no 'message'. Malcolm did sing lyrics but he was never what you'd call a lead singer, and he knew it. Malcolm usually invented his lyrics spontaneously on stage or in the studio; it was often a tangled mess. And because of the way we edited the tapes, the words were deconstructed anyway; that would be hell for a poet with any kind of ambition.

HOLGER CZUKAY I did know what was being sung about. Like on 'Yoo Doo Right' – Malcolm had got a letter from a girlfriend in America, and he quasi-read it into the microphone and added spontaneous comments about how he felt. That was his lyric, which I definitely understood. And while we were recording the song it immediately ignited the right fire inside me. I understood what it was about, from the human side.

IRMIN SCHMIDT Damo took things to extremes. Damo didn't sing lyrics; it was pure Dada. They were sound collages out of a bit of Japanese, very fragmentary German, terrible English and some kind of artificial language – mumbled syllables not from any known language. And it fitted really well with Can. It wasn't lyrics, it was music made out of vocal sounds. We just let Damo do his thing because we had no interest in being judged on our lyrics. And with what he sang, he sabotaged that approach perfectly.

HOLGER CZUKAY Lyrics were a necessary evil. That was how I felt, in any case. Damo was at his best as a singer when he used his imaginary Japanese. It really worked perfectly. Voices were instruments for us, be it Malcolm Mooney, Damo Suzuki or Irmin Schmidt now and then. In that respect, we were like Joy Division: the band didn't care what the singer thought.

IRMIN SCHMIDT Our first live shows were held in a relatively small circle. They were at unis or small clubs, rarely with many people in the audience. Most of them were students, many of whom thought we couldn't play because we didn't sound like this or that British band. For those students, we were incompetent bunglers. But we didn't make it easy for them; we performed a kind of violence at our shows.

NIKEL PALLAT At Can gigs, the monotony produced a kind of inner peace. Not like Amon Düül, who flipped out much more on stage. Can was trance, Amon Düül was ecstasy. But they were both excellent bands.

MANFRED GILLIG I can't tell you how often I listened to *Monster Movie* back then in Berlin. It was really in permanent rotation, and of course I wasn't always entirely sober. The first time I listened to it was with two guys who later founded the band Morgenrot, and a girlfriend. We used to sit down together regularly, play records and smoke joints. One of them had brought along *Monster Movie* for us to listen to. We went crazy the first time we put the record on! And then we played it all the way through again. It wasn't an intellectual approach like with Pink Floyd's *Ummagumma*, where I started analysing exactly what was happening on the left channel and what on the right. *Monster Movie* was different. There was that voice, the rawness and at the same time the repetitive aspects. It was only after listening to it several times that I started wondering how they did it. It was music you took your time with, which you could listen to ten times in a row because it was so exciting and it made you lift off, in a way. The analytical response only came later. I must have listened to it fifty times, at least, when it was brand new. And seeing Can live, later on, was a revelation too: Holger Czukay playing around with electronics, Damo Suzuki with his strange vocals, and Jaki Liebezeit's relentless beat behind it. So we were almost proud that such exciting music was coming out of Germany, for once. And that made us want to find more German bands like them.

RENÉ TINNER The main difference between the studio sessions and the live shows was the volume. Can were actually only happy making music when it was loud. In the studio, we usually worked with headphones, which made a pretty big difference. A lot of people said the gigs were much better than the records, which was partly because we took a whole lot of risks – which meant fifty per cent were very good, but the other fifty per cent were bad. You'd soon forget the bad ones and take the good ones as your yardstick. My favourite appearance was probably the one in the Arles amphitheatre in the south of France, an open-air concert in summer where everything went right. And on top of that the wonderful surroundings, I think Nico was the support act, and the red wine was great. Six thousand French hippies were in paradise.

STEFAN MICHEL A Can gig just started whenever they were ready. What they did up there didn't seem to have any structure, it was more like a session that might last two hours, or it might take five. There was hardly any light on stage, but they did those typical hippy lightshows of that era: slides with different coloured liquids projected onto the back wall. You couldn't see much, though. And if you were listening out for tracks you recognised, you'd have a long wait; they preferred to develop things out of the moment. But it's the same with albums like *Monster Movie* or *Tago Mago*, they just continued the same way on stage. A band like Guru Guru, though, was already 'performing their tracks', the stuff you knew from the LP.

HOLGER CZUKAY Can had a really mixed audience to begin with. The first Can live show was part of an evening of modern music, although obviously we wanted to do it on a different level. It wasn't a good show, though. People clapped, but I knew it wasn't great. We were on the right path, in principle, but the result could have been better. I always knew that kind of thing straight away.

IRMIN SCHMIDT The exhilarating thing about Holger was his passion; the man was really all fire. He often almost burst out in flames, he was so emphatic. Sometimes I thought: 'A fireball's coming up any minute now, he's going to explode!' Whereas Jaki was pure energy, even when he was sitting around looking grumpy; his appearance is deceptive. He could drum planes out of the sky.

SIEGFRIED SCHMIDT-JOOS Can's appearances were happenings, where you never knew what would happen. There were only a few set parameters for them. Their trance music led to incredible patterns that suddenly mushroomed. From performance to performance, completely different pieces came about, sometimes under the same name. Every show was an adventure. Inevitably, there'd be less exciting passages, phases of ebbing and fading to enable new surges. But when it got intense, it was breath-taking. And that's transported on their recordings – to this day.

IRMIN SCHMIDT We played as a support band twice. Once for Black Sabbath; that was in 1969. Farfisa donated me an organ, and the owner of a big music shop who was a big Can sponsor also gave us a lot of equipment. He set up a huge PA for the gig, but the Black Sabbath guy was on the mixing desk and he wouldn't let us play any louder than Black Sabbath. My memories of the night are limited, though, because I had to go to the dentist shortly beforehand and my dentist had slipped, pulled one of my bottom teeth and destroyed one at the top, a complete massacre; anyway, I was up to my eyeballs on painkillers and I remember the concert just as ocean waves crashing. Later on, we played a tour with Hawkwind, but we always took turns. And we only came to fruition when we got to play for a long time, at least two hours. We usually played for a good hour and then did encores. Sometimes they went on for three hours, open-ended.

HOLGER CZUKAY We played a very special gig in Stuttgart once, in the Liederhalle. We'd been invited by the SDAJ, West Germany's Young Socialist Workers party. They paid us DM2,500. It was about 1975, some party gathering or other. So when we got there, I went into the hall and took a look. First they all sang the 'Internationale', but they sang it like exhausted warlocks. I couldn't believe it. They sounded like a collection of political people singing something they didn't believe in at all, they had no fire. And then we went on stage and drove them all out of there, down to the last church mouse. There was no one left at the end. It fitted perfectly because we felt like something was going wrong with them. We had to chase them out, like Jesus expelling the merchants from the temple.

IRMIN SCHMIDT The SDAJ had persuaded me to play at their AGM in Stuttgart's Liederhalle. We weren't particularly close to them, but of course we were on the left, so we said yes, and it was supposed to be paid. When we arrived, there were a lot of people running around and it was hard to unload our big speakers from the van. We had a PA with two really heavy bass speakers at the time, which Holger had had made. It was incredibly difficult to get the equipment on stage; we had to lug it all down long corridors and up and down stairs, and no one deigned to help us, not even when we asked them. The whole, let's say, community always had more important things to do, so that got our backs up to start with. Eventually the PA was set up, but then came Franz Josef Degenhardt and various girls in knitted dresses, who sang hand-knitted songs. With all due respect, it wasn't exactly rousing stuff. We sat in the audience, me next to Michael, and people around us kept leaping up and clenching their fists, with this devout, bovine look on their faces. It made us feel sick, especially me. I thought: 'We've had this uniformed mass hysteria in this country before.' By the time we got on stage we were so worked up that we emptied the hall in fifteen minutes. Two or three thousand class warriors buggered off, leaving our little fan community, maybe about a hundred people. The organiser came running up and ordered us to stop playing immediately. We said we wouldn't go until we got our fee. That turned up pretty quickly and we broke off the gig. That was our encounter with Germany's communist youth movement. But they wanted nothing to do with us either after that.

GERHARD AUGUSTIN People danced at Can gigs.

IRMIN SCHMIDT Our live audience was partly made up of students and 1968 activists. Some of them thought you had to share absolutely everything; for instance, they'd come on stage with a drum, sit down next to Jaki and start tapping away. None of us hated that more than Jaki. Or when someone 'helped out' on Jaki's drum set during a show – it could happen that Jaki accidentally hit them on the fingers with his sticks, hard enough to get the message across. Those kinds of guys – there were a couple of them in every hippy commune in those days and they'd come crawling out of their holes on occasions like Can gigs – they had a rather, let's say, one-sided idea of sharing, to put it politely. I had more understanding for them, though, in principle, than Jaki did. If someone joined in spontaneously, I'd sometimes think: 'Why not?' But when microphones went missing after the gig, that didn't match up with my idea of sharing. Apart from that, no matter how revolutionary, radical and whatever other 1968 stuff we were, we were primarily artists. And artists perform something for other people's enjoyment. If you just share for sharing's sake, nothing good comes out of it, or hardly ever. It's similar with these joint compositions that come about these days on the internet, out of sheer enthusiasm over all the stuff you can share – it's rare for anything usable to come out of it, it's always just amorphous mishmash in the end. And even less came out of that kind of thing live. Not everyone was into it in the audience either, when people climbed on stage to join in. There was always more applause than booing when we chased them off again.

WIM WENDERS Because my good friend and film editor Peter Przygodda was a Can fan from the early days, I knew the band from their first LPs and singles. I definitely had *Soundtracks* and *Tago Mago*. And *Ege Bamyası*, of course. I never saw Can live at the time, to my great regret. I never saw the Beatles either. But when Peter Przygodda edited the Can film about the 1972 'Free Concert' in Köln's Sporthalle, I saw that several times.

HILDEGARD SCHMIDT I simply took on the job of managing Can. You just have to come up with something when you've got no money. There were hardly any managers back then; everything was run via artist agencies. So I started by sitting down, pinning a big map of Germany to the wall and looking at where the band could play around the country. And then I wrote to culture people in every interesting town and offered for Can to play there. We also arranged a lot of our own concerts in those days, and I was the promoter.

BRIAN ENO I was listening to Can from 1972 at least. I imagine John Peel probably played it on his radio show . . . that was how most of us in England heard about new music at the time. The first thing I heard from Can was *Tago Mago*. Shortly after that I got to know Holger. I think we met through our mutual friendship with Michy Nakao, a Japanese photographer.

HILDEGARD SCHMIDT There was only one time when I intervened strongly in the music – when I got them to make *Tago Mago* a double album. I thought all the material was so good that it would have been a terrible waste to shrink it down to one LP. It had to be two records! But that solution hadn't occurred to the band. Getting the record label to do the double album wasn't as easy; it was still very unusual, despite the *White Album*. But once United Artists had accepted it, they were instantly enthusiastic. You have to find the right moment, when you know quite clearly that what you're doing is right, and then you can come up with the arguments. I managed to persuade them, anyway, and I was glad of it when *Tago Mago* was a success.

IRMIN SCHMIDT When the record label heard 'Aumgn' and 'Peking O' they wondered what was going on. But Hildegard insisted on it being a double album – her first heroic deed as our manager! She came into the studio when we said the record was finished, and she listened to side one and side two. And then she listened to all the other stuff we had lying around. In the end she said that had to go on the record as well – and she was so right. We hadn't dared to offer the label a double album. When she said it, we thought it was a great idea, of course. So Hildegard persuaded them to release a double LP with those crazy tracks on it. And she was completely right about it; *Tago Mago* is our most successful record.

GERHARD AUGUSTIN Business meetings were only ever with Irmin and Hildegard.

IRMIN SCHMIDT But it's better not to endanger such risky discussions about doubling up your LPs with debates about record covers – and that's how you end up with a crap-looking 'art head'. Especially if you haven't got any better suggestions. We never wanted to make grand statements with our covers, we just wanted them to look good. So we'd usually just let the label do what they thought was best with the sleeves, partly so they'd let us get on with the music. Working with Siggi Loch was great anyway, he gave us a lot of support, and we didn't want to overstrain the relationship with long discussions about a cover picture. The sleeves weren't all that important to us. Hildegard getting them to include sides three and four of *Tago Mago* despite their disconcertment – that was important, not the stupid head on the cover.

STEFAN MICHEL Hildegard had the business side firmly in hand. That was a good thing too, because Irmin Schmidt was totally fixated on the music and he seemed to have taken lessons in chaos from Stockhausen. Hildegard was very down-to-earth, though, and knew very well that the band was Irmin's whole life. You could tell on stage, as well, that he was the musical dynamo.

HILDEGARD SCHMIDT Can's expectation was that they could all make the music they thought was good. That was the aim. Then they made a joint decision: Hildegard's responsible for the money, she gets all the income – so everything from live shows, records and the Performing Rights Society, every pfennig – and then everyone was paid the same amount monthly, like a salary. The roadie and me as well. They handed in receipts for petrol and that kind of thing to me. The only thing everyone had to do themselves was pay their rent; we all lived separately, we weren't the commune types. So I looked after the money and did the bookkeeping. On tour, it was clear that I'd pay the bills. And Jaki didn't drink wine, for example, only Coke, while Messrs Schmidt and Karoli had a very different attitude to alcohol. We'd often go out for a big meal in Paris and other places, but there were never any complaints, absolutely never, where Jaki might have said: 'Guys, it's not OK, I'm making do with a hamburger and a Coke, and you're living it up on our money,' and so on. Can never argued about money, which was a very precious thing. Things always went well with the record companies as well. The deal was that we'd deliver the finished product and they had to take it, they were pure tape-acceptance agreements. We'd never have accepted any suggestions for changes from the record label. That wasn't hard to negotiate, though, because we never got million-mark advances anyway. But we had our freedom. And the good fortune that we always dealt with labels that understood us.

SIMON DRAPER Very few German musicians spoke good English. Hildegard Schmidt, the wife of Irmin Schmidt and Can's manager, was a particularly good English-speaker.

IRMIN SCHMIDT We already had a big flat when I was still a student, and before Can we even bought a big place of our own, because I'd made pretty good money with theatre and film music. Hildegard was earning very well too. Then when Can started, we instantly stopped making money. The change in our income made a big difference; it was brave of Hildegard as well. She's proud of her husband, who's always made a very good living, and as soon as things get serious he goes and starts a rock band. Before that I'd played Brahms on the radio as a pianist, done piano recitals, conducted, founded an ensemble, done mime. I was very involved in the gallery scene as well, even wrote art reviews for a conservative broadsheet, the *Frankfurter Allgemeine Zeitung*. I gave it all up for Can. And Hildegard went along with us, even became our manager. Without her lust for adventure and her trust in us, Can would never have existed in the form it took.

HILDEGARD SCHMIDT From the point when 'Spoon' got big, everything was suddenly easier. I ended up doing less promotion and more work on contracts, and making sure the band was paid. So I'd collect the money before they went on stage, otherwise they wouldn't play. I always told the others I wasn't a professional, but I kept a keen eye on everything.

SIGGI LOCH As managing director at Liberty, my main job around 1968 largely consisted of finding new pop artists for the German market. I had old ties to Klaus Doldinger, so he was the first act I signed. Because I'd run the Star-Club label for a while, I was still loosely in touch with the German rock scene, but my focus was on jazz. But one day my old friend Kalle Freynik turned up. He'd had a go of it as a German protest singer, and I'd made the record *Ich bin ein Deutscher!* with him in 1966 on the Star-Club label. Anyway, Kalle came to see me in München and played me an album he actually wanted to release on his own label, Scheisshouse-Records – that was Can's first recording. The music knocked my socks off. The only one of them I knew was Jaki Liebezeit, who'd been active in the Düsseldorf and Köln jazz scenes before Can. Listening to Can's first record was a huge eye-opener for me, and I wanted to sign them up immediately. I'd agreed a five-thousand-mark advance with Kalle. He wanted to come to my office the next morning, sign the contract and pick up the money. But he didn't show up. Instead, Abi Ofarim called me up and said if I wanted Can, I'd have to go through him. He doubled the advance to DM10,000, a lot of money for an unknown rock band in those days. So I ended up on Ofarim's couch negotiating with him, because I was completely on fire about the band. It turned out to be a win–win situation for all involved, both artistically and financially.

STEFAN MICHEL Around 1971 Abi Ofarim had a production company, and I got a job in the press department. That was when he had a contract with Can. I remember the nonplussed faces when Can came to München to play *Tago Mago* to the executives. Ofarim and his colleagues' faces got more and more puzzled the longer the record played. Ofarim left the room after a while; he thought it was really terrible, and Irmin looked irritated as well. But the band stayed diplomatic, there was no arguing. They weren't amused, though.

HILDEGARD SCHMIDT Abi Ofarim did pretty much nothing for us. He sued us later because he thought he was owed a lot of money, but thankfully that didn't work. A wonderful man called Siggi Loch helped us, and a lawyer.

JAKI LIEBEZEIT Our German 'breakthrough', if you can call it that, came with the soundtrack for a TV crime show by Francis Durbridge [the show was a *Strassenfeger*, a made-for-TV movie called *Das Messer*, meaning 'The Knife'; Durbridge was a British novelist and dramatist, best known for the *Paul Temple* series starring Francis Matthews, popular in Germany and the UK at the time]. That was the first time the name Can became slightly better known. After that hit, a lot of people started coming along to our German shows.

IRMIN SCHMIDT It's hard to say why Can were never a success in the US. I travelled in the States back then and I thought the rock scene I found there was very conservative. They didn't have time for anything avant-garde like Can. The intellectual East Coast was an exception, and New York, with bands like the Velvet Underground. And a little bit, but really only a little bit, San Francisco. I went to both cities often; I had friends in San Francisco. And there was some stuff going on in Chicago as well, but that was all. I don't think Can would have reached a large audience in the US in those days, even if we'd played there more often, in all the college towns. And we couldn't have played ninety gigs across the country, travelling by bus. We refused to do that even in Germany. What probably made Holger believe in bigger success in the US was that our musical fodder at the time was exclusively

American, not British. We were influenced by people like Captain Beefheart, Frank Zappa, Jimi Hendrix and Otis Redding. One of the great moments that 'clicked' for me was Jimi Hendrix's 'Hey Joe'. I first heard it on a jukebox in Berlin and it was like a flaming comet for me. The jukebox was stocked by this guy who always had everything that had just come out. The pub was close to the Akademie der Künste, where my friends [Markus] Lüpertz, [Peter] Sorge and others were students at the time. They dragged me along and said: 'Irmin, you've got to hear this, it's an amazing song.' I totally flipped out as well. One day later I had a copy and I couldn't get enough of listening to it. But even Hendrix, Zappa and Velvet Underground were more successful in Europe in their early days than in the States.

HILDEGARD SCHMIDT It wasn't easy promoting Can in Germany in those days; people didn't want them. What they wanted was British and American music. That all changed when 'Spoon' was on the soundtrack for Francis Durbridge's cliff-hanger TV series. After that everything was easier. We got our first appearances in the UK very soon, and everything there was much more pleasant. Things always went great for us in France as well. One of the first gigs Can played abroad was in Paris at the Bataclan, March 1973. We sold so many advance tickets that we played two days in a row. Two months after that we played the Olympia too. France was always amazing for us. In general, we were always lucky when it came to the music industry, I have to say. There were a lot of wonderful people who looked after me when I started back then.

HOLGER CZUKAY Of course we wanted to be a success. *Monster Movie* first came out as a private pressing and sold like hot cakes. That was a pleasant surprise. I was already thinking about what might be successful in rock music. The soundtrack for Francis Durbridge was the first time we earned a lot of money, but we didn't let it go to our heads. We got a new van instead.

IRMIN SCHMIDT Up to 1973 we refused to do playback appearances on TV. We'd say: 'We'll play properly or not at all.' In retrospect that was nonsense, part of our evaporating 1968-style attitude. But it worked well in England – we were on live TV there every year from 1971, and it went fine. We did it here once on the *Beat-Club* show. It was very different to the UK because *Beat-Club* wasn't about the music, it was all about the look. The director Mike Leckebusch kept wanting another take. He wasn't unpleasant, he just had his own ideas of what he wanted. After the fourth run, we said: 'That was great, we can't do it any better than that.' But we went on doing it, and it only went downhill. Leckebusch took the twelfth version, where we were completely wiped out, and we said: '*Himmelherrgottsakra!*' I regretted afterwards that we didn't just say earlier: 'Sorry, that was our best take, *auf Wiedersehen*.' That's what we should have done. It would never have happened in the UK. They always had a different kind of respect for pop music there, which is why they've made so many great contributions to the genre. When we played at British universities, the night porter would come along and tell us how he liked it and talk about music. Nothing like that ever happened in Germany.

HILDEGARD SCHMIDT Because everyone in Can trusted me, I never got involved in internal artistic differences, I never took sides. I was only ever interested in the end result. Once when there was no sound technician in a venue, I took care of the sound from the ladies' toilet. I had a walkie-talkie in the toilet, and a roadie on the stage had one too. From the ladies', I told him: 'Turn the guitar up, bass down,' and so on. That was hard work, and I was really angry.

IRMIN SCHMIDT After Damo went and joined the Jehovah's Witnesses, we carried on without a singer, which worked very well on *Soon Over Babaluma*. Then we all took a turn at singing for a while. 'I Want More' was even a hit; we sang it together as a choir. People often present us as having had a crisis period without a singer, but that's just wrong.

HOLGER CZUKAY When we didn't find a singer for a while, I suggested we could just have the radio playing instead. I got everything ready one day to synchronise it, but the others didn't like the idea. I asked: 'Why? It's the original Can concept!' After that I knew my time with Can was nearing its end. Which was painful, of course.

SIMON DRAPER I thought it was very exciting that they brought the guy from Traffic into the band. I presume it wasn't as pleasant for them, though. Looking back, it was certainly more interesting than they may have realised at the time.

HOLGER CZUKAY The idea was to bring the unknown back into play, to reinvigorate Can. And for me, the unknown was people like Rosko Gee, a Jamaican groove-bass magician, or Reebop, the percussion magician from Ghana. Unfortunately, it didn't work the way I'd hoped. Rosko and Reebop made up a good rhythm section, but they thought and played along absolutely commercial lines. They were proper professionals; I didn't fit in with them. It was actually me who brought Rosko in. I'd met him at a TV appearance, and then he came to visit me in Köln.

IRMIN SCHMIDT A lot of things just went wrong in the late phase. Rosko insisted on claiming copyright for his lyrics for one song. That was against everything we'd agreed, but we still went along with it. We did say afterwards that it mustn't happen again, but that indecision was a sign of weakness and decay. Rosko came from Traffic, where that was just standard practice: whoever wrote something claimed the author's rights. Our collective idea was obviously alien to him. We were friends with Rosko and we remained friends, but it went against our rules. He should have stuck to them if he wanted to be in Can. But equally, we should have enforced them. Aside from that, incidents like that were just external symptoms for internal tendencies. Something was crumbling on the human side in those days. Holger stopped playing bass in favour of his electronic magic tricks. In retrospect, I often think we could have become something great if our cohesion had still been stronger. But Holger's change of instrument might have made things difficult between us musically as well, because we were starting to step on each other's toes. He did his sounds, I did my sounds. We were drifting apart in a lot of ways. Can had just had its time.

JAKI LIEBEZEIT When the two guys from Traffic joined, that was the beginning of the end. They never understood our band philosophy. It was probably impossible to get it if you'd only just joined. Anyone would think it was pure anarchy. Most people look for a leader to carry them through life.

GERHARD AUGUSTIN Czukay was the crazy sound nerd, but he was also a very nice person who made sure the band stayed in balance when things got stressful.

HOLGER CZUKAY I felt isolated and I had to deal with the fact that I didn't have a dialogue partner in the band any more. There was no one left. The crunch came at a show in Geneva, where Reebop pulled the plug on me while I was playing. I'd said beforehand that I'd put up with that exactly three times, having the plug pulled on me. Then it happened three times in Berlin, once somewhere else and then in Geneva. That was it for me. I felt like I was in the way in Can, all of a sudden. Anyway, after Geneva it was all over. I knew something would be missing when I left. Can made a mistake, in my view: we wanted to climb too high. We lost sight of the basis of our music, at some point; the commercial aspects got too important. I had to leave Can, there was no other way.

JAKI LIEBEZEIT All due respect to Holger, but he could sometimes be a problem and he did try to take power within the group. He had all the technical equipment under his control and he started to use it to pressure us; he even went on strike once. Then again, Can wouldn't have sounded the way we sounded without Holger, that's for sure. He was irreplaceable for the band. In the end he caused problems, in various ways. Schmidt as well – once he became a father all he ever did was complain. There was never actually a time limit when Can was in the studio. If something was working, we'd stick with it for as long as it took. But then Daddy Schmidt would get tired after 8 p.m. and say things like: 'I've been up since five in the morning. The baby's always screaming, wants feeding and so on. Anyway, I've got to go home now.' Who could blame him? But it did upset the group dynamic. All the rest of us were independent, didn't have families to tie us down. Once you've got children, life just doesn't revolve entirely around music any more. That's perfectly normal.

HOLGER CZUKAY My years with Can were an exciting time of learning for me, like studying under Stockhausen. He and I stayed in touch privately, and I visited Stockhausen at home a couple of times. That was great. He thought the idea of Can was interesting, but he only had a very limited interest in rock music. He asked me: 'Why don't you play all the instruments yourself? You're a better pianist than me. Why aren't you convinced that every note you emit is eminently superior to any other?' I answered that that couldn't be my line. And I asked: 'What are you doing these days?' 'I've started studying Charlie Chaplin. Every little thing he did.' Then we went outside and stopped talking, just looked wordlessly up at the sky.

JAKI LIEBEZEIT We spent a lot on equipment towards the end. Technical equipment was very expensive back then; we had to invest more and more. The PA kept getting bigger, so big that we had to buy a new van for DM120,000, a lot of money for us. At some point we realised it all gets out of date too quickly and we were losing too much money. That was partly why we stopped. It just made more sense for all of us to continue on our own. Schmidt could concentrate on his film scores, Holger on his solo records, Karoli as well, and I worked on lots of productions.

IRMIN SCHMIDT We really fell into the tech trap. When we started out we'd record on two tracks, and there was no chance to mix anything afterwards. The mixing happened in our headphones – you had to listen carefully during the recording to what the others were doing and bring yourself into the mix consciously. As the tech got better and better, we lost that practice and the sensibility that went with it. Later, whatever you did could be corrected; it was on a separate track, so you could repeat it, mix it in differently, etc. We did play the same way as before, especially live, of course, but in the studio someone would start playing an extra solo on their own. The others didn't need to be there for that either. And once Jaki had done his job we others could come along and add something. That meant a little bit of our community was lost, a little bit of our inner space where everyone was co-responsible for everything at every moment, no matter if he was sitting around quietly, splicing tapes or playing till his fingers bled. For me, the records up to *Soon Over Babaluma* are what counts. After that it gets more and more muddled. We abandoned *Out of Reach*. We turned it in and then split up. The next record was made in a small and very concentrated group again, and we just called it *Can*. We'd noticed that something had gone awry, which came together again on that LP. With the very good track title 'All Gates Open' the future had opened up again. If only Michael hadn't died, so young and so sad. That was the end after all.

JAKI LIEBEZEIT We knew we were different to most other bands. But I'd never have thought the records would have such a long life. Especially because I only ever thought in the moment. My attitude has always been: it's fine for now and I'll think about tomorrow when it comes. If it turns out now that something longer-lasting than I imagined came about along the way, that's fine too.

BRIAN ENO After hearing Can, my ears were open for what was happening in Germany.

DANIEL MILLER Respect for Can is growing and growing. What's special about their music is that it doesn't sound at all old. I hear their influence everywhere, across all genres. We used to have a stock of old records we had on our back catalogue, in our office. Whenever bands or solo musicians came to negotiate contracts or whatever, we'd invite them to help themselves to whatever they liked from our back stock before they left. Everyone, every single one of them went straight to the corner with the Can records and grabbed everything that was there. No matter if they were young or old, making rock or techno.

SIEGFRIED SCHMIDT-JOOS Just timeless music.

PLANK

'He heard things you didn't even know were there.'
FRANK DOSTAL

WINFRID TRENKLER There were only three sound engineers in Germany whom independent people wanted to work with back then: Dieter Dierks, Thomas Kukuck and, of course, Conny Plank.

HANS LAMPE Conny was actually an electrical engineer. Then he'd got a job for Radio Saarland as a sound engineer, but they soon chucked him out. He was pretty proud of that, though, because the reason they sacked him was for eating sardines and putting the empty tin on the mixing desk. In those days sound engineers ran around the radio stations in lab coats. Then he checked out the Köln and Düsseldorf scenes in the Rhenus Studio, before he ended up in Hamburg. But he kept in touch with his contacts in Köln and Düsseldorf. That was how the first Kraftwerk records happened, and the NEU! debut.

MICHAEL ROTHER As far as I know, there was no other sound recordist and producer in Germany as musically talented and excited about experimentation as Conny. After I met him in 1971 with Kraftwerk, it made absolute sense to go back to him with NEU!. Conny was the man we needed. He was willing to support us and he was on the lookout for suitable partners for putting his ideas of sound design into practice. Conny was seeking experiments, wanted to step off the beaten track and reorganise music, so NEU! were as important for him as he was for us – we were natural allies.

GABI DELGADO-LÓPEZ I couldn't stand most of what got airplay in Germany at the time. I was saved by the American military station AFN, which played great funk and soul for the GIs, things like Parliament and Funkadelic. That music was the first thing I had in common with Conny Plank; I told him how much I liked it, and he was really into it too. Our link didn't come through Kraftwerk or anything, it was Parliament and Funkadelic.

HOLGER CZUKAY After he got chucked out of Radio Saarland, Plank got a job at Windrose Studios in Hamburg. That's where he met the composer and arranger Bert Kaempfert, and they came up with this easy-listening sound together, the 'Kaempfert sound'. Pretty crazy, actually. The British and American tradition was to pick up every instrument separately and add it all together later in the mixing desk. But Conny said: 'Let's look for the spot in the room where everything sounds perfect. Where is that spot? That's where we'll put a stereo microphone.' And that was exactly what marked out that Bert Kaempfert sound. Space was an element of Can's sound too, which was a very new approach at the time. That's why the old Can recordings still sound so modern. Later on, Conny went to America and worked with Ray Conniff. The Americans were crazy for that Kaempfert sound, of course, but Conny wouldn't tell them the secret.

HANS LAMPE Plank was working in the Star Studio, which belonged to Ralf Arnie, a songwriter and music publisher; 'Tulips from Amsterdam' was one of his. He had money, but he also had a big heart for long-haired hippies. They'd record schlager tracks in the studio during the day, and at night it was open for experimentation. In return, he'd get the music made there for his publishing company. It was a fair deal, for him and for us, because we could try out so much there. Conny was an experimental engineer, constantly in search of innovative sounds.

FRANK DOSTAL Conny didn't care at all what scene you came from. He never read a pop magazine in his life; the only things he was interested in were music and people. And if the people were arseholes but made great music, he'd just focus entirely on the music. Conny was always behind his mixing desk. If you didn't keep in touch with him yourself, you'd lose contact.

HANS-JOACHIM ROEDELIUS When Conny made the first Cluster record he was still a soundman on a fixed contract. And I think he was glad to work with us because we weren't interested in making money, so he could let loose his potential. Conny was incredibly creative; he was actually the third member of Cluster. Without his work at the mixing desk, our music would have sounded different.

GABI DELGADO-LÓPEZ It was through Conny Plank that we met Can; before that we'd only known their records. Holger Czukay would often sit in on our studio sessions with DAF when we were recording LPs. He'd make the occasional comment but otherwise he was quite reserved. Conny was an open and generous person; you could just pop into his studio, say hello, watch and listen to what was going on.

HANS-JOACHIM ROEDELIUS Plank's personality was the input: the openness and generosity he embodied. He was important as a sound technician, a fellow musician, a backer, a dialogue partner and as a person. He worked his fingers to the bone; perhaps that's why he left us so early. If something made him curious, it didn't make a difference if it was night or day; he'd sit down and dive in. He was a close friend of Holger Czukay's; they'd talk for hours on end.

HOLGER CZUKAY Conny Plank was our ally.

GABI DELGADO-LÓPEZ Conny was a generous person who taught me many of his production techniques. Other people made a big secret out of them, but Conny always taught everything he knew to anyone who asked – he never showed off, he was never vain. He said things to me like: 'It's great that you're a hundred-per-cent artist, but that's not enough. You've got to be a hundred-per-cent businessman as well, you've got to know everything about contracts. That's the only way to have control of your art.' Some people abused Conny's generosity, of course, but he still stayed that way, even though it caused him a lot of trouble. He was one of those people with no fear of others.

HANS-JOACHIM ROEDELIUS He was always inventing new things that later became standard. Phasing effects, for example, which he created by running two tapes in parallel with a slight time delay. He played along, if you like, on the mixing desk; that was creative work on top of what he did as a sound engineer. He let us stay in his flat in Hamburg for a while as well, he put food on the table for us. He even went on tour with us, on the spur of the moment.

FRANK DOSTAL He'd been on a contract in Hamburg. One day he said he'd got the money together to open up his own studio, and he moved to the countryside far away from Hamburg. Urban exodus was all the rage in those days.

MICHAEL ROTHER Without Conny, we wouldn't have got NEU! going. That might sound strange because he wasn't a musician, he didn't do any composing or play any instruments. But if you leave behind the classic idea of sound composition and start to value sound design, the organisation of sound as a creative act, he was our third man. Conny played a key part, even just through the skills he had and we didn't. Neither Klaus nor I had any experience with a sound studio. There were lots of things I only learned by watching over Conny's shoulder. Then, at the end of the seventies, I opened up my own professional studio and I was able to draw on the experiences I'd had with him. Conny was a properly trained sound recordist. He was absolutely key, not only for NEU! but also for the second Harmonia album, *Deluxe*. And he worked on my first three solo records as well. It took my breath away, the precision, intuition and outstanding cognitive memory with which he got results out of multitrack recordings during the mixing process. We'd just kicked off and played; often there was nothing usable on a track for minutes, and then suddenly there was – and Conny always knew where. It was incredible, as if he could hear all the tracks in parallel in his mind. Conny always grasped early on where we wanted to get to, sometimes even before we did, and then helped us to get there. But very respectfully and subtly, just through constant encouragement. 'Right, kids, come on then' – that was a typical Conny line if we'd been messing around again. He had such a sure hand for picking the pearls out of the whole thing, it was astounding. And he created those sound paintings that are still impressive today, with such modest means. The equipment had almost nothing to offer for sound manipulation.

FRANK DOSTAL Conny was radical. He'd offer you sounds at times that were so drastic they'd shock you, because they had nothing to do with what you'd discussed earlier. He'd just turn up the knobs and present something that was entirely his. You get that sometimes. When situations like that happened, he'd fight really hard for what he'd come up with. We'd often say: 'OK, we'll leave your version as it is, but now do it the way we actually wanted it.' And if that really was better, he could definitely accept it. But we could accept his version, if it wasn't. It ended up getting us the best results.

PETER BURSCH Plank was more of a pal; Dieter Dierks was a more serious type, we weren't as close to him. He worked very well too, of course. Plank was very emotional and really into our guitar work. He produced us properly by influencing the recordings. He was constantly saying things like: 'Do this instead! Or that! It'll be a huge hit.' Plank was really immersed in the music. Sometimes he'd be so into something he'd completely flip out. He'd run around the studio, yelling: 'What a great number!' He'd fire us up while we were playing, put pressure on us to play more and longer. He was almost a band member. We'd take along sleeping bags and bed down in his studio – if the session didn't go on all night long, anyway. Once we'd started playing we stopped noticing the time. We could go on until six in the morning; that was pretty normal. That's just how we were. And he was too.

HANS LAMPE Conny was a good sound engineer who had the ability to coax things out of people that no one else could get out of them, not even themselves. He inspired and motivated people, gave them mental stimulation: 'Try it like this . . .' or 'Why don't you play it this way . . .' That's what was unique about him.

MICHAEL ROTHER When I look at what he made out of 'Hallogallo': it was a tape machine as 'echo–echo–echo' – with delay, in other words – plus a plate reverb and compressors, and that was it. The rest was the right organising of the elements, the right EQ-ing and so on. I knew I wanted to do something different to anything that had come before. And the track 'Hallogallo' was a recognisable success – although how it came about is a bit of a mystery for me to this day. Once we had the master mix we immediately knew we'd created something special with Conny. I remember it well, playing my family a copy of the *NEU!* album on a little tape player at home, and they were all enchanted: my mother, my brother, my girlfriend. It was a kind of magic that we partly owed to coincidence. Klaus and I had a vision for the track that we hadn't discussed, but it was still something we shared: something fast in E, a very nice key for guitar. Klaus on the drums, me on guitar. That's the basis, and then we'll just see what happens. The rest came about in a spontaneous process of overdubs. We had no plan at all for how the piece would ultimately sound. The vital thing was paying attention in the creative process itself, listening and perceiving what was happening around you: for example, the guitar playing backwards, or rather the reversed tape.

FRANK DOSTAL He was very receptive to musical ideas that went beyond the usual song scheme, and he also had experience with that kind of sound, as a recording engineer. So it was logical to book him for A.R. & Machines, especially for *Echo*. Sometimes he'd come to us after working ten hours on something else and then do another twelve hours with us, interrupted only by short naps. Sometimes he'd nod off at the mixing desk, just for ten minutes, then he'd be right back quick as a flash and we'd get back down to it. A complete maniac and a remarkable musician and person. He had this amazing sensibility for music. He heard things you didn't even know were there. Before we could formulate some of our ideas, he already knew what we were aiming for. Conny was always a hundred-per-cent immersed in things – sometimes he'd even sing them to you beforehand. We left his voice on the record once. He never wanted to be a singer, but we all loved it, as a gag.

ASMUS TIETCHENS Conny Plank was a man with a burning interest in experiments. He'd always find time to work with a whole lot of musicians – although not with just anyone – and often for free. Cluster and Harmonia never paid Plank anything, of course; it was pure friend-ship. He took on very different acts for money. I remember him as a really pleasant person, although I only spent six days with him. Very cooperative, very reserved about his own and the technical input. He never said: 'Guys, you've got to do it this way'; he only ever offered his advice. And that was only when he noticed it was the right moment to venture a discreet comment, with tips like 'a bit more delay' or that kind of thing.

GABI DELGADO-LÓPEZ It was actually Conny who invented the DAF sound; it was his idea to send in the Korg and the Arp. He never interfered with compositions or lyrics, though. He'd say: 'I'm your sound chauffeur.' He got the last grain of energy out of those crappy old plastic machines. And he was a master at positioning mics. He just understood like no other how electronic music works, and also its flaws and mistakes. He could work magic on some mistakes, creating a new energy level – and then they weren't mistakes any more, they were righter than right. In those days, most synthesizers were a bit weak at the knees, just beeped away. One of Conny's great achievements as a producer was to make those devices sound more powerful. When we showed up with our Korgs as DAF he laughed, said they were pretty weak and weedy. Then he positioned them far back in the room and routed them through huge Marshall guitar-amp stacks, which created this amazing sound. The direct signal – what came directly from the synth – was hardly more than twenty per cent of the sound. Even now, disappointed friends come to me after buying themselves a Korg, wondering why it doesn't sound like on our records. Conny wanted a dirty sound with power; you can hear it from Kluster and early Kraftwerk to NEU! and Devo, all the way to DAF. And of course we loved the fact that Holger Czukay was a DAF fan. We recorded a couple of DAF tracks in the Can studio later on. Holger played us the solo stuff he was working on and his crazy videos. In 1979 there was a session with Robert Görl, Jaki Liebezeit, Holger Czukay and me in the Can studio, on the margins of a recording with DAF. It was just a forty-minute jam session, with the two drummers making it extremely rhythm-oriented. You'd probably call it 'tribal' these days. Sadly, the recording disappeared after Conny's death.

MICHAEL ROTHER We've felt Conny's loss since 1987.

KRAFTWERK

'I didn't care what other bands did.'
KARL BARTOS

MICHAEL ROTHER I went to the same grammar school as Florian Schneider-Esleben. He was already playing the flute in the school orchestra, and he was very eccentric. He had an awkward way of moving, the opposite of smooth, and people laughed at him for it.

KARL BARTOS I had an A in harmony theory and I knew what a counterpoint was. The fact that Ralf Hütter and Florian Schneider came from upper-class backgrounds and I was a working-class boy didn't matter when we were making music. We were all the same. That was the time when higher education was opened up for everyone, at last – not just for the elite. In the UK, a generation before us got the benefit; otherwise John Lennon would never have been able to start at art school. It was a good thing that working-class creativity finally made its way into art. For Ralf and Florian, though, materialist thinking came ever more to the fore over time, and the differences in our social backgrounds became tangible.

MICHAEL ROTHER I'd noticed Florian but I didn't know him; then again, he was more than three years older. But I do think it's interesting that we went to the same school.

KARL BARTOS The first thing you learn as an art student is that you have to find your own language. Either you only paint hammers or you paint everything back-to-front, or whatever. I wasn't that obsessive about finding that language to begin with, but then when I heard how

310

Florian played 'Tongebirge' in the Kling-Klang studio, consciously not using any blue notes, I thought to myself: 'Yes, that's a great approach.' An approach I hadn't been looking for, but it immediately grabbed me.

HOLGER CZUKAY In the early days of Can, Kraftwerk came to our studio a couple of times. They'd suddenly be standing around and joining in, but they never imposed themselves. As long as no one wanted to take centre stage, we were open to anyone who wanted to play with us, at that early point. And they were quite reserved. They weren't called Kraftwerk yet, though; they were still Organisation. After that, Michael Karoli said to me: 'I think we'll hear more of them in the future.' He thought what they'd do would have substance. We had a fair few sessions with them; the Kraftwerk boys wanted to learn. And then once they'd learned enough they just stopped coming over.

MICHAEL ROTHER The first time I jammed with Kraftwerk there were two guys sitting on the sofa, listening. One of them was Klaus Dinger; that was the first time I met him. Ralf was playing organ, I was on bass, and then Charly Weiss was on drums. We exchanged phone numbers after the session. Two weeks later Florian called and asked if I fancied playing with them. They wanted to play live shows. I was enthusiastic about it. Then Florian said: 'We've got a gig next week. Right, let's practise "Ruckzuck" now, it's in A.' And that was about it, actually, in terms of agreements. I didn't end up taking over the part as Ralf had played it on the record, though, although I liked it a lot. I created my own part on the guitar, partly as a reaction to the group's new make-up, because it was pretty difficult to do much live with just flute and guitar. We had to play like mad to be heard. Florian played his flute, Klaus thrashed away at the drums and I kicked off on my guitar, maybe a bit too heavy, playing whatever I came up with. After that Ralf disappeared for six months. It was him who'd brought me into the band, and then he left to finish his degree. For a few months, Kraftwerk was left with Florian as musical director, with his awkward personality and his electronic flute and electronic violin, then Klaus Dinger – who completely fascinated me, he was a 'power station' in himself, I'd never seen anything like him on guitar – and me on guitar.

KARL BARTOS In 1972 Steve Reich and Musicians performed *Drumming* at the Düsseldorf Kunsthalle, and I went along of course. Ralf Hütter and Florian Schneider were there too, but we didn't know each other yet. It was a fortunate coincidence that Kraftwerk and I met later on.

MICHAEL ROTHER As I remember, most of Kraftwerk's music at the time came out of jamming, although the interaction was more limited than later on in Harmonia. That's why I was so happy with Harmonia – the mutual resonance was perfect, which led to very multi-layered music coming quasi out of nowhere. Klaus's powerful playing style had a strong influence on our live appearances as a trio in Kraftwerk, and if the flow ever came to a standstill, he'd power through and get us over the hump on his own, if need be. But he did listen very carefully to the music, and no matter how much pressure he put on, he always kept an eye on me and Florian and was permanently reacting to us. He wasn't a drummer's drummer, an engine without a car; he was a musician's drummer who saw himself as part of an overall process.

KARL BARTOS What I brought into Kraftwerk was the ability to think in musical structures. I also had the theoretical and technical knowledge to construct the music and its essence even more precisely.

WINFRID TRENKLER The record company never had the slightest say with Kraftwerk. And they didn't have a management company either; they always did everything themselves, and they were good at it.

KARL BARTOS Even in early interviews, Kraftwerk themselves said that they'd absorbed the sound and rhythm of their origins, the Ruhr region. That idea originally came from Marinetti and Russolo, though, who said a century ago that you can organise sounds into music. I once made a list of where the sounds that I first stored in my consciousness actually came from. It only started when I began to perceive music emotionally: the emotion inherent to Bavarian folk music or the echo of church bells from Lake Königssee or anything else. None of that got through to me before puberty, though. My consciousness had to be switched to 'receive' first. And I was switched on by pop music from England and the US. So a German context didn't mean anything to me, to begin with.

BERND DOPP Around the time of *Kraftwerk 2* they played at the Fabrik, which was very crowded. The crowd came for their minor hit 'Ruckzuck', but the gig was very experimental. NEU! were easier to deal with because they were so rhythmic.

MICHAEL ROTHER Klaus and Florian, those two firebrands! It wasn't just that I was much younger than them; I also had a completely different temperament. But I was always fascinated by what happened musically with them. They were constantly squabbling, but part of that was struggling with insecurities: who they were, where they came from, where they were heading. And there was constant disagreement: for example, over a gig in a discotheque called Penny Station – the same place where the album *Harmonia Live 1974* was recorded three years later, incidentally. Anyway, Klaus and I were completely in agreement, we thought it was a particularly successful Kraftwerk performance. I remember feeling ecstatic as I played, rolling on a big wave that powered us forward. Klaus had a recording of it that we'd have liked to release, but Florian wasn't interested. Florian presumably still has the recordings we made with Conny Plank in 1971 for the second Kraftwerk album, as well. They were a complete failure, though, because that ecstatic, energetic music only worked under certain conditions – in a live situation in front of an audience. When they were carried along by the wave of music and passed that escalation on to us, that was when we really hit our peak, as Kraftwerk. The music might not have been as delicate – maybe it was more like woodcuts, subsisting purely on the dynamic and the ecstasy – but it had incredible power. And that's something you couldn't reconstruct in the studio. I remember this studio situation in Ralf Arnie's studio in Hamburg; it was like playing in a vacuum. The same vacuum as in the *Beat-Club* studio when we recorded Kraftwerk's TV performance there in mid-1971. Alone in a big room with five tech guys, three cameras and two tapes. We only pretended to be losing it. We could always manage what we performed there and what you see and hear on the recording, but it wasn't anywhere near the energy that came about sometimes when the sparks flew in the right live situation, with sweat and steam and an audience. That was a rather frustrating experience, on *Beat-Club*. For the second Kraftwerk album, we only recorded about twenty-five minutes, and after that it was clear we were doomed to fail. For Klaus and me, that was the end of our collaboration with Florian, who went back to working with Ralf not much later.

BRIAN ENO Kraftwerk's *Ralf und Florian* was a hugely important record for me.

KARL BARTOS I first went to the Kling-Klang studio in 1974. My professor had said: 'Kraftwerk, you know them, they want something from you.' So I went over. Ralf and Florian were looking for another classically trained percussionist alongside Wolfgang Flür, who fulfilled the function in robotic style. What they got, though, was someone who also knew pop music and had already played a whole lot in bands, in my schooldays. On the one hand, I could play opera and knew who Arnold Schönberg was. And on the other, I also played percussion and vibraphone in a big band and knew all there was to know about Keith Jarrett, Chick Corea and Miles Davis. So I walked into the Kling-Klang studio and got out my vibraphone. They had these speakers they'd built themselves. I played a few notes and then the other two started improvising and I joined in, as I'd learned from playing jazz. Ralf Hütter was sitting at his Farfisa piano, only playing major chords. At first I thought: 'Wow, this guy can't play at all.' Florian played a scale into an echo device. But I soon worked out what they meant. We had an instant connection – because I clearly recognised their references.

WOLF SEESSELBERG Kraftwerk would stroll around the centre of Düsseldorf every day in their black leather outfits, including black gloves. They were always dressed to the nines. My brother and I used to laugh at them. I once saw two of them at one of our concerts in the Düsseldorf Kunsthalle, but we were never in contact.

KARL BARTOS The entire Kraftwerk formula is contained in 'Autobahn' – it's all in there. Conny Plank was not entirely innocent when it comes to bringing that sound aesthetic together. So-called krautrock, Faust, Klaus Schulze, Popol Vuh and all the rest had nothing to do with Kraftwerk. And we had nothing to do with the other guys in Düsseldorf either. We had different influences, in the classical music tradition, in jazz, in futuristic sound music and the continuation of that idea in electroacoustics. Not to forget minimalism, and of course the Anglo-American pop music we analysed.

IGGY POP I did have a very nice time shopping for asparagus with Florian Schneider in Düsseldorf. Naturally, we had a grocery cart, and it was a groove.

KARL BARTOS We went to the Philipshalle as Kraftwerk, to see Tangerine Dream. That was in 1976, and afterwards we analysed their concert. How they might prefer ternary time signatures, or how they sometimes didn't pay attention to the diatonic aspect when they transposed their sequences. We looked at it from a music-theory perspective.

Or I did, at least. But we never met. What Tangerine Dream were doing we called 'drone music', which wasn't meant at all negatively. The term 'ambient' didn't exist yet. We did it with Kraftwerk as well sometimes – turned on our machines, the sequencers tootled away, and we'd chat and sometimes play something. Tangerine Dream, similarly to Michael Rother, always understood their music as a 'stream', music that flows and develops. Sometimes a branch might change here and there. For me, though, some of the most important elements of our music are its clear structures. Florian was allegedly friends with Klaus Schulze. But that 'scene' that people in the UK are always asking about never existed. All I knew was that there were a few other people in Berlin.

JEAN-MICHEL JARRE I remember the first time I heard Kraftwerk; it was in the first half of the seventies and I was convinced they must be an American band singing in German, some kind of strange Beach Boys pastiche. I thought it was very cool. Of course, then I worked out Kraftwerk was a German band, but it goes to show how little we musicians knew about each other back then.

DANIEL MILLER A while ago, I picked up the original Kraftwerk vocoder on eBay. As it turned out, it came directly from Florian Schneider; we had a good laugh when that came out. It doesn't work properly, but I knew that beforehand. But Florian made me a beautiful certificate confirming the vocoder's authenticity. I've got the framed document hanging up on my office wall.

NEU!

'I love NEU! for their humour and brutality.'
IGGY POP

MICHAEL ROTHER We wanted to create something really new; Klaus and I wouldn't be happy with anything else. It had to be innovative, something no one had ever heard before. That was our aim. Hence the band name NEU!, meaning 'new' – it was just right.

BERND DOPP I was part of the minority who defined ourselves at grammar school through progressive music and thought ourselves pretty cool for it. To be precise, we defined ourselves through music no one else knew. If more than ten people listened to it, it was no longer cool. At the start of the seventies albums were key, not singles like in the sixties. The new progressive album music went hand-in-hand with consciousness-altering substances, which were pretty widespread in the target group. Suddenly, progressive music from Germany was cool. There wasn't much of it. But buying an album was expensive; they cost DM22, so it was a real investment. I could only afford it now and then. We'd exchange albums for a few weeks among good friends, and that's how I got my hands on my first Kraftwerk album or the first Ton Steine Scherben record – that wasn't krautrock but it was still cool, because of their strong political leanings. And one day someone lent me the first NEU! record. I'd heard 'Hallogallo' before on TV and I knew the names Klaus Dinger and Michael Rother from Kraftwerk. I'd seen Kraftwerk play at Hamburg's Audimax, when those two were still in the line-up. And I'd heard of Conny Plank as well, although I didn't quite know what a producer actually does. It took a while back then before everyone learned that there was an exciting new band out there.

317

MICHAEL ROTHER Our debut was the first album I made in my life. We didn't complete the album with Kraftwerk, before that. And the fact that our debut *NEU!* clearly reached people made me incredibly happy, of course; it was sensational. All you had to do was walk across the centre of Düsseldorf and you'd actually hear 'Hallogallo' and 'Negativland' coming out of discos.

STEPHEN MORRIS *NEU!* was one of the first records that made me think: 'I want to do that! And I can do it too!' It was krautrock like punk – you got the feeling you could be part of it. Exactly how and who didn't matter. It was just clear: it's possible!

BERND DOPP At the start of the seventies I had really long hair. There weren't that many gigs here back then. American artists rarely came to Germany, and British acts were rare here as well. Pink Floyd playing in Hamburg was a sensation. It didn't even matter that it cost DM17 to get in – a lot of money for us in those days – because it was such a rare occasion. So then it was great that German bands were suddenly cool and ultra-hip. Even hipper and cooler than the stuff from the States and England. On top of that, their music was complex. Another very cool thing was that you could afford their gigs because they were cheaper than the international stars'. So I went to see NEU! at the Fabrik in Hamburg.

MICHAEL ROTHER I never talked about the music itself, neither with Florian in Kraftwerk nor later with Klaus in NEU! nor with Roedelius and Moebius in Harmonia. We didn't talk about music; we made it. An idea would be thrown in and then we'd kick off. If we quarrelled about the direction of our sessions, it happened in the music itself. It was never about music theory or any musical agenda you could put into words, anything one of us wanted to impose to drag the others in their direction. Above all, in Harmonia, making music was completely democratic: one person started, the next one listened quietly and then joined in, the third one came in next. Then the ideas circulated and effected change in those of us taking part. And the sum of all those reciprocal inputs added up to Harmonia's music. If I listen to a piece like 'Ohrwurm' from the first Harmonia album, it was a brilliant five minutes of a two-hour gig at which we tortured the audience for more than ninety per cent of the time because we were seeking, seeking, seeking . . . and finding nothing . . . and seeking again . . . and then there were suddenly those five minutes in which something came together that I don't think you can come up with on the drawing board, something where all the musicians' sounds and contributions suddenly came to one point. You notice it at the time, or at least you have an inkling, but later when you listen to it, it gets even clearer. We had neither the necessity nor the wish to talk theory about music.

GABI DELGADO-LÓPEZ What I liked about NEU! was that their tracks were so long. It was music that went on and on and was constantly changing, but stayed the same. There are definitely parallels between DAF and NEU!.

HANS LAMPE Klaus had this straightforwardness in his playing that's on 'Hallogallo', this constant dynamo. A beat played straight ahead that takes you all the way to the horizon.

MICHAEL ROTHER A lot of magic came together on 'Hallogallo'. A lot of details weren't planned; they just happened. Suddenly there was guitar feedback with which I could play endless notes, and Conny had the idea of turning the tape around so I heard that backwards guitar, which really inspired me. I've always been fascinated by backwards music, perhaps because it reminds me of Indian sounds. In this case, though, perhaps it was also because of the sense of yearning transported by the long notes pulling upwards. In any case, what Conny played to me inspired me to add new melodies, and then the tape was turned around again. It was all a fluid, spontaneous process in a very short time. We only recorded for four nights, and then we spent a week mixing. The recordings were done in the Windrose-Dumont studio and the mixing in Ralf Arnie's studio. Arnie got the publishing rights, and presumably never regretted it. Those were the deals in those days. We were poor and he had the studio. We always worked at our own risk and had to scrape the money together. 'How much can we get our hands on?' I'd earned a bit of money with Kraftwerk, so I had something to put in the kitty. How Klaus did it, I don't know; maybe he borrowed some money. Anyway, we put our money together with Conny's, that was our working method: joint risk, joint output. And we only talked to record companies with a finished album.

HANS LAMPE I met Michael Rother and Klaus Dinger when they were working on the NEU! single 'Neuschnee'. It was in München, in Giorgio Moroder's Arabella studio. There was great chemistry between them in the studio. They pushed each other and made a good team. Klaus was the dynamo who laid down the beat, and Michael played the melodies to go with them on the guitar. They just complemented each other well.

MICHAEL ROTHER In later years, some tracks were much more clearly formulated before we got to the studio than 'Hallogallo'. I got a four-track recorder in 1974, and that helped. It meant I could compose the melodies to 'Isi' and 'Seeland' beforehand, and record sketches of them.

HANS LAMPE On *NEU! '75*, Klaus wanted his brother and me to play drums. Michael couldn't identify with it. Klaus's idea of working up a real steam with a second drum-set, at gigs as well, was absolutely not Michael's thing. For the *NEU! '75* album, they met in the middle: half was by Michael and the other half was as Klaus wanted it. It was a compromise. Things were still relaxed in the studio, though; they had limited time because they had to pay for studio hours. It was just too expensive to sit around arguing. Aside from that, Conny held everything together. He said: 'Come on, guys, time's running away from us. Get a move on! We've still got the mixing to do!' He was a man who spoke his mind. These days you've got computers and you send files back and forth.

MICHAEL ROTHER We did do the occasional spot of verbal arm-wrestling. Not everything went intuitively. But what triggered it wasn't musical issues, it was crises with our partners and that kind of thing. And despite all the problems I had with Klaus in later years, especially concerning how he dealt with our recordings, we almost always largely agreed on things in the studio. We got along well musically, even later. People talk a lot of nonsense, above all that we'd drifted in completely different directions on *NEU! '75* and couldn't pull ourselves together. What is true, though, is that Klaus wanted to play more live shows, and wanted to get out from behind the drums and play guitar. He felt cut off from the audience back there. Ultimately, what he wanted was to stand front-of-stage and clown about, get the audience worked up, and so on. Another thing that's true is that I wasn't all that enthusiastic about the two new drummers Thomas Dinger and Hans Lampe, to be honest. I was much more interested in making the third album with Klaus and putting the concepts I'd developed into practice with him and Conny. The compromise was: two of us on one side of the record and four on the other. I was very happy to play on Klaus's stuff: for example, the guitars on 'Hero', 'After Eight' and 'E-Musik', and also the piano; I enjoyed all of it. I didn't personally feel the frustration that Klaus yelled out on 'Hero', but I loved the dynamic, powerful music just as much as he did. Sure, Klaus wasn't yet that experienced on the guitar, he kind of went on playing drums on it – but that's great when you listen to tracks like 'Hero' or 'After Eight', where he plays those scrape–scrape–scrape riffs; I couldn't have done that. And in the other direction, I think Klaus liked the melodic stuff on the first side of the album as much as I did. Otherwise we couldn't have worked together as a team for so long, with so much success.

HANS LAMPE Klaus wanted to sing as well. You can reach people more directly with vocals. But Michael's ideas were different.

BERND DOPP In the Fabrik back then, there were rows of cinema seats in front of the stage. You didn't stand, you sat, and you had to get there early to get a good seat. It wasn't full, though, because NEU! was music for a minority. Anyway, I was sitting there, and then this guy came along who looked much older than me; he was probably in his late twenties, which seemed ancient to me at the time. In any case, he looked like he'd just arrived at the Fabrik from some kind of hippy paradise; he had a great big beard and long, long hair. I was fifteen, sitting there in my lumberjack shirt next to him, totally impressed.

MICHAEL ROTHER We only played live six or seven times as NEU!, and every time was extremely unsatisfactory for me, musically. At our first two appearances there were only two of us, with me working with a cassette recorder, so with pre-recorded material, which the audiences wouldn't yet accept back then because it wasn't live and there wasn't enough movement for them. I had no musical support – a single live guitar couldn't represent the forest of guitars I had in my mind. So we looked for people, and the first person we tried out was Eberhard Kranemann, whose visions of destruction completely collided with our idea of NEU!'s music. Klaus and I agreed it didn't work. Then we tried it with Uli Trepte from Guru Guru, who was a very nice guy but too laid back for us. So that didn't work out either.

BERND DOPP I remember thinking Dinger's drum groove was outstanding; it really drove the band. It already sounded like electronic dance music – but it wasn't even electronic! Another thing I remember is the Orange amps on stage. And Conny Plank was on the mixing desk – I wouldn't have recognised him, but he was introduced. I was really excited that Uli Trepte from Guru Guru was on the bass. The band played like crazy, like a constantly grooving machine. And the experimental sequences were great too. Tracks like 'Hallogallo' sounded completely different to the studio versions, but I was blown away. The musicians had very long hair, as did everyone in the audience, and they didn't put on a show; they just sat on stage and played their instruments. Uli Trepte was perched on an amp with his feet on a chair. No one moved around, it was very static. It felt to me like the music went on for hours and hours, but it must have been much shorter.

MICHAEL ROTHER In the UK, NEU! was a modest but clear success. I was looking for the right musicians for a UK tour, and as part of that search I went to see Moebius and Roedelius in the Weserbergland, because I'd heard their track 'Im Süden'. I knew Cluster from a legendary joint gig with Kraftwerk at the Audimax in Hamburg. In those days everything was totally democratic, so the first thing they did was think about who should play first, even though Kraftwerk were obviously the main act. Then Cluster said: 'Why don't you guys start?' Which was a big mistake, of course. We played the whole audience into a state of ecstasy with our Kraftwerk 'riot music'. They didn't want us to stop, but we said: 'Thanks very much, but here comes the next combo, Cluster.' And then Roedelius and Moebius started playing their abstract, quiet sounds, which didn't go down well. At some point the audience lost their temper and fans stormed the stage. I was afraid they'd start a punch-up. But they just turned the speakers around and unplugged the instruments – which was bad enough. It was an unforgettable experience of a stomping mass being unable to cope with calm music.

HANS LAMPE *NEU! '75* didn't do that well at first. It was only when Bowie let everyone know his *"Heroes"* was inspired by NEU!'s 'Hero' that interest picked up. Bowie wanted Michael as a guitarist; it's a shame it didn't work out. It would have been the perfect fit. The guitar on Bowie's *"Heroes"* is actually Rother-style guitar, if you listen carefully.

IGGY POP I love NEU! for their humour and brutality. And especially Michael Rother for his musicality, on his own and in all his bands.

HANS LAMPE When things stopped working with NEU! the two of them went their separate ways. Klaus started up La Düsseldorf, and Michael was on his way to the Weserbergland to work with Roedelius and Moebius. Klaus wanted to do more concept-oriented stuff so he could market the music better. That was a clear statement. If you want to make a living out of your music, you do have to take an occasional look at the market. That's how La Düsseldorf came about.

FORST

'You had to lug your shit outside in a bucket [even Brian Eno].'
HANS-JOACHIM ROEDELIUS

DIETER MOEBIUS Michael Rother came from NEU!, who were pretty wild things. I think he was looking for a bit of peace and quiet with us.

MICHAEL ROTHER Achim Roedelius once claimed in an interview that Klaus Dinger had sent me to Forst. That's not true at all, his memory's playing tricks on him. In reality, Klaus was very sceptical and said: 'Harmonia just don't rock!' Klaus and I were looking for musicians for NEU! gigs in 1973, and I liked the melodic side of the Cluster track 'Im Süden' from the *Cluster II* album. It reminded me of what Ralf Hütter did, and that was a good musical starting point for me. So I rang their place in Forst and went to the Weserbergland, where Cluster had moved from Berlin a year before. I packed my guitar to do a bit of jamming with them and find out whether they'd be a good addition to NEU! on stage. The funny thing is that I ended up only playing with Roedelius, who had his electronic piano hooked up to a delay. I played around with two or three effects on my guitar. Anyway, we clicked straight away and we both knew it was like a marriage; we complemented each other perfectly. And when Moebi came out of his den a bit later, it was clear that things would get serious. From then on, I was much more interested in developing Harmonia than in pursuing the plans for NEU! live. In Forst, we made music together that took me further and fascinated me, so I put NEU! on hold for the time being.

HANS-JOACHIM ROEDELIUS Dinger was an extremely difficult person. I didn't realise at the time that he wasn't well, so I took the things

325

he said to me personally. Once when we were living in Forst, Dinger turned up and wanted to set up a supergroup called Europa: two drummers, two guitarists, two keyboardists, practically with Cluster as the band's keyboard section. It was a nice idea and it might even have come to something, with his drive. He really put the moves on us, showed up in Forst in his Mercedes 600, doing thirty kilometres an hour on the B-roads with traffic piling up behind him. When he got to our place he withdrew to a room on his own, cooked his own food and didn't participate in the community. That was a drastic mistake, of course, because it messed up his chances with us. No sense of community? Only looking to earn money? That wasn't right for us.

MICHAEL ROTHER Klaus was not at all happy about my new connection. When he noticed he was losing me as a partner in NEU!, he reacted with his typical fight-or-flight response: a plan for a big fusion, a kind of supergroup. Everyone just hooks up with everyone else, a classic Dinger idea – but actually there was no reason not to meet up and discuss it. So he went to Forst with his guys who later became La Düsseldorf, Hans Lampe and Thomas Dinger. In reality, though, the supergroup plan failed at the first hurdle, because at the time Klaus was displaying more and more . . . well, social deficits. He was high-handed and arrogant, and that made it impossible to work with him in a team. The community in Forst rejected him. I'm not interested in apportioning blame, in putting him down and proclaiming myself right. That was pointless even then, and even more so now in retrospect when he can't have his say. You'd have to dive very deep to do Klaus justice. Let's just say: Klaus was animated and pervaded by his wish for personal greatness. I'm not entirely free of vanity myself, but I was still more interested in the music, I think. Klaus wanted to be loved; I wanted to be loved for my music. If you only see it from the outside, you draw the wrong conclusions. Our relationship is often described wrongly, especially on the internet. When it came to music our ideas were almost identical; we understood each other perfectly, while we were playing and when we were assessing the results.

HANS-JOACHIM ROEDELIUS After the Zodiak, Schnitzler, Moebius and I moved away from Berlin in 1969 and went wandering the world. Schnitzler soon gave up and went on alone in Berlin, but Moebius and I stayed on the road. First we spent two years travelling through Europe in a post-office bus. In the long run, we weren't as brutally provocative as in the beginning with Schnitzler, when the plan was to always make something happen spontaneously, Fluxus-style, and then smash it up again so that no one got to enjoy it. Moebius and I wanted to make proper music instead. We played our last gig with Conrad in Göttingen in early 1971. After that we swapped the Kluster K for a C and went back on the road as Cluster. Then we met a guy who was organising a big festival on the island of Fehmarn; he paid us decent money and also told us about an old estate on the River Weser which was abandoned and empty.

DIETER MOEBIUS In those days we were often in Kiel, where a gallery owner had discovered this big derelict grange in Forst. The guy had used his powers of persuasion to get a hundred-year hereditary lease on the place. He knew us well and asked if we wanted to take a look at it. It belonged to a foundation; he'd lured them in by saying it was going to be an artists' colony, so now he needed artists for his colony. We went out there in the middle of winter, and I remember not wanting to get out of the car. It looked so depressing: falling down, small windows, surrounded by mud, no plants or trees. It really didn't look good. It took a lot of imagination to picture ever making something inhabitable out of it. The whole thing consisted of three houses for three sets of tenants, with one water source for everyone and six outdoor toilets in the barn. But I let him persuade me to give it a try, at least. A long time ago. Now it's paradise.

327

HANS-JOACHIM ROEDELIUS We created a very special sound world when we were living in Forst, in that idyllic setting. The music reflected all the joy and fun we had in Forst. Our mental and emotional states there are reflected very nicely in the sound – and we were proud of that. But we didn't seek it consciously, it just happened to us. Just like Forst itself; it was so beautiful you just had to go there, you couldn't say no – although there was nothing there whatsoever, really nothing!

DIETER MOEBIUS Subconsciously, the place might have influenced our music, but to begin with it was less about music and more about making the buildings fit for human habitation again. We didn't really settle in there at the start because we had to keep leaving for gigs. Cluster getting gentler and more melodious later on might be related to Forst, though.

HANS-JOACHIM ROEDELIUS Our productivity in Forst was closely linked to the weather. We made more music in the winter than in summer; when it was mild we'd spend more time preparing for winter, chopping wood, making jam and so on. What we certainly did was put our feelings for the place on tape with *Musik von Harmonia* and *Harmonia Deluxe*.

DIETER MOEBIUS I can only go to Forst in summer now. I've got a huge room there with a massive fireplace, but it hardly heats the place. I don't like being there in winter; it's just too cold.

MICHAEL ROTHER Obviously, people in the village were critical of us; we were real bogeymen for them. It's no wonder – to look at, we embodied all their prejudices and suppressed sexual fantasies. In those days they still had a brothel in Forst, and another one next door in Bevern; two brothels known for miles around. 'Ah, you're from Forst?' People from the area would go right ahead and assume we must be some kind of wild sex commune. I dread to think what kind of fantasies they had. But that's all they were, I know that.

HANS-JOACHIM ROEDELIUS We didn't even have toilets. You had to lug your shit outside in a bucket. That was in 1976; I'd started to put in a little bathroom upstairs in the house to make things easier for my wife and child. We had to do everything ourselves: install wiring and plumbing, go out to the forest and chop wood, bake bread, etc. It was great, but we did it because we had to. We met Eno at a gig in Hamburg. He was on a promo tour for his solo stuff and he came to see Harmonia at the Fabrik one night. He was as familiar with our work as we were with his, and then he came on stage spontaneously and joined in. There was a keyboard that wasn't occupied all the time and he just sat down at it. He did ask nicely if it was all right, and of course we loved the idea. In those days Eno was still wearing a beret with long hair and mascara, he still looked like he was in Roxy Music, who he'd just left. We got along musically right away because we all improvised and had an open mind.

WINFRID TRENKLER I played Harmonia on one of my first Radiothek shows on WDR in 1973. The track was eight minutes long, and the production manager called in from the control room while it was still on, yelling: 'What's this crap you're playing?' I'd arranged an Eno interview in Hamburg around the same time and I knew there was a Harmonia gig at the Fabrik that night. I'd invited Eno along. He'd never heard a note from the new German bands so he had no idea what was coming his way. So I went along with Eno and my girlfriend, who took photos; the Fabrik was half full. The band wasn't that well known yet. Harmonia had put up a big garden umbrella on stage and hung fairy lights off it. And then the three of them sat underneath it on chairs with their instruments; that was their whole stage show.

BRIAN ENO I don't recall anything! It's true . . . just a small stage with some amber lights. I can't even remember if I actually played, and if I did, what I played.

WINFRID TRENKLER Eno seemed perfectly sober to me and my girlfriend. We were with him before and afterwards. Not a trace of him being high. After the show I asked him how he'd liked it, and he said: 'This is the most important rock music being made in the world right now.' I wouldn't have thought he'd be so enthusiastic about it. I'd hoped he'd like it, but I hadn't expected such a strong reaction. Then he asked me for the Harmonia musicians' addresses: 'I want to do something with them.' The three Harmonia guys lived together in Forst, in a house Albrecht von Wallenstein once used as quarters in the Thirty Years' War, back in the seventeenth century.

DIETER MOEBIUS Brian Eno came from Roxy Music and was look-ing for a 'new music'. He didn't bring his ambient sounds to us; we brought them to him. We met him at a Harmonia gig in Hamburg, at the Fabrik. He'd just been doing something at NDR, knew our name and came to see us play. In the break he came backstage and asked if he could join in. You don't say no to that! And then he just joined in with the show. We were in contact from that moment on. Eno came to visit us in Forst, later on. Our projects with him always had to go quickly because Eno never has time. But he did stay with us in Forst for a week. Michael already had an eight-track recorder, so we just kicked off. We created enough material in that time for three LPs.

HANS-JOACHIM ROEDELIUS Eno came along during the phase when Harmonia was actually already over. He revitalised us, but in Cluster style! *Cluster & Eno* is a Cluster record, and *After the Heat* is an Eno record. Together with Michael and Eno, Harmonia rose from the ashes again in Forst. Everyone had his own track; there was a four-track tape machine and no overdubs, nothing! Everyone took a turn with everyone else. I don't think that was Eno's intention; he just had to go along with it because everyone had to go out to work during the day to pay for us to eat. I think he'd actually come more as a producer, which he was already doing by then. But that didn't work with us. So he had to go along with us, which was good for him, and for us as well. Sometimes the sound was instantly right, but sometimes we had to try a lot of things out, to change certain places and get them right. I got bogged down a lot to begin with, but I learned a lot from Eno in that respect. If there are twenty-four tracks, I tend to fill at least eight of them right up and then sit there clueless and wonder what it is that doesn't fit. With Eno, everything went very fast because he put limits on himself. The three albums we produced with him were made in a week. I hardly did anything on *After the Heat*; Eno and Moebius had a full concept for it. When it comes to marketable concepts, Moebius is much closer to the mark than me. I tend to daydream with my stuff, but Moebius is a realist, and an eternal punk as well. He does his thing consistently, makes no compromises. We complemented each other well in Cluster: I was the melodic one and he was the structuralist. Of course, that only made sense for a certain length of time.

DIETER MOEBIUS On *Before and After Science* I was the medium between Conny and Brian, guiding their communication. I was important there somehow, I don't know why. Maybe I was a benevolent guiding spirit.

HANS-JOACHIM ROEDELIUS Then my wife Martha asked him: 'Eno, where are you going?' He was on his way to Bowie, to work on *Low* and *"Heroes"*. Staying with us was a crossroads for him: 'What shall I do in the future? Do I stay the producer and rock star I am now, or do I indulge in fun and games like with Harmonia and make it better?'

BRIAN ENO I loved working with the Clusterites. I suppose what I liked about German music in general then was its rigour, its commitment to innovation and experiment. It wasn't about pop, but broader – it was about art . . . It seemed very natural to me that you could take the innovations of mid-twentieth-century concert music – people like Stockhausen, Cage, Riley, etc. – and marry them with the technologies that pop musicians had developed and mastered. I also liked the fact that the resulting music was presented as something you could actually enjoy, in casual situations (i.e. not sit-down concerts). That sense of audience enjoyment wasn't a priority with avant-garde musicians at the time – in fact, it was almost regarded with suspicion.

HANS-JOACHIM ROEDELIUS Brian wrote us letters later: for example, when he was in Canada with Daniel Lanois to produce U2. He wrote that he got joy out of my music every morning because it's so lovely and simple, which gives the listener freedom. We come from free improvisation, after all; we only tried with Michael Rother to repeat certain patterns to create song-like forms. Harmonia was an attempt at commercial success. Moebi and I thought: 'Now we've got Michael, he's such a wonderful guitar player and he writes such beautiful tunes.' And we succeeded with the *Musik von Harmonia* album. But then when we went on to *Harmonia Deluxe* and the tracks took on real pop forms so that we could repeat them recognisably on stage, we stopped enjoying it. Cluster didn't want that. We didn't want to have to sit down and practise forever, just to reproduce the same piece a hundred thousand times. What for? That's why we ended up going our separate ways.

BRIAN ENO Staying in Forst influenced my later work in two ways. First, I was pleased to find a group of people who seemed to want to do some of the same things I wanted to do. And secondly, I discovered some things I didn't even know I wanted to do. For example, the 'classicism' that Roedelius brought to the music was a surprise to me. It didn't sound coy and retro, and it didn't sound sweet or historical. It sounded modern and fresh.

HANS-JOACHIM ROEDELIUS The record companies just let us get on with it. I think the idea was that they could probably make money out of it one day, if they just went about it consistently enough. But then they never were consistent enough; they hardly ran any advertising for our records, the budgets were small. Harmonia only got bigger budgets because Michael Rother was with us, who'd been more successful with NEU!. They thought they had something really special. And what came out of it? Well, at least Rother's famous all over the world now. Moebius and I always went by our gut feeling. That meant we were most consistent as a duo, and we still are now. Cluster have only ever done what we thought was right, and not what the industry thought was important. We've always avoided clichés. We didn't care whether the audience danced or whether the hat was full at the end. As long as we managed to survive somehow – and that worked pretty well in Forst.

ASMUS TIETCHENS Our contact with the guys in the Weserbergland was always very warm and friendly. I spent a good few weeks on the farm in Forst, in the summers. I'd read *The Lord of the Rings* in 1968, and the first time I went to Forst I thought: 'Oh yes, it's the Shire – gentle hills and a river right outside the house! Never-ending sweetness and charm.' The thing is, my motto was always: 'Don't trust the idyllic!' And when you looked out of the window in the Harmonia studio, you had this extremely gentle landscape right there: hills! Meadows! Peaceful! Beautiful! I said to myself: 'What kind of music can possibly come out of it?' I did enjoy the landscape, but it didn't inspire me at all. I need the city, tobacco and a dimly lit room – that's what inspires me! I can't let myself get distracted by optical impressions. The studio I work in now is underground with artificial air conditioning. I need that kind of thing to release stuff. There were no musical overlaps between Roedelius, Rother and me, none at all, to this day. When Michael's in Hamburg we play pool once a week and we're good friends, but we've never even thought of making music together. Actually, we did once:

he helped me with a side project, the Hematic Sunsets, played guitar on one track, but that's it.

MICHAEL HOENIG Moebi and Achim Roedelius stayed true to themselves, in a wonderful way.

HANS-JOACHIM ROEDELIUS When I started a family I dropped out of the whole communal life thing, moved away from Forst and eventually ended up in Austria.

BEYOND GERMANY

'We'd never have got far without going abroad.'
JEAN-HERVÉ PERON

WERNER 'ZAPPI' DIERMAIER We never actually made it in Germany. That's how it was then, and it still is.

SIEGFRIED SCHMIDT-JOOS Other countries weren't just more interested in our music; they were into everything from Germany, including visual arts and literature.

LÜÜL We thought it was sad that interest in our music inside Germany was always more restrained. They always liked us in France, for instance. Germany's just a very conservative country.

PETER BAUMANN You'd hear about Amon Düül, Can or Kraftwerk now and then, but there was way less going on in Germany than in the UK or the States.

HARALD GROSSKOPF All the Nazi crap had given me a real inferiority complex; I felt part responsible for everything, somehow. My first trip abroad was to Sweden at the age of nineteen, and I got a very friendly reception. On tour with Ash Ra, the French really loved and admired us in particular. It was a young generation who didn't have a problem with Germans. Maybe it's that the French have always loved comics and science fiction. They're more open to modernist culture. Ash Ra played at a science-fiction festival in Metz in north-eastern France; there were three thousand people there. Our records were more successful abroad than in Germany too.

JAKI LIEBEZEIT The reactions to Can from abroad improved our reputation here.

PETER BRÖTZMANN Germany was always difficult territory – I was more successful abroad, from the very beginning. Audiences in the UK and Holland were much more open, it would be mostly young people. But Holland was tricky too. I went to every last one-horse town with Han Bennink and Willem Breuker, and I kept having trouble as a German. There's an artists' bar in Amsterdam called De Kring, a real night bar; I'd often head over there late at night after gigs. The regulars were intellectuals, journalists, writers, artists, many of them with Jewish backgrounds. They liked to give a German guy making my kind of music a hard time. It often wasn't easy. Then again, I forged a lot of contacts there to Jewish painters and writers, many of which have become deep friendships over the years. But Holland was difficult. France was never a problem, and there were no problems at all in Russia. In the UK they'd make their jokes. You get used to it; you couldn't laugh about it but you could put up with it.

IRMIN SCHMIDT From the very beginning, Can reaped far more attention abroad than in Germany. And that's true to this day. The Dutch were the only ones who didn't like us. We never played live in Holland. Or in Scandinavia.

HANS-JOACHIM ROEDELIUS We noticed fairly quickly that we were perceived differently abroad to in Germany, because the only real reactions came from elsewhere. The first from Japan, where we're still seen as 'the originators of the space age', which is a fitting classification. We toured Japan twice, most recently in 2009. In the seventies we went on tours of the UK, Italy and Holland. I put feelers out early on for people who wanted to play freely and try out experiments, despite being trained musicians. But there weren't very many of them, and they were scattered across all the countries.

JEAN-HERVÉ PERON We got more respect abroad than in Germany, no matter if it was France, Britain or Italy. In Germany we weren't just ignored; no, people absolutely hated us. We had a terrible reputation, like a commercial boy band or something. I never actually thought Faust were all that commercial. It was impossible to get live shows in Germany back then. The audience for our first shows, like the one in Hamburg at the Musikhalle, was bought and paid for, all pretend. We'd never have got far without going abroad.

GÜNTER SCHICKERT The first time I saw what sold-out gigs looked like was when I was on the road with Klaus Schulze in Italy. I wasn't jealous; just amazed.

IRMIN SCHMIDT Can's reception was very much via the UK. We did have a reputation in Germany at the end of the sixties, which we'd built up playing live at universities and through early film scores, especially for Ronald Klick's *Deadlock*, which was a good success. And our album *Soundtracks* sold well, even more than *Monster Movie*. 'Mother Sky' was on heavy rotation in progressive German discos and was on a British soundtrack. In the UK itself, though, the atmosphere was different from the outset. That first UK tour was still very difficult, in fact. But no one in the audience wanted to play along with us like they did in Germany, and after the show they rushed on stage and hugged and kissed us, even at our very first gig at London University. Then it turned into a triumph and was very overwhelming. We weren't playing gigantic venues, just universities and smaller clubs, but people were always knocked out, in the best sense of the phrase. Of course, not everybody there loved it, but there was a large section at every show that completely flipped out. We were such a success that someone came on stage in Glasgow, on our second UK tour, and hugged us so hard he broke one of my ribs. I played the rest of the tour with a broken rib.

JAKI LIEBEZEIT A lot of people in Germany thought Can were no good. They'd say: 'They're not as good as the Brits. They sound really different.' But that was presumably why we were so successful in the UK – because we really did sound different. And the Brits appreciated exactly that; we were exotic for them, if you like. There were a lot of German bands that sounded so British that no one noticed them when they played in England. People noticed Can in the UK because we were different. We first went over there in 1972. It was great; we felt very much at home there. It was partly because the audiences totally appreciated us. We had to wait for that in Germany.

IRMIN SCHMIDT It was always strange. When it came to public recognition and awards, we were almost showered with them in the UK or France, compared to Germany. When a CD box of my solo LPs came out in 2015, I was on six radio shows on big stations in Paris alone. It was similar with the press. The box was reviewed in all the major newspapers and magazines, and it was similar in the UK. In Germany, though, there was next to nothing. It's very surprising because a lot of my solo work is film scores, and almost always for German TV films. I've almost never won any awards here, either. Whether it's just the general phenomenon of a prophet having no honour in his own country, or it's something specific to so-called krautrock, or even specific to me, I can't say. I register it as strange, but that's the way it is. It was similar with Can. We had a hit here in 1972 with the song 'Spoon', but nothing else happened. My friend Wim Wenders once called me from Tokyo and said: 'I'm in a record shop and they've got almost all Can's records in stock.' He was thrilled and couldn't believe it, because you'd never find them in record shops in those days. When I went on a promotional trip to Japan a lot of people actually recognised me: 'Oh! Oh! Oh! Irm . . . Irm . . .!' Obviously Germany has taken notice of Can in the meantime, but it used to be different. We had to get famous in England and France first, before we made it here.

ACHIM REICHEL Germany was generally more uptight. In my youth I'd often hear people complaining about what they called 'negro music'. People in other countries were much more tolerant, more relaxed. And I never experienced any hostility on foreign tours back then either, amazingly enough.

KLAUS SCHULZE When it comes to music, the French, British and Americans were much further along than us. After the war the Germans just started adapting everything; no one dared to make anything new. There wasn't a lot of scope to develop something of their own – they had the direct consequences of the war to deal with first. But that led to cultural rigidity, and in that atmosphere it was hard at the end of the sixties – and later even harder – to be accepted by a broad German audience if you did something musically progressive, especially with the German progressives themselves. A band like Pink Floyd was much more interesting to them than some crazy German band from Berlin; they couldn't possibly be any good. For most people, the only things they took seriously were things that came from far away. And we were just too close, perhaps; you could come up and talk to us in the uni cafeteria, and you couldn't do that with Syd Barrett. But for that exact reason, we soon realised either we do our own thing or we don't do anything at all. It sounds absurd, but especially if you did something of your own as a German in those days, you almost became a foreigner in Germany, and that in itself made you interesting for other countries.

DANIEL MILLER I remember very well that the krautrock bands were far less well known in Germany than in the UK. I had a German girl-friend at the time, and every time I mentioned the bands to her friends they just gave me this look, really perturbed that I liked their music. They expected you to listen to Bob Dylan and Jimi Hendrix. It was a mystery to them why anyone would listen to German bands. It was as if they were somehow ashamed of German culture. Some kind of post-war inferiority complex. I don't think they rejected the bands because of the music; it was more the fact that they didn't come from the UK or the States. German artists didn't fit into their worldview back then.

KLAUS SCHULZE One of the first people from outside who realised something was happening in Germany was Richard Branson from Virgin. He heard that a special sound was coming out of Germany and he thought: 'This is new, I'll take it!' Branson soon had a whole catalogue of German artists, which was a rarity for a British label at the time, but that's exactly why it worked for him. For us, that was our first step into the professional league; that was when we started to live off our music. My album *Moondawn* got me to number two in the French charts; not bad. But in Germany things were tough for a long time. Now and then I'd get an offer to play at the National Gallery in Berlin, the Robert Schumann Hall in Düsseldorf or the Frankfurt opera. But it wasn't like the music had suddenly been accepted. That didn't actually change until 1978, when my double album *X* went into the German charts. That's when I knew things were kicking off here as well. We all liked going into record shops to see ourselves. When *X* came out I went to check, but the section was empty, so I went to the guy behind the counter and said I was looking for Klaus Schulze's new record, and he said: 'Look, it's right here next to the till – it's selling like hot cakes.' But I've never really cared that much how many people listen to my music.

JÜRGEN DOLLASE In the first half of the seventies German bands' live shows were always a bit pathetic because they had such terrible equipment. The strategies for overwhelming the audience that were such a big part of British and American bands wouldn't work for German bands. Gigs where the PA alone had enough power to put a venue under real pressure weren't the norm in early-seventies Germany.

KLAUS SCHULZE Obviously, other countries still had major reservations towards Germans from the time before 1945, and we did feel them sometimes. When the Goethe-Institut invited us to play in Norway, locals came along who said they only knew one German word: *Passierschein* – from having to show permits under the German occupation. And the first time we went to Normandy we found that people didn't like us there, even though we didn't exactly look like the Wehrmacht. It didn't matter, we were still *boches* to them.

JEAN-HERVÉ PERON I'm a Frenchman who lives in Germany and a big defender of Germany, because I pick up on what my children and grandchildren get thrown at them abroad. My wife's been insulted in France. A woman looking at our daughter just went ahead and said she didn't know Germans could have beautiful children. What's my wife got to do with the war? And my fifteen-year-old daughter was insulted as a 'shitty German' on a Dutch campsite. It annoys me. French people who can't even speak decent French tell me German's a harsh language. Pardon? I ask them to say a sentence in German, but they never get any further than *Achtung*. I've stopped tolerating that kind of prejudice, and I immediately confront it when I come across it.

KLAUS SCHULZE In Holland, a guy from the record company said he wanted his bicycle back. I didn't get it right away. 'Sorry, mate, I haven't got your bike.' Until someone told me the Germans had confiscated all the bicycles in Holland during the war. So it was a serious comment. And it was deadly serious. In the late sixties, early seventies, the war had only been over for two decades; plenty of people had experienced it first-hand. There were a lot of people in their fifties and sixties in the record companies, who could have strange reactions to us. There was a big generation gap abroad: the young audiences were really into us when we played live, but the older people said: 'Not the Germans again!' It was never a big deal, but you'd notice a lot of subtle jabs. The blanket talk about 'evil Germans' could be annoying sometimes. It was all the more surprising in Poland; I had close ties to the place. I played a big venue in Gdańsk in 1983, where Lech Wałęsa had held his famous speech. A lot of Solidarność people were at the gig and were really into me; they all knew me from their student days.

HOLGER CZUKAY The first time we went over to the UK we got both a friendly reception and insults; regardless of all the ovations, we were still just krautrockers in the end. I noticed people had certain reservations towards Germans in general. The first time we played in London the audience didn't seem to believe what we were doing on stage. I remember it was a really great gig. Impossible! We couldn't be Germans. At the same time, I knew: if you do what we're doing right, you can't go wrong. Stockhausen always used to say: 'Don't worry! You can't do anything wrong.' Why should that be any different in England?

ACHIM REICHEL I had this experience with a very nice radio presenter who suddenly mentioned that she'd pretend to be Danish every time she went abroad, because we Germans weren't always very popular. I couldn't understand that. You have to face up to it. I've never seen any point in denying my origins; the opposite, in fact. As an artist, you can make your contribution towards processing these things, perhaps. That's why being a musician is my dream job.

PUBLIC ENEMIES

'I didn't even throw stones.'
MICHAEL ROTHER

IRMIN SCHMIDT In Köln, the poet Rolf Dieter Brinkmann would come to the Can studio sometimes. But that brought me up against my boundaries, especially when Brinkmann expressed his solidarity with the Baader–Meinhof gang; only verbally, of course, but he was still really radical. I had a lot of rows with a few people on that subject, because I always vehemently resisted the idea that the Red Army Faction was essentially doing the right thing. And with Brinkmann in particular it was extreme; there was a time he stormed out really angry after one of those arguments and was never seen again. It was a shame because I thought some of his stuff was really wonderful, even though he wasn't easy to get along with. But I had the same deep ideological divisions with a lot of people at the time, probably precisely because I was the most approachable one in Can for ideological questions. There was no need to talk to Holger or Jaki about the Red Army Faction. No discussion.

KLAUS SCHULZE We never had contacts with terrorists – aside from when they stole the takings from a Tangerine Dream gig in Frankfurt once because they said the money would be better used for political purposes. We were just these crazy potheads who no one took seriously, so naturally it was fine for the proletarian revolution to confiscate our night's pay; you had to start somewhere. But there was no serious contact with the Red Army Faction; that was more of a thing with political rock bands like Ton Steine Scherben or Floh de Cologne. As a counter-culture to the establishment, we weren't actually as unpolitical as others accused us of being at the time, and as we thought ourselves, perhaps; because we were pretty far removed from the mainstream in every respect. We were at least as hard to reach for 'the system' as any left-wing grouping. And people on the street thought *we* were terrorists, not the real terrorists.

HANS-JOACHIM ROEDELIUS Andreas Baader and guys like that used to come by occasionally. But I thought the Red Army Faction was terrible, later on. And what I experienced when I was looking after the children in the commune went against all my principles. They spent all their time talking and left their children alone. When there was a thunderstorm and the kids were scared, they'd come into our bed because their parents were off talking somewhere. Just for that reason, I had less and less patience with all the anarchist crap people talked; there was often nothing behind it. I was immune to communist slogans as well; I'd had to wave the flag for the party chairman Walter Ulbricht at East German demonstrations, and that was enough for me.

IRMIN SCHMIDT I conducted the stage score for a play at the Residenztheater in München, and the director asked me to rearrange the original score by the left-wing Jewish composer Paul Dessau. I didn't want to do it at first, but the director said: 'You're allowed to!' I answered: 'But only if Dessau gives his permission.' After I'd rearranged the music I still thought Dessau's original was much better than mine, but they wanted it to be modern, with keyboards and so on. Anyway, at the end of that process we went over to East Berlin to get Dessau's blessing. There was this gathering there with the playwright Heiner Müller, I think at the director Fritz Marquardt's apartment. Just before we made the trip, I'd given Hildegard a very nice rabbit fur, all in white, very glamorous, and she looked amazing in the coat, with fancy boots. We hadn't quite worked it out, anyway, and we felt rather uneasy, especially because I felt like a complete idiot next to all these geniuses – but only until the moment when Heiner Müller announced there'd soon be a civil war in West Germany. That's when I woke up from my admiration and said: 'What? Are you crazy?' But Müller had his total understanding of the situation: 'The Baader–Meinhof gang will lead to civil war, and that's coming up now. It'll be a year away, at most.' And he thought that was a very good thing. I admire him to this day, but he could be pretty wrong about things. I knew the commune on Türkenstrasse and the scene around Andreas Baader, and even then it was clear they'd never prompt a civil war. It might come to a bloody end, but expecting a civil war from them was just rubbish. But the conversation ended abruptly anyway when Marquardt went to the window, looked out and announced: 'He's coming!' He meant Dessau, clearly recognisable by the brand-new white Mercedes parked outside the house. Then in came Dessau, an imposing figure: quite tall, good-looking and charismatic, short white hair; he dominated the room, wearing a tailored Chairman Mao suit of the finest blue cloth. I thought it was pretty good, quite funny that Brecht's friend the Stalin Prize-winner Dessau had a huge white Mercedes and hand-made brogues – he looked great, dressed to the nines! Anyway, then we talked about all sorts of things: an upcoming premiere of Heiner Müller's play *Prometheus* where he wanted us – Can, I mean – to do the music, and a lot of other things. I spent the whole time glancing nervously at my cassette and eventually I said: 'Herr Dessau, we've rearranged your music for *Mann ist Mann*.' He gave me a quick look and then he said in the broadest Berlin accent: 'Give it here, young man. But one thing's for sure: you won't get a performance fee for your arrangement. Those performance fees are all mine! You do whatever you like with it but don't make me listen to the bloody thing.' And then the scales fell from my eyes. He didn't give a toss what I'd done to his Brecht score, all he wanted was his share of the West German income – which he was perfectly entitled to, but it was still disillusioning. In the other direction, you have to imagine how it was for me. My share of the performing rights fee didn't matter to me because I was making a mint in West Germany with my theatre commissions at that time. The theatres were throwing money around in those days. I did that *Mann ist Mann* arrangement in one afternoon; I was a trained conductor. I looked through the score to magic it into something for two keyboards, and then I wrote a '1' next to some instrument parts and a '2' next to others, and that was all I did. Then I got myself a conducting student from the München conservatory and said to him: 'You play that part, and I'll play this part.' I got DM4,500 for that artistic masterpiece alone, one afternoon's work. Then we rehearsed it, and I got another ten thousand for that. I got three hundred and something marks for every subsequent performance, and there were twenty-eight performances. On top of that, I got them to pay for a hotel if I was staying for one day, and for two days they paid for a flight from Köln to München. Then I got new instruments for DM4,000, so the theatre ended up spending about DM100,000 on the music alone. I earned about DM50,000 in six months with that type of thing, which was a big financial help in the early days of Can. I feel bad even saying that in the Spotify era; even Dessau's GDR-level luxury lifestyle must make today's musicians green with envy.

RENATE KNAUP We got home from some tour at five in the morning and found Gudrun Ensslin and Andreas Baader in Falk's and my bed, with Ulrike Meinhof upstairs. I flipped out and yelled at them: 'Get out of my bed right this minute – who do you think you are?' And Chris, who was the world's least assertive person, complained: 'There's some of them up in my room as well.' So I went upstairs and sorted it out, and they got up right away as well. We were so tired we fell asleep the minute our heads hit the pillows.

CHRIS KARRER That was bad. We came back from a gig completely wiped out, all we wanted was to get some sleep, and there were these complete strangers in our beds. We kicked them out, believe you me. Then that same night they drove their stolen Mercedes into the lake and we had to tow them out with our Cadillac. We didn't even know who they were, at first. Dieter had stayed home and he was trembling and shaking with fear: 'Don't you know who they were? That was the Baader–Meinhof gang, they turned up and threatened me with a gun.' But when the rest of us came back and got angry, they did show some respect. I hadn't recognised them anyway, all I saw was that someone was in my bed. We were always left-wingers, we still are, but not like them.

RENATE KNAUP They were already on the run when it happened. They disappeared while we got some sleep; we'd been on the road for twelve hours. I remember that a lot of the men's clothes went with them; they just stole them. They certainly creeped me out but I wasn't scared of them. I was in such a bad mood I'd have beaten them out of my bed. I didn't care who took care of them. I had nothing else to do with them, didn't pay much attention to what they were doing, but I did know it went too far for my taste. All right, at the beginning it seemed pretty cool, robbing banks and all that, the whole 'take from the rich and give to the poor' attitude, that made sense, but what came next – kidnappings, blackmail, violence – that was all crap! And it led nowhere, or only to things like the abduction of Hanns Martin Schleyer; it all got really terrible. We discussed it in the commune, of course, but we all rejected it. The only person with a weapons obsession was Peter Leopold. He once shot a rifle at the wall, but other than that he was a total softie.

CHRIS KARRER We often got arrested for supporting terrorism. The police once broke into our house and tied us to trees and searched the place. They came with loaded guns, which was pretty scary. They really thought we were terrorists. It turned out that a guy living with us had supplied weapons to the Red Army Faction, so we'd been under observation for months. We really didn't know anything about it. But they soon worked out we had nothing to do with all that.

CHRISTIAN BURCHARD Our commune was in München Haidhausen, number 15 Metzstrasse. Brigitte Mohnhaupt from the second-generation Red Army Faction lived two floors down. We were neighbours but we never had a lot of contact. We'd go round to borrow some salt or onions, but none of them ever wanted anything from us. It was only ever us going down to them, and I remember Mohnhaupt and her friends were always listening to the Stones. But we never had any real contact; they were like on another planet, even though we thought they were rock 'n' roll. They just thought we were crazy. And one day they were gone. Just like that, gone! The next day this huge load of police turned up. All they'd left behind was their cat, running around the place all confused. So we took in Brigitte Mohnhaupt's cat. We called it Hutze, and when she had kittens not long after, we said they were all little Red Army Faction kitties.

IRMIN SCHMIDT I once saw Andreas Baader lounging on a sofa in the commune on Türkenstrasse in München; he kept dropping grand political statements that were abysmally stupid. He was an unpleasant macho man. But we never really had much to do with them. Two or three people from the Türkenstrasse commune liked Can, so we went round there. But I spent much more time at Giselastrasse, where the crazier people lived, the funnier guys like Fritz Teufel and Rainer Langhans. None of them wanted to throw bombs around.

MICHAEL ROTHER We did get our house in Forst searched once, a kind of raid in search of Baader–Meinhof people. Someone from their fringes, Bommi Baumann, had come to visit us once. I didn't have any contact with them. I couldn't kill people; I didn't even throw stones. Despite all the criticisms I had of society, violence wasn't my solution, it wasn't my way.

IRMIN SCHMIDT We'd get held up for a long time crossing the border, in East Germany but also on the West German side. Rock musicians automatically fell under suspicion of 'drugs and terrorism'. Especially at the border crossing in Aachen, on the way back from tours, they'd regularly pick on Michael. He must have had something about him that annoyed the police. Jaki and I rarely got searched. And I always wore extremely civilised clothes for crossing borders; I couldn't be bothered with that nonsense. I'd hide my ponytail under a cap to make me look like I had short hair, with a neat jumper and jacket over my jeans. That made me look fairly normal, not at all like a hippy. It helped at stations and airports as well. I'd always turn up with one hand in my pocket, suit jacket on, back straight and a very firm gaze, trying to give off a firm but friendly air. I'd be quite snobbish to the customs officers, nod at them and pass through without being stopped, like all the major criminals in their suits and ties. The bourgeois imagination sought evil among the freaks, so looking as un-freaky as possible in transit zones was a good technique for not getting harassed. It was also down to my degree and my work as a conductor. You learn to radiate a certain confidence. 'I beg your pardon? I'm the conductor!' When you step onto the podium for your first rehearsal with a symphony orchestra, as a young person, the musicians start by sizing you up. They try out what they can get away with, so you learn to express without words: 'Go ahead and check me out, but if you don't play along, it'll get difficult for you; so difficult that it's best you play along right away, OK?' That's why they left me alone at airports. Michael and Damo, of course, had more problems – the guards would always beckon them over.

ACHIM REICHEL It was always worst on the way to Berlin. I played a few RIAS gigs there with A.R. & Machines. What happened at the border there was pretty extreme every time.

MICHAEL ROTHER We went to Brussels with Harmonia for a gig in 1974. That was at the height of the Baader–Meinhof mania. We were sitting in our old Mercedes and suddenly we were surrounded by police with machine guns. They searched us all. Then they took us in.

It was frightening; don't make a false move. We looked different, and that apparently made us suspect. Us just wanting to make our art and live our private alternative lifestyle, they didn't care about that. We couldn't make them understand it, and they weren't interested in it. Society just viewed us with suspicion, that's how it was.

JÜRGEN DOLLASE The first wave of terrorism was a disaster for us. We kept getting stopped and checked. When we drove home from gigs at night – and we often went home straight afterwards instead of booking a hotel, to save money – we'd often have very unpleasant experiences. A van full of long-haired men was suspicious on principle. We'd be stopped and suddenly surrounded by ten to twenty policemen with machine guns. Then you'd look into the faces of family men pointing their machine guns at you. And you'd just think: 'For God's sake, make sure you walk slowly and don't make any sudden movements.' It was pretty bad sometimes. We ended up in every police check.

MICHAEL ROTHER We were on our way to a festival in Carinthia once, driving to Austria. Moebi drove the band van and I was in front in my VW Variant; I had a girl with me. I got to the festival, and after a while I started wondering where the others had got to. We didn't have mobile phones, obviously, so you couldn't just ask. Anyway, a plain-clothes policeman had overtaken Moebi and seen him sitting at the wheel with his hash pipe. The Austrians were very uncool about that kind of thing. Allegedly, they'd been alerted to a big upcoming drugs transport. The police took the whole van apart, unloaded all the instruments, searched everything, and then they found a few trips on friends who'd come along for the ride. So we did get a taste of the general terrorism hysteria, not just in terms of the zeitgeist but also first-hand.

JÜRGEN DOLLASE I'm not sure whether I had anything to do with terrorists, but if I did, then they weren't any of the top people. I might have met a couple of lower-level guys. I can't remember any names.

There were a few strange types when I was an art student, people who'd turn up out of nowhere and stay a week or so in some commune, ominous people with a lot of rumours floating around them, and then they'd vanish without a trace just as suddenly. It was quite an opaque situation. But there were very few close links between the hedonist rock 'n' rollers and the political faction, at least not among people I knew. I did have liberal attitudes but I wasn't really politically active. There were rock bands who seemed to do quite well out of socialist slogans. They played at all the left-wing events, where we were occasionally roped in, but not very often.

IRMIN SCHMIDT A number of Can shows were very aggression-laden. Sometimes that was great, but sometimes less so. We played a great gig in Berlin in 1970, when things were really extreme there. Malcolm had just left and Damo hadn't joined yet. We played at the technical college auditorium, a huge space filled to bursting with people. We had a good reputation at unis, but people rarely expected political statements; they just wanted great music. They'd pass joints onto the stage, as they did this time. The police were posted outside but they weren't allowed inside the uni for some reason. We played for five and a half hours flat, one of our longest shows ever. It was winter, bitterly cold outside. We'd started late, so we weren't finished until just about two in the morning. And the police had to wait outside in the cold. The plan was not to stop until they froze into blocks of ice. We were musically very aggressive as well that night. By the time we came out at the end there were really only a few of them left; it was a triumph of sorts. What wasn't fun at all, on the other hand, was another gig in Berlin, at the old Sportpalast, where Free were on first, then us and then the Flock. The Flock had difficulties because they got there too late, and then they insisted on us lending them our speakers. We didn't really want to but we let them talk us into it, and then they ruined our speakers good and proper. But even getting into the venue was hell; you had to pass through a two-hundred-metre police cordon, hundreds of police

351

lined up three-deep on either side, all with helmets and unmoving like gladiators or showroom dummies. We had to lug our stuff past them to the stage, and it was humiliating, very humiliating, in fact. The whole audience had to pass through as well, like running the gauntlet. So the atmosphere was charged from the very beginning, the audience and the musicians. And then when the Flock had difficulties, the first few people started smashing things up. The Flock stopped playing very early on and then a massive fight started in the venue. We found out later that the person who triggered it was an agent provocateur, a plain-clothes policeman. So it was the police who'd started the fighting! From up in the sound booth, I watched in horror as the police clubbed young girls between the legs, clearly enjoying it, in plain clothes. Of course, you start to think there's a lot wrong with our society, God knows! If not then, when? And, of course, your impotent rage quickly makes you say: 'Enough of this! It's us or them! Take up arms!' But I still wouldn't support Baader–Meinhof. A situation like that was intolerable, but it had to be solved differently. And quite a lot did change, even without the great revolution. At some point many people realised that violence only begets even more violence.

KARL BARTOS We used to enjoy driving around at night, in Kraftwerk, listening to music in the car in the early hours after we left the studio. The police must have stopped us at least four times or more. The police car would pull in ahead of us, one officer would stand behind our car, one in front, and one would ask: 'What are you doing here at this time of night?' It was pretty threatening. We were the right age to appear suspicious. Our reaction to these checks was always to turn on the light in the car and put our hands up right away. Then we'd say: 'We're musicians, we've just finished work.' You didn't get cynical; naturally, I was afraid of the policemen standing there with their guns locked and loaded. But they were scared too, of course; they were terrible situations.

352

IRMIN SCHMIDT We'd get stopped by the police all the time in Köln. Three or four long-haired guys sitting in a car listening to loud music at two in the morning – extremely suspicious. Didn't they have anything better to do?

HARALD GROSSKOPF At the end of Ash Ra's French tour in 1977 we played in Mülhausen, on the border. They'd just recently found Hanns Martin Schleyer dead in a car boot right nearby, after his abduction. We played in place of Ritchie Blackmore, who'd had to cancel, which was a terrible fit; people wanted Rainbow and they got Ash Ra. But it was great, tip-top equipment, and the organiser knew me from my Wallenstein days. He'd booked a whole restaurant for us; we smoked joints and drank alcohol. After that we weren't completely wasted but we certainly shouldn't have been driving. But of course we drove off in our big fat Daimler, Manuel had this second-hand 280 S-Class with double headlamps, and the three of us cruised around Mülhausen with the wind in our long hair. Suddenly this Peugeot overtakes us with screeching brakes, pulls up in front of us, and four guys with guns leap out and aim at our heads. So we wound the windows down very cautiously and Lüül, who spoke pretty good French, said he'd take his ID card out of his pocket very slowly. Then there was a bit of toing and froing with their walkie-talkies, they checked our ID and let us go again. They didn't care that we were drunk and stoned. It was the manhunt for Schleyer's kidnappers. And when someone points a gun right at your head you definitely get scared. We had the same thing a few years earlier with Wallenstein, at a motorway service area near Wuppertal. We were just about to get out of the car when we saw ten guys with machine guns surrounding us. All they wanted was to check our ID. As hippies, we felt a bit elitist and we'd find incidents like that amusing. That's how it was, the square capitalist world, and we wanted nothing to do with it.

IRMIN SCHMIDT We'd often get asked to take a political stance on stage, like after that Berlin show where the police had surrounded us.

But we never did. We didn't make statements. I think sometimes the wordless presence with which we performed was enough. Even the very idea of our music gave other people ideas; at least I hope so.

HARALD GROSSKOPF The security forces sometimes had no idea, though. In Wallenstein, we often travelled in closed vans. Three men in the front, the roadies, and behind them in the back of the van we'd be lying on top of the equipment in sleeping bags with our girlfriends, obviously smoking joints like they were going out of fashion. Then one time in Mönchengladbach, the van did an abrupt brake, the doors opened and there was a policeman. I just thought: 'Oh God, the game's up,' batted away the smoke and said hello as politely as I could. And the policeman gave us a nice friendly answer, told us his daughter was a fan of ours and would never forgive him if he came home without an autograph. We were very happy to help him out. Either he really didn't pick up on how stoned we were or he loved his daughter more than the law. My money's on the first option.

ROLF-ULRICH KAISER

'LSD in every tea.'
BERND WITTHÜSER

WINFRID TRENKLER We just called him RUK.

GERD KRAUS Kaiser was the most-hated man in pop.

FRANK FIEDLER People thought of him as a freak, but he came across like a businessman. Maybe he was a bit hip. He did release our music, at least.

GERD KRAUS A tie-wearer. He didn't run around like us, he wore better clothes. He made a strange impression, to be honest.

KLAUS BRIEST We didn't want anything to do with anyone who looked straight, with suits and ties or bow ties; they were squares who couldn't give us no satisfaction, because they didn't smoke the same cigarettes as us. Rolf-Ulrich Kaiser walked around like that but he still didn't come across as a square. He seemed very lively, talked fast and loose.

NIKEL PALLAT As a journalist, Kaiser was always very busy, a bit of an institution. From the mid-sixties he wrote the most interesting articles about music, which made him very prominent in the scene. He reported on the latest musical developments, from Germany or the States or the UK, it didn't matter; he had a broad range, did books about political folk music, about the Mothers of Invention, the Fugs, plus a 'protest ABC' and a book about communes, and then his *Buch der neuen Pop-Musik*, and that made a wide audience see him as a mouthpiece. He had such an exciting style that I'd often be dying to listen to the music he wrote about.

GIL FUNCCIUS Kaiser had a Beatles bowl cut back then; he didn't seem like the type to do drugs.

BERND WITTHÜSER I was never interested in beat music. But then the songwriters [Franz Josef] Degenhardt and [Hannes] Wader came along. I started to sing like them as a teenager, doing protest songs. I made everything that was on my mind into songs. My family got pretty angry with me over the lyrics. They'd have preferred a nice schlager singer like Peter Alexander. But I was singing about smoking joints and having sex, and my mother would tell me off: 'It's just not done, Bernd!' I got pretty well known in the Ruhr region after a while. When I got even better known the girls started coming along at last, after I'd waited so long for them. And that was when I met Rolf-Ulrich Kaiser, who was a journalist for the *Westdeutsche Allgemeine Zeitung*. Kaiser would come to my gigs quite often and write a lot about me. He was in with an intellectual crowd at the time, so he had great connections. I came from this folk club scene and I was hanging out with people like Kaiser and [the writer] Henryk M. Broder, which was very exciting. We became friends, I'd say.

PETER BURSCH In 1968 Rolf-Ulrich Kaiser organised the Essener Songtage with Henryk M. Broder and the cabaret collector Reinhard Hippen. That was how everything started in Germany; it brought the scenes together for the first time and it gave everyone a sense of cohesion, despite all the controversies that came out of it. Kaiser offered us a record contract right after we came off stage. He didn't promise us anything unusual, he just had a good overview.

GERD KRAUS Because he was so well known as a journalist, all the musicians threw themselves at him. Kaiser had something to say and he had good connections. You'd have his books on your shelves. And his record company Ohr was the first big German rock label.

HARALD GROSSKOPF He was definitely an important figure. After the cultural disaster of the Third Reich, Kaiser was the first journalist to hear something unique in German music. And he decided to foster that, first as a critic and then soon as a producer, by founding his own record labels, first Ohr, then Pilz and then the Kosmische Kuriere. It was all part of his mission as Germany's pop Kaiser.

ULRICH RÜTZEL Compared to his musicians, Kaiser looked like a civilised human being. He didn't have a wild look to him, he was quite inconspicuous. He had no desire to look like the artists he worked with. Kaiser was a jovial, extremely nice man. Very funny and chatty.

BERND WITTHÜSER I met Walter Westrupp in 1969, in this little club where I used to play. Walter was a DJ there. Then the band Insterburg & Co. came along, who did this really impressive comedy pop stuff. So I stopped doing protest songs and started an Insterburg-like combo with Westrupp. The two of us, me in black with my guitar and Westrupp doing a kind of one-man band with all sorts of instruments and nonsense. And that same year, Kaiser said: 'Let's make a record!' 'That's crazy,' I thought, 'a working-class lad from the Ruhr region like me getting a record contract out of the blue.' It was a huge deal, and it only confirmed my 1968 decision to change my life. That liberation was amazing.

GERD KRAUS Kaiser came up to us after a Limbus gig and talked his head off to stress that he did everything really professionally. He said Ohr was part of the big Metronome label, which was international, and he said we could use a studio in Hamburg. A lot of it was rubbish, of course. But it was funny that the flyers were literally cut out as ear-shapes, like the name of the label.

MANI NEUMEIER Kaiser had a great ear for music, which is why Guru Guru signed our first record contract with him. But he also chased after us; he knew us from the Irène Schweizer Trio. He asked us if we wanted to make a record for him, and *UFO* became one of the first releases on Ohr. We hesitated at first because we didn't actually want to make any records; the idea was for Guru Guru only to exist live. But then we realised you can't get your name out there very well without records, because nobody knows you. Kaiser paid DM1,000 per band. We turned it down at first and said everything was different with Guru Guru: 'We want a thousand marks each!' Kaiser's boss – I'll just call him that, I mean the guy from Metronome, the parent label that financed Ohr entirely – he just sneered and said: 'OK, you can have your thousand marks each.' He earned much more than that out of us later on, it was peanuts for him. But we'd got what we demanded!

NIKEL PALLAT Heinz Trenczak was this very young guy, studying under the composer Mauricio Kagel in Köln. Kagel wanted his students to try out working in broadcasting, so Trenczak got a trainee post at WDR editing the TV show *Ende offen*, and his first show was the one we were on. It was a fairly common but crazy talk-show format, an open-ended discussion on the minor channel WDR 3. It started at eight and went out live. The official subject was 'Pop & Co. – the "other" music between protest and market forces', and they'd invited controversial guests: [rock band Gila's] guitarist Connie Veit, the music scholar Wolfgang Hamm – another guy from Kagel's coterie – then Heinz-Klaus Metzger, a pompous Neue Musik pundit who made a very good opponent, and also Bodo Albes, the manager at the time of Inga Rumpf's band Frumpy, who were playing at the same time as the programme, so they cut to live footage now and then, plus Rolf-Ulrich Kaiser and me. The host was the ultra-avant-gardist Hans G. Helms, a terrible choice; he was an Adorno man, like Metzger. So it all added up to a very crude mixture, and then it went on for hours. By the time I brought out my hatchet it was eleven o'clock at night.

It was easy enough to get the hatchet into the studio; no one did any checks at WDR in 1971, or on my flight out from Berlin to Köln. But I mean, who would have expected a talk-show guest to bring along a hatchet in those days? They ramped up the security checks after the incident. It wasn't a sure thing that I'd get the hatchet out in the first place; we'd discussed it beforehand and decided to play it by ear. I was standing in for Rio Reiser, who had the flu. If the conversation hadn't escalated the way it did, I'd have left the hatchet unused. But the escalation began with Kaiser co-opting the discussion. He'd started moaning about the media, about their lack of support. That old chestnut. We'd prepared for the show and we had our sights set on Kaiser. Our attitude was: we're Ton Steine Scherben, and we won't be co-opted by people riding the avant-garde Neue Musik wave. We had our own label, David Volksmund Produktion, and we wanted to do our own thing completely independently, whereas Kaiser had a deal for his allegedly oh-so-progressive Ohr label with the major producer Peter Meisel, who made his money out of schlager, and ultimately with BASF. We wanted to draw a line between us and then react if Kaiser used certain terms. So I asked what all Kaiser's moaning would change about the fundamental situation. We had a heated exchange for two or three minutes, and then I'd had enough of it! My indignation was definitely genuine, but of course it was also a role I was playing and a happening; I made conscious use of the live-show situation. I don't actually have a short temper and aside from that I'm a pacifist – waving that axe around in the studio was the first time I was armed in my life, but I can get drawn into things. What annoyed me the most was that the studio table turned out to be so stable. It was glued so firmly I couldn't get the blade through it. I whacked away at it three times to start with and realised: nothing's happening! Then I put my back into it and nothing happened again – it was appalling! I thought: 'Am I too weak to smash up a table?' The other guests had leapt up in outrage and were staring at me, shocked. I gathered up their microphones; we wanted to donate them to a band in the juvenile prison in Berlin. After they broke off the show there were three minutes of silence. Then the first journalists came along and asked what had happened. After a while a nice elderly gentleman came up and said: 'It's time to calm down now – and I'm afraid you'll have to give the microphones back.' Apart from that, it all ended quietly. It was attempted criminal damage, but the police didn't come. A pharmacist from Remscheid called up the WDR right then and said he'd never seen such great television, and he'd be happy to pay for all the damage. It's a YouTube classic these days but hardly anyone saw it live at the time. Who'd be watching WDR 3 just before midnight? But even now, people shouldn't just look at the hatchet; it was really about something, there were a whole load of objective contradictions between those people: the artsy-fartsy twelve-tone Marxists with zero relation to reality, then Gila's stoner psychedelia and party rockers like Frumpy, and then the shitty liberal but at least liberal WDR, plus Kaiser's pandering to commercialism, and last of all Ton Steine Scherben – it was a totally controversial discussion, and that had to be made clear and slugged out. At least that was still possible back then.

JÜRGEN DOLLASE I first met Rolf-Ulrich Kaiser at an open-air festival in Landshut. We'd barely played a handful of gigs by then. The festival had a good line-up, with Amon Düül and Krokus from Switzerland. Anyway, Kaiser approached us there. We had a local bar-owner looking after us at the time, so I wasn't really part of the negotiations with Kaiser. I wasn't a good friend of his, let's put it like that, because Kaiser was a rather strange guy. His girlfriend Gille Lettmann always came along with him. They were joined at the hip.

ULRICH RÜTZEL Kaiser and his girlfriend Gille Lettmann weren't joined at the hip, as people often say. Rolf-Ulrich was usually alone when it came to business. She wasn't interested in that side of things. He planned everything precisely, and Gille only came along when it benefitted him. He was a professional; he just went over the top by neglecting the pragmatic side of business. But actually Kaiser was a businessman who wanted to make big bucks.

BILL BARONE Kaiser was OK, in principle. His girlfriend Gille Lettmann was the strange one of the two, the space queen. Things never went smoothly when she was around.

GERD KRAUS I never noticed his girlfriend. Maybe she was too ethereal?

MANI NEUMEIER The esoteric side of Kaiser only came later. In the early years he took everyone he could get and let them do their thing in peace. He just needed too many bands, so he took a few bad ones, and then sadly he smoothed everything into monotonous mush. I won't name names but there was a folk duo that was just as important to him as Amon Düül or Guru Guru.

HARALD GROSSKOPF His record company was based at his place in Köln. That was the headquarters of Ohr and Pilz-Musik. We went there a lot. A two-storey house stuffed full of records, with a stock area and an office. I presume we also took LSD with him there.

PETER BURSCH I often visited him at home. He had a huge book collection. Lots of books about folk music and bands like the Grateful Dead. I borrowed a lot of books from him. You could tell he knew exactly what he was talking about. But he just let us make our music. Before we went to the studio he booked us a big hall in the Remscheid conservatory for a week. We rehearsed there, lived together and ate in a proper canteen, so we could work on our tracks undisturbed. Kaiser popped in now and then to check we were all right. Sometimes Bernd Witthüser or one of Guru Guru would come by. That was a good thing because we were still young and we had no studio experience at all. Kaiser was listed as our producer on the record even though he didn't produce a thing, hardly came to the studio during the recordings. He took care of the press instead, and he'd given us the contract. He just let us get on with it.

GIL FUNCCIUS I was in my mid-twenties and I urgently needed a job. A friend of mine knew Kaiser and told me he was looking for cover illustrators. There were other things I'd rather have done but I needed the money. I'd been in the political scene before that, but when I started working as a graphic designer for Kaiser the whole scene turned its back on me. I didn't particularly like him either; maybe he was quite nice. Kaiser was a typical businessman, his whole habitus was mercantile middle-class. He was my age but he came from a completely different world; the political scene was very picky about people like him. And young people can often be arrogant. We rejected anything bourgeois like the plague. I didn't take his Deutschrock at all seriously at the time. Working with Kaiser went fine, though, because he let me do what I liked. Which I exploited thoroughly to begin with, of course. After the third commission he said it was all too expensive, but to begin with I ran riot. I loved the gatefold cover for the first Annexus Quam LP, *Osmose*, even though it was a hell of a lot of work. The second thing I did was Floh de Cologne, *Rockoper Profitgeier*, the one with the guts spilling out of the bird. I obviously loved being able to do things like that and get paid for it. But after a while Kaiser decided it was all too expensive.

GERD KRAUS The record covers for the bands on Ohr had terrible graphic design – apart from Limbus, because I insisted on influencing them myself. Even the colours: murky green wasn't OK, I wanted a nice colour. Unfortunately, I couldn't do anything about the limp balloon hanging out of a slit in the cover, but these days I wish I had an intact original cover with the balloon; they cost a lot of money now. I still don't know what that balloon was supposed to mean, though. That's something I'd ask Rolf-Ulrich Kaiser, if I could.

ULRICH RÜTZEL I joined BASF as a label manager for Kaiser's second label Pilz – meaning 'mushroom' – in January 1972. It had been set up a year before, but it was pretty stagnant, and Kaiser insisted on Pilz getting its own label manager. I'd known Kaiser for a year and a half before that because he'd booked me as a jazz pianist for concerts in stately homes. He was booking and staging folk and jazz events at the time. Most of the artists on Pilz, with the exception of Wallenstein and Popol Vuh, came from the folk scene. The Pilz catalogue turned into a clever combination of the rising electronic music scene and the ebbing hippy folk movement. But everything that wasn't schlager and didn't come from the UK or the States was a hard sell in Germany in those days, and the PR pressure on Pilz was enormous.

GIL FUNCCIUS I didn't know any of the bands on Ohr and Pilz before I started. Kaiser gave me information on them. I went from West Berlin to Essen to work with Witthüser & Westrupp, in the days when Kaiser still paid for trips like that. Two loveable weirdos, incredibly nice. After I worked on the cover they invited me to stay overnight and come along to a friend's place. I did, and then we ended up at the Kippenbergers' place. The painter Martin Kippenberger was only eighteen back then, cheeky and arrogant.

ULRICH RÜTZEL Kaiser recognised how important PR is, and I think you can say he was an absolute marketing genius, but he wasn't actually a great music aficionado. You can tell from the Pilz label; a lot of what came out there wasn't exactly the finest of the fine. There were a lot of good-natured chancers under contract, people who liked more than one joint a day. They'd take the occasional tab of LSD with Kaiser and me. But the conjunction of German folk and synthesizers was something entirely new, ultimately an evolution in music history. Tangerine Dream or Klaus Schulze only did electronic stuff, but Kaiser went one step further with Witthüser & Westrupp and Bröselmaschine. [The bands] Emtidi and Hoelderlin were more folk ponytail guys – bringing them together with electronic music was a historical coup. Kaiser recognised that synthesizers could create a certain mood and you didn't have to be a good musician to work them. You just smoked a couple of decent joints and off you went.

BERND WITTHÜSER Our first record for Kaiser, *Lieder von Vampiren, Nonnen und Toten*, was still fairly straightforward. After that things got more interesting; that's when LSD and mushrooms came into it. Then we did records like *Der Jesuspilz*, and Westrupp and I performed in churches. We'd adapted the Bible into songs; not all the clergy were into it but they had a full house for a change when we played. For a while there were churches all over the place calling to book us for gigs. It was crazy – you're standing at the altar tripping your face off.

ULRICH RÜTZEL Kaiser was a folkie at heart; he came from Burg Waldeck originally, and he stayed that way in the end. His bad reputation with some people is down to them not counting him as part of music's high culture. I was fortunate enough to be a label manager for the jazz label MPS as well; I didn't have to bribe any editors there. If I gave Siggi Schmidt-Joos from *Der Spiegel* magazine a new MPS record, I knew he'd be interested. It was just all good stuff, from Oscar Peterson to Sun Ra to Wolfgang Dauner. But Joos definitely didn't want anything from Pilz; he avoided Kaiser's things as far as possible.

SIEGFRIED SCHMIDT-JOOS Kaiser? A totally tone-deaf nerd.

GERD KRAUS Kaiser didn't get involved in the music; we wouldn't have put up with it. We did want to be on Ohr, but we got taken for a ride with the record contract. Once we'd signed he stepped away entirely. Kaiser had a way of evaporating decorously when things got tricky; he'd utter a few cryptic sentences, poetic fluff that sounded like castles in the air – and then he was gone. He'd either just leave or drop out of the conversation. Once the record contract was signed we got nothing more out of him; from then on, Kaiser was a phantom.

ULRICH RÜTZEL Kaiser's basic idea was to be constantly present on the market, just pump stuff out – no matter if it was good or not. He didn't give a fig if critics panned the records. He'd just say: 'Ulli, we've got to be present all the time. And to do that, we have to do all kinds of stuff.' Kaiser invented the forerunner to viral marketing, if you like. As a former booker, he thought shows were very important. You sell records by doing shows. That worked then and it still works now. Kaiser pushed that principle to the brink of insanity.

JÜRGEN DOLLASE He seemed like a bit of a fanatic to me, though who knows what about. But of course he infected other people with his enthusiasm and the visions he had of all the things you could do. That meant he could easily convince people of his ideas, which was pretty astounding.

ULRICH RÜTZEL We'd often talk about what we wanted to do next. I'd go to Berlin a lot, where we'd meet up at Peter Meisel's music publishing office; that was Kaiser's official address for a long time. Kaiser wanted to do pop like the Brits, but he rightly said: 'We can't do things the same way as the Brits!' He didn't want his bands to sound like Nazareth or Status Quo; he wanted a new form of German popular music, rock music with German lyrics, and that was really new at the time. Udo Lindenberg wasn't around yet; if he was singing at all back then, it was in English, if he wasn't still just drumming.

STEVE SCHROYDER I met Kaiser and his partner Gille at a hotel in Köln and we instantly had this incredible connection. I used to read the tarot for all sorts of people in those days. I'd learned it on my trip to Finland, where I'd got hold of a deck of cards and spent a long time with them before I started laying other people's cards for them, partly to take it further myself. Anyway, I had my tarot cards with me that first time we met, and I read the cards for Kaiser and Florian Fricke from Popol Vuh. I'd lay the cards before every gig with Tangerine Dream as well; Edgar liked it. He and his wife Monique consulted me regularly on things like that. Kaiser and Gille were also extremely interested in tarot.

HARALD GROSSKOPF Tarot was a trend in the seventies; people were looking for answers to the trauma of the Nazi era, and back then the cards offered fast answers and solutions for a lot of people. Our parents' generation didn't want to talk about any of it, and tarot filled that gap. Then there was our wish for rebellion, which a lot of people fulfilled with drugs, even if they didn't think drugs were all that great; the gap had to be filled.

ULRICH RÜTZEL Later on, Kaiser and his girlfriend Gille Lettmann even brought out their own deck of tarot cards.

STEVE SCHROYDER I wasn't that into them bringing out their own tarot deck soon afterwards. It's secret knowledge, you know, you have to treat it with respect; you shouldn't just commercialise it.

HARALD GROSSKOPF They did all this esoteric stuff, but we all went along with it. Gille was an attractive woman, it was just that her esoteric leanings were much worse than his. It was all part and parcel back then, but after a while the two of them really wouldn't do anything without laying the tarot cards; studio dates at full moon and things like that.

PETER BAUMANN Kaiser got a tad too deep into Timothy Leary. At some point all they talked about was cosmic couriers, in a very metaphysical way – which became uncomfortable for us in Tangerine Dream.

JÜRGEN DOLLASE I don't think they thought very long about the idea of the Kosmische Kuriere. It was just something that Rolf-Ulrich Kaiser came up with one day, probably through his links to Timothy Leary in America and Sergius Golowin in Switzerland, but also to the psychedelia guy Brian Barritt, who was Leary's right-hand man for a while; he was part of it too. They were the gurus, more responsible for our minds than for the music. But it worked pretty well because they were all impressive people who just came along to the sessions. Sometimes it was a bit strange, though.

HARALD GROSSKOPF For the sessions with the Kosmische Kuriere, we'd all rock up to Dieter Dierks's studio in Stommeln. I lived not far away in Mönchengladbach and I came on my moped, Witthüser and Westrupp came from the Hunsrück on motorbikes, even in the depth of winter, and Schulze and Tangerine Dream came by car from Berlin. Then we'd all down the stuff, dissolved in little sparkling-wine glasses. And then we'd wait. After a while someone would pick up a random instrument and get started. And then the others would join in bit by bit. Sometimes we'd swap instruments. I had the feeling I had nothing more to do with the sound's creation but that I did influence the sound, so I could guide the drums purely mentally – that was how far it went with LSD. But then I also drummed myself free, found my own voice, which was very liberating. Perhaps that was how I developed my own style, which I was later able to put into practice on recordings with Klaus Schulze.

JÜRGEN DOLLASE The Wallenstein drummer Harald Grosskopf and the Dutch bassist Jerry Berkers were in charge of the concrete side of the 'cosmic sessions'. It was mostly down to me that the stuff ever turned into tracks suitable for release on albums, like the one with Sergius Golowin or the one with Walter Wegmüller. I was the only one who brought any structure into the chaos so that it sounded at least a bit like music. But the reason why some of the cosmic records later became so influential was not least thanks to Harald Grosskopf's drumming. In the sessions, which mostly went on forever, he ensured a continuous beat that somehow held it all together.

WINFRID TRENKLER I was at one of those sessions. Everyone was given something to drink. Harald Grosskopf was still thirsty and asked me for another drink. I passed him my glass, which Kaiser might have put acid into as well. Then Grosskopf had two highs, and I was lucky to have dodged that bullet.

HARALD GROSSKOPF I always felt that everyone knew they were getting drugs. There may have been other situations, but I never took anything if I didn't know what it was. Actually, there was one exception: Winfrid Trenkler was at one of those big night sessions with Kaiser and had a glass with a drink in it, and I was crazy thirsty after six hours of drumming. I pointed at the glass and he gave it to me. I'd already taken one LSD trip, and then after I downed Trenkler's glass it made two. Oddly enough, it didn't double the effect.

PETER BURSCH Kaiser always had thousands of ideas. He came to ask us if we wanted to join his Kosmische Kuriere. We did go to Dierks's studio once, a big session with lots of bands. He put LSD in our drinks without telling us – a terrible experience.

HARALD GROSSKOPF As I see it, everyone was high at the sessions. We didn't know much about LSD, so we just tried it out as an adventure. Gille Lettmann and Rolf-Ulrich Kaiser brought it in from Switzerland, super-clean and straight from the source. It was fantastic quality, not like the stuff you got in bars, with strychnine or other crap in it sometimes.

JÜRGEN DOLLASE The material Rolf-Ulrich Kaiser distributed was very good quality, but by then I wasn't having hallucinations any more. A lot of people who have had long periods taking LSD or similar things will tell you: after a while the hallucinations stop, then all you get is that sharpened, hysterical perception. The sessions would go on all night. There were no discussions or other kinds of talking, it was all about playing music. If you wanted to stop, you stopped, did something else and then joined in again later. The tape was running the whole time. Then Dieter Dierks would edit it together later with Kaiser for the records.

HARALD GROSSKOPF There were no instructions at all, it was all total chaos, but in a good way. You'd just sit down and do something, on the piano or the guitar or whatever. Time didn't matter, you wouldn't even notice you'd been making music for twelve hours straight. Sometimes you'd just stare at the wall for an hour, watch imaginary rays of sunshine and listen to the others playing, and then join back in afterwards. But you did notice occasional climaxes. There was often a strong sense of forming a unit with the others, almost more than with yourself. I had very strange fantasies, where I could watch myself playing from two metres above – I was playing down there, but I was also the other person watching on from above. I thought to myself while I watched from up there that I knew exactly what the guy down there was playing. That was a typical LSD experience, and it's strongly linked to your own perceptions. If you have a lot of fear inside you, it can be hugely amplified, up to the worst horror projections combined with very realistic fantasies.

JÜRGEN DOLLASE The spark didn't catch with me until Kaiser's Kosmische Kuriere sessions. We were sitting around in Dieter Dierks's studio and the music that was playing had this surging rhythm, probably down to Klaus Schulze's keyboards. I was playing bass and watching Brian Barritt sitting in the middle of the studio rocking on a chair – in the same rhythm as the music. It gave me this typical LSD idea: is he really rocking to the music? Or is it him that's making the rhythm? So I went over and stopped him – and the music collapsed at the same moment. There were so many coincidences like that that you did start to think: 'What's going on here?'

HARALD GROSSKOPF An LSD trip lasted about twelve hours. It took about sixty to ninety minutes to kick in. After half an hour it started with this strange pressure at the back of your eyes, and then reality started dissolving slowly. And at some point it got so huge that all sorts of things from the past could suddenly come back up. I had a few pretty bad experiences, and also some very good ones. But it's dangerous stuff – looking in a mirror on LSD isn't a good idea, for example. I once felt like I was going through the genetic code of my entire existence; that's attractive and frightening all at once. But it can also have really bad effects on your heart and circulation, or cause lasting psychological damage. I wouldn't recommend it, in general. When we were taking LSD we didn't know what it might bring; no one explained it or warned us. And people did die of it.

STEVE SCHROYDER That studio session in Switzerland with Timothy Leary was an ultra-unusual situation. Ash Ra Tempel had come with a crowd of about twenty hangers-on, and Leary's retinue in Switzerland consisted of maybe fifty people who lived in a village there. Leary had bunkered down in Switzerland after he escaped from prison in the US, with the help of the Black Panthers. Anyway, that whole retinue was in the studio in Bern, but there wasn't much contact with Leary himself; he was welling over with ideas, which he announced wherever, whenever. Being a quiet, contemplative person, it was all a bit much for me; eye contact was enough for me in those days. You could communicate fine just via your eyes, and I got on very well with him like that. He did record a few spoken lines, but I wasn't sure what else he did there. But then when I heard his words on the record we made together it was great, really amazing. The hard core of Ash Ra Tempel consisted of ten people who'd come to the studio in the centre of Bern. A lot of them had been dosed with LSD without knowing, and they still complain about it now. But you've got to be a bit strange to complain about being given LSD at a recording session with Timothy Leary.

WINFRID TRENKLER The musicians liked the fact that Kaiser got Timothy Leary involved. The first time I interviewed Ash Ra – in this case Manuel Göttsching and Hartmut Enke – at their place in Berlin, they were over the moon about it.

STEVE SCHROYDER But a lot of them really didn't notice and then wondered why they suddenly felt so weird. One girl burst into tears in the studio. Her boyfriend was sitting there saying: 'Timothy Leary's the devil and we're all going to hell!' The album we were working on was called *Seven Up*, because of the seven levels of consciousness, and because they passed round cans of 7 Up at the recording sessions, laced with LSD. Before we kicked off we were told to each take a can of 7 Up. And then we recorded the album in two days in Bern, although we wasted most of the time on side one. We'd actually had a few practice sessions for it in the old Wrangelstrasse police barracks in Berlin. Side two was good old improvisation; Manuel had set the theme, but we still played absolutely freely. And it was perfectly fine, unlike the first side, which was edited and processed over and over in the studio; it was just the wrong music for an LSD record. Anyway, when it was all over and everyone was squatting on the floor, happy as Larry with ourselves and the world, Kaiser came in and yelled: 'Lads! Get off your backsides and record something decent at last!' It was totally out of order; I guess he wanted to act the music mogul. I really hated him for that.

HARALD GROSSKOPF Kaiser and Lettmann were always at the sessions, laying the tarot. We all kind of joined in because we had a bit of an esoteric streak as well. Then again, I thought it was embarrassing that they were always consulting the tarot about every little thing. 'Is this OK? Is that OK? Right, let's ask the cards first!' Then we'd all look at the cards they'd laid and say: 'All right, we'll do a session on the Chariot.' That was the spirit in which the *Tarot* album was made. There were twenty-one basic cards, which the music refers to. The album was made with Walter Wegmüller, a Roma artist from Basel who painted pictures to match the subject. We were all on acid at the session, looked at the tarot cards and made music to go with them.

BERND WITTHÜSER One day, Sergius Golowin turned up from Switzerland and told us a fairy tale while we were necking the stuff. There was LSD in every tea, and everyone knew it. It was OK for a while, didn't become a problem for me until later.

JÜRGEN DOLLASE For the record with Sergius Golowin, we were at a farmhouse in the Westerwald hills, where Witthüser and Westrupp lived. We had a planning meeting, where we obviously took a trip. There was a thunderstorm that night, and at some point, when all of us were tripping, Sergius Golowin said: 'Come on, let's go outside.' Whereupon we left the farmhouse and went out to a hill. And I was thinking to myself that it might actually be a bit dangerous. Then Sergius Golowin started telling a story, about powers and his brothers and sisters and all sorts of things. Anyway, from a certain point on, you got the impression that Golowin had something to do with the thunder and lightning out there. The joke was, the next day the villagers said they'd never seen such a terrible storm in all their lives. For us, there seemed to be a link between Sergius Golowin's energy and the thunderstorm. That's what it looked like to us, at least. I thought it was astounding, at any rate, and very entertaining.

BERND WITTHÜSER Klaus Schulze was there as well, on that stormy night. We were all sitting on the floor, terrified. We'd dropped acid, toadstools and all sorts of things. In that state of mind, thunder and lightning make a pretty strong impression. Then Golowin went outside and came in again fifteen minutes later, and then the storm was over, and I wondered if he'd been talking to the gods. It calmed down after that, anyway.

HARALD GROSSKOPF Then everyone played until the stuff wore off. That would often be when the sun went up in the morning. You couldn't sleep straight away when it was over, you'd have these extreme waking dreams. It took one or two days to get back to your normal level. But then there were people like Hartmut Enke, who didn't come down again from one of his last sessions. He told me once, perfectly serious, that he'd discovered the sound of all sounds, and if you put that sound out as a single, it would be a huge hit. He wanted to go to Rome to convince the Pope of the idea. He was actually a great creative musician who was already playing his bass with a compressor back then; it gave it his very own sound, which really fascinated me. But at some point, all he did was laugh away to himself, like in a bad movie. I found it sinister. They found the Wallenstein singer Jerry Berkers dead of an overdose one day in his home town in Holland. At some earlier point, he'd also taken too much and he came to me, looked at me sadly and said: 'Hey, Harald, I'm dying!' I was shocked. He disappeared in the break at a Wallenstein gig at the Fabrik in Hamburg once, because he allegedly had too much blood on his face, and he didn't turn up again for two weeks.

JÜRGEN DOLLASE Sadly, our Wallenstein bassist Jerry Berkers got screwed up by the whole thing and ended up psychotic. We played a few more gigs but it got worse and worse for him. One night he was on stage singing 'Mother Universe' and he started pulling at his hair and saying you couldn't sing about Mother Universe – it was too much. He ended up in an institution, couldn't play with Wallenstein any more. There was someone else from Berlin who had so many problems from those psycho-sessions that it made him ill as well. I didn't have any trouble with them. I experienced them as very intense, but above all as exciting.

ULRICH RÜTZEL Of course the Kosmische Kuriere sessions were extreme. Kaiser got most of them produced by Dieter Dierks; it wouldn't have been possible without him. He had a great ear for that kind of thing and he didn't just work in the studio; he also took a financial risk – first he did the work and then he had to wait until the money came in. Kaiser had to keep applying for it through his publisher Meisel – Meisel had the final say when it came to money. I presume that's why the whole thing imploded. It's not easy to recoup those kinds of production costs. They usually paid the artists an advance, and they only got royalties once the costs had been recouped. But Kaiser wasn't the only one who did that. Unless you were a big-name artist – then your manager would make different arrangements.

PETER BURSCH Kaiser had a deal with Dieter Dierks, who was setting up a studio near Köln. The studio was still very spartan. A rural area outside of Köln, and he'd converted his parents' pigsty into a studio. The place was so small we had to go outside to sing. You can hear all that on our first record: cars driving past and a church bell ringing. But we didn't care – it was great there. The mood in the band was good and Dieter was very creative. He was the first person to have a multitrack machine, which meant we could experiment. His mum cooked meals for everyone; it was a great atmosphere.

HARALD GROSSKOPF Dierks fused those sessions into albums. He never took drugs, only drank a bit of alcohol. Now and then he'd pick up the bass during the recordings. We did so much there, we must have recorded about sixty hours of music. It's all either lost or just never came out. Including a lot that was better than what's on the Kosmische Kuriere records; I was a bit disappointed by them. The only one I liked is *Cosmic Jokers*, or at least the A-side. I thought everything else was just weird, out-of-it music made at dawn, when no one was really high any more. And then that was the stuff they brought out! I was pretty frustrated.

WINFRID TRENKLER Then Kaiser played the music to journalists at a press conference in Dieter Dierks's studio in Stommeln. Gille Lettmann was walking around doing her 'star girl' thing. There were little stars stuck wherever you looked. Not everyone was impressed by that kind of thing, though. I thought all that sugary frosting was inadequate, and I wrote critically about that whole staging aspect in the press. Later on, Kaiser resented me for finding it all so ridiculous. The records to go with it, the music – I gave that positive reviews, of course, called it 'pioneering'.

ULRICH RÜTZEL Sure, Kaiser was hyped up, but weren't we all hyped up in those days? It's one of those black-and-white stories. The managers who had a say at the big German record companies were pretty much the opposite of Rolf-Ulrich Kaiser. He was like a hyped-up musician, and he'd play that role for the boring BASF managers, who were pretty dull guys from the chemical industry. The three managers based in Hamburg were great, though, maybe because they didn't have that chemical background. They understood Kaiser, but when the other guys came in from Mannheim and Ludwigshafen, the fun was over. They held their meetings in the mornings, and not with cognac and whisky. We did – in our coffee, obviously.

JÜRGEN DOLLASE Kaiser had some really insane ideas. For instance, he once held a press conference on the high-speed train from Hamburg to München. He planned a show at the Deutschlandhalle in Berlin, where various bands were supposed to play on different floors, and he thought up a crazy stage rig for it. Nothing came of it, as was often the case.

HARALD GROSSKOPF Kaiser once rented a dining car from the railway company as a PR gag, and it went all across Germany picking up journalists along the way. They were wined and dined, and we were available for interviews. It worked – the press reported on it, there was even a piece in *Der Spiegel*. We took it all for granted at the time, thanks to Rolf-Ulrich Kaiser.

ULRICH RÜTZEL The PR campaign in the Wuppertal suspension railway with Witthüser & Westrupp was a stroke of genius. Kaiser said we had to do things that went beyond treating editors to a bottle of whisky. That wasn't enough any more. Obviously, they'd still get the whisky, but we'd smoke a joint with them as well. What we wanted was really big stories. So we booked a carriage on the suspended train in Wuppertal to launch a Witthüser & Westrupp album. It was a dining car and we invited journos along. The trip started at eleven in the morning, breakfast with wine, beer and whatever. The carriage soon filled up with the usual clouds of smoke. From there, we took a coach to the farm from the song 'Bauer Plath', somewhere in the Westerwald, and we arrived there stoned out of our minds. Kaiser was always coming up with unusual PR ideas. Just keeping people talking about us all the time.

HARALD GROSSKOPF Klaus Schulze was supposed to call himself 'Klaus "Quadro" Schulze' because Kaiser thought quadrophonics would be the next big thing. Schulze thought it was stupid, obviously.

BILL BARONE Kaiser saw quadrophonic sound as the technology of the future and the next media revolution, so we recorded a Wallenstein album using four-channel equipment. But as we know, not much ever became of quadrophonic sound.

HARALD GROSSKOPF There was even a plan for 'cosmic fashion' – but I didn't want to walk around dressed like that, neither on Earth nor in the cosmos. I worked on my costume until I liked it and felt able to wear it, but it was a compromise with Gille Lettmann, who wanted us to dress like that all the time, at least on stage. As a marketing idea to create a corporate identity, it was an interesting approach, of course, but those cosmic robes were too kitschy for me in the end.

BILL BARONE The two of them were always trying to convince me to wear make-up on stage. But I said I was a rock guitarist and I wasn't going to put on make-up; I wasn't into all that cosmic crap. My compromise was to wear the funny costumes Lettmann invented for us, now and then. But I refused to shave off my beard and change my hairstyle. The costumes were actually all right: a black suit and a weird jacket with silver decorations over the top. There were much worse stage outfits at the time.

HARALD GROSSKOPF No one wore the stuff in the long run. The two of them were constantly making new suggestions, but that ultimately only led to everyone leaving, one by one.

JÜRGEN DOLLASE Kaiser was a promotional genius, but perhaps he failed in the end because his ideas were a bit too crazy. Apart from that, there was the contradiction that we were poor as church mice, barely making ends meet, no money for equipment, no money for anything – and then I'd spend days in a luxury Paris hotel for some marketing campaign, doing one interview after another; it was absurd. We did get a bit of money but it bore no proportion to our fame, which was pretty decent. None of us had a proper manager, or I didn't have anyone to take care of things like that for me, at least, stuff you'd probably do through a lawyer these days. It was all organised pretty unconventionally back then.

BERND WITTHÜSER Kaiser did some great advertising for us. Everything was fine at the beginning: Kaiser had big plans and did his best to put them into action. But after a while far too much LSD turned up in the place, and all the mushrooms as well – God, we tried all sorts of things, it was pretty intense. One day Kaiser just flipped. He was still organising things, but it all got way too esoteric for me; I wasn't into the whole cosmic thing.

MANI NEUMEIER We laughed at him when the cosmic thing came along; we thought it was terrible. And the music to go with it was awful too. Going 'quack, quack' and putting it through an echo machine is miles away from cosmic. You need a different musical force. We talked about it at the time, me and Irmin Schmidt and Edgar Froese, and they thought it was stupid as well. But you had to start somewhere and no one else would have set up a label so quickly with that music, the way Rolf-Ulrich Kaiser managed it. If you look at that achievement, his cosmic excursions at the end don't make much difference.

IRMIN SCHMIDT We had to resist that drugged-up mysticism at times, Herr Kaiser's 'cosmic' nonsense. You had to fight against being dragged into his stupid world. It was another romantic illusion. I never even uttered the phrase 'consciousness-expanding'. We expanded each other's consciousness by making music.

JÜRGEN DOLLASE A lot of it was just ridiculous hippy populism. We are all one? Thanks, but no thanks! We did play sessions together, but the thought was always at the back of my mind that none of them were proper musicians. I found an appropriate term for it later, which I now use about cuisine: 'projective triviality'.

BERND WITTHÜSER I'd had enough of them by the end of 1972. Westrupp had had enough as well; he wanted to go home. I didn't want to go back to Essen, so I got on my NSU Supermax, rode to Berlin and carried on as a busker. I made enough that way and it was another act of liberation. I was still in contact with Kaiser for a while, but he was on a different trip; I could hardly talk to him. That was early 1973, about then.

ULRICH RÜTZEL At some point, Kaiser started running out of bands. There were rumours that he hadn't done his accounting properly. The artist royalties weren't always done right either, I heard. But those were the kinds of details he just didn't have an eye for; he wasn't a cheat. You mustn't forget he'd spent huge amounts of money on the productions. Kaiser lost control of the whole business side after a while; by the beginning of 1974 at the latest it had all slipped away from him.

JÜRGEN DOLLASE He could have been a great impresario, but the economic basis of the whole industry was too fragile. If the records had sold double the numbers, it might have worked. But sadly he was inherently underfinanced. I can't remember when I last had anything to do with Kaiser. Of course, we ended up in a legal dispute over accounting, and from then on it got chaotic. We went to RCA in Hamburg for our fifth Wallenstein album. That was the end of our contact with Kaiser, there were no ties after that. All we heard was that he was in considerable financial trouble, which didn't surprise me.

ULRICH RÜTZEL The sad end was partly due to his ineptitude in business matters. Someone should probably have been employed to get a proper grip on the finances. People who work creatively like that shouldn't have to take care of the books as well. BASF and the publisher Meisel kept completely out of the artistic side. I spent nights and nights debating with Kaiser how to pick the quality up a bit. I didn't have a perspective for how to continue. We couldn't go on bringing out Bröselmaschine forever. I suggested moving a bit more towards jazz. But at some point, he ran out of steam. The contract between Pilz and BASF wasn't extended after 1974, and then I lost touch with Rolf-Ulrich Kaiser. BASF-Musikproduktion in Hamburg went back home to the massive chemical production plant in Ludwigshafen and I moved on to Phonogram. We never saw each other again after that.

PETER BURSCH We left him as well, later on. We turned down his offer to make a second record with him. He just freaked out one day, kind of drifted off. We left in 1973, anyway. We weren't interested in him after that. I never saw him again. All I heard is that he's allegedly in an institution. Dierks bought a lot of the recordings after that.

KLAUS BRIEST At some point everyone was mad at him. I can't remember exactly why – in our case, it was to do with us wanting to release a double LP on the Ohr label, which Kaiser wouldn't accept. That's why the single LP we did bring out was called *Hau RUK* – a play on words, with *hau ruck* meaning 'heave-ho' and *hau* meaning 'hit', i.e. hit Rolf-Ulrich Kaiser.

HARALD GROSSKOPF Things went too far when they offered us five-year contracts with really bad conditions. Ash Ra, Schulze and Tangerine Dream left Kaiser and went to Virgin, where they got decent advances and were very successful.

PETER BAUMANN After *Zeit* and *Atem* we'd had enough of Ohr, and Rolf-Ulrich Kaiser as well. We went to court to get out of the contract, it worked, and then we got a call from Richard Branson.

WINFRID TRENKLER They all fell out after a while. Tangerine Dream and Schulze felt Kaiser had ripped them off; it was about money, nothing to do with drugs by then. Then again, it must have been difficult for musicians to accept a negotiating partner who was often off his head.

HARALD GROSSKOPF All that was presumably very hurtful for Kaiser, though, because he was actually a really nice guy, very intelligent. Gille was the seemingly naive girl who made a name for herself by his side, probably dominated him a bit as well.

BERND WITTHÜSER I still met Kaiser sporadically in Berlin, later on. He always wanted to persuade me to do something else with him, but it was over for me. These days, forty years later, I play different versions of the old songs, which gets some fans angry. But I'm very happy as a busker.

MANFRED GILLIG In the early days, *Sounds* magazine opened up its doors to him. The records he brought out in the early seventies had stickers on them saying 'Recommended by *Sounds*'. But there was a break at some point, and then *Sounds* wanted nothing more to do with him. I think he'd promised all sorts of things and not kept his promises, and he got increasingly strange.

HARALD GROSSKOPF He wanted to use American PR methods to get success, but he went about it too naively. He wanted to do huge releases – think big! – but sadly he went over the top, including with the musicians. Most people didn't want to go along with it. It was just too exaggerated, and there were never any limits. A very sad story, which ultimately broke him.

KLAUS BRIEST I heard he ended up with such major problems that he had to go into an institution. A few people crashed and burned back then and never got back on their feet. But that's just what I heard.

WINFRID TRENKLER One day, he was just gone.

GERHARD AUGUSTIN He downright fled the industry. Apparently, Dieter Dierks knows where Kaiser is. Somewhere near Köln, I've heard. But it's interesting, isn't it, that someone can disappear without a trace to this day, so thoroughly that all we have are rumours.

HARALD GROSSKOPF Allegedly, he renamed himself Meson Cristallis and is living in a church-run institution somewhere in Bergisches Land. He's become a hermit, like a guru, and Gille is his messenger to the outside world. She was sending esoteric circulars to industrialists for a long time. But they don't have an internet connection or any contact with the outside world.

ULRICH RÜTZEL Later on I moved from Hamburg to Eslohe in Sauerland, up a remote hill. I heard that Kaiser had lived there with Gille for a few years. It's pretty crazy. I don't really care about the rumours, but from the big city to the middle of nowhere was quite a major change.

SIEGFRIED SCHMIDT-JOOS A tragic figure; he seems to have been mentally ill and then disappeared out of sight for good. The tendencies were noticeable from the beginning, in his overheated ego.

MANI NEUMEIER Of course Kaiser was strange and we didn't like him much, but he raised awareness for the new music more than anyone else in Germany; nothing would have happened if it wasn't for him. He ran around all the newspapers for his artists and managed to make people sit up and pay attention to the music. Without him, it would have just passed by unnoticed. A lot of German bands that are big today profited from Kaiser's pioneering work.

GERD KRAUS The rumours of what became of him are incredible. Some say he's in a mental institution, others say he's in a sanatorium, and then another lot claims he's in a commune. People I trust have told me he was in rehab and had mental health problems. But who knows for sure? I don't wish him ill; I have memories of him that range from melancholy to unbearable. I know others feel similarly.

NIKEL PALLAT I kept asking people if they'd heard anything from Kaiser, but all I got was conjecture, conjecture, conjecture.

ULRICH RÜTZEL His achievements are still monumental. Those were the years when we veered out of the goodie-two-shoes Germany of the early sixties. When we left our parents behind us and joined the extra-parliamentary opposition. Rolf-Ulrich Kaiser's releases were part of the score. And a good share of the music we listened to came from Rolf-Ulrich Kaiser.

HARALD GROSSKOPF The last time I saw him was at a petrol station just outside Köln, heading to Frankfurt. It must have been around 1993 or '94. He looked just like he used to, actually, just a bit greyer; he was with Gille. They got petrol and then drove off in a little car. I didn't say hello; I didn't want any contact with them. The whole thing with them was still too close and I wanted nothing more to do with them. It's got better now, though.

GIL FUNCCIUS Looking back, you have to admit that Kaiser made a lot of things happen back then – but we didn't appreciate it.

DEUTSCH

'Can could never have happened in the UK or France.'
IRMIN SCHMIDT

JEAN-HERVÉ PERON Faust were German through and through: I was French, Zappi was Austrian, Rudolf was half Russian, plus a Swabian and a Friesian. And people say we're a model German band. Absurd.

LÜÜL I think there is a German sound.

SIMON DRAPER Electronic music was moved forward in Germany back then, and I do think there's a sound that tied them all together. Whether that happened consciously or unconsciously is obviously hard to say. Is it a coincidence that Giorgio Moroder had a similar background?

DANIEL MILLER I don't believe in a German sound, although there are common factors between bands like Can and NEU! and Kraftwerk. But what do they have to do with Popol Vuh, Klaus Schulze or Tangerine Dream? It's more like a German approach that unites many of the bands, an attitude or a concept. But the results sound very different.

IRMIN SCHMIDT All right, we had Malcolm, a Black American singer who'd experienced violence at first hand; he fit directly into our perception of the world. Damo wasn't German either, of course, and neither were Rosko and Reebop. Can was open internationally; perhaps that's no coincidence. But I still think the hard core of Can could only have come about in Germany, not in the UK or France, or in San Francisco either. From my point of view, the music, the way it is, could only be invented by people who had that very personal experience, a history influenced by parents who were all very respectable, or seemed so, but at the same time had been either Nazis, actively or passively, or anti-Nazis. That fundamental moral issue was everywhere and yet was rarely mentioned – and that leaves its mark. Apart from that, all of us but Michael had consciously experienced the late war years and the post-war years, that country in ruins, and thus a ruined culture and society. Outwardly, a lot was soon rebuilt and ran like clockwork, but culturally that 'zero hour' seemingly never ended, so we had to find cultural nourishment abroad, to begin with. And that became a key factor, I think, for people like us who wanted to do something new – that proto-experience that our own thing couldn't be something we found as an existing 'own tradition', ready for us to draw upon; it was something we could only get via diversions. Not through mere adaptation, like everyone from Peter Kraus to the Scorpions, but only through a profound dynamic of reflection and intuition, of maximum material distance and syncretism on one side and maximum immersion and coalescence on the other. In concrete terms, that means we had to reinvent absolutely everything for ourselves, the collage technique of *musique concrète* or the Dadaists and the groove of Africa or James Brown, Hendrix's Marshall power and West Coast psychedelia or the coincidences and silences of John Cage. You had to know and learn a lot to do it, but also always be able to forget everything. That was the only way to develop anything of our own in that German vacuum, the only way Can could become Can. And all those layers of experiences united us, regardless of whether they were consciously formulated or not; we just grew up that way. Other people may have perceived what came out of it as Teutonic and heavy, sometimes with a certain aggression, but that wasn't what was German about us. The allegedly 'proto-Germanic' elements of Can were essentially foreign projections, where people didn't know our real conditions, or didn't want to know them; they were more interested in imagining us as some kind of *Asterix* Visigoths or Faustian silver-screen Nazis. That was a complete misunderstanding of the specifically German aspects that really did exist in Can, of making something out of the cultural poverty of a total breakdown of civilisation. But that could have happened in Berlin or München instead of Köln. The only key factor was the urban aspect; it wouldn't have worked in a rural community – Can was just too modern.

STEVEN WILSON Those endless repeated sounds seem Teutonic to me, even if that might be a cliché: Kraftwerk, Can, NEU!, they all had them. Outside of Germany, the Germans are seen as incredibly effective, and the krautrock sound is just kind of effective as well. Rammstein are similarly effective with their industrial-stomp sound. Brits just sound different.

NIGEL HOUSE There definitely is a German sound from those days. The recordings Bowie and Eno did in Berlin in the seventies sound somehow German to me too. The German side to it begins where rock 'n' roll ends. The German element was more psychedelic and very, very eccentric. Musicians like Einstürzende Neubauten, Liaisons Dangereuses, Die Krupps, Der Plan, Andreas Dorau or Die Tödliche Doris continued in that spirit.

BRIAN ENO I think there is a characteristic which runs through much German music: it's economical, spare, austere, focused. It's the opposite of a lot of Anglo-American pop, which delights in density and decoration. It's another way of thinking about how you make music – by reduction as well as addition.

HARALD GROSSKOPF The German sound is electronic and lives on in techno.

GABI DELGADO-LÓPEZ 'Vorsprung durch Technik' is the German sound; people in Germany have a special affinity to technology.

HANS-JOACHIM ROEDELIUS Our sound wasn't German, it was universal. An electronic sound world which hasn't yet been researched at all. The only really interesting thing, though, is that they're all people who don't care whether what they do is interesting for a market, who just do what they feel like. People who live lives they see as meaningful, and consciously pursue that.

ASMUS TIETCHENS The Krauts' electronica wanted to overcome the Anglo-American musical hegemony. And it did, through long pieces with only one harmony and stubborn rhythms. Like the punks who wanted to overcome all the fiddly art rock, which they did too. They're all useful, correct and good developments in that they made people's ears fit for more extreme regions, which open up beyond harmony and rhythm, posing and rock 'n' roll macho. As soon as I heard the music, I was aware that it was a clear beginning of something entirely new; there'd never been anything like it. It was really new – no matter how it was played. Klaus Schulze was just as new as Kraftwerk, Conrad Schnitzler was just as new as Can. And it created a new audience, which was willing to accept more remote things. Suddenly, the least academic and pretentious people were able to listen to things like Stockhausen and Pierre Schaeffer, voluntarily and intensively. I've been at home in that grey zone between popular and classical music since 1984, and there's an audience for it around the world.

END

'The dream was over.'
LUTZ LUDWIG KRAMER

ACHIM REICHEL Krautrock was over at some point. Around the mid-seventies there was no going on. It was an exciting period, but it wasn't clear to us at the time that we'd opened up a gateway that many others would later pass through.

PETER BAUMANN No more new bands came along. The movement had passed its prime.

GÜNTER SCHICKERT Society changed. Suddenly all people cared about was money.

HARALD GROSSKOPF For me, krautrock ended in the early eighties. That was when it finally fell flat.

MANI NEUMEIER It was all over by the start of the eighties; punk and Neue Deutsche Welle came along and no one cared about our music any more. Guru Guru went on playing anyway, but most of the other bands gave up. I saw no reason to stop, I fought for my place. The audience got smaller, of course, and we didn't have as many opportunities to play. But after a while a lot of them came back. These days we have a loyal audience and more and more young people come along.

LUTZ LUDWIG KRAMER Krautrock is long gone, on the shelf. People like Klaus Schulze, Tangerine Dream or Manuel Göttsching became clichés of their former selves. It's got little to do with what was going on back then. Göttsching, for example, is still a great artist but what he does these days is nothing like krautrock. I got frustrated at some point, took refuge in hard drugs and left Berlin. The dream was over, as John Lennon once sang. Most of us got burnt.

HOLGER CZUKAY At some point the whole movement, if you can call it that, just folded. The eighties brought us a lot of strange music, although a band like DAF were much closer to me than Kraftwerk ever were. Kraftwerk are a designed band; DAF was a genuine experiment, as you could tell by the way their shows were all very, very different. We wanted to change things, that was the idea. It was about leaving space for spontaneity, but not losing ourselves in it. I was in the studio the other day with a young band who brought everything they wanted to record with them, ready-made. I got them to rethink the whole thing. In the end it was a very different record to what they'd expected. The band was amazed and grateful. They said: 'Holger, that was magical.' For me, the old spirit of Can had reawakened.

JÜRGEN DOLLASE I don't care whether people discover my old music or not. I've gone further than that, it's in the past. But people still ask about my music at haute cuisine events. I walked into a place somewhere and they were playing this odd music. I just thought: 'What's this crazy stuff?' Really odd music. And then they told me it was me – the Wallenstein song 'Lunatics'. But of course a lot of good tracks were made in those days. That's why I've still got all my records.

JAKI LIEBEZEIT The rock music that's selling in Germany these days sounds like forty years ago, except that the 'message' and the lifestyle have gone missing since then. Rising up and revolution – all that is over. Ultimately, today's rock music has really gone downhill, to schlager level. Rock is no better than schlager. Even hip-hop has petrified into formality.

MICHAEL ROTHER To be honest, I find a lot of what was produced back then rather uninteresting. I was only focused on the work of people around me. And people I played with: Kraftwerk, Klaus Dinger, Harmonia and Cluster. I found Can interesting to a certain extent, especially Jaki Liebezeit's drumming. But aside from that sound cosmos, there wasn't much that interested or inspired me.

SIMON DRAPER The music just changed, developed. What we call 'krautrock' didn't disappear altogether, it just took on a different form. And adapted to the times. The electronic experiments of those early years turned into pop, in the form of Giorgio Moroder or the Human League.

ASMUS TIETCHENS I do get the impression that the musical movement ended at some point. It was pretty much over at the end of the seventies. But, of course, it still influenced the present and the future. Think of all the people who credit Klaus Schulze and Kraftwerk as an inspiration these days. If you listen to the Cluster albums – and I'm not just saying this as a friend of theirs – you hear something unique.

TODAY

HILDEGARD SCHMIDT We often get enquiries for advertising, because the so-called creatives and cool kids are often Can fans. But the projects tend to fall at the client hurdle; they think the music's too difficult. Sadly. The director of a big TV ad for Chanel was a huge Can fan, and they played 'Vitamin C' over speakers all the way through the shooting. The team wanted to use it as the soundtrack for the ad. But the powers that be at Chanel decided against it and went for Serge Gainsbourg instead, like every other perfume ad. How boring, and what a shame. But constant dripping wears away the stone; no matter whether we're featured on the soundtrack of a Sofia Coppola film or a band like Radiohead refers to us, it's always good marketing. And the fact that Can have long been regarded as a classic band is obviously a good thing.

IRMIN SCHMIDT In terms of attitude, I found strong echoes of what Can did in Sonic Youth. Like me, they were influenced partly by John Cage. Or Tortoise – but Sonic Youth gigs especially remind me a good deal of familiar approaches. I saw them in Barcelona, where they claimed to be playing a Cage piece. It was more of a piece by them, but it was still great. Sonic Youth reminded me of Can mainly in their attitude, and in the way they played together; it had that same radicalism. I've seen a whole lot of British bands citing us, ever since the eighties. There's no German band I could say the same of. Actually, no, there is one, Die Goldenen Zitronen; I've heard they talk about us, and you can spot our influence in some of their music. But they're much more politically explicit than we ever were.

JAKI LIEBEZEIT It's impossible to state Can's influence on the present because the spirit of those days has evaporated. If at all, I find hints of us in the contemporary electronic scene, because they're also trying to take new paths.

HOLGER CZUKAY My studio is used exclusively by me these days. The Beatles would have been thrilled to have a studio like mine.

JAKI LIEBEZEIT I don't listen to the old stuff any more. I've only ever looked ahead. But I'm still glad Can's not forgotten, of course I am. The interesting thing is that these days, long after the end of the band, I earn more from Can than when it was still going. It doesn't make me rich, but it's a reliable small income, which grants me a certain freedom for my current projects. There's a lot of things you only become aware of when the performing rights and royalty payments come through. An American by the name of Kanye West – no idea how to pronounce it – took something or other from a Can track for his music, which then sold incredibly well. And a bit of the money made its way to me, even though you can't even hear me on the track. But the good thing is that we were always registered as composers, all of us. I was happy to hear of an American magazine called *Spin*, where they listed the hundred best 'alternative' drummers. For some reason, number one was the guy from Nirvana. Number two was Tony Allen. And I was number six. There was a Roland drum machine at the end of the list; thank God I made it on there ahead of that. So I can't complain about any lack of recognition. In the nineties I was at the top of a list in a British magazine, I think it was the *NME*, of the most influential drummers of all time. That was a bit of a surprise.

IRMIN SCHMIDT I don't hear Kraftwerk influences on any German bands either, by the way. I mean, there's a lot of synthesizer–sequencer noodling, wallpaper music, but that's not on Kraftwerk's conscience.

Kraftwerk got a lot more of a response abroad than in Germany. Like Can did too.

GERD KRAUS There's been a huge amount of interest in the music made here, for a few years now – all over the world, from America to Japan.

RENATE KNAUP I think it's great that the musicians of the 1968 generation have left their mark. None of us had any idea it would turn out that way. But we did have phenomenal chemistry; that's what made Amon Düül the band we were, and it's still productive when we go on stage today. It's great. A surprising number of young people come to see us play. And, I'm pleased to say, a lot of young women. But the women come because of me, not because of the men. Eighteen-year-old American fans send me emails: 'Hello, Renate, may I talk to you?' With this incredible reverence. In Germany people just say: 'Amon Düül? Never heard of him.' But there's a new generation now that do know us. Then there are people who work out there's a singer at the table and say: 'Go on, sing something for us.' It's so amazing. 'Hmm, what shall I sing, without the seven crazy men who always accompanied me?' In the end I don't do it.

CHRIS KARRER I can tell by my rights statements that interest in our music has been building for a while now. And at our shows, I see that our generation's sons and daughters have discovered it now. There are some krautrock bands that get bigger crowds now than they did in the old days.

KLAUS SCHULZE People often tell me my music inspired later generations. All the bands on the Warp label and that kind of thing. Of course, I notice the interest when younger musicians get in touch. Like the stuff I did with the Dead Can Dance singer Lisa Gerrard. The first time she got in touch I was really surprised she'd even heard of me.

She said she'd told friends and colleagues she was coming to see me in Germany, and they were all impressed. 'They all know you,' she said. I got an inkling of it when I got an offer to do a remix for David Lynch, and ended up on the soundtrack of Sofia Coppola's film *The Bling Ring*. I take all the hip-hop samples in my stride by now.

MICHAEL ROTHER You can hear the echo around the world. Elements of our music are cited and adopted. I listen to Stereolab and think: 'Oh yes, I know exactly where that comes from.' But in general, people often misunderstand what was actually meant. I often wish for more artistic obstinacy and ambition. A lot of people these days cite Klaus Dinger's Motorik beat, for example, because it's in fashion right now. And purely superficially, it's easy to imitate. But the magic's not that easy – without the combination with all the other elements of NEU!'s music, there's not much point to that beat. No one would talk about the ten-minute drum track on 'Hallogallo' if my guitars and Conny's mix weren't there too. A lot of enthusiastic fans don't realise that what they're enthusiastic about is a whole entity; you can't just rip single elements out of it without losing the substance and the effect. But copying a whole track, 'Hallogallo' for instance, doesn't get you far either. Why should anyone do that? It already exists. And even if you want to take your own new paths, that's nothing more than a good starting point. In the end, though, all that counts is what innovation you really achieve, whether with or without a vision of a new music, with or without a Motorik beat. And even having that idea that you want to take your own new paths is no use in the abstract sense. In the end, what matters is what you really create of your own. But I don't want to complain about it; I do realise how much I profit from all the attention. And of course I'm glad of the great esteem we get; there are musicians in the world more misunderstood than me.

ACHIM REICHEL When my daughter was about sixteen, friends of hers asked her to tell me that *Die grüne Reise* was an awesome record.

I couldn't believe it: 'Darling, are you trying to get more pocket money out of me?' 'No, my friends are really into it.' I hadn't even realised the music had reached a new generation through the internet. That was around the year 2000, and it started getting more and more interest. It was clear that the music was spreading without record-label support, in a generation that wasn't even alive when it was made. I was pleased, obviously. I don't make a lot out of it now, sadly, and back then people couldn't stand my stuff.

HANS-JOACHIM ROEDELIUS It's a school, and it's alive. All sorts of people credit us. From Daniel Lanois and Brian Eno all the way to Stereolab. And more and more young people are joining them. The principle we worked on is so dynamic that we covered a whole world. We were given that freedom and we accepted it as a task, consciously and lovingly. If you can accept it that way, you have the most fun. But it always starts all over again from the beginning with new young people.

LUTZ LUDWIG KRAMER When I work with young bands and play really freely, they often say: 'Wow, that's amazing, what are you doing there?' And I answer: 'That's how it was with krautrock.'

LÜÜL They've even got a waxwork of me in Tokyo. It's a funny feeling, looking at it.

ALWAYS

'It was cool to drop names like Michael Rother.'
STEPHEN MORRIS

BRIAN ENO Whereas most English pop music grew out of other pop music, it seemed to me that what was happening in Germany had grown out of contemporary art. That made a difference because it didn't see 'entertainment' as its only job. Perhaps you could say it expected its audiences to be more adventurous.

DANIEL MILLER I presumably first heard krautrock on John Peel, but only the music – the name and the genre didn't yet exist. I was looking for something new and exciting, and I heard Can's 'Yoo Doo Right'. At around the same time, I happened to discover Amon Düül's album *Phallus Dei*, because it leapt out at me visually. That record's got a really strange cover. I was a student at the time, in pretty conservative Guildford, and the Amon Düül record was on special offer in a department store. I had no idea who they were but I marvelled at the strange cover and saw the German words on the sleeve. It all looked very interesting, so I bought it. Along with Can, Amon Düül showed me there must be an interesting scene in Germany.

STEPHEN MORRIS The fascinating thing about krautrock was that it sounded unique. That attitude of taking a new path just grabbed me. I had to know what was going on there. And after every record you listened to and got halfway familiar with, you wanted more: another record, another band. So you'd keep checking the krautrock section for new deliveries: Guru Guru, Popol Vuh and so on. I discovered so much amazing music.

DANIEL MILLER Most music produced in the UK and the States at the time bored me. I grew up in the sixties and that was a really exciting time for a while, including music-wise. But from 1968, rock music started to drift in the wrong direction, for my taste, and got more and more pompous. In the UK rock music seemed to care increasingly about musical virtuosity, which clogged up all the energy and creativity of the previous years. With Can, though, I heard the music and the musicians' freedom; their music was a revelation to me. Rhythmic music reduced to the bare necessities, with no idiotic solos and that kind of crap. Plus those crazy vocals, free from all logic. The music had no references to what I knew from America and the UK; the closest comparison was Captain Beefheart.

GABI DELGADO-LÓPEZ The first time I heard Can, I felt like it sounded different to anything I'd heard before. What I liked so much was that the song structures were largely disintegrated. I particularly loved Jaki Liebezeit's drumming. The vocals were mostly spoken, almost breathed. And the production wasn't polished to death. The music sounded rough and free, a raw, unpolished sound. It was an approach a bit like punk. Don't forget, at that time, in the early seventies, production tended to be really bombastic. Over-produced bands like Yes and Genesis. Music with too much decoration and too much ballast. Can's music was light, in comparison. Nothing was overloaded, no detail unnecessary. And I liked that.

STEPHEN MORRIS I presume I first read something about krautrock in *Melody Maker* or *New Musical Express*. One day I stumbled across the term in some record-dealer ad. I used to study those ads fastidiously as a teenager. Anyway, one day there was a new section called 'Krautrock', full of strange band names like Amon Düül, Tangerine Dream and Guru Guru. And the 'cosmic' thing was enticing too – 'cosmic music', what a promise!

DANIEL MILLER I didn't read any interviews with the 'krautrock-ers'. So I didn't know if they had some kind of common objective, but I sensed that they were changing the language of music by showing what was possible. The more I found out about the political and artis-tic scene in Germany, the more sense the whole thing made to me. I was less interested in the music's political aspect – but just like in the UK and France, there was a student rebellion going on in Germany; I picked up on that much. I didn't really care what the bands and musi-cians thought politically, but the political context they were embedded in was fascinating, of course.

NIGEL HOUSE You'd find out about Can and bands like that from John Peel and the *NME*. It was on the BBC now and then as well. In one programme they mentioned that the Baader–Meinhof gang had lived in the same building as Amon Düül – what an incredible link! Before I discovered punk, my favourite band was Hawkwind. I liked Can as well, as a teenager, but it was hardcore stuff; *Ege Bamyası* was my fave.

STEPHEN MORRIS The interviews I read with German bands were completely different to what you were used to. It was always made very clear that these musicians were trying to go new ways, that they avoided anything that sounded British or American. I found that very appealing.

DANIEL MILLER A band like Amon Düül sounded like they couldn't play all that well but they had a lot of fun trying. It wasn't about per-fection, it was about a feeling they wanted to express. A feeling I always liked a lot in early-sixties music.

STEPHEN MORRIS It was such a fluid sound; it didn't seem like something someone had composed very strictly. The music often reminded me of people sitting down in a room with instruments and just letting fly.

DANIEL MILLER I used to play in a school band; I was an untalented musician, which was very frustrating. In a way, I empathised with the people from Amon Düül and identified with them. Why they sounded so weird, I don't really know. Maybe they were great musicians who just made their records completely off their heads. It doesn't matter – their music was exciting.

STEPHEN MORRIS The names of the band members sounded mysterious as well. Sometimes they looked like they were full of typos. Or with a band like Amon Düül, the members changed so often you could hardly keep up. But I didn't care much who exactly was playing; the music was what counted.

GABI DELGADO-LÓPEZ We listened to things like Düül II and the early Kraftwerk albums as well. I first heard Can on the soundtrack for that famous TV movie; the song was called 'Spoon' and I liked it a lot. I was still a kid at the time, taping music from the radio on my Grundig tape recorder.

DANIEL MILLER I soon became a real fan. Klaus Schulze's first album, *Irrlicht*, was incredibly important to me. Can's *Tago Mago* was another really important one. I still took a critical perspective; I didn't just like things because they were 'German'. As soon as it got rockier I lost interest. I wasn't into that many things, in the end. But what I did take a shine to I loved with a passion, and it influenced and inspired me.

JULIAN COPE I discovered Amon Düül II and Can first because John Peel played them both on his show from 10 p.m. to midnight every weekday. It had a depth and a fury that transcended all the British bands I knew and made a lot of the so-called progressive rock sound unhewn and poorly finished. The twin drums of Amon Düül II really showed up some of the lame-duck rhythm sections like [Nick] Mason and [Roger] Waters, and Can was James Brown on LSD.

STEPHEN MORRIS Although the krautrockers did have a very disparate sound, there was a spirit that united them all. It was music lacking any warmth, nothing about it was the least bit cuddly, their sound was cold. But that was exactly what I wanted – to hell with warm and cosy! There was depth to it too, which always left you puzzled. You didn't just put a krautrock record on, listen to it and work out what was happening right off the bat. You were actually forced to think deeply about the music. It took several plays before you'd gradually pick up on what happened on a record like that. You couldn't ignore it.

JULIAN COPE Most of my friends listened, and it was the older heads that got me into the stuff. Growing up in the industrial Midlands, I had friends and associates who demanded tough sounds – Black Sabbath, of course, but other spiky stuff.

STEPHEN MORRIS A schoolmate's big brother had *Yeti* and *Carnival in Babylon*, *Tago Mago* and *Monster Movie*, records that spoke to me; they came across like a new version of the Velvet Underground. I only realised over the years that the bands were actually very different. They were sold in the UK as a single phenomenon, and it was only later that I learned that that single big movement never existed. But obviously that applies to all scenes and phenomena. Bands are individual and difficult; I know what I'm talking about. Every single band is riddled with tensions. The myth of four friends going through thick and thin against all odds was always a pile of nonsense. All punk bands hated each other.

JULIAN COPE I'd see a copy of Amon Düül II's *Yeti* at every party I went to, and a copy of *Tago Mago* at the same parties.

STEPHEN MORRIS I always wanted to play like Jaki Liebezeit from Can. His hypnotic style seriously impressed me. I must have a couple of hundred krautrock records, but the one I always come back to is

Can's *Tago Mago*. When I was still in a school band, three boys making noise in a room, we covered Can's 'Oh Yeah': a song we were all really into. When we played it we felt a bit like Can.

JULIAN COPE Faust's debut would be used to hijack parties. It was easy to get the records. At the big Virgin Records in Birmingham they had aircraft seats with headphones, and you could listen to a whole side of vinyl while you decided. *NEU! 75* never achieved a UK release and neither did Amon Düül I's *Paradieswärts Düül*, so they were always in the import racks.

DANIEL MILLER I tried to get my friends into the music as well. I kept on preaching about how great the records were, brought people back to my student digs and turned the records up to the max, but most of them just looked horrified. Some of them liked a few things, but I couldn't get anyone into the music the way it had grabbed hold of me. I was pretty much the only one with a passion for krautrock.

STEPHEN MORRIS It was a time when you got to know people because they had similar taste in music. If someone liked bands like Hawkwind, they might be interested in krautrock, heavy psyche-delic rock. You'd discover a record like NEU!'s first album because Dave Brock from Hawkwind had written the sleeve notes for it – only krautrock was even more mysterious. And NEU! came out on United Artists, which we thought was a cool label. Can and Amon Düül were on UA as well, and Dave Anderson from Hawkwind even played bass on *Yeti*. German stuff wasn't the slightest bit uncool. It was new and unfamiliar, and attractive.

DANIEL MILLER The German world wasn't that far away for me; I've got family roots in Austria. I was familiar with German from my younger days, and with the culture and politics as well. So all the superficial factors, the German song titles or musicians' names, didn't come across as mysterious or exotic to me like it did for others; what fascinated me was really the music.

STEPHEN MORRIS It definitely helped that the music was mainly instrumental, so there was no language barrier. The minimal language used by bands like Kraftwerk sounded more like mysterious instruments.

NIGEL HOUSE A few of the more experimental things were a bit too arcane for me, though. If you couldn't find them in the shops, you could get a lot of the records via mail order. But of course, the fact that you couldn't get hold of it immediately made the music even more exciting. It was a well-kept secret that you had to discover. Even the idea of what these mysterious bands' records might sound like was exciting in itself. Imagining that unlistenable stuff might have been more inspiring for people who were creative themselves than any obvious influence.

STEPHEN MORRIS A lot of the records were compared at the time to Frank Zappa, but I think that's far too simple. It was more of a misunderstanding by the British music press, with their narrow horizons and lack of imagination.

NIGEL HOUSE You'd only know a couple of band names and none of the musicians behind them. The first musician I picked up on was Holger Czukay with his *Canaxis* album, which I loved.

STEPHEN MORRIS I didn't make sense of the details of the various German bands until much later. But the more I got into the music, the more I wanted to know. What I wanted most of all was more of these mysterious records. How were you supposed to know who the Cosmic Jokers were? Over the years I've collected a good bit of krautrock. Some of it's stunning, some of it's terrible. The people behind the music were pretty obscure for a long time. The first ones who seemed really tangible and came over here were Faust, on tour with Gong.

DANIEL MILLER I saw Faust live a few times; it was incredible, every time.

STEPHEN MORRIS The first krautrock record that left a lasting impression on me was Faust's debut album. The transparent vinyl looked spectacular in itself. And the music was stupendous; they weren't real songs, it was something unique and a kind of opposite to everything the Rolling Stones, the Beatles and that lot were doing. It completely grabbed me, anyway. There were a couple of like-minded people in Macclesfield, thankfully. Five or six friends in my neighbourhood were as into it as I was.

DANIEL MILLER I wasn't interested in Kraftwerk to start with, but the first time I heard *Autobahn* it changed my life. I was really impressed with Faust as well, especially their first album. I couldn't believe what I was hearing.

STEPHEN MORRIS Kraftwerk were cool too. It was cool to drop names like Michael Rother, NEU!, Roedelius. They were all musicians we thought were acceptable. I once played Amon Düül tapes on the Joy Division tour bus, and they got thrown straight out of the window; I can't remember who it was, but it wasn't me. Ian Curtis always pretended to be pretty into krautrock, but he wasn't really all that fired up about it.

NIGEL HOUSE For me, Tangerine Dream were always hippies, guys who played endless lullaby tunes in quadrophonic sound for a cross-legged audience in churches. That had nothing in common with my definition of exciting music. I just thought: 'No! Not like that!' But I never understood Harmonia or Cluster either. It was all too cosmic for me.

DANIEL MILLER I'd noticed the soundtracks that Popol Vuh composed for Werner Herzog as well. So I tried to get hold of more records from Germany. A few record shops had imports. And I pieced together an idea of this unusual German music scene, bit by bit. I was a film student, so I was already aware of the young German film-makers like Rainer Werner Fassbinder, Wim Wenders and obviously Werner Herzog, before it dawned on me what was happening in the German music world.

STEVEN WILSON I remember watching Werner Herzog's *Nosferatu* on TV one night as a teenager and wondering who the hell had made that incredibly touching and hypnotic music. That was how I discovered Florian Fricke and Popol Vuh.

STEPHEN MORRIS We never talked about the music we liked in Joy Division. Musical taste was a controversial subject in our scene: 'What? You've got a Genesis record? Burn it, right now!' Everyone pretended they only liked the Velvet Underground and Iggy Pop. Bowie was OK as well. Especially because he'd been in Berlin and made music there with Eno, which you could imagine as a kind of more accessible form of krautrock.

IGGY POP David Bowie introduced me to krautrock. It sounded like reality, even outside Germany. Within Germany, that vibe was so obviously in the air. In the blood too. I think it influenced David Bowie in the music he wrote for me, and through him, it influenced me. Germany in general sifted the crap out of me. Every day in Berlin was a kraut encounter. I loved Kraftwerk for their humour and melody. Well of course the krauts are taking over, aren't they? Seriously, I hear it with FKA Twigs, LoveDragon and many others. Goat is, I think, a lot like Amon Düül. Aside from that, I listen to any other German music you like: the usual Brecht, Weill, classical, etc.

GABI DELGADO-LÓPEZ Like so many krautrock musicians, DAF got their opportunity in the UK, not in Germany. We had no chance here. They let us play once a year in clubs like the Ratinger Hof in Düsseldorf, SO 36 in Berlin or Hamburg's Markthalle. We didn't get to play any other places. We went to record companies like EMI in Köln, who said: 'Guys, listen, that's not music. You've got to learn what music is first.' That's exactly how it was. Then we scraped the last of our money together and went to England. Through the Rough Trade people, we met Daniel Miller, who'd just done his own first single as the Normal. Anyway, he said: 'Amazing! I'll make a record with you!'

DANIEL MILLER The krautrock bands helped me to understand what kind of music I wanted to make. You can hear elements of Can and Kraftwerk and all the other bands on my first single, 'Warm Leatherette'. I incorporated it all and I can hear it clearly on there.

GABI DELGADO-LÓPEZ The Germans were too fixated on music from the UK and the States. But once we'd got good reviews in the *NME* and other British papers, suddenly the German critics wanted to talk to us too. They put little stickers on our records in Germany that said 'Top hit in England'. They don't do that these days, thank God.

DANIEL MILLER A lot of the musicians I've worked with in my life were also influenced by krautrock. From Depeche Mode to the young bands I work with now. I can't imagine my record company Mute would even exist without the German artists that gave me so much inspiration. I still can't believe the Can re-releases are on Mute.

PAUL WELLER I started listening to so-called 'krautrock' because a reviewer mentioned that a couple of tracks on my then new album sounded like NEU! and Cluster. I didn't know the bands, so I went out and bought some of their records. I liked the NEU! albums the most, though. By *NEU! 75* they sounded pre-Sex Pistols.

STEPHEN MORRIS Klaus Dinger was also impressive, of course. But we only worked out much later that Klaus Dinger even existed. It was always just NEU!. You couldn't decipher what it said on the record sleeves, anyway. Does it say who plays the drums? Don't know! Maybe a machine? A robot? No idea!

PAUL WELLER In recent years I've met and spoken to Michael Rother, and he played with us in Hamburg this year. I've heard the 'kraut-rock' influence a lot in recent years, from the Horrors, Toy, in some independent dance music, Primal Scream in the 'noughts', Andrew Weatherall, Broadcast and Death in Vegas. I have that reviewer to thank for that piece of my education. I hope to do a track with Herr Rother some time. I'd love to see what we can come up with.

STEVEN WILSON I was fourteen when I discovered krautrock. I never thought much about Germany as the birthplace of krautrock. In eighties UK you'd immediately think of divided Berlin, so I always connected Germany with the Berlin Wall. We knew Klaus Schulze and Tangerine Dream came from Berlin. A sixteen-year-old friend of mine had a couple of Tangerine Dream records and one by Klaus Schulze.

JULIAN COPE My mate Rizla Deutsche and my drummer Rooster Cosby restarted my krautrock fire in 1989. They'd both grown up with the same stuff, so we had a big theory emerge about what made a German band 'krautrock'. We decided that the Scorpions and Birth Control were just West German rock. To be krautrock involved (we believed) evincing a genuine Germanic take on rock 'n' roll, and the autobahn drones and sounds of big industry added to that colossal vibration. Eventually, our theories obliged me to remind my generation of their krautrock roots by writing a book, which sold a lot of copies.

NIGEL HOUSE Julian Cope's book changed so much. Our krautrock sales in the shop went through the roof when it came out. It really appealed to a whole new audience. I couldn't hear a lot of what Cope celebrates, but his book's momentum was tremendous.

STEVEN WILSON There's so much boring, samey music that you're grateful for every adventurer. Musicians who seek their own paths are rare and precious, as is music that sounds like it's taking a risk. Ideally, krautrock would be even more influential. There's a clear krautrock aesthetic that's very distinct from British progressive rock. Prog rock was linked to the structures of classical music and the virtuosity of jazz, whereas krautrock was often sustained by a kind of primitivism, with a focus on sound and textures, less on virtuosity. I liked the British progressive bands' virtuosity and musicality, but ultimately I preferred the refreshingly unpretentious aspects of krautrock. I still do.

NIGEL HOUSE We sell a lot of krautrock to a young crowd. There are a few older buyers, obviously, but lots of young ones. Can and Kraftwerk always do well, preferably on vinyl. They're classics that sell reliably. The records have sold well as far back as I can remember. Krautrock was always cool. Partly because people like John Lydon kept saying they listened to Can and bands like that.

STEVEN WILSON Discovering music used to be more exciting than it is now, when everything seems to be just a click away. It's boring. You had to spend a lot of time looking for krautrock, and once you found something, it was precious. I used to go record-hunting with my friend Simon. We lived thirty miles outside London and we'd take the train once a week to the Virgin Megastore on Oxford Street to invest our savings. I discovered Ash Ra's *Correlations* there, and Can's *Future Days*. They were exciting records; I'm afraid that feeling of discovering such exciting music doesn't exist these days.

NIGEL HOUSE The audience for krautrock is very mixed. There's a big City lawyer who gets us to put every re-release aside for him. Can's

Tago Mago, Kraftwerk's *Trans-Europe Express* and the first NEU! LP are in our canon of the 200 essential albums in music history. I was sixteen when I discovered Can, and it's important to me to pass that knowledge on to the next generation of teenagers.

STEPHEN MORRIS It wasn't actually relevant that they were Germans. The musicians weren't the same people who'd flown the bomber planes or sent them over, were they? Not at all – they were the rebellious children of the people who'd done so much harm. And that rebellious aspect was a really exciting element of the music. You could hear that those musicians wanted to be well away from what their parents had done. I wanted that for very different reasons, to get far away. It's an age thing, obviously, but not just that. People will always want to get well away.

BIOGRAPHICAL NOTES

(Key recordings are full albums, except where noted)

GERHARD AUGUSTIN He wasn't a musician but he had a good ear for new and interesting things, Gerhard Augustin once said. Born in Hagen in 1941, the music manager, producer and pop-culture pioneer was one of Germany's first DJs. He and Michael 'Mike' Leckebusch developed the concept for *Beat-Club*, the first German TV show to feature UK and US musicians, which ran from 1965–72, sometimes with Augustin presenting. In the seventies he worked with artists like Can, Amon Düül and Popol Vuh for the United Artists label. He had a longstanding friendship with Florian Fricke, which also led to Augustin producing music by Popol Vuh. He went on to work with Ike and Tina Turner, producing several of their albums and managing them. He has published several books, including *Der Pate des Krautrock* (The Godfather of Krautrock). Gerhard Augustin died in 2021 in Bremen.

Popol Vuh: *Affenstunde* (United Artists/1972, producer)

WILLIAM 'BILL' BARONE Born in Philadelphia in 1951, the guitarist tried out for the Rascals in 1970 but didn't get the job, and ended up in Germany a year later instead, with Wallenstein. He returned to the States in 1975, shared a stage with Chuck Berry and was most recently on the road with his band Sylvia Platypus. He is now living in Philadelphia again.

Jerry Berkers: *Unterwegs* (Pilz/1972, electric guitar)

KARL BARTOS If his parents had had their way, he'd have become a telephone engineer. Instead, the musician, producer and songwriter, born Karlheinz Bartos in Marktschellenberg in 1952, studied piano, vibraphone and percussion at the Robert Schumann Conservatory in Düsseldorf. His professor recommended him to Ralf Hütter and Florian Schneider when they were looking for a drummer. Bartos was a member of Kraftwerk from 1975–91 and co-wrote songs such as 'The Model'. He followed that with solo projects and collaborations with musicians like Johnny Marr, Bernard Sumner and OMD. His autobiography *The Sound of the Machine* (also translated by Katy Derbyshire) came out in English in 2022. Bartos lives in Hamburg.

Kraftwerk: *Die Mensch-Maschine* (Kling Klang/1978, electronic drums/ co-writing)

PETER BAUMANN Born in 1953, the Berliner met Christopher Franke at an Emerson, Lake and Palmer show in 1971 and joined Tangerine Dream shortly afterwards. The line-up of Edgar Froese, Franke and Baumann, which many fans consider the best in the band's history, reaped worldwide success and influence with albums like *Phaedra* and *Rubycon* in the first half of the seventies. Baumann left the band in 1977 to start a solo career. In the eighties he moved to San Francisco, where he set up the Private Music label, making best-selling New Age productions. Since he sold the label in 1996, he has worked mainly on his Baumann Foundation, a think tank researching the experience of being human.

Peter Baumann: *Romance 76* (Virgin/1976, electronics/producer/writing)

HANS 'LAMPE' BIERMANN Born in Hamburg in 1952, the drummer set up Conny Plank's studio in Wolperath along with the famed producer himself. He played drums on the album *NEU! '75* and was a founding member of Klaus Dinger's La Düsseldorf. After more than two decades as head of the sound department at the RTL TV channel in

Köln, Biermann toured the world with Michael Rother from 2012–20, and also performed with him in Seoul in September 2023 as part of his touring band.

La Düsseldorf: *La Düsseldorf* (Nova/1976, percussion/electronics)

KLAUS BRIEST Playing covers with the band Soul Caravan soon got boring for the bassist, born in Wiesbaden in 1944. He and two pals changed the name to Xhol Caravan and the sound to free improvisation in 1967. To avoid confusion with the British band Caravan, they pruned the name down to Xhol. Their albums, including *Motherfuckers GmbH & Co KG*, came out on Rolf-Ulrich Kaiser's Ohr label. Xhol went their separate ways in 1972. Briest now plays bass in the band Groove Collection.

Xhol: *Hau RUK* (Ohr/1971, bass/effects)

PETER BRÖTZMANN Born in Remscheid in 1941, Brötzmann wanted to liberate the saxophone, beginning in the jazz club he set up at school. He went on to study art in Wuppertal and work as a graphic designer. At a Berlin jazz festival in 1966 he co-founded the Globe Unity Orchestra. Brötzmann's uncompromising style made him one of Europe's most influential free-jazz musicians; his 1968 album *Machine Gun* is considered a classic. He has released a series of solo works and also worked with his son Caspar Brötzmann. Peter Brötzmann died in Wuppertal in 2023.

Peter Brötzmann Octet: *Machine Gun* (Brö/1968, saxophone/producer)

CHRISTIAN BURCHARD Born in 1946 and brought up in Hof in Bavaria, the drummer and multi-instrumentalist studied in Erlangen and then decided against bourgeois life, as he puts it. Instead, he went to München and started the band Embryo with Edgar Hoffman in 1969, bringing together jazz, rock, world music and a free lifestyle. For

411

decades the band has played beyond all trends and styles around the world, directed by Burchard until his stroke in 2016. More than 400 musicians are said to have been part of Embryo over the years, with the band now led by his daughter Marja. Christian Burchard died in München in 2018.

Embryo: *Opal* (Ohr/1970, drums/keyboards)

PETER BURSCH Born in 1949, Bursch, with his fellow musicians, had started playing folk cover versions as Les Autres, discovering their joy in free improvisation as Bröselmaschine, the band he set up in 1969 – named after a device used in his commune for rolling joints. After their slot at the Essener Songtage, Rolf-Ulrich Kaiser offered them a record contract, and their debut album *Bröselmaschine* was released in 1971. Since then the band has split up numerous times but keeps getting back together. The guitar textbooks Bursch has been publishing since the mid-seventies became a huge hit and earned him a reputation as Germany's 'guitar teacher of the nation'.

Bröselmaschine: *Bröselmaschine* (Pilz/1971, guitar/vocals/flute/sitar)

JULIAN COPE Born in 1957, Cope made a splash in the late seventies as the singer and songwriter for the Liverpool post-punk band the Teardrop Explodes and has been a successful solo artist since the early eighties. In the mid-1990s he published the book *krautrocksampler*, presenting bands from Faust to Harmonia, though he took a few liberties with the truth. The book had a massive effect, introducing the veteran krauts to a new, younger audience. To top it all off, Cope offered a coherent definition of what is actually krautrock – and what is not. With Cope sadly refusing to allow reprints, his standard work has become a much-sought-after rarity.

Julian Cope & Donald Ross Skinner: *Rite* (Ma-Gog Records/1993, synthesizer/keyboards)

HOLGER CZUKAY Born in Danzig as Holger Ekkehard Schüring in 1938, Can's bassist took a joyful and imaginative approach to life, often juggling fact and fiction. For instance, his relatives kindly point out that the surname Czukay was his own private invention and the family was actually called Schukey until 1935. Holger Czukay's light-hearted attitude towards biographical details was ultimately an artistic decision. What we do know is that he studied composing under Karlheinz Stockhausen in sixties Cologne, where he met Irmin Schmidt. He had a long and internationally successful solo career, with albums including *Movies* and *Der Osten ist rot*. As a soloist, Czukay worked with such celebrated musicians as David Sylvian, Jah Wobble, Brian Eno and the Eurythmics. He is also regarded as a sampling pioneer. Holger Czukay died in 2018; his grave in Köln is diagonally opposite Jaki Liebezeit's last resting place.

Holger Czukay: *Movies* (Harvest/1979, vocals/bass/synthesizer/writing)

GABI DELGADO-LÓPEZ Born Gabriel Delgado-López in 1958 in Córdoba in Spain, he came to Germany with his family in 1966. In Wuppertal in 1978 he co-founded the band Deutsch Amerikanische Freundschaft (DAF for short), gaining fame far beyond Germany with brawny and provocative electropop songs like 'Der Mussolini', long since recognised as classics of the genre. Gabi Delgado-López died in 2020.

Deutsch Amerikanische Freundschaft: *Alles ist gut* (Virgin/1981, vocals/writing)

WERNER 'ZAPPI' DIERMEIER As a drummer he has a feeling for rhythm and power, so he was utterly serious when he one day spontaneously invited a builder with a pneumatic drill on stage with Faust at a show in Birmingham. It was such a resounding success with band and audience alike that they made a permanent feature of such special guest appearances. Aside from Faust, Diermeier, born in Gutau in Austria in

1949, was also involved in the experimental schlager project known as derschlaeger, experimented with construction and printing machinery in the eighties, and instigated a Faust reunion in London in 1994. He is currently working on the percussion project Monobeat Original.

Faust: *Faust* (Polydor/1971, drums/writing)

JÜRGEN DOLLASE Born in Oberhausen in 1948, the musician and writer is presumably the only artist in this book who signed up voluntarily for two years in the German army, specifically in the Federal Border Guard. After getting his A-levels in Viersen, Dollase studied art, music and philosophy at the Düsseldorf art academy, and it's up to experts to decide whether the band he started in 1971 as Blitzkrieg – which then became Wallenstein – played art rock, krautrock or just plain rock. Whatever the case, the first Wallenstein long-players came out on Rolf-Ulrich Kaiser's Pilz and Kosmische Kuriere labels, which eventually led to Dollase playing at Kaiser's legendary 'cosmic sessions'. Wallenstein split up in 1982; Jürgen Dollase left music behind him and has been a successful restaurant critic for years.

Wallenstein: *Cosmic Century* (Kosmische Musik/1973, vocals/synthesizer)

BERND DOPP The Hamburg music manager began his career in a music shop, joined WEA Records in 1984 and became CEO of Warner Music Central Europe. In early-seventies Hamburg, he saw one of the seven live shows NEU! ever played. He retired in 2021.

FRANK DOSTAL Born in Flensburg in 1945, the Hamburg-based songwriter, musician and producer knew Achim Reichel from their time together in the Rattles. The two of them ran the legendary Star-Club for a while and then made pop music as Wonderland. At the start of the seventies, the adventurous pair launched the experiment A.R. & Machines, for which Dostal wrote lyrics. They went on to produce children's songs and shanties together before parting ways, after which Dostal became a very successful lyricist. His best-sellers include the German Smurfs theme tune and the Spanish pop duo Baccara's 'Yes Sir, I Can Boogie' (the best-selling single of all time by a female group) and 'Sorry, I'm a Lady'. As a board member of the German collecting society and performance rights association GEMA, he was a passionate fighter for copyright payments from internet giants. Married to Mary McGlory, bassist for the Liverpool band the Liverbirds, Dostal died in 2017.

Wonderland Band: *N°1* (Polydor/1971, vocals/writing/producer)

SUZANNE DOUCET Born in Tübingen in 1944, the artist came to fame in sixties Germany as a schlager singer, actress and TV presenter. At the end of the decade she moved to München and then studied at the Sorbonne for a while. The avant-garde album she recorded with her sister under the pseudonym Zweistein was released in 1970. In the mid-seventies Doucet relocated to Los Angeles and became a pioneer of the New Age genre. Finding out by chance a few years ago that her Zweistein album had had a renaissance with a younger audience, Doucet revealed the secret of who was behind its experimental sounds. She still lives and works in the United States.

Zweistein: *Trip* • *Flip Out* • *Meditation* (Philips/1970, writing/vocals/instruments)

SIMON DRAPER Many experts immediately connect Virgin Records with Richard Branson, who had the idea for the record shop that became the label. If you talk to the artists who brought fame and fortune to Virgin in the seventies, though, you'll hear the name Simon Draper over and over. Branson ran the business side, but Draper, who is his cousin, took care of the music. Born in 1950 and brought up in South Africa, he had studied English and politics, and would look after artists like Mike Oldfield, Gong, Robert Wyatt, XTC, Simple Minds and the Sex Pistols for Virgin. But also Tangerine Dream, Faust, Can and later DAF, in the days when barely anyone was interested in them in Germany. When the label was sold in 1992, he left the industry. Since then he has published beautiful books, collected art and regretted not buying the Bridget Riley illustration used on the cover of *The Faust Tapes*.

BRIAN ENO Born in 1948, Brian Peter George St John le Baptiste de la Salle Eno began making music as the keyboardist and songwriter of Roxy Music in the early seventies, leaving the band in 1973 to start a solo career as a musician, producer and jack-of-all-musical-trades. In the first half of the seventies Eno and his pal David Bowie discovered bands like Harmonia, Tangerine Dream, NEU!, Cluster and Kraftwerk, and were bowled over. It takes no great leap of the imagination to guess what inspired them for the instrumental tracks on Bowie's *Low*. A fortunate coincidence took Eno to a Harmonia gig in Hamburg's Fabrik venue. Eno rarely talks publicly about his past, so the fact that he provided statements for this book on his adventures with Harmonia in Forst shows just how important that episode still is for him.

Cluster & Eno: *Cluster & Eno* (Sky Records/1977, electronics/writing)

FRANK FIEDLER Born in Kiel in 1945, the cameraman, director and musician studied at the Berlin film academy and worked with Florian Fricke on various Popol Vuh productions.

Popol Vuh: *In den Gärten Pharaos* (Pilz/1971, mixing)

LIMPE FUCHS For the composer and musician, born in München in 1941, university was a long-sought escape route from the working-class Catholic world of her childhood. She met the sculptor Paul Fuchs after her A-levels, started a family and the band Anima with him, and moved to Italy. Rolf-Ulrich Kaiser offered them a record contract, followed by albums like *Stürmischer Himmel* and projects with Friedrich Gulda and Albert Mangelsdorff. Now a solo artist, Fuchs lives in Germany. She has her home and studio in the former stables next door to the parsonage in Peterskirchen where Florian Fricke produced. Limpe Fuchs is still searching for sounds, developing instruments and teaching music – and also producing new records.

Anima: *Anima* (Pilz/1972, vocals/zither/electronics/percussion)

GIL FUNCCIUS Born in Stuttgart in 1942, the illustrator was looking for a job when she ran into Rolf-Ulrich Kaiser at the start of the seventies. Kaiser got her designing audacious record covers for bands like Annexus Quam, Witthüser & Westrupp, Embryo, Wallenstein and Amon Düül. Funccius lives and works in Berlin.

MANFRED GILLIG Born in 1950, the journalist and author moved from Kronach in Upper Franconia to Berlin with his mother in 1963, going on to see bands like Tangerine Dream playing in bars in their early days. Later, he wrote for the German music mag *Sounds*, became editor-in-chief of *Musikwoche* and worked for the Hannibal publishing house. He is a judge for the German Record Critics' Award and has retired to northern France.

KURT GRAUPNER Born in Holzminden in 1943, the sound engineer made mixing desks at Telefunken and converted old mono recordings into stereo before accepting an offer to provide technical support to Faust. Part of the job was converting an old schoolhouse into a state-of-the-art studio. After Faust he worked in TV and film before retiring in 2002.

Faust: *Punkt* (Bureau B/2022, engineering)

HARALD GROSSKOPF Born in Hildesheim in 1949, Grosskopf, like so many krautrockers, started his career in a beat band. He very nearly joined the Scorpions, helping out on drums fairly often in their early years. Instead, he ended up as drummer and/or keyboardist in the art-rock band Wallenstein, followed by episodes with Klaus Schulze, Ash Ra Tempel and Rolf-Ulrich Kaiser's Kosmische Kuriere. Grosskopf is presumed to be the first drummer to play to electronic music. It's a minor miracle that he can remember the turbulent sessions with Kaiser with such precision. His 1980 solo album *Synthesist* is considered a classic of its genre. Harald Grosskopf has produced seven solo albums, played on more than 100 records, and still regularly releases new music.

Harald Grosskopf: *Synthesist* (Sky Records/1980, writing/electronics/drums/producer)

HELLMUT HATTLER It was in a basement in Ulm that a young Hellmut Hattler discovered his love of bass-playing. Born in 1952, he was a founding member of the band Kraan, which has been juggling fusion, jazz and art rock since 1970, and earning itself a reputation for virtuoso performances. Despite taking time out and sporadically announcing its end, the band is still active. It releases records on a regular basis and always seems to be playing somewhere. Hattler recorded an album in the mid-seventies with Dieter Moebius, Asmus Tietchens and Conny Plank under the moniker of Liliental.

Liliental: *Liliental* (Brain/1978, bass/writing)

MICHAEL HOENIG Born in Hamburg in 1952, Hoenig grew up in Berlin, where he studied sociology, theatre studies and journalism and also met Thomas Kessler, who was running the Electronic Beat Studio at the time. Hoenig recorded two albums with Agitation Free. In Tangerine Dream, he replaced Peter Baumann for an Australian tour in 1975. He was also part of a duo with Klaus Schulze, known as Timewind. His solo debut *Departure from the Northern Wasteland* was released in 1978. He later moved to Los Angeles and wrote successful soundtracks for films, TV series and computer games. He has been living and working in Ibiza for some years.

Michael Hoenig: *Departure from the Northern Wasteland* (Warner Bros. Records/1978, electronics/writing/producer)

NIGEL HOUSE Born on a farm in Somerset in 1958, he was studying landscape architecture when he was offered a job at the legendary Rough Trade record store. House and two partners took over the company from its founder Geoff Travis in 1981. He now runs several branches around the UK, plus one in New York and one in Berlin. If you're lucky enough to bump into House in one of the shops, make sure to ask him for recommendations.

HANS-JOACHIM IRMLER Born in Sigmaringen in 1950, the musician started experimenting with sounds at an early age. In 1969 he started an art degree in Hamburg, where the mother of TV show *Beat-Club*'s co-founder Mike Leckebusch wangled him a trainee position in television. Irmler was a founding member of Faust in 1971, giving him an opportunity to indulge his passion for challenging sounds. He now runs his Faust Studio in Scheer, teaches keyboard workshops, releases solo material and still plays live.

Faust: *So Far* (Polydor/1972, electronics/writing)

JEAN-MICHEL JARRE Born in Lyon in 1948, he is the son of the world-famous soundtrack composer Maurice Jarre. In search, like the krautrockers, of new musical forms of expression, he discovered electronic music in the early seventies. He happened by chance to go to the legendary 1974 Tangerine Dream show in Reims Cathedral. Jarre became a global star with his debut album *Oxygene* in 1976. Since then, he has sold more than a hundred million albums, played spectacular live shows and become a pioneer of electronic pop. Jarre produced music with Edgar Froese of Tangerine Dream shortly before Froese's death.

Jean-Michel Jarre: *Deserted Palace* (A Sam Fox Production/1973, electronics/writing)

CHRIS KARRER Born in Kempten in 1947, the multi-instrumentalist discovered that playing jazz was a liberation for him. He was a founding member of Amon Düül and Amon Düül II, toured with Embryo and released a number of solo albums. He passed away in 2024.

Amon Düül II: *Phallus Dei* (Liberty/1969, guitar/writing)

THOMAS KESSLER Born in Switzerland in 1937, Kessler moved to Berlin to study composing after studying German and French literature in Zürich. The Electronic Beat Studio, which he set up in the basement of a school in Berlin-Charlottenburg in 1965, became the nucleus of the 'Berlin School'. Musicians from Tangerine Dream, Agitation Free and Ash Ra Tempel took their first steps towards electronic music there on an EMS Synthi-A. Kessler returned to Switzerland in 1973 to set up a studio in Basel. He has composed numerous avant-garde works over the decades. Kessler is still bemused by the overwhelming gratitude of the musicians who recorded in his Berlin studio: 'What on earth did I do for them?'

Thomas Kessler: *Thomas Kessler* (Musiques Suisses/2006, composition)

RENATE KNAUP Born in the Allgäu region in 1948, her brothers being the well-known actors Karl and Herbert Knaup, the singer went to London as an au pair and then in 1968 to München, where she ended up in the commune that gave rise to Amon Düül. Using the aliases Renate Knaup-Krötenschwanz and Henriette Kroetenschwanz, she has been productive and successful with Amon Düül II since the seventies. Knaup had a spell as a singer with Popol Vuh, also in the seventies. She lives near München.

Amon Düül II: *Yeti* (Liberty/1970, vocals/tambourine)

LUTZ LUDWIG KRAMER Born to an opera singer and a film producer in Potsdam in 1954, Kramer's musical starting point was the beat band the Ugly Things. Before discovering beat, he'd made a few minor movie appearances. At the age of sixteen in 1967, he moved into Kommune 1 and kicked off as the frontman of Agitation Free. He was the band's radical young thing, rejecting the idea of making a record as selling out and leaving before they released their debut album in 1970. He lived in Thailand for a while in the seventies, began painting and did all kinds of jobs. He made another live appearance with Agitation Free at a reunion concert in Berlin in 1997. He has released two solo albums this century, and is spending a lot of time in Thailand again.

Ludwig: *As We Are Drifting* (self-released/2016, vocals/guitar/writing)

GERD KRAUS Born in the Odenwald region in 1939, the multi-instrumentalist founded the band Limbus 3 (later Limbus 4, when a fourth musician joined them) in 1969; Rolf-Ulrich Kaiser signed them to his label. Kraus now works as a director, visual artist and playwright and lives in Bad Berneck and Santiago de Cuba, where he has produced two documentaries about the Santiago de Cuba music scene.

Limbus 4: *Mandalas* (Ohr/1970, instruments/writing)

HANS 'JAKI' LIEBEZEIT He always seemed so relaxed that he wouldn't drop a beat in an earthquake. Born in Dresden in 1938, Liebezeit ended up in Köln at the age of twenty, on drums in Manfred Schoof's and Alexander von Schlippenbach's bands. But jazz became too much of a restriction for him, so he was glad when Irmin Schmidt asked him to recommend a drummer for Can – and suggested himself. The groove he brought into Can was influenced by his love of jazz and African music. After Can, Liebezeit helped out musicians like Brian Eno, Depeche Mode, Eurythmics, Gianna Nannini, Trio and Michael Rother, and worked on his own projects with Jah Wobble and Burnt Friedman. It was always important to him never to stand still, he said on a sunny day in his Köln studio. That joy in constant change was what drove him. He reacted with his typical dry humour to various placings in 'best drummer of all time' lists: 'At least I ended up ahead of the drum machine.' Jaki Liebezeit died in 2017 and is buried in Köln, diagonally opposite Holger Czukay.

Burnt Friedman & Jaki Liebezeit: *Secret Rhythms* (Nonplace/2002, drums)

SIEGFRIED 'SIGGI' LOCH Born in Pomerania in 1940, Loch became managing director of Liberty/United Artists Records Germany in 1966, a job that brought him into contact with bands like Can and Amon Düül II. As the founding managing director of WEA Music, he also distributed products from Klaus Schulze's record label IC-Records. Loch fulfilled his dream of his own jazz label in 1992 with ACT-Records.

LÜÜL (LUTZ GRAF-ULBRICH) Born in 1952, he started his first band at school in Berlin-Charlottenburg with Christopher Franke, later of Tangerine Dream. The next stage for Lüül was the beat band Agitation in 1967. They transformed into Agitation Free and played regularly at the Zodiak Free Arts Club. Lüül was one of those experimenting with electronic sounds in Thomas Kessler's Electronic Beat Studio, the nucleus of the 'Berlin School'. In the early seventies Agitation Free went on a tour of the Middle East for the Goethe-Institut, discovering other musical cultures. After Agitation Free, he worked with Ash Ra Tempel and the Velvet Underground icon Nico (with whom he also had a relationship). Over the past years he has released solo albums, made music with the band 17 Hippies and written his memoirs. There is a waxwork of Lüül on display in Tokyo.

Agitation Free: *Malesch* (Vertigo/1972, guitar)

STEFAN MICHEL Born in Gera in 1946, the journalist and label manager witnessed the Schwabingen riots and was hired by Liberty/United Artists in 1971, taking care of bands like Can, Amon Düül and Popol Vuh under the watchful eye of Gerd Augustin. He then switched to

WEA Music, where he was a manager until the early nineties. He has run his own PR agency in Hamburg since 1994.

DANIEL MILLER Born in 1951 to the actors Martin Miller and Hannah Norbert, who had fled the Nazis from Austria to the UK in 1938, Miller grew up in London and was an early fan of bands like Can, Faust and Kraftwerk. Inspired by punk's DIY euphoria, he released the single 'Warm Leatherette' in 1978 under the pseudonym the Normal on the label he started especially for the purpose, Mute Records. The musician and producer was also in the Silicon Teens and Duet Emmo. Mute Records have brought out a raft of acts, including Depeche Mode, Yazoo, Fad Gadget, Erasure, Moby and Nick Cave. Miller is thrilled that Mute now has Can on its books.

Robert Rental & The Normal: *Live at West Runton Pavilion 6/3/79* (Rough Trade/1980, electronics)

DIETER MOEBIUS Born in St. Gallen in Switzerland in 1944, Dieter Moebius moved to Berlin at eighteen to study art. He met Conrad Schnitzler and Hans-Joachim Roedelius in the Zodiak Free Arts Club and with them founded the band Kluster in 1969. Berlin soon got too restrictive for him and he left the city with Cluster, now sans Schnitzler. From 1973 he was part of Harmonia with Roedelius and Michael Rother, working in their shared studio in Forst, where Brian Eno paid a brief but productive visit. After that came records with Conny Plank, Asmus Tietchens and Mani Neumeier, numerous solo projects – and many tours. Dieter Moebius died in 2015.

Cluster: *Zuckerzeit* (Brain/1974, writing/electronics)

STEPHEN MORRIS Born in Macclesfield in 1957, drummer and composer in the bands Joy Division, New Order and the Other Two, Morris dreamed as a teenager of one day playing the drums like Can's Jaki Liebezeit.

New Order: *Movement* (Factory/1981, drums/writing)

MANI NEUMEIER Born in München in 1940, he was, he claims, the first free-jazz drummer in Germany. Over the course of his career, he has played with jazz icons like Philly Joe Jones, Yusef Lateef and John McLaughlin. Neumeier went in a different direction in 1968 with the band the Guru Guru Groove, which then became Guru Guru. While the line-up constantly changed, Neumeier has remained the band's beating heart and frontman over the decades, earning them an excellent reputation as a live act far beyond Germany. Guru Guru are still releasing albums on a regular basis and touring the world. Few artists of his generation have stayed as true to their earlier life plans as Mani Neumeier.

Guru Guru: *UFO* (Ohr/1970, drums/writing/electronics)

NIKEL PALLAT Born in Potsdam in 1945, he allegedly got the worst A-level results in his year and went on to work as an accountant, at least for a while. Then Ton Steine Scherben got in the way, with Pallat as their 'organiser' – some say their manager. He also joined them on stage occasionally as a musician and looked after the band's own record label. Pallat co-founded the independent music distributor EFA Medien and later worked for Indigo Distribution. He published his memoirs in 2023.

Ton Steine Scherben: *Keine Macht für Niemand* (David Volksmund Produktion/1972, writing/voice)

JEAN-HERVÉ PERON Born in Casablanca in 1949, Peron grew up in France and went to the United States as a teenager. He saw Europe's 1968 student uprising on TV there and promptly returned to France. After two years of busking around Morocco, Scandinavia and the rest of Europe, he ended up in Hamburg in the early seventies – 'because of a girl' – and settled down there. The singer, guitarist, composer and trumpeter was a founding member of Faust. The original line-up went their separate ways in 1975, and Peron and Werner 'Zappi' Diermeier are currently continuing the band in their own version. Peron has been running an avant-garde festival in Schiphorst since 1998; he lives in the north German town. His cement mixer has been on display in a series of museums.

Faust: *Faust IV* (Virgin/1973, vocals/bass)

IGGY POP Born James Newell Osterberg in Muskegon, Michigan, in 1947, the singer, songwriter and rocker with the Stooges came to fame and infamy at the end of the sixties. Celebrated as the godfather of punk with occasional self-destructive tendencies, Pop ended up in Berlin with David Bowie in 1977, living there while recording solo albums like *The Idiot*. He wrote his biggest hit 'The Passenger' after riding the city's U-Bahn, and discovered bands like Kraftwerk, NEU! and Tangerine Dream there. Iggy Pop has long since returned to the States, but his love for music from Germany is just as strong. He still plays krautrock tracks on his occasional BBC radio shows. He was inducted into the Rock & Roll Hall of Fame in 2010.

The Stooges: *The Stooges* (Elektra/1969, vocals/writing)

ACHIM REICHEL Born in Wentorf in 1944 and brought up right by the River Elbe in Hamburg's St. Pauli quarter, this son of a seaman became a sixties German star as the singer of the Rattles, touring the UK with Little Richard and the Rolling Stones. His meteoric rise came to an abrupt end when he was drafted into the German army in 1966. He was replaced in the Rattles by Frank Dostal (with whom Reichel later started the band Wonderland), before undergoing a radical shift in style to his avant-garde project A.R. & Machines. Their debut album *Die grüne Reise* came out in 1971 and amazed his audience. It was followed a year later by the double album *Echo*, which Conny Plank worked on. These days *Echo* is a coveted collectors' item; back then, it was not a commercial success. Reichel once again changed tack, producing folk bands like Ougenweide and recording sea shanties that sailed up the charts. He has had constant success as a solo artist ever since. To celebrate the re-release of their now-classic albums in 2017, A.R. & Machines played the sold-out Elbphilharmonie in Hamburg. Achim Reichel, who published his autobiography in 2020, no longer lives on the Elbe, but he's still a Hamburg boy.

A.R. & Machines: *Die grüne Reise* (Polydor/1971, writing/instruments)

HANS-JOACHIM ROEDELIUS Born in 1934, Roedelius lived through the final war years in Berlin, having previously been a child actor in movies such as *Es leuchten die Sterne* and *Verklungene Melodie*. He wanted to be a doctor but became a masseur, then met Conrad Schnitzler in the sixties while doing roofing jobs in Corsica. Roedelius and Schnitzler opened up Berlin's Zodiak Free Arts Club in 1968 and started the band Kluster with Dieter Moebius – renamed Cluster after Schnitzler left. Later, Roedelius made music as Harmonia with Moebius, Michael Rother and temporary input from Brian Eno. The hugely productive musician, also a successful solo artist (*Durch die Wüste*), is regarded as a pioneer of ambient music. He lives in Austria and recently published his autobiography, *Das Buch*.

Harmonia: *Deluxe* (Brain/1975, electronics/writing/vocals)

MICHAEL ROTHER Born in Hamburg in 1950, Rother ended up in Düsseldorf in the mid-sixties after spells in München, Winslow and Karachi. After starting out in beat bands, in the early seventies he found himself in a Düsseldorf studio by the name of Kling-Klang, which led to a short but formative episode with Kraftwerk. It was there that he met the drummer Klaus Dinger, with whom he started the duo NEU!. He went on to work with Harmonia and start a successful solo career (*Flammende Herzen*). These days, Rother is still making music in his legendary studio in Forst, and usually plays far away from

Germany. The guitarist, songwriter and producer's celebrity admirers include David Bowie, Brian Eno and the Red Hot Chili Peppers. His most recent solo album is 2020's *Dreaming*. His work always got more recognition abroad than at home and he is doubtless recognised more often on the streets of Hamburg by Japanese fans than by Germans.

NEU!: *NEU!* (Brain/1972, guitars/writing)

ULRICH RÜTZEL Born in 1944, pianist, composer and producer Rützel joined BASF as a label manager in 1972. Rolf-Ulrich Kaiser, founder of the Ohr and Pilz labels, had booked him as a jazz pianist for festivals, and in the early seventies Rützel became product manager in charge of Pilz. He was also responsible for the legendary jazz label MPS, later working for other record companies and as a successful music producer, as well as founder of the renowned Ars Electronica festival in Austria.

Conrad Schnitzler: *Auf dem schwarzen Kanal* (12", RCA/1980, producer)

GÜNTER SCHICKERT Born in Berlin in 1949, the trumpeter and guitarist switched allegiance from free jazz to beat and then became a regular at the Zodiak Free Arts Lab, where he met musicians like Klaus Schulze and Edgar Froese. His first solo album, 1974's *Samtvogel* – which he recorded entirely alone – is considered a classic. He followed it up with LPs with the band GAM, solo work and live shows. An album with Klaus Schulze, *The Schulze–Schickert Session*, was released in 2013.

Günter Schickert: *Samtvogel* (Brain/1976, electronics/guitars/writing)

ALEXANDER VON SCHLIPPENBACH Born in Berlin in 1938, the jazz pianist, composer and arranger knew Jaki Liebezeit from their jazz days. Regarded as a pioneer of European free jazz, Schlippenbach played with Gunter Hampel and Manfred Schoof and started the Globe Unity Orchestra at the age of twenty-eight. He co-founded the Anti-Festival in Köln in 1968, featuring Amon Düül. Over the past decades, Schlippenbach has recorded four solo albums and toured on a regular basis. He was awarded Germany's Cross of the Order of Merit in 2017 and lives in Berlin.

Alexander von Schlippenbach: *Globe Unity* (SABA/1967, piano/writing)

HILDEGARD SCHMIDT Born in 1939, Can's manager Schmidt played a vital role in their success, defending a sound regarded as challenging in the male-dominated music industry. It was due to her diplomacy that they stayed together so long, despite bringing together several large egos. She stayed out of musical matters but it was her idea to make *Tago Mago* a double album; she loved the music so much that she persuaded the record label a standard LP would be too short. Since the band's split, she and her daughter with Irmin Schmidt, Sandra Podmore, have run the record company Spoon Records UK Ltd and Can's management, continuing to represent the musicians' interests while nurturing a constantly growing audience for Can across the generations.

IRMIN SCHMIDT The composer and keyboardist calls setting up Can a typical 1968 decision. A freshly trained conductor, Schmidt abandoned a potential career in classical music to start a rock band. Born in Berlin in 1937, he had studied composing from 1964–66 under Karlheinz Stockhausen in Köln, where he met Holger Czukay. He then invited Jaki Liebezeit and Michael Karoli to join them – and Can was born. He has written more than forty scores for TV and cinema, including *Knife in the Head* (1978) and *Palermo Shooting* (2008). His most recent release was the 2020 solo album *Nocturne*. Irmin Schmidt and his wife Hildegard live in Germany and France.

Can: *Tago Mago* (United Artists Records/1971, piano/organ/writing)

SIEGFRIED SCHMIDT-JOOS Born in Gotha in 1936, the journalist worked for *Der Spiegel* magazine and the radio station RIAS Berlin, among other outlets. He has authored numerous books.

STEVE SCHROYDER Born in Stadtoldendorf in 1950, the musician rang Tangerine Dream boss Edgar Froese's doorbell one night and introduced himself as 'your new organist, appointed by the cosmos'. Froese was impressed, and Schroyder worked on the albums *Alpha Centauri* and *Zeit*. He shared Rolf-Ulrich Kaiser and his partner Gille Lettmann's passion for tarot and took part in the recordings for Ash Ra Tempel's *Seven Up* with the cosmic crew around Kaiser and Timothy Leary. Schroyder went on to compose music inspired by plants and the cosmos. Alongside solo projects, this century has also seen him tour with Anne Clark. Steve Schroyder's most recent project is the band Dream Control, with former Birth Control member Zeus B. Held.

Tangerine Dream: *Alpha Centauri* (Ohr/1971, organ/electronics/percussion)

KLAUS SCHULZE Born in Berlin in 1947, the keyboardist, producer and composer started out on drums in Tangerine Dream and can be heard on their first album, *Electronic Meditation*. He quit to start Ash Ra Tempel with Manuel Göttsching and Hartmut Enke. After one album and countless live shows, Schulze launched his solo career in 1971, buying his first synthesizer a year later and releasing numerous solo albums. His classic albums include *Irrlicht*, *Timewind* and *Moondawn*, and he came to be seen as an electronic music pioneer, especially of the 'Berlin School'. He saw success abroad, especially in France, before finding a sizeable audience in Germany, and collaborated with younger fans such as Schiller, Alphaville and the Dead Can Dance singer Lisa Gerrard, while his tracks have been used by Hollywood directors like Michael Mann and Sofia Coppola. His final album would be *Deus Arrakis*. Klaus Schulze died in 2022.

Klaus Schulze: *Timewind* (Brain/1975, electronics/composition)

WOLF SEESSELBERG Born in Hamburg in 1941, he has been so successful as a film architect, set designer and university professor that it has overshadowed the one Seesselberg album, *Synthetik 1*, recorded with his brother Eckart – yet this abstract electronic album, self-released in 1974, has long been considered a classic.

Seesselberg: *Synthetik 1* (self-released/1974, writing/electronics)

DIETER SERFAS Born in 1946, the drummer went to school in Hof an der Saale, where he made friends with Christian Burchard. He was part of Amon Düül II for a while in its early days and regularly performed with Embryo. Serfas spent many years working in journalism and released the solo album *Ear-Trance-Port* in 1997.

Amon Düül II: *Phallus Dei* (Liberty/1969, drums)

ASMUS TIETCHENS Born in Hamburg in 1947, Tietchens trained as a shipping clerk and spent a while writing advertising copy before he switched to music and sound art in the mid-seventies. He started cutting and splicing tapes at the age of ten, for which he blames the *musique concrète* he'd discovered on the radio one night. His tracks fall somewhere on the cusp of industrial and electronica. He recorded an album as Liliental with Dieter Moebius, Hellmut Hattler, Okko Becker and Conny Plank in 1976, which came out two years later. Always dressed in black and also using the pseudonyms Hematic Sunsets and Club of Rome, Tietchen has a loyal audience around the world. Despite having no musical training, as he emphasises, he has a sizeable discography. He has also taught sound design at Hamburg's University of the Arts.

Asmus Tietchens: *Biotop* (Sky Records/1981, electronics/writing)

RENÉ TINNER Born in St. Gallen in 1953, he was desperate to get out of Switzerland and leapt at the chance to become Can's road manager in the early seventies. What excited him most, though, was the idea of working with the band in their Köln studio. He produced Can's albums from 1974 on. Tinner has gone on to work on more than 200 productions, including with Lou Reed, Trio, Jim Capaldi and, of course, many of the Can members' solo projects.

Can: *Saw Delight* (Harvest/1977, recording/producer)

WINFRID TRENKLER Born in 1943, the journalist was one of the first in Germany to get into the new music that seemed not to fit into any pigeonhole. Trenkler wrote about it in the German *Sounds* magazine and ended up at WDR radio, where he confronted a large audience with NEU!, Kraftwerk, Tangerine Dream, Cluster and Harmonia, among others. His WDR show *Schwingungen* is considered ground-breaking. It was the euphoric music-lover Trenkler who took Brian Eno along to a Harmonia show in Hamburg in 1975 and introduced the artists. Trenkler now lives in Sweden, producing his shows for loyal fans on his own initiative. His work as a musical pioneer has not gone forgotten by artists such as Kraftwerk, who invite him to their shows to this day.

PAUL WELLER Born in 1958, the British guitarist and songwriter with the Jam and the Style Council, now a solo artist, is venerated as 'the Modfather'. Weller came late to krautrock but was so enthusiastic that he got Michael Rother to remix his song 'Around the Lake'.

Paul Weller: *Sonik Kicks* (Island Records/2012, writing/singing/guitar)

WIM WENDERS Born in 1945, the film-maker (*Paris, Texas*) saw Amon Düül live and is a friend of Irmin Schmidt.

STEVEN WILSON Born in London in 1967, the guitarist, singer, songwriter and producer made a name for himself in the progressive rock band Porcupine Tree in the late eighties. He was fourteen and music-obsessed when an older friend played him Tangerine Dream and Klaus Schulze, who made a deep impression on him. Besides Porcupine Tree, he has worked with bands like No-Man, Blackfield and Bass Communion. Celebrated as the 'king of prog rock', he is also in demand as a remixer, restorer and refiner of historic recordings, having worked on albums by King Crimson, Jethro Tull, Roxy Music, Yes and many more. Tangerine Dream's *Zeit* is one of his favourite records of all time.

Steven Wilson: *Tape Experiments 1985/1986* (Tonefloat/2010, electronics)

BERND WITTHÜSER Born in the Sauerland region in 1944, the bard refused to learn a decent trade like his mother wanted. Instead, he took inspiration from Bob Dylan and began playing his own German songs in cafés and bars around Essen, aiming to escape the grey coal-mining area. With Walter Westrupp in 1969 he started the anarcho-folk duo Witthüser & Westrupp, which Rolf-Ulrich Kaiser signed up to his Pilz label. The duo caused a stir playing live in churches in the early seventies. After they split up in 1973, Witthüser went to India, lived in Berlin for a while and then moved to Tuscany, where he played regularly as Barnelli. He drove his motorbike to all his gigs, even the most distant. Bernd Witthüser died in Italy in 2017.

Witthüser & Westrupp: *Trips + Träume* (Ohr/1971, writing/singing/guitar)

WRITER'S ACKNOWLEDGEMENTS

I'd like to thank everyone who granted me an interview for this book. Every single conversation was fascinating. And I wouldn't have got far without those (too many to list here) who helped me with tips, advice, contacts and their valuable time. Thanks as well to Stefanie for her endless patience. To Hildegard and Irmin Schmidt, whose invitation was ultimately what got me started, and to Gunther Buskies, Andreas Dorau, Renate Knaup, Maren Kumpe, Johannes Ullmaier, Winfried Hörning and Harald Grosskopf: *DANKE!*

For the UK edition: DANKE to Katy Derbyshire for the miracle of bringing all these unique German voices to the English language and managing to keep their individual vibes! And, of course, *DANKE* to Dan Papps for his trust and enthusiasm in this book. Not forgetting Rachael Williamson and Mark Sinker at Faber for their support! And, finally, Jack Smyth for the stunning cover.

TRANSLATOR'S ACKNOWLEDGEMENTS

Many thanks to Andy Sier for his expert eye on the muso-speak. All remaining mistakes are my own. And thanks, of course, to Christoph Dallach for his support and enthusiasm!